The Economic Development of Latin America in the Twentieth Century

André A. Hofman

Researcher, Economic Commission for Latin America and the Caribbean, Chile

Edward Elgar

Cheltenham, UK • Northampton, MA, USA

© André A. Hofman 2000

Published by
Edward Elgar Publishing Limited
Glensanda House
Montpellier Parade
Cheltenham
Glos GL50 1UA
UK

Edward Elgar Publishing, Inc.
136 West Street
Suite 202
Northampton
Massachusetts 01060
USA

A catalogue record for this book
is available from the British Library

Library of Congress Cataloguing in Publication Data

Hofman, André A., 1953–
    The economic development of Latin America in the twentieth century
/ André A. Hofman.
        1. Latin America—Economic conditions—20th century.   I. Title.
    HC125.H645 1999
    338.98—dc21   98–27904
                                                                        CIP

ISBN 1 85898 852 7

Printed and bound in Great Britain by Bookcraft (Bath) Ltd.

Contents

List of Figures

List of Tables

Acknowledgements

I am greatly indebted to a large number of people in the preparation of this book; I will never be able to repay these debts. My interest in Latin America and its economic history started towards the end of my studies at the University of Groningen, while I was working on Mexico's economic development, under supervision of Angus Maddison, and continued with a study on demographic decline in Latin America after the European conquest. Fernando Fajnzylber's interest in comparing Latin America with countries outside the region and Angus Maddison's unreserved support, were great sources of motivation in the preparation of this book.

I am very grateful to many of my colleagues at ECLAC in Santiago, Chile. Oscar Altimir has been a constant motivational force and Barbara Stallings gave me the opportunity to finish this study. I am grateful to the following for their comments or other assistance; Asdrubal Baptista, Renato Baumann, Gloria Bensan, Ricardo Bielschowsky, Jorge Bravo, Ruud Buitelaar, Rodrigo Carrasco, Juan Chackiel, Ricardo Crosa, Pascual Gerstenfeld, Gunther Held, John Hennelly, Sebastián Herreros, Felipe Jiménez, Graciela Moguillansky, Guillermo Mundt, Marcelo Ortúzar, Igor Paunovic, José Miguel Pujol, Carlos Rodríguez, Mónica Roeschmann, Gert Rosenthal, Pedro Sáinz, Horacio Santamaría, Osvaldo Sunkel, Rosemary Thorp, Daniel Titelman, Raffael Urriola, Víctor Urquidi, Andras Uthoff, Miguel Villa, Richard Webb and Jürgen Weller.

I am also grateful to Derek Blades, Alberto Ffracchia, Alan Heston, Daniel Heymann, Mark Keese and Michael Ward for assistance on methodological issues. I owe thanks to Ricardo Ffrench-Davis, Simon Kuipers, Juan Carlos Lerda, Nanno Mulder, Joseph Ramos and Bart van Ark who kindly read substantial parts of the book and commented extensively on many chapters. Mario Castillo was helpful at the initial stage of the research project and Sergio Zamora helped with the capital stock estimation. I am very grateful to Ana María Amengual and Christine Boniface who helped in the final editing of the book. I have received continuous support from colleagues all over Latin America, with whom I made contact when I visited their countries, or when they visited ECLAC in Santiago. Without their support this book could not have been completed.

Being a member of the Groningen ICOP (International Comparisons of Output and Productivity) team has been very stimulating and I have been working with several of its members. I am very grateful to Bart van Ark for efficient, graceful and continuous support, and to Peter Groote for comments and advice. I would particularly like to thank Dirk Pilat on whose support I always could count. I have had a very fruitful relation with Nanno Mulder with respect to capital stock estimation.

Angus Maddison has been my main source of inspiration. In spite of the long geographical distance he always provided guidance, redirecting my efforts where appropriate. Probably more than he is aware, his support, new ideas and challenges have been a major source of professional satisfaction, and his untiring and timely comments during all stages of the preparation of this book was admirable.

I dedicate this book to my wife and children who accepted, although not always without protest, the many hours of work on this book that should have been dedicated to them.

1. Introduction

This book provides an assessment of Latin America's[1] twentieth-century economic performance and policy from a comparative and historical perspective. The theory and empirics of economic growth have come to be the focus of attention once again. Surveying the literature, one sees many new interesting ideas and the rediscovery of older, somewhat forgotten ones. The empirical work – and this book is in that tradition – concentrates on determining trends and main sources of growth in a cross-section of countries. Economic growth in Latin America is explained on two levels: (a) proximate and measurable influences which are captured in the growth accounts; (b) causes of a more ultimate character, that is, qualitative and institutional influences which are more difficult to measure.

The analysis of economic performance concentrates on the quantification of economic growth, long-run estimates of GDP growth and the measurement of factor inputs and total factor productivity. Another important element of this study is an international comparison with countries outside the region, both developed and developing. Maddison (1991a) defines proximate causes of growth as:

> those areas of causality where measures and models have been developed by economists and statisticians. Here the relative importance of different influences can be more readily assessed. At this level one can derive significant insights from comparative macroeconomic growth accounts. (p. 11)

Through growth accounting it is possible to identify and quantify the proximate causes of growth but no light is shed on the ultimate causes of growth.

This study is for the most part eminently empirical in nature, and presents long-term series not available until now for several variables which can serve to analyse Latin American growth, levels of performance, and phases when growth accelerated or decelerated. For the 1950–94 period, a growth accounting analytical framework is presented using a total factor productivity analysis in which step-by-step explanatory factors are listed, and given their weight in 'explaining' economic growth in the sample of countries. Growth accounting shows the contribution of factor inputs (capital, labour and land) and total factor productivity to output growth. For these quantitative growth accounts long-term GDP and capital formation series were required which permit analysis of GDP (per capita) and labour productivity developments since 1900.

1

This kind of growth accounting exercise may serve different purposes such as explaining differences in growth rates between countries, illuminating the process of convergence and divergence, assessing the role of technical progress and calculating potential output losses. Growth accounting cannot provide a full causal explanation. It deals with 'proximate' rather than 'ultimate' causality and records the facts about growth components: it does not explain the underlying elements of policy or circumstance, national or international, but it does identify which facts need further explanation.

Ultimate causes are those factors related to economic growth which are difficult to quantify in economic or statistical models. They include the role of institutions, ideologies, pressures of socioeconomic interest groups, historical accidents, and economic policy at the national level (Maddison, 1991a). They also involve consideration of the international economic order, foreign ideologies or shocks originating in friendly or unfriendly neighbours. The ultimate sources of Latin American performance are less clearly established than its proximate causes and constitute an extremely interesting area for further research. The contribution of this book to the understanding of the role of these ultimate sources in economic growth is only modest. Chapter 2 analyses some of the topics to be included in the realm of ultimate sources, such as the institutional set-up, social capabilities and path dependency. In Chapter 7 policy and international context are analysed.

It should be stressed that the proximate causes are not independent of the ultimate causes of growth. To a rather significant degree proximate causes are dimensions through which ultimate causes can be seen to operate. However, the importance of interaction and interdependency between the different sources of growth is emphasised. On the proximate level the interaction between capital accumulation and technological progress is an example of this interdependence. On the ultimate level there exists interaction between the institutional framework of a society and the implementation of economic policy. An example of interdependence between the ultimate and proximate levels is the relationship between technological progress and the institutional context.

In this book Latin American performance is compared with three other groups of countries: (a) two rapidly growing Asian countries (Korea and Taiwan) whose economic growth in the past couple of decades has been remarkably fast; (b) Portugal and Spain, whose institutional heritage had a good deal in common with Latin America; and (c) six advanced capitalist countries (France, Germany, Japan, the Netherlands, UK and USA), whose levels of income and productivity are among the highest in the world.

Judging from the performance of several countries in the early 1990s, it would seem that Latin America is now climbing out of the depths of one of the most profound crises of the twentieth century. The 'lost decade' of the 1980s was characterised by low or negative real economic growth, huge external indebtedness, great macroeconomic instability represented by two to three digit inflation, fiscal crisis, and great distortions in resource allocation. Some lessons can be learned from studying Latin America in a comparative perspective.

- There are lessons from the lost decade, which was a period of stagnation rather than growth. The situation in Latin America in the 1980s was highly unusual, with slow or negative growth. Although other regions also experienced lower growth, this did not lead to negative total factor productivity. The implication is that policy at that time was less efficient in Latin America than in many other areas.
- In the period 1950–80 Latin America was not an outlier. Total factor productivity was then positive as it was in other regions. Total factor productivity growth was fastest in Europe, followed by the Asian developing countries and the Latin American countries. Growth accounting, of course, accounts only for the so-called proximate causes. An evaluation of policy, institutions and shocks of an internal or external character is important, in order to be able to get a fully rounded view of growth performance and of the efficacy of countries.

Previous work on economic growth accounting in Latin America has concentrated mainly on detailed studies of specific country experience. This book, by contrast, takes a comparative view of a substantial array of countries, within and outside Latin America. Unlike some recent econometric analysis it does not use a maximalist approach, where available data are used without regard to their quality. In this study great attention is given to the construction of comparable series, which data are reasonably reliable. A very important element of this study is the transparency of the methodology used. The complete description of the sources gives the reader the opportunity to judge the quality of the available information. This is the reason for the inclusion of appendices in which the basic series are given together with a description of methodology and sources.

In Chapter 2 some of Latin America's most salient characteristics, such as unequal income distribution, persistent macroeconomic instability and the institutional context, are analysed in a historical perspective. This historical perspective is important because some of the roots of these characteristics might be found, for example, in pre-Columbian society, the colonial period or in the relatively early independence of Latin America compared to other developing regions. This study provides a short, not exhaustive, description of some of the most important characteristics of Latin America in comparison especially with the United States. In this context it is interesting to compare Latin America with the United States because both belong to the same hemisphere, were 'discovered' at the same time by European countries, and had very substantial natural resources endowment by world standards. Now, however, income levels in Latin America and the United States are quite different and the latter leads the world in productivity. The first element to be analysed is the physical endowment of Latin America followed by the institutional framework, inequality, human capital, debt, foreign trade and inflation to finish with policy and ideology.

A long-run perspective of growth acceleration and slowdown in Latin America compared with the other groups of countries is presented in Chapter 3. Labour productivity for the 1913–94 period shows some additional evidence concerning the cycles of acceleration and deceleration of growth in the twentieth century. Per capita GDP showed recovery in the 1989–94 period after the negative growth in the lost decade of the 1980s. The analysis of the business cycle and comparison of similarities and differences in the periods commonly used are also studied in this chapter. The main causes of cyclical instability, either of an internal or external nature, are identified.

In Chapter 4, which deals with the human capital dimension, I analyse the results with respect to employment, unemployment and annual days worked. This section also takes into consideration the quality aspects of the population as reflected in educational levels. The results with respect to physical capital are the subject of Appendix G and Chapter 5. Appendix G gives a systematic comparison of previous capital stock estimates in Latin America. The lack of comparable estimates of fixed capital stocks for Latin American countries has long hindered analysis of economic development within the region as well as comparison with other developing and developed countries. Chapter 5 attempts to fill this gap by providing estimates of gross and net fixed capital stock for the six Latin American countries selected. The estimates have been generated by employing the 'perpetual inventory method' currently used by most OECD countries to estimate their capital stocks, and hence the most appropriate in an international comparison.

Chapter 6 presents a causal analysis of Latin American post-war development using the methodology of the growth accounts, providing for labour and capital a detailed breakdown of their components and indicating the weighting procedure of all inputs (including land) into a measure of augmented total factor input. Performance and policy of Latin America in the post-war period is analysed in Chapter 7. An overall description of policy and performance in the Latin American region is given. The chapter concludes with a description of the major policy issues on which consensus has been reached and the ones which are still subject to debate.

In eight appendices, the complete series, sources and measurement procedures are presented. Appendix A contains long-term population series from 1820–1995. Appendix B provides time series for GDP, levels of GDP and GDP per capita both in national currencies and international dollars. Some basic quantification with respect to the labour market is given in Appendix C, which presents activity rates, employment, educational level of the population and labour productivity series from 1950 onwards, as well as estimates of hours worked. Estimates for total and disaggregated capital formation for the 1900–1994 period, which are the essential building blocks for the construction of capital stock estimates using the 'Perpetual Inventory Method', are presented in Appendix D. Appendix E presents the standardised estimates with respect to the fixed capital stock, both in national currencies and international dollars. Appendix F presents import and export series in current dollars as well as indices representing volume movement. Appendix G gives the evolution of consumer prices on a year-to-year basis. Appendix H consists of previous non-standardised capital stock estimates and examines in some detail the history of capital stock and national wealth estimation in Latin America in the twentieth century.

NOTE

1. Latin America refers, if not indicated otherwise, to: Argentina, Brazil, Chile, Colombia, Mexico and Venezuela, which cover around 80 per cent of Latin America's population, territory and GDP, see also Chapter 3 for a description of our sample. The origin of the term Latin America is not totally clear. Bushnell and Macauly (1988) attribute it to the Colombian José María Torres Caicedo in 1856 while Annino (1995) gives France as the origin, citing one of Napoleon III's advisors on imperial projects as having used the term.

2. Some Distinctive Characteristics of Latin America over the Long Run

There is a consensus among analysts that the origin of some of the most pressing problems of Latin America, for example unequal income distribution and macroeconomic instability, can be found in its history. It is for this reason that I do not keep as strictly to the twentieth century in this chapter as I do elsewhere. The colonial period and the achievement of independence, which came rather early in Latin America compared to other developing regions, are important in understanding the Latin American reality. A short description is presented of some of the most important characteristics of Latin America especially in comparison with the United States, another ex-colony in the same hemisphere. The initial situation as regards natural resources endowment was not better in the United States than in Latin America, but the United States became the world productivity leader.

NATURAL RESOURCE ENDOWMENT

The relationship between the natural resource endowment of a country and its economic development is not straightforward. Long-run empirical evidence shows that the availability of natural resources is not a decisive factor in economic development. There are examples of resource-rich countries that have grown rapidly over the long term while others have had only a modest economic performance. On the other hand there are examples of countries, despite being very poor in natural resources, that have grown at a spectacular pace.

In economic theory, the classical economists assigned a very important role to the impact of natural resources on the growth potential of an economy. Adam Smith stressed the availability of land as a factor in economic growth.[1] Ricardo and Malthus were quite pessimistic about the availability of natural resources for growth. More recent studies, like those prepared by the Club of Rome, stress the same point. However, it has become clear that technological advances have increased the productivity of agriculture enormously and that technology and geological prospecting have also increased proven reserves and the yield of mineral resources.

7

A great variety of arguments are presented in the literature about the effects, both positive and negative, of natural resources on development. On the positive side the availability of minerals, fertile soil, climate or geographic location present the opportunity to capture economic rents to be used for accelerated economic growth. Negative elements regularly mentioned are the effect of deterioration due to the structural transformation process, affecting a country's pattern of international trade, hindering efficient resource allocation, inducing rent-seeking behaviour, formation of dual economies and Dutch disease effects.

In a comparative perspective the Latin American advantage in natural resources is overwhelming. Total land area per head in 1950 in Latin America was two or three times the level in the United States (which is the best endowed developed country among those considered), and more than 20 times that of South East Asia (see Table 2.1).

Table 2.1 Total Land Area per Head of Population, 1900–1994 (hectares per capita)

	1900	1950	1994
Argentina	58.3	16.0	8.0
Brazil	47.3	15.9	5.3
Chile	25.2	12.3	5.4
Colombia	26.0	8.7	3.0
Mexico	14.0	6.9	2.1
Venezuela	34.7	17.3	4.1
Korea	1.1	0.5	0.2
Taiwan	1.3	0.5	0.2
Portugal	1.7	1.1	0.9
Spain	2.7	1.8	1.3
France	1.4	1.3	0.9
Germany	1.1	0.7	0.5
Japan	0.9	0.5	0.3
Netherlands	0.7	0.3	0.2
UK	0.6	0.5	0.4
USA	12.5	6.3	3.7

Source: Appendix A, FAO, *Production Yearbook*, various issues and Maddison (1995).

The Western Hemisphere together with Australia is often referred to as 'empty'.[2] They are 'countries of recent settlement'. Land was obviously the most abundantly available natural resource in these 'empty' countries and offered a great opportunity for economic development. Mineral resources have also had a great impact on economic development in Latin America since the colonial period.

Adam Smith (1776) was one of the first writers to emphasise differences in the use of the land between the English and the Spanish colonies, and the relationship between land use and economic development. Among the factors limiting productive use of land he mentioned engrossment, rights of primogeniture, taxes and levies and a restrictive trade system. The land system introduced by the Spanish, the 'encomienda', granted large properties to 'conquistadores' as well as the right to exploit indigenous labour more or less like serfs. The 'encomienda' was gradually replaced by the 'hacienda' which was the form of landownership that prevailed at the end of the colonial period.

However, it is important to note that during the colonial period Spain was not at all interested in agriculture and most part of its energies went into obtaining gold and silver. The first source was, of course, the gold already found by native Americans from alluvial sources. The second step was to expand alluvial gold mining. The third step was the introduction of the mercury amalgamation technique which improved the efficiency of extraction and made the mining of lower grade silver ore possible. Mining developments generally created mineral rents that helped to maintain external equilibrium. But it produced a pattern of resource use that made the distribution of income worse, the economy less diversified, export earnings more concentrated on primary products. Mineral development may well have caused a lower growth rate in the non-mining sectors of the economy than otherwise would have occurred (Lewis, 1984).

In the colonial period, the Southern Cone countries, Argentina and Chile, established a system of great landed estates, haciendas or latifundios. Argentina (Río de la Plata in colonial times) was an impoverished colony. It was only during the second half of the eighteenth century that exports of hides provided an indication of the enormous potential of this rich and fertile country (Díaz-Alejandro, 1983 and Cortés Conde, 1985). Chile, which had some mining but nothing on the scale of the silver mines of Peru and Bolivia, experienced a great expansion of livestock herds in the seventeenth century to meet the strong demand for leather and for fats for making candles and soap. The eighteenth century saw the transformation of Chile's pastoral economy when it captured the Peruvian market for wheat (Cariola and Sunkel, 1985).

Brazil was somewhat different as it was colonised by Portugal and mining was, initially, relatively unimportant. Portugal did not exercise as strong an authority as Spain did on its colonies. The plantation economy introduced in the sixteenth century, when Brazil became the world's most important producer and exporter of sugar, also had distinct characteristics compared to the rest of Latin America, particularly the use of slave labour on a great scale. Like the Southern Cone countries, Brazil was only sparsely populated at the time of conquest. Two centuries after Columbus' discovery of the Americas, gold was found in Minas Gerais and the subsequent discovery of diamonds in 1729 generated an era of spectacular opulence that lasted into the second half of the eighteenth century (Cardoso and Helwege, 1992).

Agriculture in Mexico towards the end of the colonial period was a hacienda system with great church estates. Production on these haciendas was mainly self-sufficient and only partly directed to the market. Most agricultural production was for domestic consumption. There were also a few export crops such as dyes for the booming European textiles industry, cacao, vanilla and henequen. These haciendas were not 'feudal' as was originally claimed, especially by the Berkeley school (Borah, 1951), as they were connected to domestic markets, especially in supplying workers for the mining industry and urban settlements. Although some plantations were developed in Mexico, for example for sugar cane, these were never as important as in Brazil. Mexico's agriculture was basically oriented to the domestic market.

Independence was seen by many as a great opportunity for Latin America to accelerate its economic development.[3] The new opportunities for trade, now that the region was no longer hindered by Spanish regulations, and access to international capital are regularly mentioned as potentially the most important factors for inducing faster development. Most scholars point to the beginning of the nineteenth century as the starting point of accelerated capitalist development, with much faster growth than in the 'protocapitalist' period from 1500–1820 (Maddison, 1991a). However, Latin America did not enjoy the same acceleration as achieved in Europe and the United States, because the first half of the nineteenth century was devoted to political consolidation of independence and the formation of more stable political and economic regimes. Brazil and Chile were the first to form stable regimes and suffered less from political instability than other countries, especially Mexico, Colombia and Venezuela.

During the first half century after independence, Argentina's considerable land-based natural resources remained undeveloped, as the country was immersed, most of the time, in political turmoil. Díaz-Alejandro (1983) claimed that a political and social framework compatible with export-oriented growth was established in Argentina only shortly after the middle of the nineteenth century. By 1880 the best land on the Pampas had been appropriated in a manner leading to concentrated ownership. All exports were based upon natural resource wealth, especially land, and the first exports were wool, hides and salted meat, to which wheat, corn and linseed were added. Later on frozen beef exports became important. Brazil experienced an agricultural revival at the end of the eighteenth century based on its plantation economy. First sugar, later cotton and, at the end of the colonial period, coffee were to become extremely important in Brazil.

Mining, which had not been particularly important in Chile during the colonial period became prominent after independence. Chile then experienced an expansion based on exports of gold, silver and copper, followed in the 1850s and 1860s by substantial trade in grain. The grain exports originating from the area around the capital, Santiago, and the south, were very important during parts of the nineteenth century. This expansion was ended by the War of the Pacific in 1879. After the war, with the incorporation of the provinces of Tarapacá and Antofagasta, a second major cycle of expansion began. This cycle reached its height about 1920 and ended with the Great Depression of the 1930s. The boom in nitrate production in the provinces of the Norte Grande relegated grain and flour exports to a secondary role (Cariola and Sunkel, 1985).

The export-oriented development strategy of Latin America continued at least until 1913. It was after the Great Depression of 1929–33 that the debate on industrialisation as a development strategy assumed importance in many countries. Industrial development was promoted after the Great Depression and during World War II as imports became scarce. This policy was at the expense of agricultural exports though mining exports remained important. Many authors have indicated that the process of industrialisation had already started long before the Great Depression[4] but the import substitution strategy was intensified after the World War II and was maintained longer than many commentators, often in retrospect, thought necessary.

In the economic development of Latin America in the twentieth century, natural resources remained a very important element. Currently in all countries the single most important export product is a primary product.[5] Several countries have added manufactures to their exports, but only in Mexico and Brazil do these represent more than 50 per cent of total exports. Recently, since the debt crisis of the 1980s, there has been some indication of change in Latin America's development strategy. Chile is the prime example of a country which, after a process of macroeconomic stabilisation and economic restructuring, adopted a strategy based upon its abundant natural resources. The growth of the natural-resource based export sector has given new momentum, through forward and backward linkages, to the entire economy which has been growing at a rate of over 6 per cent for more than 10 years.

INSTITUTIONS

The institutional set-up and its relation to economic growth, a subject normally located in the sphere of the so-called ultimate causality, is extremely important and, in the case of Latin America, further study of the relationship between growth and institutions can be very useful. Institutions provide the incentive structure of a society and they comprise the formal rules, constitutions, laws and regulations; and informal constraints, conventions, norms of behaviour and self-imposed codes of conduct, and their enforcement characteristics (North, 1993). In a historical context the comparison between Latin America and the United States in terms of the institutional set-up might explain part of the difference in performance. North refers to the idea of path dependence, originated by David (1985) and Arthur (1988), and applied it to institutional evolution, indicating that once on a particular path economies find it very hard to fundamentally change direction because of the built-in characteristics of institutions. His striking comparison between the institutional evolution of Spain and England and the consequences for the subsequent course of events in Latin and North America provides a striking illustration of the role of path dependency (see also North, 1990).

In this respect the 'social capability',[6] that enhanced growth in the successful Asian countries, is deficient in Latin America. 'Social capability' refers to different elements such as the adequacy of the institutional framework, the role of government in designing and implementing economic policy and the skill level of the population.

During the conquest and the colonial period, Spain was to a large degree isolated from the forces important to modernisation in the rest of Europe, especially in Northern Italy. The Renaissance and Enlightenment made possible recognition of man's ability to transform the forces of nature through rational investigation and experiment. But Spain retained, to a great extent, medieval thinking and medieval ways. The wars of Reconquest against the Moors had allowed the Castilian Crown to obtain great wealth. Agriculture, crafts and commerce took second place to armed conquest as sources of wealth in the eyes of both hidalgos (noblemen) and peasants. It was this way of thinking which induced the followers of Hernán Cortés and Francisco Pizarro to seek fame and fortune in the new world. This behaviour and its modern, rent-seeking variant, is still, in many Latin American countries, an important component of the behaviour of economic agents.

In a comparison of institutional development in Latin America and the United States during their respective colonial periods, several features become clear.[7] The level of interference by the colonial power was much lower in the case of the English than in the case of the Spanish. As Smith (1776) noted:

> The Spanish colonies, therefore, from the moment of their first establishment, attracted very much the attention of their mother country; while those of the other European nations were for a long time in a great measure neglected. (p. 612)

Spain deliberately followed a policy of total conquest, modelling the colonies on the institutional structure of Spain and destroying the indigenous political and cultural institutions, together with indigenous religion and architecture. The other colonial powers had a much stronger tendency to a system of coexistence with indigenous institutions.

The Spanish Crown established a centralised, hierarchical system with several viceroys,[8] who also had responsibility for appointing bishops and therefore exercised control over the church. The authority of these viceroys was hardly challenged during the whole colonial period.[9] Underneath this centralised structure there was a complicated method for dispensing favours, land mineral concessions and so on, which made it important to be close to power and which partially explains the absentee character of landownership.

The indigenous population was considered and treated as inferior. They were subjected to military oppression and faced unknown diseases like measles and smallpox that caused epidemics with extremely high death rates (Maddison, 1995). Later they were subject to cruelty, racism, injustice and indifference, elements characteristic of colonial Latin America which continued to be a feature of the independent Latin American countries.

The labour relations established under Spanish colonial rule were of an extremely dependent, debt peonage, and oppressive character. This impeded practically all forms of labour mobility and stands in marked contrast to the conditions experienced by settlers in the English colonies, who were basically independent, working their own land.

An important distinction between the English and Spanish colonies concerns the fiscal burden imposed upon them by the colonial power. There are very clear indications that taxes in the Spanish colonies were much higher than in the English ones. The Crown taxed the production of agricultural estates and mines by levying a 'fifth'. Remittances of profits to Spain were quite high. In the case of the English colonies taxes were much lower and basically trade related. There was a big difference in the style of government between the English and the Spanish colonies in the Americas. The English colonies of North America were split up into 13 virtually autonomous colonies, while the Spanish featured a highly centralised power structure, and their top officials had a sumptuous lifestyle.

The mercantilist restrictions imposed on Latin America by the Spanish were much tougher than those on English colonies. They confined all their trade by their colonies to a particular port in the mother country; ships were obliged to sail from that port, in convoy at a particular season, or, if on their own, only once a special licence had been granted, which in most cases was very expensive. Trade was limited to a few ports in Latin America and Cadiz and Seville in Spain. The monopolistic character of this trade had very detrimental effects on prices, production and trade.[10] The mercantile policy of Spain and Portugal practically prohibited the development of manufacturing industries in Latin America.

One of the institutional arrangements that changed as a result of independence was the new ability to raise capital on the international financial market, which had been impossible during the colonial period. It is interesting to note, however, that all Latin American governments were in default by the end of the 1820s for a myriad of reasons. The colonial period did not prepare them for financial independence.

The origins of fiscal irresponsibility can be traced to Spain's own practices. It is an irony of history that when Spain conquered Latin America, its relative power was already on the decline in Europe. One reason for this was the establishment of more efficient institutional arrangements in several European countries, such as the Netherlands and the UK, which were the world productivity leaders until the beginning of the twentieth century. The institutional systems of Portugal and Spain were very different from those in the more advanced northern European countries in terms of religious practice, centralisation of power, the role of science and technology and the degree of fiscal responsibility.

Argentina was created as a nation, in the sense of definitively bringing the national territory under a single regime, in the third quarter of the nineteenth century. Formal political unity was achieved between 1859–62, with the accession of Buenos Aires province to the Argentine Federation. But the issue of governance was only resolved in the following two decades, with the closing of the Indian frontier in Patagonia, the suppression of the last regional revolt and the creation of a federal district separating the city of Buenos Aires from the province of the same name in 1880. Díaz-Alejandro (1970) states:

> From 1860 to 1930 Argentina grew at a rate that has few parallels in economic history, perhaps comparable only to the performance during the same period of other countries of recent settlement. (p. 18)

Differences in the role of central government in the economies of Latin America can be explained partly by political considerations, as well as by differing relations with the world economy. The state in Brazil was internally strong and internationally respected, while in Mexico the state was internally fragmented and internationally dependent. The republicans who took power in Brazil in 1889 inherited a state with fairly strong institutions that had the support of the elite, since Brazil's path to independence had been smooth. A weak church and the social cement of slavery tended to convince the country's ruling class of the necessity to maintain a united front. Arguably, a nation was built and a state formed earlier in Brazil than anywhere else in Latin America.

Brazil experienced a peaceful transition to independence. It was much more dependent on the world economy than Mexico, its ratio of exports to GDP was twice that of Mexico, and exports were concentrated in two commodities, coffee and rubber. The Brazilian state relied upon taxes on international trade to a much greater degree than Mexico. Foreign exchange was a more pressing concern, since Brazil's foreign debt was twice the size of Mexico's.

The transformation and the strengthening of the economies of Latin American countries occurred at different moments in their national histories, depending on the export commodities involved and their relative success in state-building. Chile's economy was affected by overseas demand as early as the 1850s (copper exports to Europe and wheat to California), and Argentina and Brazil followed in the 1860s. These countries, along with Mexico, then felt the full impact of the combined effects of the European economic expansion, which, as far as Argentina and Brazil were concerned, triggered an unprecedented level of European immigration. Chile established a constitutional regime in 1833 and was widely admired in Spanish America for its stability. Mexico and Argentina were not to have stable regimes until the late 1860s.

In Colombia the doctrine of economic liberalism went unchallenged from the late 1840s until the 1880s. The basic tenet of economic thinking in Colombia until the 1940s was economic liberalism. Independence brought a more general commitment to economic liberalism in the 1820s by the Colombian government. It adopted free trade and attempted both to reform some taxes and to privatise Indian communal holdings in accordance with liberal prescriptions. The state that Porfirio Díaz seized in 1876 was less secure; Mexico before Díaz had been plagued by civil wars, regional rivalries, and foreign invasions. The treasury was plundered, foreign credit scant, power splintered and sovereignty mocked. Internal peace and external pressures were constant concerns of Díaz.

INEQUALITY OF INCOME AND WEALTH

The distribution of income and wealth in Latin America is extremely unequal in comparison with most of the rest of the world, and these levels of inequality have been persistent over time. The roots of this situation can be found in the distribution of land, mineral rights and education during the colonial period.

Labour relations inherited from the system of landownership, which tied the workers and their families to the land, also caused very uneven initial conditions and proved to be a major obstacle to a more equal distribution of income. Education of the masses was completely neglected during the colonial period; Spain even tried to prevent the population from becoming literate because this was deemed dangerous for religious and political reasons. Two particular facets of the colonial period provide a partial explanation of the uneven income distribution in Latin America. Unequal income distribution was a legacy from the old colonial system of labour exploitation, with slavery in Brazil and peonage elsewhere. Restricted access to education was another cause of inequality, and was more important than in many Asian countries (Maddison, 1989).

Cardoso and Helwege (1992) describe the roots of inequality as follows:

> The colonial division of property had implications not only for the usage of land but for the political structure of the region as well. The encomienda system established a landed aristocracy that dominated political life for centuries and then shared power as industry displaced agriculture as the central economic activity. It established a sharp division between the haves and the have-nots, creating a class structure that is extremely bifurcated by comparison to other cultures. Problems of unequal income distribution and widespread rural poverty that face the region today are rooted in events of the sixteenth and seventeenth centuries. (p. 37)

The problem of inequality in income and wealth was inherited from the colonial period, in which the distribution of assets (principally land) favoured a concentration of income, and for most of the post-independence period the dynamics of the dominant model of economic development have either preserved the existing level of inequality or have exacerbated it (Bulmer-Thomas, 1994).

A long-term view of Latin American income distribution is very difficult to obtain because of huge methodological difficulties.[11] In Table 2.2 Gini coefficients[12] are presented for the 1950–90 period based upon a methodology of linking appropriate pairs of Gini coefficients.

Altimir (1987) describes these pairs which were selected on the ground that they are comparable with regard to the concept of income, the procedure used for measuring income and the geographical coverage of the surveys used to collect the data, as well as the units and criteria used by the respective authors in processing or adjusting the survey data (see also Altimir, 1992).

A first step in the preparation of Table 2.2 was the selection of a base period Gini for which there were reliable estimates of income distribution in the specific country. This base period Gini estimate was linked over time to the other available estimates. The results indicate that income distribution in Latin America in the post-war period either remained the same or worsened. The worsening of the income distribution was especially marked after 1980.[13]

Table 2.2 Latin America: Inequality in Pre-tax[14] Income Distribution, 1950–90 (Gini coefficients around benchmark years)

	1950	1960	1970	1980	1990
Argentina	0.400	0.419	0.412	0.472	0.423
Brazil	–	0.570	0.630	0.619	0.631
Chile	–	0.459	0.473	0.522	0.520
Colombia	0.513	0.542	0.516	0.566	0.494
Mexico	0.516	0.606	0.586	0.478	0.523
Venezuela	0.613	0.462	0.494	0.390	0.442
Average Gini	0.510	0.509	0.518	0.507	0.506

Source: Oscar Altimir kindly provided access to his extensive database on income distribution (see also Altimir 1997 and 1998). The 1950 estimate for Venezuela is a direct interpolation based upon estimates for 1944 and 1962 from Baptista (1991).[15]

In Table 2.3 the Latin American countries are compared with the other countries of our sample, and the results show markedly higher inequality in Latin America than in all the other country groups. There are also reasons to presume that these differences have persisted over time. Inequality may have risen somewhat in recent decades in the advanced countries.

Table 2.3 Inequality of Pre-tax Income of Households around 1970

	Year	Gini coefficient	Top decile per capita income as multiple of that in bottom deciles
Argentina		0.412	11.2
Brazil		0.630	20.0
Chile		0.505	21.3
Colombia		0.539	21.8
Mexico		0.586	25.5
Venezuela		0.494	25.0
Arithmetic average		0.528	20.8
Korea	1970	0.351	7.6
Taiwan	1959	0.396	7.0
Arithmetic average		0.374	7.3
Spain	1965	0.393	
France	1970	0.416	14.4
Germany	1973	0.396	10.5
Japan	1969	0.335	7.5
Netherlands	1967	0.385	10.5
UK	1973	0.344	9.1
USA	1972	0.404	13.5
Arithmetic average		0.382	10.9

Source: If not otherwise mentioned, from sources given in Maddison (1989) and (1995). See Table 2.2 for Latin American Gini coefficients. Gini coefficients for Spain from Jain (1975).

HUMAN CAPITAL

The renewed interest expressed by the 'new growth' theorists in human capital highlights once again the importance of this factor in improving productivity and growth. A higher level of education permits faster incorporation of technical progress and most growth analysts, since Schultz (1961) and Denison (1962), attribute an important weight to this factor. Education had an extremely low priority during the colonial period in Latin America. Far fewer universities were established than in the United States even though the population was much larger. To a great degree, the indigenous population went uneducated during the entire colonial period. Argentina had moved toward mass primary education as early as 1860 (Bulmer-Thomas, 1994), and was the first country in Latin America in the twentieth century to provide compulsory primary education, paid for by the State, for all of the population (Cortés Conde, 1985).

Brazil's educational system lagged behind those of most Latin American countries. Women were almost totally left out until well into the twentieth century. At the end of the colonial period the whole rural and urban population was illiterate. The situation had improved somewhat by the end of the nineteenth century, especially with respect to the urban population, whose literacy rates reached a figure of just below 50 per cent. Education in Chile became a priority during the government of José Manuel Balmaceda (1886–91) and major progress was made at the primary level (Blakemore, 1992). However, primary education became compulsory only in 1920 (Mamalakis, 1976).

The rural indigenous population of Colombia received almost no formal education during the colonial period. From the middle of the nineteenth century some increase in elementary education took place and the proportion of the population able to read reached about 30 per cent at the beginning of the twentieth century. The National University was founded in 1867 but most professionals received their education abroad (see Orlando Melo, 1987 and Safford, 1976).

In Mexico the indigenous population was almost completely denied education during the colonial period. The education of the middle and upper classes was entirely dominated by the Catholic Church. After independence there was little change in education policy. An educational reform was initiated in 1833 but could not be fully implemented. During the second half of the nineteenth century education was reformed and removed from clerical control, and there was some state intervention in favour of popular education. After the Mexican Revolution, free compulsory education was introduced but initially coverage was extremely low. Table 2.4 shows the evolution, during the second half of the twentieth century, of the situation in Latin America as regards years of primary, secondary and higher education.

Table 2.4 Average Years of Formal Educational Experience of Population Aged 15–64, 1950–90

	1950			1970			1980			1990		
	I	II	III	I	II	III	I	II	III	I	II	III
Argentina	3.9	0.8	0.1	4.7	1.5	0.2	5.0	2.0	0.4	5.1	2.7	0.7
Brazil	1.5	0.2	0.1	2.2	0.6	0.1	3.2	0.9	0.1	3.9	1.3	0.2
Chile	3.6	0.7	0.1	4.4	1.4	0.3	4.9	2.1	0.3	5.3	3.0	0.4
Colombia	2.0	0.3	0.1	3.0	0.9	0.1	3.4	1.4	0.2	4.4	2.4	0.4
Mexico	1.9	0.2	0.0	2.9	0.5	0.1	4.2	1.3	0.2	4.6	1.9	0.4
Venezuela	1.7	0.2	0.0	2.8	0.6	0.1	4.1	1.2	0.2	5.4	2.3	0.4

Note: I refers to primary, II to secondary and III to higher education.

Source: Appendix C.

INFLATION

The issue of inflation has generated intense debate in Latin America, especially between the so-called monetarists and structuralists. The former see inflation as detrimental, and contend that a stable price level is a necessary condition for economic growth, whilst the structuralist school regards inflation as an inevitable byproduct of economic growth. Simonsen (1964) differentiates the monetarist and the structuralist school by the sign of the correlation between growth and inflation. For the structuralists this is positive while the monetarists expect it to be negative.

Table 2.5 Experience of Inflation, 1900–1994 (annual average compound growth rates)

	1900–13	1913–29	1929–38	1938–50	1950–73	1973–80	1980–94
Argentina	n.a	2.2	-0.7	30.6	30.5	189.1	629.1
Brazil	-1.6	6.4	-0.2	12.3	31.6	47.0	748.6
Chile	7.3	5.1	6.5	16.4	48.6	236.2	22.3
Colombia	4.6	7.7	3.1	11.7	10.8	27.2	26.4
Mexico	5.3	2.9	2.2	10.0	5.7	22.5	58.9
Venezuela	3.0	1.7	-4.4	6.0	1.8	11.3	28.9
Arithmetic average	3.7	4.3	1.1	14.5	21.5	88.9	252.4
Korea					30.1	20.0	8.7
Taiwan					7.2	13.0	3.2
Arithmetic average					18.6	16.5	6.0
Portugal					3.4	23.9	16.7
Spain					6.7	19.6	9.7
Arithmetic average					5.0	21.7	13.2
France	0.9	12.1	1.4	28.1	5.0	11.1	5.5
Germany	1.3	2.5	-2.2	3.8	2.7	4.8	2.8
Japan	2.8	4.8	1.2	82.4	5.2	9.7	2.1
Netherlands	1.1	2.0	-2.1	7.4	4.1	7.1	2.6
UK	0.9	3.3	-0.7	5.3	4.6	15.8	6.4
USA	1.3	3.1	-2.1	4.5	2.7	8.9	4.5
Arithmetic average	1.4	4.7	-0.7	21.9	4.1	9.6	4.0

Note: For the Asian and the Iberian countries, no information for the pre-war period was available.

Source: Maddison (1989), IMF (various issues) and Appendix G.

In comparative terms Latin American inflation has been higher than in OECD countries, particularly since World War II. One of the most interesting findings is the fact that the acceleration of inflation had started well before the 1950s, as a matter of fact the starting point is similar to that documented in Table 3.4, which shows the growth acceleration in GDP per capita and labour productivity.

Table 2.5 presents the inflationary experience in the twentieth century of a sample of 17 countries, and shows that Latin America had the highest inflation of all regions in most periods. It also makes clear that the Latin American inflationary experience was, surprisingly, not very different from that of the advanced countries during the first half of the twentieth century. The advanced countries witnessed more or less the same levels of inflation before the Great Depression, and the acceleration of inflation during the 1938–50 period was greater than in the case of the Latin American countries. However, with the exception of Japan (the country that had by far the highest inflation in this period), inflation in the advanced countries was somewhat less than in Latin America.

Table 2.5 shows that the big difference occurred after World War II when all areas, except Latin America, experienced a reduction in inflationary momentum. In the period 1973–80 inflation accelerated in all countries, with Latin America again recording the highest rates. While inflation abated in the rest of the world after 1980, Latin American inflation accelerated further. In the early 1990s, in the context of economic stabilisation and restructuring, most Latin American countries were able to drastically reduce their rates of inflation. In particular, Argentina and later Brazil which had recorded extremely high rates succeeded in stabilising their economies; Chile and Colombia reduced inflation even further, while in Mexico and Venezuela inflation increased somewhat.

DEBT PROBLEMS

The recent debt crises of the 1980s and the 1990s are not unprecedented events, but part of a chain of recurrent crises throughout the history of Latin America. During more than a century and a half the Latin American nations have repeatedly experienced international financial storms that greatly damaged their economies and strapped them into an apparently irrevocable succession of boom and bust cycles that reinforce underdevelopment (Marichal, 1989).

Foreign capital can foster economic development in various ways, for example through increases in the rate of growth of the capital stock, mitigating payment problems and helping technology transfer. However, Latin America's experience has been one of booms and crises. Productive use of foreign investment very often did not have priority; indeed the first inflow of capital into Latin America shortly after independence was used principally for military expenses. Defaults were usually followed by a 20- to 30-year drought in access to private credit.

One of the first significant financial waves came in 1822 as newly independent Latin American countries attracted European capital for the consolidation of independence and trade promotion.[16] The financial boom was short-lived, however, as debtors and investors overestimated the region's export earnings potential and were also adversely affected by the European financial crisis of 1825–26; servicing problems and financial panic occurred shortly thereafter in 1827. The severe losses experienced by creditors helped keep foreign investors away from the region for more than two decades. Nevertheless, foreign capital returned with some enthusiasm in the 1850s due to expansive forces in some European capital markets and the fading memories of the past losses. The second wave of credit was also followed by severe payment problems: 58 per cent of Latin American public debt to Great Britain was in default by the end of 1880 (ECLAC, 1965a).

Notwithstanding these earlier problems foreign capital flowed into Latin America during the rest of the nineteenth century and the early part of the twentieth century, although there were other payments crises in the 1870s, triggered by the world crisis of 1873, and in 1890, as a result of the Anglo-Argentine financial panic of that year (Marichal, 1989). During this period Latin America managed to attract a steadily increasing number of foreign investors, and by the eve of World War I the region had become the target of keen competition among the great international financial centres.

During World War I capital flows to Latin America slumped, but serious payments problems did not develop, in part because exports and payments capacities were boosted in wartime. In the 1920s another investment boom ensued, followed by the famous crash of the 1930s, which was brought on by the Great Depression and the dramatic fall in the region's export prices. Private capital flows dried up almost completely in the fifteen years following the 1929 depression due to defaults. It was only after World War II that Latin America's access to private international capital began to be gradually restored.

Immediately following World War II, the region's foreign finance was heavily dependent on direct foreign investment flows and bilateral lending. This was complemented by World Bank funding at the end of the 1950s, as that institution turned its attention from the reconstruction of Europe to development finance. Additional multilateral finance became available in the early 1960s with the establishment of the Inter-American Development Bank. Private commercial banks had a very low profile in the region's external finance situation, generally limiting themselves to export credits guaranteed by their own government and relatively risk-free short-term trade credit. Meanwhile, bond issues were for only limited amounts due to investors' lingering memories of the 1929 crash, and the institutional restrictions that limited access to these markets.

The picture changed radically in the 1970s. Capital flows boomed, partly as a result of increased liquidity due to the first oil crisis and partly because of increasing Latin American demand. These new inflows were largely provided by private commercial banks. A good deal of the flow was in the form of bank credits at floating rates of interest, most of them denominated in dollars. The situation turned around abruptly in 1981 as world trade prices in dollars fell and interest rates increased dramatically (see Table 2.6). From one year to another, net transfers to Latin America became negative. The debt crisis of the 1980s caused Latin America to change its development strategy. Most countries became involved in efforts to achieve stability and made structural changes in their economies.

At the beginning of the last decade of the twentieth century, several Latin American countries which had seemingly mastered the crisis of the 1980s, stabilised their economies and introduced or deepened structural reforms, once again became attractive to foreign investment. The big inflow of foreign capital in the early 1990s took a variety of forms, for example short-term bonds (Mexico), investment in assets in the stock markets (most countries) and also some foreign direct investment (Chile).

Table 2.6 Average Real Annual Percentage Interest Rate on Developing Country Floating-Rate Debt

1977	1978	1979	1980	1981	1982	1983
-11.8	-7.4	-9.7	-6.0	14.6	16.7	15.9

Source: Reisen (1985).

In December 1994 and early 1995 it seemed that Latin America was again headed for crisis, triggered once more by Mexico.[17] On 20 December, the newly elected Mexican government devalued the peso and, having accumulated large external liabilities, provoked a tremendous fall in confidence in Mexico and in the rest of Latin America. This caused a 'tequila' effect, entailing the reversal of capital flows in some countries and a massive sell-off of assets in the stock markets which fell steeply in almost all countries.

Some countries are in better shape than others, for example Chile, because it had already introduced profound economic reforms and had a positive, copper influenced, trade balance; and Brazil, still on the path of reforming the economy, but having rather high reserves, as well as a positive trade balance and a relatively low current account deficit compared to Argentina and especially Mexico. The renewed reversal of capital flows to Latin America and the increase in interest rates caused negative effects in several countries, particularly in Mexico and Argentina, which both went into recession, and Venezuela and Colombia, both immersed, for different reasons, in severe political crises.

THE MOVE FROM OPEN TO CLOSED ECONOMIES – 1929–1980s

Latin America's role in the world economy is a story of ups and downs. During the colonial period trade was officially limited only to Spain and Portugal, although smuggling became increasingly important. After independence there was freer trade and although initial political instability did not help the export sector, exports increased in some countries, for example Chile, and Latin America's terms of trade probably improved as prices of imports fell after the termination of the colonial monopoly.

Table 2.7 Variations in Volume of Merchandise Exports, 1870–1994 (average annual compound growth rates)

	1870–1913	1913–50	1950–73	1973–94
Argentina	5.2	1.6	3.1	5.8
Brazil	1.8	1.7	4.7	8.9
Chile	3.4	1.4	2.4	8.8
Colombia	2.0	3.9	3.8	5.7
Mexico	5.9	-0.5	4.3	9.7
Venezuela	4.1	5.4	4.1	-1.9
Arithmetic average	3.7	2.3	3.7	6.2
Korea	0.0	-1.3	20.3	12.6
Taiwan	4.8	2.6	16.3	10.8
Arithmetic average	2.4	0.7	18.3	11.7
Portugal	n.a.	n.a.	5.7	8.5
Spain	n.a.	n.a.	9.4	8.2
Arithmetic average	n.a.	n.a.	7.5	8.4
France	2.8	1.1	8.2	4.4
Germany	4.1	-2.8	12.4	4.0
Japan	8.5	2.0	15.4	6.2
Netherlands	2.3	1.5	10.3	4.3
UK	2.8	0.0	3.9	3.9
USA	4.9	2.2	6.4	5.1
Arithmetic average	4.2	0.7	9.4	4.7

Source: Maddison (1995).

At the end of the nineteenth and the beginning of the twentieth centuries, Latin America was relatively open to world trade, exporting primary products and importing capital goods and consumer durables. The Great Depression marked a change in trade history as, first, the de facto exclusion from the world market, and second, import substitution policies caused Latin America to turn away from international trade. More recently, as a result of the debt crisis but also due to severe problems with the import substitution strategy, there has been a renewed trend to use trade as an engine of growth.

Latin America has always been an exporter of primary commodity exports: in the colonial period, first minerals like silver and gold, and later on agricultural products like sugar and coffee. Surprisingly, for all the countries of our sample the first export product, by value, is actually still a primary commodity: coffee in the case of Brazil and Colombia, oil in Mexico and Venezuela, maize in Argentina and copper in Chile. In the section dealing with natural resources, it was pointed out that some Latin American countries had been quite successful in entering the world market on the basis of agricultural and mining products.

In Table 2.7 the export performance of Latin America, in terms of volume growth rates, is compared with other regions. At the beginning of the century Latin America's performance was similar to the rest of the world. The 1913–50 period was much better for Latin America, among other reasons because it was not that directly affected by the World Wars.

In 1950–73 the export performance of Latin America in comparison with the rest of the world was extremely poor. Latin America did not profit from the rapid expansion of trade opportunities, indeed Latin American trade barriers and protection were increased. The data presented for the 1973–94 period were disaggregated in the case of Latin America to show somewhat higher overall growth rates in the 1980–94 period. Argentina, Colombia and Venezuela had higher growth rates in 1980–94 than in 1973–80. Brazil had similar growth rates in both periods and Chile and especially Mexico had lower growth rates in the 1980–94 period.

POLITICAL AND POLICY INSTABILITY

One of the points stressed by many authors is the importance of ideology in Latin America's macroeconomic management as opposed to the more pragmatic approach followed, for example, by some Asian newly industrialising countries.

As has been indicated above, in the discussion on institutions, economic policy in Latin America during the colonial period was guided principally by the mercantilist doctrine imposed by Spain. After independence a shift can be observed towards a more laissez-faire orientation. At the end of the nineteenth century free trade and liberal commercial policies had favourable effects on economic growth. However, Latin America already had quite high levels of protection compared to other regions in the world.

The 1930s are widely regarded as a major turning point in Latin America's development. The decade marks the acceleration of import-substituting industrialisation and the start of public policy more concerned with growth and social objectives. An important element was the emergence of strong protectionism and nationalism in most of the advanced countries. By the end of 1931 most Latin

American countries were experimenting with balance of payments measures previously regarded as heterodox.

As a result of the unfavourable shocks of the Great Depression, the Latin American policy mix changed more by force of circumstance than deliberate strategy. The countries of the region abandoned the gold standard, imposed exchange controls and discriminatory trade restrictions (such as quotas, tariffs, and multiple exchange rate systems) on imports of consumer goods, and adopted countercyclical fiscal and monetary policies. This set of policies has been called the model of domestically-oriented growth. Import-competing manufacturing activities were given an advantage not only through protective trade policies, but also through tax and credit incentives. Specifically, the dynamic growth component, instead of being the export sector as it was before the Great Depression, was private and public investment in import-substituting industries and public investment in infrastructure geared to these industries' needs (Corbo, 1988).

Latin America abandoned economic orthodoxy in the beginning of the 1930s with remarkable success. Most Latin American countries had by 1932 erected exchange control barriers, raised tariffs, devalued very substantially and begun to default on foreign debt. In thus breaking away from the liberal international economic order and gold standard rules they felt able to follow expansionary fiscal and monetary policies to promote recovery (Maddison, 1985). The drastic experience of recession in the independent countries of Latin America had induced a change in attitudes towards the liberal international economic order, and an inward-looking approach to development which had its first successes in the 1930s (Maddison, 1985).

After World War II, when the advanced countries embarked on a period of growth characterised by dismantling of barriers to international trade and capital and so on, Latin America's policies did not change much and came to be characterised as 'structuralism' (Corbo, 1988). The main characteristic was promotion of industrialisation for the domestic market. Import substitution was implemented by a set of policies designed to shift the domestic terms of trade between agriculture and industry in favour of the latter. The major tool was the trade regime. Moreover, in these years of increasing intervention, the state itself often became directly involved in import-substitution industrialisation by setting up public enterprises in highly protected sectors, such as steel, petroleum, and chemicals. One of the major results of this policy was discrimination against exports (Corbo, 1988).

In the late 1940s and the 1950s the Santiago-based Economic Commission for Latin America and the Caribbean (ECLAC) worked on the theoretical foundations of what was to be called the structuralist position in economic development. Raúl Prebisch, one of the most controversial and influential intellectual leaders in Latin America, formed a team in the late 1940s and onwards at ECLAC and produced a series of studies of which the one by Prebisch (1991) is the best known.[18] Here the influential concept of the 'centre-periphery system' in economic relations was revealed for the first time.

Prebisch's best known academic contribution is the so-called Singer–Prebisch thesis (see also Singer, 1950) on the secular deterioration of terms of trade which led him to advocate industrialisation in Latin America and for a long time made ECLAC and import substitution inseparable. Many of these ideas were initially developed as a result of analysis of problems of inflation. Structuralist analysis attempted to identify specific rigidities, lags, shortages and surpluses, low elasticities of supply and demand, and other characteristics of the structure of developing countries that affect economic adjustments and the choice of development policy (Chenery, 1965). Structuralist analysts emphasised, among many other factors, the role of the state in economic development, the structural shift from agriculture to industry, and the lack of economic surplus for accumulation; they became influential in many countries in Latin America, particularly in Brazil and Chile.

A more critical analysis, also with respect to import substitution industrialisation, was provided by the Marxist structuralist interpretations, of which André Gunder Frank (1969) and Paul Baran probably offered the best known. The relationship between the 'core' and the 'periphery' is not one of mutual benefits but of exploitation. The surplus in the periphery will be caught by foreign capital or by the local elite. The basic theory is that import substitution increases dependency on imports and increases the power of the industrialists and multinational corporations at the expense of the poor and the rural peasants.

In the mid 1960s, both at ECLAC and elsewhere, another more sociological and political line of interpretation was developed to be known as 'dependency theory', which tried to explain why some of the presumed consequences of industrialisation for the periphery were not being produced. One of the basic economic arguments was that the industrialisation that took place in Latin America was largely limited to the production of consumer goods. The fruits of the dynamic capital goods sector where technical progress was concentrated went once again to the centre nations (Cardoso and Faletto, 1969).

Another set of ideas was developed at ECLAC to counter the foreign exchange constraint through economic planning and economic integration of the Latin American market, in order to be able to move to a second, more difficult stage of import substitution which could not be enacted at the national level alone. This analysis, together with the structuralists' view on inflation, was very influential in the 1960s and has been labelled Structuralism II (Corbo, 1988).

From early on several critics, within and outside Latin America, criticised the import substitution strategy. As early as 1950, Viner (1950), had rejected most of the arguments for protecting import-competing industry and recommended elimination of discrimination against exports. Another influential critic was

Roberto Campos (1967), who questioned the emphasis in favour of industry at the expense of agriculture, and the confidence in the theory that, by substituting public for private initiative, new resources would be created, and the assumption that inflation could be used to increase capital formation in a sustainable way.

Around the middle of the 1970s, a group of Southern Cone countries started to experiment with new policies which abandoned import-substitution policies and government intervention. These so-called neoconservative experiments were inspired as much by political and ideological as by economic factors and were implemented under the reign of military governments. Although many observers acknowledged serious problems in Latin America's development strategy in the mid 1970s, including the inefficient role of the state, the application of a radical anti-interventionist model paid very little attention to the limits of the market and the private sector (Ramos, 1986).

The debt crisis of the 1980s caused many Latin American countries to rethink their development strategy due to the economic necessity of debt servicing and external constraints; many countries started to implement neo-liberal policies consisting of economic adjustment, stabilisation and outward orientation, and also including policies to reduce state intervention, promotion of private enterprise, fiscal discipline, getting the prices right and improving allocation in the product, factor, and financial markets. Most of these policy elements were included in the 'Washington Consensus' (Williamson, 1990); additional themes like income distribution and social issues have been added to the agenda in the 1990s.

NOTES

1. Smith (1776, p. 617): 'Plenty of good land, and the liberty to manage their own affairs their own way, seem to be the two great causes of the prosperity of all new colonies'.
2. The term 'empty' countries, used for the American hemisphere and Australia, was of course not appropriate as both areas had significant indigenous populations. North America, the Southern Cone and Australia were sparsely populated. The more densely populated parts of the Americas experienced very drastic reductions in their population in the first decades after the conquest
3. Most Latin American countries became independent during the first half of the nineteenth century. All countries, except Brazil, declared their independence in 1810 and won it soon after: 1816 in Argentina, 1818 in Chile and Colombia and 1821 in Mexico and Venezuela. Brazil became independent from Portugal in 1822.
4. See in the case of Argentina (Díaz-Alejandro, 1970 and 1983), in Brazil (Suzigan, 1976), in Chile (Palma, 1979 and 1984), and in Colombia (Ocampo, 1987).
5. In the case of Argentina, maize (8.0 per cent) and beef (6.7 per cent) are the first and second export products and 68 per cent of all exports are of primary origin. The respective figures for other countries are: Brazil, coffee (8.5 per cent) and iron ore (5.2 per cent) and 40 per cent; Chile, copper (42.9) and grapes (4.6 per cent) and 81 per cent; Colombia, coffee (49 per cent), oil (12.6 per cent) and 69 per cent; Mexico, oil (43.6 per cent), coffee (3.5 per cent) and 47 per cent; and Venezuela, oil (79.1 per cent), aluminium (4.2 per cent) and 86 per cent (Bulmer-Thomas, 1994 and World Bank, 1995).
6. A term introduced by Okhawa and Rosovski (1973) but recently emphasised especially by Abramovitz (1986, 1990).

7. The comparison by Adam Smith (1776) of colonies in the Western Hemisphere was not the first but he concentrated on economics while other comparisons, for example Buffon (1761), de Pauw (1768) and Hegel (1820) were more of a theological–philosophical nature (Annino, 1995).
8. Around 1800 Latin America was divided in the Viceroyalties of New Spain, New Granada, Perú and Rio de la Plata (Lynch, 1991).
9. Between 1535 and 1816 there was a steady succession of 60 viceroys in New Spain (Maddison, 1995).
10. However, these detrimental effects of mercantilism on Latin American production, trade and development should not be overestimated; see the careful summary in Cardoso and Helwege (1992), emphasizing that mercantilism may not have been as important in slowing industrial and agricultural growth as the distorting nature of the mineral boom itself. They also stress that most European countries were extremely protectionist until the late nineteenth century. This makes it difficult to assess how much trade would have occurred in the absence of mercantilism.
11. Among those most mentioned are: underestimation of income that affects differently both income level and their concentration, the technique for measuring income and the geographical coverage of the surveys, see Altimir (1987) for a review and discussion of the income measurements from different types of surveys in Latin America and their comparability problems.
12. The Gini coefficient is a measure of income concentration that ranges from 0 to 1, the larger the coefficient, the greater the inequality. Thus 0 represents perfect equality and 1 represents perfect inequality.
13. It cannot be stressed enough that these estimates give only an indication of a tendency as the linking procedure involved linking series of different coverage, definition and quality.
14. In the strict sense it is difficult, especially in the case of the Latin American countries, to differentiate between pre- and post-tax income distribution, again; see Altimir (1987).
15. I did not use the 1957 estimate (0.802) of Baptista (1991) because it seemed unreasonably high, especially compared with his 1962 estimate (0.462).
16. The following description of Latin America's history of capital flow and debt is based largely upon Devlin (1989), ECLAC (1965a) and Marichal (1989).
17. By the middle of 1995 things had settled again; the major countries affected by the crisis were Mexico and (to a lesser extent) Argentina, both entering into recession. The repercussions in the rest of Latin America were relatively minor and most countries recovered part of the losses, especially those on the stock markets. However, on a negative note, several observers have commented that the crisis of the 1980s started the same way, through a number of minor crises in several countries. On the other hand, more optimistic observers suggest that the situation in Latin America is now structurally different from the 1980s as many countries have restructured their economies. In fact, only a few countries have advanced far in structural reforms, notably Chile, but several others are in the process of restructuring and it is to be hoped that economic growth will resume (or continue) in Latin America as restructuring is always much easier in times of economic growth but is extremely painful in times of crisis. It should also be stressed that structural reforms do not prevent crisis *per se*, as Chile found out so painfully in the early 1980s.
18. Many studies could be mentioned; of special importance were a series of country studies titled, *"The Economic Development of ..."*, which used what for that period were quite advanced techniques: capital stock estimation, econometric analysis and extensive data collection, and which are up-to-date valuable statistical sources for historical research due to their excellent empirical base. Other important ECLAC studies dealt with external financing, inflation and industrialization.

3. Economic Performance in Latin America – A Comparative Quantitative Perspective

A primary purpose of this book is to provide a new quantitative assessment of Latin American economic growth performance in the twentieth century. For the period after 1950 a growth accounting framework is presented in Chapter 6. Chapters 4 and 5 provide the necessary basic series for capital stock and labour input.

In this chapter the growth performance of Latin America throughout the twentieth century is treated from a comparative perspective using indicators of demographic development, growth rates of GDP and GDP per capita and labour productivity. Our sample covers only six of the 44 countries of Latin America and the Caribbean – Argentina, Brazil, Chile, Colombia, Mexico and Venezuela – but these had in 1994 a combined population of 359 million, equivalent to 75 per cent of the total for Latin America. They cover about 80 per cent of Latin American territory, and about 85 per cent of Latin America's GDP. Two major biases of the sample should be emphasised. First, it excludes the smaller countries of the Latin American continent which generally have a (much) lower per capita GDP. Second, it also excludes all 23 islands of the Caribbean which make up for around 5 per cent of GDP in the area, and of which 15 have higher than average per capita GDP.

Latin America's performance is compared with three other groups of countries: (a) two Asian countries (Korea and Taiwan) whose economic growth in the past couple of decades has been remarkably fast; (b) Portugal and Spain, whose institutional heritage had a good deal in common with Latin America; and (c) six advanced capitalist countries (France, Germany, Japan, the Netherlands, the United Kingdom and the United States), whose levels of income and productivity are amongst the highest in the world.

AGGREGATE GROWTH PERFORMANCE

The GDP growth rates presented in Table 3.1 show a quite respectable performance by Latin America for the whole of the twentieth century. The slowest growth was in Chile and Argentina, with Brazil and Venezuela having the best overall performance. A comparison of these results with the other countries of the sample shows that the average growth of 4.2 per annum was faster than the advanced and Iberian countries, which both grew at an average of 2.8 per cent a year. Growth in Latin America was slower than in the Asian group, which grew at 4.8 per cent in the twentieth century.

Table 3.1 Latin America: Total GDP, 1900–1994 (average annual compound growth rates)

	1900–13	1913–29	1929–50	1950–73	1973–80	1980–89	1989–94	1900–94
Argentina	6.4	3.5	2.5	4.0	3.0	-1.0	6.1	3.5
Brazil	4.5	4.7	5.0	6.9	7.2	2.3	0.9	5.0
Chile	3.7	2.9	2.2	3.6	2.8	2.9	6.4	3.2
Colombia	4.2	4.7	3.6	5.1	5.0	3.3	4.3	4.4
Mexico	2.6	0.8	4.0	6.5	6.4	1.4	3.0	3.7
Venezuela	3.3	8.2	5.9	6.4	4.1	-0.1	3.6	5.2
Arithmetic average	4.1	4.1	3.9	5.4	4.8	1.5	4.0	4.2
Korea	2.0	3.0	0.7	7.5	7.1	8.7	7.6	4.5
Taiwan	1.8	3.8	1.8	9.3	8.3	7.4	6.3	5.2
Arithmetic average	1.9	3.4	1.3	8.4	7.7	8.0	6.9	4.8
Portugal	1.7	0.6	2.6	5.5	3.2	2.5	1.5	2.8
Spain	2.3	2.4	0.1	6.1	2.1	2.8	1.5	2.7
Arithmetic average	2.0	1.5	1.4	5.8	2.7	2.7	1.5	2.8
France	1.7	1.9	0.6	5.1	2.8	2.2	1.1	2.4
Germany	3.0	1.2	1.4	5.9	2.2	1.9	2.7	2.8
Japan	2.5	3.7	1.1	9.6	2.9	4.0	2.2	4.2
Netherlands	2.3	3.6	1.5	4.7	2.4	1.8	2.1	2.9
UK	1.5	0.7	1.7	3.0	0.9	2.9	0.6	1.8
Arithmetic average	2.2	2.2	1.3	5.7	2.3	2.6	1.8	2.8
USA	4.0	3.1	2.6	3.7	2.1	3.0	1.7	3.1

Sources: Latin America from Appendix B and other countries from Maddison (1995). Korea updated to 1994 with growth rates from IMF (various issues) and Taiwan from Council for Economic Development (1994), 1994 updated using growth rate for 1992–93.

In Chapter 7 policy regimes in Latin America in the post-war period will be analysed together with their role in the performance of the region. In this section I give only a condensed description of the performance of the different countries during the twentieth century. The periodisation and the appropriateness of my benchmarks are discussed in the section of this chapter on fluctuations in growth.

In the twentieth century most of our countries performed best in the 1950–73 period. Of the 16 countries in our sample, 10 experienced the highest growth of the century in this period. These include all the advanced countries, with the exception of the United States and three Latin American countries. Three countries of the sample group are currently experiencing their best growth period of the twentieth century, with two of them, Korea and Taiwan, coming, not very surprisingly, from Asia. The other one is, quite significantly, Chile, which managed this performance amid one of the worst crises for Latin America in the twentieth century. However, one must take into consideration that Chile's performance in the past has been extremely weak; its overall performance in the twentieth century is the worst for the Latin American sample. For two countries, Argentina and the United States, the first part of the century, 1900–1913, was their best period in terms of total GDP growth. Finally, there is a clear distinction between developing and advanced countries in 1973–80. Growth performance deteriorated abruptly in all advanced countries after the OPEC crisis, while the pace of growth remained high in Latin America and Asia.

The inter-war period was by far the worst in terms of total GDP growth for most countries in the twentieth century. Six countries (France, Japan, the Netherlands and Spain of the advanced countries, and Korea and Chile) experienced their lowest point in the 1929–50 period, while the United Kingdom, Germany, Portugal and Mexico had their low period from 1913–29. Latin America, with the exception of Chile and Mexico, experienced its major crisis during the lost decade of the 1980s.[1] For the Asian countries 1900–1913 and 1929–50 were the worst periods.

PER CAPITA GROWTH

Table 3.2 shows the long-term per capita growth record since 1900. The final years of the liberal world order were years of prosperity for most countries in our sample. On a comparative basis it was the best period of the twentieth century for Latin America, but per capita growth was very slight in the Asian developing countries, which grew at a rate of 0.6 per cent before World War I. The Iberian countries grew at 1.3 per cent, about the same rate as the more advanced European countries. The United States did even better with a growth rate of 2.0 per cent.

The period 1913–50 can usefully be divided into three different sub-periods with benchmark years in 1929, the year the Great Depression began, and 1938, the dividing point between the Great Depression and World War II.

From 1913–29, when the liberal world trading order broke down, the expansion of per capita real income in different regions was quite similar, with Asia as the laggard. Latin America experienced fast growth during the first years of the twentieth century. In the period 1929–50 when growth was interrupted by the collapse of international trade and World War II, most areas suffered major setbacks and their growth performance was generally very poor, or, in the case of

Asia,[2] negative. Several primary exporters in Latin America had already experienced difficulties in the late 1920s; Brazil lost control over the coffee market and Chile lost ground as a result of the introduction of synthetic nitrates.

Table 3.2 GDP per Capita, 1900–1994 (average annual compound growth rates)

	1900–13	1913–29	1929–50	1950–73	1973–80	1980–89	1989–94	1900–94
Argentina	2.5	0.9	0.6	2.3	1.4	-2.5	4.8	1.3
Brazil	2.3	2.5	2.6	3.9	4.7	0.2	-0.8	2.6
Chile	2.4	1.6	0.6	1.4	1.2	1.3	4.6	1.5
Colombia	2.1	2.1	1.6	2.2	2.7	1.3	2.5	2.0
Mexico	1.9	0.1	1.6	3.3	3.5	-0.8	1.1	1.7
Venezuela	2.3	7.3	3.8	2.6	0.5	-2.5	1.2	2.9
Arithmetic average	2.2	2.4	1.8	2.6	2.3	-0.5	2.2	2.0
Korea	0.8	1.3	-1.3	5.2	5.3	7.4	6.6	2.7
Taiwan	0.4	2.1	-0.9	6.2	6.2	5.9	5.2	3.0
Arithmetic average	0.6	1.7	-1.1	5.7	5.7	6.6	5.9	2.8
Portugal	0.9	-0.1	1.5	5.4	1.3	2.6	1.4	2.2
Spain	1.6	1.5	-0.7	5.1	1.0	2.3	1.4	1.9
Arithmetic average	1.3	0.7	0.4	5.3	1.2	2.5	1.4	2.0
France	1.5	1.9	0.5	4.1	2.3	1.7	0.8	2.0
Germany	1.6	0.8	0.4	4.9	2.3	1.8	1.8	2.1
Japan	1.3	2.4	-0.2	8.3	1.8	3.4	2.0	3.1
Netherlands	0.9	2.1	0.3	3.4	1.7	1.3	1.6	1.7
UK	0.7	0.3	1.3	2.5	0.9	2.7	0.4	1.4
Arithmetic average	1.2	1.5	0.4	4.6	1.8	2.2	1.3	2.1
USA	2.0	1.7	1.5	2.2	1.0	2.0	1.2	1.8

Source: See Table 3.1.

In contrast with most of the rest of the world, 1929–50 were remarkably good years in Latin America. Unlike other areas, GDP per capita accelerated. The general trend towards import substitution and expansionary fiscal and monetary policies produced impressive results by world standards. If there was an engine of growth in Latin America during the 1930s, that engine was import-substituting industrialisation.

There is truth in the assertion that the Latin American countries that performed reasonably well during the 1930s were those which had large domestic markets and some industrial base prior to 1929, as was the case in Argentina, Brazil, Colombia and Mexico. One may conclude that a substantial domestic market and a degree of autonomy with regard to exchange rates, fiscal and monetary policy were conditions required for industrialisation in Latin America in the 1930s.

Table 3.2 shows GDP per capita growth rates. Latin America averaged 1.8 per cent per capita growth a year, compared with a mere 0.4 per cent in Europe, and - 1.1 per cent in Asia. The USA grew by an average of 1.5 per cent for 1929–50 as a whole, but the average includes the depressed 1930s and the wartime boom. Analysis of Table 3.3, on comparative levels of performance, clearly reveals that the whole period 1900–1950 was, comparatively, a very prosperous one for Latin America. Its per capita GDP increased somewhat compared to the United States whilst all other countries show a relative decline. The figure for the Asian group fell from an average of 17 per cent in 1900 to 8 per cent in 1950. The Iberian level had fallen to 21 per cent by 1950. Also, the advanced countries' level had fallen drastically. The detrimental effects of World War II on most countries, and the relatively sheltered position of Latin America, explain this performance to a great extent.

Table 3.3 Levels of per Capita GDP, 1900–1994 (international 1980 dollars, USA = 100)

	1900	1913	1929	1950	1973	1980	1989	1994
Argentina	52	55	49	41	42	43	29	34
Brazil	10	11	12	15	22	29	24	22
Chile	38	40	39	33	27	28	26	31
Colombia	18	18	19	19	19	22	21	22
Mexico	35	35	27	27	35	42	33	33
Venezuela	10	10	24	38	41	40	26	26
Arithmetic average	27	28	28	29	31	34	26	28
Korea	19	16	15	8	16	22	35	45
Taiwan	15	12	13	8	19	27	38	46
Arithmetic average	17	14	14	8	17	24	36	45
Portugal	25	22	16	16	33	34	36	36
Spain	43	41	40	25	48	48	50	50
Arithmetic average	34	31	28	21	41	41	43	43
France	55	52	54	44	68	74	73	71
Germany	58	55	47	37	69	75	74	76
Japan	23	21	24	17	64	67	77	80
Netherlands	74	64	69	53	71	74	69	71
UK	96	81	65	62	68	67	72	69
Arithmetic average	61	55	52	43	68	71	73	73
USA	100	100	100	100	100	100	100	100

Source: Table 3.1.

Since 1950, Latin America's performance has been systematically much worse than that of almost all the other areas. The period 1950–73 witnessed great expansion in Latin America, with growth per capita averaging 2.6 per cent a year (faster than the 1.8 average for 1929–50). However, most other areas had a golden age with a much greater acceleration of growth. Asian growth averaged 5.7 per cent a year from 1950–73, Iberia 5.3 per cent, and the advanced European countries 4.7 per cent. US performance was much more modest at 2.2 per cent a year.

In the post-war period Latin America did not enjoy positive growth to the same extent as other countries which were enjoying reconstruction and catch-up, rapid expansion of international trade and the commercial exploitation of a backlog of technological advances made during the war. An additional important factor in explaining Latin America's lacklustre performance was the fact that Latin America had grown faster than any other region during the first half of the twentieth century and was thus much closer to its potential, while many other countries had much larger scope for recovery.

In 1973 the period of post-war expansion abruptly came to an end. The advanced and the Iberian countries settled into a much lower pace of growth. The Asian countries continued growing at extremely high average per capita rates of above 5 per cent. Latin America experienced a modest slow-down between 1973–80 but a complete collapse in the 1980s.

The crisis of the 1980s was triggered off by the rapid increase of interest rates in the international market and affected Latin America profoundly as many of its countries had rapidly increased their foreign debt in the 1970s when international liquidity was very high. The debt crisis forced them to reevaluate their development strategy and in many cases a more outward looking, private sector oriented strategy was adopted. Table 3.4 presents labour productivity in Latin America for the 1913–94 period (1913 being the earliest year for which data were available).

One of the most important findings is that the process of acceleration of GDP growth and labour productivity had already started in Latin America around 1938, when per capita GDP and productivity growth accelerated with growth rates about three times as high as the previous 1929–38 period. It should be noted that growth was more homogeneous compared to the 1913–29 period when average per capita growth was also relatively high in Latin America. Growth accelerated from 1938 onwards, especially in Argentina, Chile, Mexico and Venezuela. It was during this period that the combined effect of expansionary fiscal and monetary policy and import substitution resulted in high growth of productivity per man hour and per capita GDP, some countries also benefiting from the positive effect of World War II.

*Table 3.4 Latin America: Labour Productivity Growth and Levels, 1900–1994
(average annual compound growth rates and USA = 100)*

	1913–29	1929–38	1938–50	1950–73	1973–80	1980–89	1989–94	1900–94
Labour Productivity (GDP per Man Hour)								
Argentina	1.6	-0.2	2.7	2.6	2.2	-2.1	4.6	1.7 [a]
Brazil	5.2	3.0	3.9	3.9	4.0	0.1	-0.6	3.4 [a]
Chile	2.3	-0.7	2.0	3.0	1.0	-0.2	3.2	1.8 [a]
Colombia	4.2	0.6	2.3	3.0	1.9	1.3	2.1	2.5 [a]
Mexico	2.4	1.0	3.4	4.2	2.7	-1.1	0.4	2.2 [a]
Venezuela	11.1	1.4	4.9	3.5	-0.9	-1.8	0.2	2.7 [a]
Arithmetic average	4.5	0.9	3.2	3.4	1.8	-0.6	1.6	2.4 [a]
Levels of Labour Productivity (USA = 100)								
	1913	1929	1938	1950	1973	1980	1989	1994
Argentina	53	51	44	41	40	45	32	38
Brazil	9	15	17	18	24	30	26	24
Chile	42	46	38	32	35	35	30	33
Colombia	18	26	24	21	23	24	24	25
Mexico	37	34	32	33	45	52	41	39
Venezuela	24	37	37	45	53	48	35	33
Arithmetic average	31	35	32	32	37	39	31	32
USA	100	100	100	100	100	100	100	100

Note: [a] refers to the 1913–94 period.

Sources: Appendix A and B for population and GDP. Appendix C for employment and hours worked for 1950 onwards. Annual hours worked were estimated at 2588 in 1913 based upon Maddison (1991a, p. 255) and interpolated to 1950. Employment 1925–50: from ECLAC (1965b) except for Argentina 1913–50 from IEERAL (1986). Employment before 1925: Chile from Ballesteros and Davis (1965), Mexico from INEGI (1985) and Brazil, Colombia and Venezuela retrapolated.

FLUCTUATIONS IN GROWTH

In order to be able to compare Latin America with countries outside the region, the benchmarks which are almost universally accepted by the scholars in this field have been analysed. For the twentieth century these benchmarks consist of the years 1913, 1950 and 1973. With these benchmarks four different phases of growth can be distinguished in the twentieth century, that is a first phase until 1913,[3] a second phase from 1913–50, a third from 1950–73 and the fourth and last phase covering the period since then. However, it is necessary to ascertain whether this chronology, specifically developed for the advanced countries, also fits the Latin American case and, if not, which countries are the main exceptions, in what period, and what is the effect on the analysis. Table 3.5 and Figure 3.1 give an indication of the shifting weights, in terms of total GDP, of the sample countries from 1900–1994.

The most important country of the sample in 1900, in terms of GDP, was Mexico. In the mid-1920s, Argentina had the biggest weight. During the 1940s, Argentina, Brazil and Mexico had very similar shares. Lastly, from the end of the 1940s until 1994, Brazil was the most important economy in the region.

Table 3.5 Latin America: Share of Each Country in Total GDP of the Six Countries, 1900–1994 (per cent)

	Argentina	Brazil	Chile	Colombia	Mexico	Venezuela	Total
1900	21.9	16.4	10.2	6.3	43.1	2.2	100
1929	31.2	21.9	9.4	8.2	25.1	4.3	100
1950	24.3	28.0	6.9	8.0	26.3	6.6	100
1980	13.4	38.6	3.4	6.5	31.5	6.6	100
1994	12.5	37.5	4.6	8.1	31.3	6.0	100

Source: Appendix B.

Figure 3.1 Latin America: Share of Individual Countries in the Six Country Total GDP, 1900–1994 (in percentages)

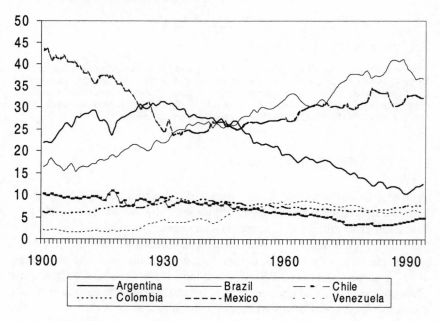

Source: Same as Table 3.5.

In Table 3.6 the annual fluctuations in GDP are presented on the basis of aggregating total GDP of the six countries. The 1950 benchmark is not very clear in terms of fluctuations of GDP growth, as Latin America continued the growth process initiated in the late 1930s. It can be concluded that growth in Latin America from 1950 onwards was more stable than in the period after the Great Depression.

The 1900–1994 period will be analysed graphically for each country on the basis of yearly GDP estimates for each country in order to see whether the individual country cycles coincide with the phases distinguished above. For each country we will also analyse the sensitivity of changes in the benchmarks to growth rates.

Table 3.6 Year-to-Year Percentage Change in Aggregate GDP of the Six Countries, 1900–1994 (annual growth rates)

1900		1914	-3.2	1930	-4.4	1950	5.4	1973	8.9	1981	0.7
1901	8.1	1915	-0.2	1931	-5.3	1951	6.0	1974	6.6	1982	-0.7
1902	-1.6	1916	2.0	1932	-4.1	1952	3.2	1975	3.7	1983	-2.4
1903	8.6	1917	0.5	1933	9.5	1953	4.8	1976	6.2	1984	3.8
1904	3.8	1918	5.3	1934	8.2	1954	6.9	1977	5.0	1985	3.3
1905	8.5	1919	0.3	1935	4.9	1955	6.2	1978	4.9	1986	3.5
1906	2.0	1920	6.0	1936	6.4	1956	4.2	1979	7.1	1987	3.1
1907	5.7	1921	0.4	1937	5.2	1957	7.3	1980	7.1	1988	1.0
1908	1.4	1922	6.2	1938	2.5	1958	5.3			1989	1.6
1909	4.6	1923	8.6	1939	4.6	1959	2.6			1990	0.4
1910	4.6	1924	3.3	1940	1.5	1960	7.4			1991	3.3
1911	1.1	1925	3.1	1941	6.0	1961	7.1			1992	2.7
1912	5.7	1926	4.8	1942	0.2	1962	4.0			1993	3.1
1913	1.5	1927	3.4	1943	3.5	1963	3.5			1994	4.5
		1928	7.8	1944	8.0	1964	8.0				
		1929	2.0	1945	2.7	1965	5.4				
				1946	9.5	1966	4.6				
				1947	5.8	1967	4.8				
				1948	6.7	1968	7.9				
				1949	4.1	1969	7.6				
						1970	5.1				
						1971	6.7				
						1972	7.6				

Source: Appendix B.

CAUSES OF CYCLICAL INSTABILITY

There are many factors, external or internal, which may cause instability. Of course, they cannot be separated completely and a combination of the two can generate all kinds of different results. A good example of the combined effects of internal and external factors was the first oil crisis in 1973 which caused distinct domestic reactions with different results in terms of economic stability. Most countries experienced a fall in growth rates as they adopted policies to adjust to the change in relative prices. Latin American countries, including the non-oil exporters, borrowed heavily, with only minor adjustment to changes in relative prices, and the growth process continued. In the 1980s the combined effect of lack of price adjustment and heavy indebtedness caused the 'lost decade'.

Here we will give a description of the most recurrent causes of cyclical fluctuations in Latin America.[4] Several causes of instability of external origin can be identified:

– As already indicated in Chapter 2, the sudden drop in capital and trade flows due to external reasons represents a major cause of instability in Latin America. The crises of the 1820s, the 1870s, the 1930s and the 1980s were caused predominantly by such developments.
– Another relevant factor producing instability is extreme dependence on one or a few primary commodities, with fluctuations in demand or supply factors generating instability. This factor is quite important in Latin America as the single most important export product is still a primary commodity in all countries of our sample.
– External factors of a non-economic character, like war or extreme political unrest, influence stability through falls in exports and deterioration of the terms of trade.

Many internal factors are also important:

– Climatic variations can create instability in countries specialising in agricultural primary products. Droughts, with their effects on harvests or energy generation; extreme temperature changes, either at sea or on land; storms; and earthquakes, still have significant influence.
– A traditionally important cyclical factor in Latin America is the political process, where electoral considerations often have powerful economic effects. This has been the case in countries with relatively high political stability, for example Mexico, or countries with higher instability and more populist political processes.
– Another cause of economic instability stemming from internal political events comes in the form of extreme situations such as military interventions. This has been the case in Chile, Argentina and many other countries. Arguably, other extreme cases fall into this same category, like the Unidad Popular experiment of President Allende in the early 1970s in Chile.
– Some crises in Latin America can be clearly attributed to mistakes in domestic economic policy. Populism and neo-conservative experiments in Argentina and Chile in the 1970s and the Mexican crisis in the 1990s are examples.

INDIVIDUAL COUNTRY EXPERIENCE OF INSTABILITY

In Figure 3.2, concerning Argentina, one can observe clearly that 1913 was the last year of a phase of rapid growth. This growth, the fastest in Latin America, was export-led, especially by agricultural products (see Díaz-Alejandro, 1970), and was accompanied by high (foreign) investment and large immigration from Europe.

Argentina's impressive per capita GDP growth between 1900–1913 declined rapidly during the 1913–29 period, caused, in the view of some commentators, by the lack of government support for industry. These commentators have called this period 'the Long Delay', to be situated between Rostow's 'Preconditions' and 'Take-off'.[5] Díaz-Alejandro (1970) provides some strong arguments against this thesis, indicating that the 1913–29 period can be divided into two sub-periods (1913–19) and (1919–29). The first period of economic depression started before World War I, and was touched off by the decline in foreign capital due to monetary restrictions in Europe, aggravated by the bad harvest of 1914, and of course the onset of World War I. From 1917 onwards foreign capital and exports recovered, and GDP grew rapidly especially in manufacturing and construction.[6]

During 1929–50 Argentina's growth performance was the worst in our sample of Latin American countries, GDP growth being negative (-0.8) during the Great Depression and growing at 1.7 per cent during 1938–50. Argentina was a prototype country of the liberal world order, and was hit extremely hard by the depression, which cut its markets for exports and foreign capital and reduced migration to a minimum. As a result of the depression, there was a change in Argentina's long-run economic policies, with more emphasis on import substitution and less on export promotion.

In the period 1913–50, the crises of World War I and the Great Depression figure clearly, but the contractionary effects of World War II are not that evident. In fact, the growth rates for the 1938–50 period (around 1938, Argentina again reached pre-Great Depression GDP levels) and the 1950–73 period are similar (see Table 3.4). From 1973 onwards, there is a clear drop in growth rates which lasted until the 1980s, and negative growth rates until the early 1990s. It can be concluded that 1913 and 1973 are reasonable benchmarks for Argentina. The 1950 benchmark cannot be clearly distinguished, but 1980 represents a turning point for Argentina.

It is also evident that the performance in the second half of the twentieth century until recent years was significantly below the performance of the first half, and that, as will be discussed in Chapter 7, during the 1970s and 1980s external instability was compounded by domestic policy errors.

Brazil

Brazil experienced a period of rapid growth at the beginning of the twentieth century, following important political changes during the last quarter of the nineteenth century such as the abolition of slavery and the establishment of the Republic. As in the case of Argentina this growth was export-led, based upon exports of agricultural products such as coffee and rubber, but the Brazilian government also initiated a programme of public works. Unlike in Argentina, this was the starting point of a period of rapid growth which was to continue until the 1980s (see Merrick and Graham, 1979 and Villela and Suzigan, 1977).

Brazil's performance was among the best in Latin America during the 1913–50 period. Of particular note is the fact that the country recovered relatively rapidly from the adverse effects of the Great Depression. One element that has been stressed is the coffee support programme which had some countercyclical effects of a Keynesian nature.[7] The promotion of industry through import substitution was not a deliberate policy choice; however, the industrial sector benefited indirectly from the coffee support programme and the various stabilisation programmes, for example from the protection offered by the numerous exchange-rate devaluations and the tariffs on imports.

Although 1913 and 1929 are years characterised by slower growth and even economic recession, it is hardly possible to conclude that the 1900–1913 period is distinctively different from 1913–50. During the whole period Brazil experienced a growth rate of around 2.5 per cent and the crises of 1913 and 1929 only interrupted this growth process briefly. In the second half of the twentieth century Brazil experienced an acceleration in growth to rates around 4 per cent while the 1973–80 period shows even higher rates of growth.

Figure 3.2 shows very clearly that Brazilian growth accelerated after the Great Depression and continued growing until the crisis of the 1980s. External factors had a major impact on economic growth in Brazil in the twentieth century; however, in the 1980s and also 1990s internal political and policy factors limited growth (see also Chapter 7).

Chile

As Figure 3.2 shows conclusively, Chile is by far the most vulnerable country in Latin America in terms of GDP fluctuations. At least six major economic crises can be identified during the twentieth century. The first was related to World War I, a second occurred at the beginning of the 1920s and the Great Depression also hit hard in Chile. From the middle of the 1930s, Chile experienced a rather stable low growth path until the early 1970s. In the 1970s and the 1980s, another pair of profound crises beset the Chilean economy.

Economic growth in Chile during the first years of the twentieth century was influenced by the natural sodium nitrate boom which had started in the 1880s. The enormous expansion in production and exports of nitrate transformed Chile's society and economy as documented in Cariola and Sunkel (1985) and Mamalakis (1976). Per capita GDP grew at a fast rate that would not be repeated until very recently in the twentieth century.

During 1913–50 Chile's growth performance can be divided into the 1913–29 period of somewhat higher than average per capita GDP growth for Latin America, and the 1929–50 period of much lower comparative performance. The nitrate boom was affected by the outbreak of World War I and the contraction of European markets; however, the rapid growth of the North American market compensated for the loss of European markets and the boom apparently continued until the 1930s when the combined effect of the discovery of artificial nitrate and the low technological level caused the industry to collapse. Copper production and exports entered a new period of expansion after the great decline from 1880 until the 1920s; however, the interactions between large-scale copper production and the rest of Chile's economy were limited, and fewer linkages were established than in the case of nitrate. Chile was hit hard by the Great Depression and average per capita GDP fell between 1929–38. This development prompted the government to adopt a policy designed to reduce external dependence, and industrialisation became an important instrument for attaining economic growth.

Again it becomes clear that 1913 and 1973 are good benchmarks. Since the beginning of the 1980s, following a severe crisis, Chile is experiencing high economic growth, compared with the rest of the century. Chile is the country where external dependency and domestic policy errors caused extremely high economic volatility, as will be documented in Chapter 7.

Colombia

In complete contrast to Chile in terms of volatility is Colombia, which has experienced by far the most stable economic growth of all Latin American countries during this century. Growth accelerated in Colombia at the beginning of the twentieth century, after the period of stagnation caused by the War of a Thousand Days. The pace set between 1900–1913 was to continue throughout the rest of the twentieth century, and during certain periods growth was even faster (see McGreevy, 1985). World War I did not affect Colombia very much, and 1913 was not a crisis year in Colombia.

Figure 3.2 Latin America: Volume Movements of GDP, 1900–1994

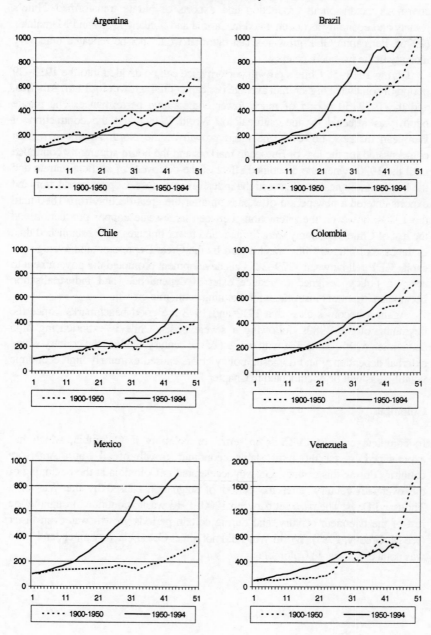

Figure 3.2 (continued)

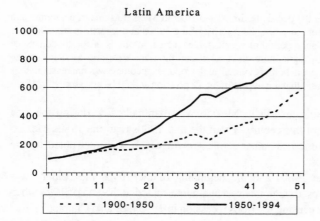

Latin America

Source: Appendix B.

However, the Great Depression negatively impacted the growth process and for the only time in the twentieth century, the country experienced negative growth. The recovery from the recession has been comparatively swift in Colombia owing partly to an anti-cyclical policy (at the national and especially the local level) and partly to exports of gold and coffee (see Maddison, 1985). During World War II per capita GDP remained stable, but from 1945 onwards growth resumed. Colombia is the only country in our group to record lower growth rates in the 1938–50 period compared to the 1929–38 period, as a result of the fall in economic growth in the early 1940s. From then on, the country recorded uninterrupted growth until the early 1980s when the debt crisis caused the country to experience a fall in growth rates.

Mexico

During the final years of the 'Porfiriato' (1876–1910) growth was relatively fast in Mexico but this process was interrupted by the Mexican Revolution and later by the Great Depression. Mexico's growth performance during 1913–50 was of course greatly affected by the revolution and the civil war. Our figures show constant per capita GDP for 1913–29 and an average performance between 1929–50. During the later period per capita GDP was stagnant from 1929–38 when the first reaction to the Great Depression was to enforce a restrictive monetary policy, but during the Cárdenas government (1934–40) a more Keynesian policy was followed. Growth sped up from 1938–50, especially as a result of World War II, which improved exports from, and tourism to, the United States and boosted remittances from temporary workers in that country.

However, Fitzgerald (1984) emphasises that:

the orthodox view of the decade leading up to 1929 in Mexico as one of economic and institutional stagnation, awaiting the reforms of the 1930s and growth in the 1940s, is not correct. It is in fact a period of considerable change: the basis of the modern State was laid; commercial agriculture and manufacturing were emerging as new leading sectors; and pressure on both peasants' and workers' incomes was increasing. It is against this background that the impact of the Depression should be assessed. (p. 248)

Therefore, economic growth in Mexico was extremely low during the first three to four decades of this century. From the mid-1930s until the 1980s Mexico experienced a long period of rather stable growth which was interrupted by the debt crisis of the 1980s.

At the end of the 1980s and the beginning of the 1990s the country was growing at modest rates, though this was again interrupted at the end of 1994 when a new crisis broke out causing a serious recession in 1995 (see also Chapter 7).

Venezuela

During the first two decades of the twentieth century Venezuela experienced fairly low growth rates. This changed in the 1920s when the country, boosted by the oil sector, began to experience extremely high growth rates. The period 1913–50 was a very prosperous one for Venezuela, with growth rates of per capita GDP well above the Latin American average. The acceleration of the growth process initiated in the second and third decade was very closely associated with foreign firms' (particularly Anglo-Dutch and US) exploitation of the oil reserves (Quero Morales, 1978). From 1913–29 and 1938–50, Venezuela grew at the unprecedented rates of 7.3 and 5.0 per cent per capita, respectively. Growth rates were somewhat lower in the 1929–38 period as the country was severely hit by the Great Depression, followed by swift recovery until a new crisis at the end of the 1930s caused negative growth; but the rest of the 1940s were again years of extremely high growth. From 1950 onwards growth rates tended to fall and between 1980–94 there was a tendency towards recession. However, the overall growth rate recorded in the twentieth century has been the highest of all countries in our sample.

The above analysis indicates that, for the first half of the twentieth century, the benchmarks normally accepted do fit the Latin American situation to a reasonable degree. In almost all cases 1913 is a crisis year (except in Colombia and Venezuela). Looking at the two major crises that affected the world in the 1913–50 period, Latin America was hit on a comparable scale during the Great Depression, although the region recovered fairly quickly, but World War II did not have as devastating an effect on Latin America as it had on the rest of the world, and in several countries in Latin America it provided opportunities for growth.

It therefore seems reasonable also to include 1938 in the case of Latin America, since its growth performance was quite different from the rest of the world between 1938–50. In the post-war period the 1973 benchmark seems quite acceptable, as argued for above; but it is also necessary to include 1980 as a benchmark in the case of Latin America because the beginning of the 1980s marked one of the most profound crises in Latin America.

The main conclusions which can be drawn from the above discussion are reflected in the Latin American total in Figure 3.2. The years 1929, 1980 and, to a lesser degree, 1913 show recessions. Slower growth occurred around the 1940s, and 1973 marked a slowdown in growth in most sample countries outside Latin America. In Latin America 1950 is not as clear a benchmark year as in the other countries in our sample. As a general conclusion, it seems acceptable to use the benchmarks identified for the international comparison, although it would be reasonable to include two additional benchmarks in the case of Latin America: 1938 and 1980.

In order to be able to combine the results obtained by other scholars, I have chosen to present a combination of the phases identified for the rest of the world and those for Latin America. A good case can be made, on the basis of empirically measurable characteristics, for the following phases in the cases of Latin America. A first phase ended in 1929 with very similar overall growth rates in the periods 1900–1913 and 1913–29. Argentina and Mexico slowed down while Venezuela accelerated, starting its oil based growth boom. A second phase from 1929–50 was characterised by a sharp recession as a result of the Great Depression but also a fairly quick recovery, compared to the rest of the world. During this period Latin America was forced into a strategy of import substitution. This was especially due to external conditions such as the protective measures adopted by many countries in the 1930s and the de facto trade contraction caused by World War II.

A third phase can be identified from 1950 to 1980, with relatively stable growth rates, although with a slight trend towards slowdown at the end of the period, especially since 1973. In this phase most Latin American countries adopted a development strategy based upon import substitution. A final phase started in 1980, showing a drastic slowdown in economic growth and the start of a process of changing the development strategy towards a more outward-oriented one. From the late 1980s (in some countries even earlier) and the 1990s onwards several countries are growing again, and the benchmark adopted for this recovery period is 1989.

NOTES

1.   This result is, of course, dependent on the periodisation since the 'Great Depression' in Latin America was rather short-lived, and by 1938 most countries were approaching or above the previous total GDP peak level (see also Table 2.5). In the 1980s the crisis lasted much longer, and several countries only recovered to pre-crisis levels at the end of the decade.
2.   The Asian countries selected are, of course, not at all representative of Asia, and therefore summarizing them as 'the Asian case' is misleading. This is even more the case in the period before 1950 when Korea and Taiwan were colonies of Japan.
3.   This phase started much earlier than 1900, possibly around 1870. See Maddison (1995) for a description of phases of growth in the nineteenth century, in which he distinguishes a first growth acceleration in Europe and its 'offshoots', Australia, Canada, New Zealand and the USA, starting around 1820 when Europe had more or less recovered from the previous period of revolution, war and economic blockade affecting it since the 1790s. Another well-accepted benchmark, also especially relevant for Latin America, is around 1870 when a sharp growth acceleration occurred in a much greater area of the world compared to the 1820 acceleration. For Latin America, as for most other countries, growth acceleration happened around this benchmark, in the case of Chile, Brazil and Argentina probably somewhat earlier, and Mexico, Colombia and Venezuela somewhat later (see Reynolds, 1983). So also for Latin America a case can be made for 1870–1913 as a period of growth acceleration which ended with the outbreak of World War I.
4.   There are many sources for cyclical analysis in Latin America, one of the best known is the *Economic Survey*, which ECLAC has published since the end of the 1940s; for many countries and for the first half of the century there exists an ever growing literature. See for a classification of business cycle causality, Maddison (1985).
5.   See Di Tella and Zymelman (1973) who situated this period from 1914 to 1933.
6.   See Díaz-Alejandro (1970) pp. 61–65.
7.   In the study of the economic development of Brazil, the anticyclical Keynesian policy followed during the Great Depression is a topic of great debate: see Fishlow (1972), Furtado (1963) and Villela and Suzigan (1977).

4. New Standardised Estimates of Labour Input and Human Capital

INTRODUCTION

Traditional analysis of growth performance always included measures of employment and labour productivity, and Denison (1962 and 1967) was one of the first to present a more sophisticated analysis of labour input, considering length of the work year, disaggregation of inputs by age and by levels of education. Since then most growth analysts have emphasized the importance of taking a broader view of human capital, though large series cross country econometric work has often used rough proxies for education – enrolment rates – rather than educational stock. Here we have followed the Denison tradition to ensure that the components of our labour input analysis are robust.

Recently, the human capital dimension to economic growth has again returned to centre.[1] As Denison (1993) observed in one of his last contributions:

> If one were forced to choose a single growth source as most important in the long run, the choice would have to be advances in knowledge. (p. 58)

Appendices A and C present a comprehensive set of tables on population and employment, the number of days and hours worked per person and data on sectoral employment and educational level of the population. The main conclusions that can be inferred from this database for the six Latin American countries are commented on, and the existing empirical material reviewed to corroborate our results. The basic sources are national censuses, population censuses, agricultural censuses and so on, and the surveys (for example household surveys) which are conducted regularly in each country. However, these censuses contain big differences between countries and I attempt to make adjustments in order to make the series as comparable as possible for the Latin American countries.

This chapter also includes disaggregated estimates of employment for 1950–94 broken down into agriculture, industry and services. It presents estimates of the average number of years of formal education of the population. The quality of human capital is affected by many other factors such as health and nutrition. Widespread schooling and good health care and nutrition early in a country's development have a positive effect on its economic performance. There is a

47

growing consensus in Latin America and elsewhere that investments in schooling, training, health and nutrition are important elements of a successful development strategy.

The past four decades of development show that appropriate government policies for human capital development are just as critical as macroeconomic stability, global competitiveness and physical infrastructure. Human resource investments are required both to facilitate the adjustment process in the short term, so that production and employment can adapt to the changing national and international economic picture and to increase the prospects for sustained productivity growth over the long term. Moreover, better schooled and trained people are more likely to explore and share market and technological innovations. Furthermore, overall social reform can be pursued more effectively, through such investments, providing opportunities for all members of society to participate in the benefits of development (IDB, 1993).

POPULATION

Table 4.1 presents population growth rates for the sample of countries. This table reflects the process of demographic transition that has been taking place since the beginning of the twentieth century.[2] Average growth rates rose till the late 1960s and started falling afterwards. The last column of Table 4.1 shows the average population growth from 1900–1994. The country that grew fastest at the beginning of the century (Argentina), is currently growing at the slowest pace. On the contrary, Venezuela, the slowest growing country at the beginning of the century, has been the fastest growing country in the last decades.

As indicated above, population grew at very different rates in the various countries of Latin America during the 1900–1913 period, when the highest growth rates were experienced by Argentina with an average annual growth rate of 3.8 per cent. This was due in large part to immigration from Europe which accounted for more than 50 per cent of total population growth. About half of all immigrants came from Italy while around 30 per cent came from Spain.[3] In 1914, foreigners made up about 30 per cent of the total population (Sánchez-Albornoz, 1991).

Brazil also had rather high population growth rates, though much lower than Argentina. An important reason for this was the much lower, though still significant, influx of foreigners. This accounts for almost 15 per cent of population growth (Merrick and Graham, 1979). Between 1880 and 1930, Brazil received around four million immigrants from Italy (36 per cent), Portugal (29 per cent), Spain (14 per cent), Germany (5 per cent) and Japan (3 per cent), as documented in Sánchez-Albornoz (1991).

Table 4.1 Population (average annual compound growth rates)

	1900–13	1913–29	1929–50	1950–73	1973–80	1980–89	1989–94	1900–94
Argentina	3.8	2.6	1.9	1.7	1.6	1.5	1.3	2.1
Brazil	2.1	2.1	2.3	2.9	2.4	2.1	1.8	2.3
Chile	1.2	1.3	1.7	2.2	1.6	1.6	1.7	1.7
Colombia	2.0	2.6	2.0	2.8	2.2	2.0	1.7	2.3
Mexico	0.7	0.8	2.4	3.1	2.8	2.1	1.9	2.0
Venezuela	0.9	0.8	2.1	3.7	3.6	2.6	2.4	2.3
Arithmetic average	1.8	1.7	2.1	2.8	2.4	2.0	1.8	2.1
Korea	1.2	1.7	2.1	2.2	1.7	1.2	0.9	1.7
Taiwan	1.5	1.6	2.7	3.0	1.9	1.4	1.0	2.1
Arithmetic average	1.3	1.7	2.4	2.6	1.8	1.3	0.9	1.9
Portugal	0.7	0.7	1.1	0.1	1.9	-0.1	0.1	0.7
Spain	0.7	0.9	0.9	1.0	1.0	0.4	0.2	0.8
Arithmetic average	0.7	0.8	1.0	0.6	1.5	0.2	0.2	0.8
France	0.2	-0.1	0.1	1.0	0.5	0.5	0.6	0.4
Germany	1.4	0.4	1.0	0.9	-0.1	0.1	1.5	0.6
Japan	1.2	1.3	1.3	1.1	1.0	0.6	0.3	1.1
Netherlands	1.4	1.5	1.3	1.2	0.7	0.5	0.7	1.2
UK	0.8	0.4	0.5	0.5	0.0	0.2	0.5	0.4
USA	1.9	1.4	1.1	1.4	1.0	1.0	1.0	1.3
Arithmetic average	1.2	0.8	0.9	1.0	0.6	0.5	0.8	0.8

Sources: Latin America from Appendix A and other countries from Maddison (1995). Korea and Thailand updated to 1994 with growth rates from IMF (1995a) and Taiwan from Council for Economic Planning and Development (1994), 1994 updated using growth rate for 1992–93.

Chile's population grew at a slightly lower rate partly because immigration was less important; significantly lower growth rates can be found in Mexico and Venezuela. Colombia grew by 2.0 per cent a year between 1900–1913. In Mexico the low growth rate was due to the effects of the revolution from 1911–21. From 1900–1910, the growth rate was about 1.6 per cent (INEGI, 1985). The population grew very slowly in Venezuela but the low growth rate of 0.9 per cent does not seem very plausible and may be due to errors in the census estimates.

In Argentina, the birth rate began to fall rapidly in the first half of the twentieth century while the death rate continued falling, although not as rapidly. There were major changes in net migration. After the unprecedented increase during the first years of the twentieth century, net migration was negative from 1915–19, only to resume growth in the 1920s and then taper off to much lower rates in the 1930s and the 1940s. Population growth rate went down from 3.8 per cent during 1900–1913 to 2.6 per cent for 1913–29 and 1.9 for 1929–50. In 1950 Argentina was the first country in Latin America to reach the final stage of the demographic transition, recording more or less stable, low crude birth and death rates.

Brazil continued the trend of 1900–1913 in terms of a constant birth rate and a slightly falling death rate. Net immigration came to a halt during World War I but resumed during the 1920s faltering, as in Argentina, in the 1930s and 1940s.[4] The population growth rate was 2.1 per cent for 1913–29, the same as during 1900–1913, and a slightly higher 2.3 per cent for 1929–50. From 1920 onwards Chile experienced an accelerated decline of its rather high, by Latin American standards, crude death rate. Initially the birth rate also tended to fall, but later stabilised, rising somewhat at the end of the 1940s. In the case of Chile, immigration was not as important in size as in Argentina and Brazil, although entrepreneurs seeking fortune in Chile have had a great impact on its economic development. The population growth rate rose somewhat from 1.2 per cent between 1900–1913 to 1.3 per cent between 1913–29, and reached 1.7 per cent in the period 1929–50.

Demographic developments in Colombia closely resembled those in Brazil, except for the migratory movement. The crude birth rate was stable during the first half of the twentieth century, while the crude death rate experienced a slow but constant decline. The resulting growth rates were 2.6 per cent between 1913–29 and 2.0 per cent between 1929–50. Population growth in Mexico was of course strongly affected by the Mexican revolution. Starting in the 1920s, the birth rate remained at a high level for much of the twentieth century while the death rate showed a systematic decline. In the case of Venezuela the long-run population estimates do not seem to be very reliable. However, the figures indicate a constant crude birth rate during the first part of the century, even showing a tendency to rise from the mid-1930s onwards. The crude death rate started to decline from the 1920s onwards resulting in a growth rate of 0.8 per cent between 1913–29 and about 2.1 per cent between 1929–50.

At the beginning of the 1950s, most Latin American countries were still in the first phase of demographic transition. However, in most countries the growth acceleration between 1950–73 was more accentuated than between 1929–50, and this was principally due to the fall in mortality. The Southern Cone countries were at a more advanced stage in the demographic transition, especially Argentina, which was growing at less than 2 per cent; and, to a lesser degree, Chile, which still had rather high birth and mortality rates.

The 1973–80 period shows a uniform tendency in all Latin American countries towards a fall in population growth. This indicates that all countries are now at a more advanced stage of demographic transition, in which the fertility rates also start to fall. During the 1980–94 period, the abovementioned trend continued and all countries (except Chile, whose population growth rate had fallen strongly from 1973–80), experienced lower population growth.

The growth rates of the population presented in Table 4.1 are the result of a myriad of underlying processes, some of which are reflected in Table 4.3. The birth rate fell on average from 41 per 1000 to around 26 at present. Mortality rates are now half those of the 1950s. Life expectancy has risen from 54 to 69 years in the second half of the twentieth century. The most drastic trend concerns infant mortality which fell to a third of the rate recorded in the 1950s. At the beginning of the century birth rates were somewhat higher, mortality rates were much higher, and life expectancy at birth was around 35 or lower (Maddison, 1995).

As can be seen in Table 4.2, the total population of the Latin American sample countries was 359 million people in 1994, compared to 121 million in 1950. This increase of 238 million people in 44 years is the result of high rates of population growth, close to 3 per cent in the 1950–73 period. Those rates resulted from constantly falling death rates, observed since the end of World War II or even earlier, and persistently high birth rates.

High population growth was accompanied by a rapid urbanisation process that involved massive movement from rural areas to cities. In 1950, nearly 60 per cent of Latin Americans lived in rural areas, but in 1990 less than 30 per cent lived in those areas. This is a characteristic trait of Latin America, which has distinguished it from other developing regions for many years (CELADE, 1993).

Table 4.2 Total Population, 1900–1994 (in thousands at mid-year)

	1900	1913	1929	1950	1973	1980	1989	1994
Argentina	4,693	7,653	11,592	17,150	25,193	28,114	32,114	34,587
Brazil	17,984	23,660	32,894	53,444	102,982	121,286	145,803	161,790
Chile	2,974	3,491	4,306	6,082	9,992	11,147	12,883	14,210
Colombia	3,998	5,195	7,821	11,946	22,778	26,525	31,739	35,101
Mexico	13,607	14,970	16,903	27,737	55,539	67,570	81,666	91,145
Venezuela	2,542	2,874	3,259	5,094	11,796	15,091	19,025	21,844
Total	45,798	57,843	76,775	121,453	228,280	269,733	323,230	358,677
Korea	8,772	10,277	13,397	20,557	33,935	38,124	42,380	44,389
Taiwan	2,864	3,469	4,493	7,882	15,427	17,642	20,006	20,983
Total	11,636	13,746	17,890	28,439	49,362	55,766	62,386	65,372
Portugal	5,450	6,004	6,729	8,512	8,630	9,819	9,795	9,850
Spain	18,566	20,263	23,210	27,868	34,810	37,386	38,888	39,205
Total	24,016	26,267	29,939	36,380	43,440	47,205	48,683	49,055
France	40,598	41,463	41,230	41,836	52,118	53,880	56,423	58,022
Germany	34,666	37,843	40,595	49,983	61,976	61,566	62,063	66,802
Japan	44,103	51,672	63,244	83,563	108,660	116,800	123,120	125,188
Netherlands	5,142	6,164	7,782	10,114	13,439	14,150	14,849	15,389
UK	38,426	42,622	45,672	50,363	56,210	56,314	57,236	58,702
USA	76,391	97,606	122,245	152,271	211,909	227,757	248,781	261,558
Total	239,326	277,370	320,768	388,130	504,312	530,467	562,472	585,661

Sources: See Table 4.1.

In the 1970s a slowdown in population growth was observed in Latin America, caused by a decrease in fertility in most of the countries, and in all strata of the population. The growth rate declined from an average of 2.4 per cent in the 1970s to 1.9 per cent in the 1980s and to 1.8 per cent at the beginning of the 1990s. These growth rates are similar to those in Asian countries, but much higher than in the advanced countries.

Table 4.3 compares birth rates, mortality rates and life expectancy around 1950 and 1990. All countries, with the exception of Argentina, show a drastic fall in birth rates as well as mortality rates, with a subsequent rise in life expectancy at birth from an average of 54 years to 69 years.

Table 4.3 Comparative Characteristics of the Demographic Situation around 1950 and 1990

	Birth Rate (per thousand)		Life Expectancy (years)		Mortality Rate (per thousand)		Infant Mortality (per thousand)	
	1950	1990	1950	1990	1950	1990	1950	1990
Argentina	25.4	21.3	62.7	70.6	9.2	8.6	63.6	32.2
Brazil	44.6	26.7	51.0	64.9	15.1	7.8	134.7	63.2
Chile	37.2	23.8	53.8	71.5	14.3	6.1	126.2	18.1
Colombia	47.3	25.9	50.6	68.2	16.7	6.4	123.2	39.7
Mexico	45.5	30.0	50.8	68.8	16.6	5.9	113.9	41.3
Venezuela	47.0	28.5	55.2	69.7	12.4	5.4	106.4	35.9
Arithmetic average	41.2	26.0	54.0	69.0	14.1	6.7	111.3	38.4
Korea	37.0	16.5	47.5	69.4	32.0	6.1	115.0	25.0
Taiwan	46.6	15.7	47.2	73.7	9.9	5.1	n.a.	6.0
Arithmetic average	41.8	16.1	47.3	71.5	20.9	5.6	115.0	15.5
Portugal	24.1	12.4	59.3	73.8	11.8	9.8	91.0	14.0
Spain	20.3	10.9	66.5	77.0	10.2	8.2	62.0	8.0
Arithmetic average	22.2	11.7	62.9	75.4	11.0	9.0	76.5	11.0
France	19.5	13.8	66.5	76.0	12.8	9.6	45.0	8.0
Germany	16.0	11.1	67.5	74.8	11.1	11.6	51.0	8.0
Japan	23.7	11.1	63.9	78.3	9.4	6.3	51.0	5.0
Netherlands	22.1	12.7	72.1	76.8	7.5	8.5	24.0	9.0
UK	15.9	13.6	69.2	75.0	11.7	11.5	29.0	9.0
USA	24.3	16.0	69.0	74.9	9.5	8.8	28.0	10.0
Arithmetic average	20.3	13.1	68.0	76.0	10.3	9.4	38.0	8.2

Note: n.a.: not available

Sources: CELADE (1993), Council for Economic Planning and Development (1994) and United Nations (1993).

The increase in life expectancy of about 15 years was mainly due to the reduction in death rates in the early years of life and, especially, infant mortality, the decrease being much less among older people. The reduced incidence of infectious diseases (diarrhoea, acute respiratory infections and immune-preventible diseases) in infant and child mortality, as well as reduced death rates related to chronic diseases in adulthood such as cancer and cardiovascular disease, have been two of the most significant factors in the so-called epidemiological transition (CELADE, 1993).

Comparisons of the levels of, and trends in, Latin American death rates and those of the other countries in the sample show that the gap in life expectancy has fallen from 13 years to 5 years. Nevertheless, current levels of life expectancy are similar to those experienced in the United States 40 years ago, when there was neither the current knowledge nor the means of preventing and treating a large number of diseases (CELADE, 1990).

Table 4.4 Total and Sectoral Employment (thousands of persons)

	Argentina	Brazil	Chile	Colombia	Mexico	Venezuela
Agriculture						
1950	1,723	10,606	722	2,164	5,338	710
1973	1,429	14,199	626	2,577	6,032	782
1980	1,333	13,078	540	2,524	7,221	731
1989	1,464	13,527	709	3,004	6,076	780
1994	1,508	13,243	822	3,258	5,645	845
Industry						
1950	2,141	3,116	684	700	1,464	315
1973	3,182	7,911	1,011	1,498	4,211	851
1980	3,654	12,596	984	2,204	5,239	1,341
1989	3,033	13,226	1,031	2,501	6,542	1,364
1994	2,673	13,056	1,054	2,642	7,568	1,438
Services						
1950	2,957	3,935	850	980	1,963	546
1973	4,791	11,055	1,257	2,541	4,937	1,705
1980	5,078	17,417	1,794	3,685	7,162	2,554
1989	7,233	27,893	2,563	4,982	11,701	3,578
1994	8,302	33,610	3,078	5,770	14,804	4,441
Total						
1950	6,821	17,657	2,256	3,844	8,765	1,571
1973	9,402	33,165	2,894	6,616	15,180	3,338
1980	10,065	43,091	3,318	8,413	19,622	4,626
1989	11,730	54,646	4,303	10,487	24,319	5,722
1994	12,483	59,909	4,954	11,670	28,017	6,724

Sources: Appendix C.

This circumstance implies that the region could have made even greater progress than it has to date, especially since the gains achieved by the Asian countries of our sample were bigger than those of Latin America, with the former reaching a life expectancy of about 70 years, while the level at the beginning of the 1950s was about 7 years lower than the average for Latin America.

Another area where substantial progress has been made is in infant mortality which has declined, especially due to mass vaccination, oral rehydration and expanded health services, and again it becomes clear that in a comparative perspective the Latin American countries performed worse than the other countries in our sample, regardless of whether, at the initial point, those countries were below the level of Latin America, at the same level or above it.

LABOUR INPUT

For the Latin American countries total and sectoral employment was estimated separately for agriculture, industry and services (according to the International Industrial Uniform Classification IIUC Rev. 1, see Table 4.4). I have used the following statistical sources: (i) population estimates by the Latin American Demographic Centre (CELADE); (ii) specific participation rates of the male and female population derived from Population Censuses and Household Surveys; (iii) employment rates obtained from Population Censuses; and (iv) 1990 estimates of the economically active population generated by CELADE (1992) were used and the ECLAC Projections Centre provided us with estimates of total employment based upon national surveys. The benchmark years used in this study that did not coincide with census and survey years were intrapolated and 1994 was extrapolated.

Methodology and Results

The methodology for estimating the employment series consisted of the following steps: estimation of the economically active population (EAP) for the 1950–80 period; estimation of total employment for the 1950–80 period; estimation of sectoral composition of employment; and estimation of the EAP and employment for 1990. For each country, the EAP was estimated on the basis of population data and participation rates, for the age group ten years and older (see Table 4.5). The data on population aged 10 years and over was obtained from CELADE (1993). The participation rates were obtained from a study by ECLAC (1985). These were updated to 1990 using the CELADE (1992) study on the economically active population. Some cases showed rather big differences in trends (for example, Argentina and Mexico) and the specific adjustments made are commented on in Appendix C on human capital.

The ECLAC (1985) study, based upon population censuses and household surveys, presents a homogeneous series of specific participation rates of the economic active population aged 10 years and over for 1950, 1960, 1970 and

1980 in the Latin American countries. The study also presents all procedures used to adjust the information to the same benchmark years, to standardise the age groups and to make the definitions of the EAP homogeneous. For 1990, the same adjustments were made, as far as possible, in order to create a consistent data base.

Table 4.5 Determinants of Total Employment, 1950–90 (in thousands of persons and as a per cent)

	Total population	Participation rate (%)	Labour force	Employment rate (%)	Total employment
Argentina					
1950	17,150	40.9	7,017	97.2	6,821
1960	20,614	39.1	8,059	97.4	7,849
1970	23,962	38.9	9,318	98.0	9,132
1980	28,114	36.3	10,218	98.5	10,065
1990	32,546	37.8	12,313	92.2	11,932
Brazil					
1950	54,444	33.3	17,799	99.2	17,657
1960	72,594	32.1	23,325	99.2	23,138
1970	95,847	31.6	30,249	98.0	29,643
1980	121,286	36.3	44,060	97.8	43,091
1990	148,477	39.1	58,023	96.7	56,108
Chile					
1950	6,082	37.6	2,290	98.5	2,256
1960	7,608	32.6	2,478	95.0	2,354
1970	9,496	30.5	2,894	94.3	2,729
1980	11,147	31.6	3,519	94.3	3,318
1990	13,100	36.4	4,772	92.8	4,429
Colombia					
1950	11,946	32.5	3,887	98.9	3,844
1960	15,939	29.5	4,704	96.0	4,516
1970	21,360	29.1	6,217	96.0	5,968
1980	26,525	33.0	8,763	96.0	8,413
1990	32,300	36.8	11,889	90.4	10,747
Mexico					
1950	27,737	32.0	8,881	98.7	8,766
1960	36,945	29.2	10,771	98.4	10,600
1970	50,596	27.9	14,136	96.2	13,599
1980	67,570	30.2	20,396	96.2	19,622
1990	83,226	30.8	25,649	97.1	25,905
Venezuela					
1950	5,094	32.9	1,677	93.7	1,571
1960	7,579	31.2	2,364	87.4	2,066
1970	10,721	28.5	3,055	95.0	2,902
1980	15,091	32.6	4,921	94.0	4,626
1990	19,502	34.9	6,812	86.0	5,859

Sources: 1950–80 from ECLAC (1990c) and for 1990 estimate see the sources in Appendix C.

In Appendix C tables are given with all relevant data starting from population and ending with the total amount of hours worked in the benchmark years. In this Appendix I also indicate for each country what specific adjustments have been made in each case.

The step from the economically active population to total employment was made by estimating employment rates. The employment rates were obtained from population censuses based upon a uniform definition of the working population for the entire 1950–80 period. In order to obtain this uniformity, a thorough analysis of all definitions used in the population censuses was made, especially concerning period of reference, the inclusion in the category unemployed of those who seek work for the first time, the minimum age to be included in the EAP and the minimum time worked in order to be included. The uniform census employment rates therefore have a standard definition for all countries except in some, explicitly mentioned, cases.

Table 4.6 presents the sectoral composition of agriculture, industry and services. The distribution was estimated using information on the sectoral economically active population obtained from the population censuses. The information for 1990 was obtained, where possible, from the same census source as the 1950–80 estimates. If the census for 1990 was not available, an estimate by ECLAC's Projections Centre was used.

It was necessary to standardise the sectoral distributions in line with the International Industrial Uniform Classification, revision 1 (IIUC 1). In those cases where the censuses used revision 2 (IIUC 2) the necessary adjustments were made, and when the censuses were conducted in different years, the percentile distribution data were intrapolated to obtain homogeneous series.

The employment estimate for 1990 was based upon a study by CELADE (1992) which provided estimates of the economically active population. These estimates are projections made by CELADE based upon assumptions with respect to population growth and male and female participation rates, and do not completely reflect changes in demographic and participation rates tendencies. This is clearly shown in some cases where the population census for around 1990 is available. In the case of Chile the estimates are rather precise but in the case of Mexico it was shown that the 1980 population census contained substantial errors and new estimates were provided by CELADE.

The ECLAC Projections Centre estimated total employment based upon National Household Surveys. Disaggregated unemployment was assumed to be 2 per cent in agriculture, and unemployment for the remaining sectors was then estimated assuming equal unemployment rates in the other sectors. I also assumed equal unemployment rates for female and male workers as it is extremely difficult to obtain data on disaggregated employment rates.

Unemployment is normally somewhat higher in the case of women and Arriagada (1994) presents the results for three capital cities in our sample countries, reporting higher female unemployment rates in two cases, with 20 per cent higher unemployment rate on average. Unemployment estimates for 1990 come from the population censuses or from national sources as indicated in Appendix C.

Table 4.6 Sectoral Composition of Employment, 1950–94 (per cent)

	Argentina	Brazil	Chile	Colombia	Mexico	Venezuela
Agriculture						
1950	25.3	60.1	32.0	56.3	60.9	45.2
1973	15.2	42.8	21.6	38.9	39.7	23.4
1980	13.2	30.3	16.3	30.0	36.8	15.8
1989	12.5	24.8	16.5	28.6	25.0	13.6
1994	12.1	22.1	16.6	27.9	20.1	12.6
Industry						
1950	31.4	17.6	30.3	18.2	16.7	20.1
1973	33.8	23.9	34.9	22.6	27.7	25.5
1980	36.3	29.2	29.7	26.2	26.7	29.0
1989	25.9	24.2	24.0	23.8	26.9	23.8
1994	21.4	21.8	21.3	22.6	27.0	21.4
Services						
1950	43.4	22.3	37.7	25.5	22.4	34.8
1973	51.0	33.3	43.4	38.4	32.5	51.1
1980	50.5	40.4	54.1	43.8	36.5	55.2
1989	61.7	51.0	59.6	47.5	48.1	62.5
1994	66.5	56.1	62.1	49.4	52.8	66.0
Total						
1950	100	100	100	100	100	100
1973	100	100	100	100	100	100
1980	100	100	100	100	100	100
1989	100	100	100	100	100	100
1994	100	100	100	100	100	100

Source: Derived from Table 4.4.

In order to check the results a comparison with alternative estimates was made. The economically active population and employment were compared, using as additional sources CELADE, ILO and national studies. The results show some differences in the cases of Mexico and Colombia. With respect to the EAP, there exist two other estimates, one by CELADE (see CELADE 1985a and 1985b) and the other by the International Labour Organisation (ILO, 1986). The estimates of the EAP made by CELADE and ILO correspond to a comprehensive and consistent set of data, based on uniform concepts, methods and classification schemes for all countries. The data take into account information on the economically active population obtained from national population censuses, labour force sample surveys and other related surveys conducted during the period 1945–85.

In general the levels are rather similar, though the estimates of this study are somewhat closer to those of ILO. The greatest differences with respect to CELADE's EAP concerned Colombia with a difference of 9.5 per cent in 1980, and Chile, with 7.5 per cent, also in 1980. In the case of the ILO's measure of the EAP, the biggest difference was in Mexico, with a 9.4 per cent difference in 1980, and Chile, with a 6.7 per cent difference in the same year. Another comparison consisted of the sectoral composition of the EAP compared with the ILO. The comparison showed both to be very similar, with the exception of Colombia in 1980 and Mexico in 1960, with differences of 4.2 and 5.6 per cent in agriculture, respectively.

Finally, with respect to the comparison of the employment series, two sources were used; first, an estimation of employment series on the basis of ILO data and second, estimates based upon national case studies. The procedure followed to estimate the employment series on the basis of ILO data was as follows: (i) the basis information was the EAP of the ILO disaggregated in agriculture, industry and services; (ii) an unemployment rate was chosen on the basis of the available information of the censuses and PREALC; (iii) the non-agricultural unemployment rate was estimated on the basis that the agricultural unemployment rate was half of the non-agricultural rate; (iv) it was assumed that the ILO estimate of EAP correspond to employment in the latter sector since population censuses tend to overestimate unemployment in agriculture, due to the type of questions used in rural areas.

Hours worked

The measurement of labour inputs for growth accounting purposes can be done either in terms of the number of persons employed or number of hours worked. In Latin America the first method has been used almost exclusively, because of its simplicity and the easier availability of statistics. It is obvious, however, that the second method is preferable for our purposes, the measurement of productivity, comparing not only countries within the region, which may themselves feature substantial differences in hours worked, but also with countries outside the region where the variation is known to be large.[5]

Table 4.7 shows the summary results on working hours per person per year for the period 1950–94, indicating a clear downward trend for all countries[6]. The average decline was about 200 hours or around 10 per cent. The extent of the decline varied from 122 hours in Mexico to 348 hours in Colombia. The Latin American sample shows remarkable homogeneity, at the end of the reference period, in terms of the number of hours worked per person. The standard deviation was somewhat less than 20 per cent in the 1950s, and fell below 10 per cent in the 1980s.

Summary Table 4.8 shows total hours of labour input for 1950–94. Remarkable differences in growth rates are evident, with Argentina's labour input growing a mere 69 per cent while Venezuela's input grew 375 per cent. The high increase in hours of labour input is explained in great part by the growth of persons employed. The latter is related to high rates of population growth, with relatively stable participation rates (see Table 4.9). The changes in the amount of hours of work per person per year are also relatively small.

In Table 4.9 the total participation rates of Table 4.5 are disaggregated in terms of female and male participation rates. Although total participation rates do not show a specific tendency, the picture is distinctly different on a more disaggregated level. Male participation rates fell in all countries with Argentina experiencing the greatest fall (8.9 percentage points) while Brazil and Colombia showed only small reductions. Female participation rates rose in all countries, with the biggest increases in Brazil, Colombia and Venezuela.

Table 4.7 Total Hours of Work per Person per Year, 1950–94

	1950	1960	1970	1980	1990	1994
Argentina	2,034	2,073	2,006	1,974	1,850	1,875
Brazil	2,042	2,134	2,145	1,985	1,879	1,860
Chile	2,212	2,031	1,962	1,938	1,984	2,002
Colombia	2,323	2,218	2,170	2,074	1,969	1,975
Mexico	2,154	2,150	2,066	2,051	2,060	2,032
Venezuela	2,179	2,024	1,951	1,997	1,889	1,910
Average	2,157	2,105	2,050	2,003	1,939	1,942

Sources: Appendix C.

Table 4.8 Total Hours of Labour Input, 1950–94 (thousands)

	1950	1960	1970	1980	1990	1994
Argentina	13,871	16,271	18,322	19,868	20,997	23,406
Brazil	36,053	49,367	63,571	85,517	105,954	111,429
Chile	4,991	4,351	5,361	6,430	8,851	9,918
Colombia	8,930	10,017	12,950	17,445	21,159	23,049
Mexico	18,442	22,404	27,865	39,788	52,354	56,943
Venezuela	3,424	3,801	5,662	9,181	10,931	12,842

Source: Table 4 of Appendix C.

Measuring the labour force in developing countries on the basis of demographic censuses and household surveys raises some specific problems, depending on the concepts and definitions used, as well as problems of classification of specific groups. The male and female participation rates used here are based on an ECLAC study that presented a homogeneous series of specific participation rates (ECLAC, 1985). Table 2 of Appendix C presents absolute employment figures. Estimating the unemployment rate for developing countries is one of the trickiest problems in this kind of statistical exercise. Generally speaking census material has been used (see Appendix C for explanation for each country).

Table 4.9 Female and Male Participation Rates (percentage of total population)

	1950	1960	1970	1980	1990	1994
Argentina						
Total	40.9	39.1	38.9	36.4	37.8	38.4
Male	64.1	61.6	58.6	54.1	55.5	56.0
Female	16.3	15.9	19.1	19.1	20.8	21.5
Brazil						
Total	33.3	32.1	31.6	36.3	39.1	40.2
Male	56.5	53.0	50.3	53.3	55.1	55.9
Female	10.0	11.2	12.8	19.3	23.1	24.7
Chile						
Total	37.6	32.6	30.5	31.6	36.4	38.6
Male	57.8	51.4	48.0	48.4	52.0	53.3
Female	17.9	14.2	13.4	15.2	21.2	24.3
Colombia						
Total	32.5	29.5	29.1	33.0	36.8	38.4
Male	55.1	49.4	46.4	50.9	54.8	56.2
Female	10.3	9.9	12.0	15.3	19.2	21.0
Mexico						
Total	32.0	29.1	27.9	30.2	30.8	31.1
Male	55.8	48.1	44.7	48.3	47.6	47.2
Female	8.3	10.3	11.1	12.1	14.3	15.3
Venezuela						
Total	32.9	31.2	28.5	32.6	34.9	35.9
Male	54.9	51.9	45.3	48.1	49.3	49.9
Female	10.4	8.3	11.3	16.8	20.3	21.9

Source: Table 1 of Appendix C.

In Latin America there are no national institutes or international organisations which systematically gather and analyse this type of data and there are no sources of information common to all countries (except for some ILO estimates). The estimates presented here have been gathered from different sources, each with a different methodological approach, and tend therefore to be only very rough, initial estimates. For a summary of the findings on annual hours of work per employee, see Table 3 of Appendix C. Mexico is the only country where the variable remained stable, while Brazil showed a rising trend until the 1970s, followed by a remarkable slowdown. The other countries show a steadily declining trend.

Human Capital

In growth accounting considerable effort has been devoted to capturing quality changes in labour input.[7] The most important of these, considered to have a direct effect on productivity, is the level of education and its rate of change. There are, as mentioned in the introduction, other aspects which have an important effect on increasing productivity and reducing poverty, such as health care and nutrition, but no estimates for these are provided in this chapter. Some factors which do have an effect on the productivity of the labour force are not included in the quantification. For example, one factor already considered by Denison (1967) is work effort. Denison cites industry observers which indicate that the pace of work in Canada and the United States is markedly faster than in Western Europe. It would not be too difficult to arrive at a similar opinion with respect to the Latin American countries, and making a case for a much wider gap than exists between Europe and the United States. However, these differences are very difficult to quantify, insofar as they are not due to differences in working hours or education, and belong largely to the realm of the ultimate causes of economic growth. Another factor is the general health of the population and the labour force; however, the impact of malnutrition and disease on labour input and productivity in developing countries has until now largely gone unmeasured.

Length of work year
One factor which has been considered by Denison (1967) and some other growth analysts is the length of the work year, measured by hours worked. They assumed that, above a certain level, decreases in time worked were fully compensated by increases in work intensity and, up until a level of about 1700 hours a year, a partial compensation was used. Currently, most growth analysts do not include this kind of analysis, maybe because of the relative uniformity of working hours in the advanced countries. This issue might be again of interest in comparisons between advanced and developing countries, marked by huge differences in annual working time. However, in this study I have assumed, as did Maddison (1987), that a reduction in working hours leads to an equiproportionate cut in labour input.

Education
In the advanced countries and successful 'late industrialisers', there is a clear recognition of the central role that education and the generation of knowledge play in the development process, and this attitude has been spreading gradually to the countries of Latin America. In most countries of the region the systems of education, training, and scientific and technological development have undergone noteworthy expansion in the last decades. However, they still display shortcomings in terms of the quality of their results, their degree of adaptation to the

requirements of the economic and social environment, and the extent to which they
are accessible to the different strata of society (ECLAC, 1992).

The rise in the average educational level of the population in the post-war
period has had a crucial effect on the quality of labour. An individual's level of
education affects the type of work he or she can do and the efficiency with which
work is performed. In all countries in our sample the population's average number
of formal years of education has risen rapidly (see Table 4.10). However, the most
rapid growth was experienced by the developing countries, with the Asian
developing countries growing at by far the fastest rate. In a recent publication
concerning the rapid growth of some East Asian countries, several explanatory
factors were put forward to explain the fast growth in human capital. These were
identified as rapid economic growth, the decline in population growth, the
relatively equal income distribution, and policies with respect to human capital
formation (World Bank, 1993a).

*Table 4.10 Average Years of Formal Educational Experience of the Population
Aged 15–64, 1950–94*

	Argentina	Brazil	Chile	Colombia	Mexico	Venezuela
Total						
1950	4.72	1.83	4.46	2.45	2.06	1.93
1973	6.87	3.23	6.46	4.41	3.81	3.94
1980	7.41	4.22	7.34	5.07	5.72	5.51
1989	8.38	5.25	8.65	6.91	6.78	7.76
1994	8.96	5.93	9.48	8.20	7.45	9.38
Primary						
1950	3.86	1.53	3.65	2.04	1.88	1.74
1973	4.92	2.41	4.55	3.19	3.14	3.11
1980	4.97	3.22	4.91	3.45	4.17	4.11
1989	5.09	3.87	5.30	4.29	4.60	5.23
1994	5.15	4.29	5.54	4.83	4.86	5.98
Secondary						
1950	0.77	0.25	0.70	0.34	0.16	0.16
1973	1.68	0.69	1.55	1.06	0.56	0.74
1980	2.04	0.88	2.12	1.40	1.32	1.20
1989	2.65	1.23	2.93	2.27	1.83	2.16
1994	3.01	1.48	3.45	2.93	2.16	2.90
Higher						
1950	0.09	0.05	0.11	0.07	0.03	0.03
1973	0.27	0.13	0.35	0.15	0.11	0.09
1980	0.40	0.12	0.31	0.22	0.23	0.20
1989	0.63	0.15	0.42	0.34	0.34	0.36
1994	0.81	0.16	0.49	0.44	0.43	0.51

Source: Appendix C.

The number of formal years of education enjoyed by the population aged between 15 and 64 years is probably not the most adequate measure of quality change. First, some authors consider the labour force as the more relevant unit of analysis and, second, important elements such as on-the-job training are not taken into consideration. On the one hand, unfortunately, in Latin America, the only data available for the whole period and all countries of coverage concerns years of formal education of the population. However, it is also true that higher levels of education of the population as a whole have positive effects, especially in terms of adaptability to changing markets and new technologies; these factors assume greater importance in the global integration process marked by rapid changes in markets and technologies and, in the case of Latin America, export-oriented development strategies.

Table 4.11 presents a comparison of formal years of education of the total population and of the labour force. The general conclusion is that differences are small at the primary level but can be significant at the tertiary level. This information, obtained from population censuses, is only available for a few benchmark years in a limited number of countries. Hence, I have opted for average years of formal education of the population as the best proxy available for human capital improvement.

As regards on-the-job training, Psacharopoulos (1993) indicates that there exists strong education–training complementarities. Psacharopoulos and Vélez (1992), using data for Colombia, found a strong positive interaction between training and years of formal education in determining earnings. They concluded that training really has an effect on earnings only after a worker has eight years of formal education. A study by Mingat and Tan (1988) confirmed the above-mentioned findings since they concluded that training was particularly productive when a country's educational system is highly developed. The rate of return on training was, according to their most conservative estimate, in the order of 20 per cent, assuming that 50 per cent of the population is literate.

Unfortunately, as education expanded in Latin America, its overall quality declined and the educational system became more inefficient. Several factors can be identified. One was the explosion of social demand for education, which led to the incorporation of more and more children, without redefining the educational content or increasing resources to meet expanded enrolments. Moreover, the traditional preference for physical investments over qualitative ones and the lack of interest in education also contributed to a poor implementation of the growth of the educational system, with the corresponding deterioration in results. In Latin America, it is of fundamental importance to design and put into effect a strategy for promoting the transformation of education and training and increasing the scientific and technological potential of the region which makes sustained growth possible on the basis of the incorporation and spread of technological progress (ECLAC, 1992). A very important consideration is whether the quantity indicator of years of education also reflects the quality changes, which have occurred in the sample countries. The crisis of the 1980s has affected the quality of education in countries of Latin America while, for example, the Asian countries may well have improved their educational systems, but this is not reflected in our data. Although it is very difficult to make an assessment of quality changes, I will analyse some aspects of deteriorating education in Latin America, together with policies for improving the quality of education.

One striking difference between Latin America and the other regions is its much higher level of grade repetition, especially in the first grade; 50 per cent in 1980 and 42 per cent in 1988.[8] There is some grade repetition in any school system because some students are not yet mature enough to be promoted or show some learning disability. Students then benefit enough from repetition to make it efficient from an economic viewpoint. However, the high repetition rates suggest a major problem. The greatest problem lies not in the lack of schools but in the quality of education. High repetition rates limit access to education, delay entrance, and have high resource costs. Some rather simple measures have been suggested for the schooling system, such as wider provision of textbooks and writing materials, which could reduce the enormous amount of resources now devoted to grade repetition (IDB, 1993).

Some micro-evidence on the effects of schooling indicates that the impact of educational attainment on wages and economic productivity is considerable. One important element, as indicated above, is the fact that schooling has both important private and social returns. In fact, the IDB (1993) study indicates that private returns are lower and social returns higher than in standard estimates.

Psacharopoulos gives a brief summary of the recent research on returns to investment in education; primary education continues to be the number one investment priority in developing countries; educating females is marginally more profitable than educating males; the general secondary school curriculum is a better investment than the technical/vocational track; and the returns to education obey the same rules as investment in conventional capital, that is, they decline as investment expands (Psacharopoulos, 1993). One of the conclusions with respect to differences in pay between different segments of employment, self-employment and dependent employment, is that empirical studies generally find no significant difference in income between the two as documented by Psacharopoulos (1993). This result, although important in itself, is also useful with respect to the determination of the respective factor shares.

The estimates of educational levels are presented for each country as a whole and in this sense the wide variations within countries in average years of education are not taken into account. For example, in Brazil, there are huge educational differences between the north-eastern region and other parts of the country. In Latin America, the quality of schooling and attendance rates tends to be systematically lower in rural areas and for the indigenous people.

Hours worked by males and females, and within each sex by individuals of different age, change over time. Women do proportionally more temporary or part-time work, and their labour market participation and skill acquisition is interrupted by child bearing and raising, resulting in lower compensation rates. Lower compensation for women is partly due to discrimination, which therefore exacerbates the quality differential between men and women. Psacharopoulos and Tzannatos (1992) estimate that women's pay is 70.5 per cent of men's for Latin America as a whole, with a somewhat higher figure for our sample countries.

Table 4.11 Comparison of Educational Level of Total Population and Labour Force (years of formal education)

Year	Country	Type of education	Total population (15–64)	Labour force	Difference (%)
1951	Colombia	Primary	2.07	2.04	-1.3
		Secondary	0.35	0.35	0.0
		Higher	0.07	0.07	0.0
		Total	2.49	2.46	-1.2
1961	Venezuela	Primary	2.14	2.19	2.3
		Secondary	0.24	0.27	14.1
		Higher	0.05	0.07	31.0
		Total	2.43	2.53	4.1
1970	Chile	Primary	4.42	4.40	-0.5
		Secondary	1.43	1.46	2.1
		Higher	0.28	0.37	32.1
		Total	6.13	6.23	1.6
1980	Argentina	Primary	4.97	5.07	2.1
		Secondary	2.04	1.98	-3.0
		Higher	0.40	0.49	22.8
		Total	7.41	7.54	1.8
1981	Venezuela	Primary	4.27	4.32	1.2
		Secondary	1.28	1.43	11.8
		Higher	0.22	0.26	16.3
		Total	5.77	6.01	4.1
1990	Mexico	Primary	4.63	4.73	1.7
		Secondary	1.90	2.36	24.2
		Higher	0.63	0.50	38.9
		Total	7.16	7.59	6.0
1992	Chile	Primary	5.44	5.44	0.0
		Secondary	3.14	3.20	1.9
		Higher	0.44	0.58	31.8
		Total	9.02	9.22	2.2

Source: Elaborated by the author on the basis of population censuses.

In a comparison between the age-participation profiles of women in advanced countries and Latin America, two facts stand out. First, the participation rate of women in developed countries is higher than in developing countries. Maddison (1991a) shows that the average female participation rate in the labour force was almost constant at around 30 per cent during the first half of the twentieth century, for a sample of 16 developed countries. From 1950 to the late 1980s, the female participation rate in the labour force increased to over 40 per cent. It is somewhat surprising that our sample of Latin American countries has not yet reached the level which the advanced countries attained as early as 1910 (see Table 4.12). However, the increase in women's participation rates has been much higher in the developing countries than in the developed countries.

Second, the age profile of female participation in advanced countries is characterised by a double peak: the first peak occurs just before childbearing starts, while the second peak is reached once the last child begins going to school. In contrast, there are no indications that women re-enter the labour market after an interruption in employment in Latin America (see Psacharopoulos and Tzannatos, 1992).[9] On average, about two-thirds of the female workers in Latin America work in the services sector, especially domestic work, compared to about one third of male workers. However, the increase in women's participation as a result of fewer household responsibilities, fewer children to take care of, higher education and other factors, has been the principal cause of the increase of participation rates of some age groups, especially women of 35–44 years of age whose participation rate increased as much as 10 percentage points between 1980 and 1990 (Arriagada, 1994).

Table 4.12 Females as a Proportion of Total Employment, 1950–90

	1950	1960	1970	1980	1990
Argentina	19.4	20.0	24.5	26.6	28.0
Brazil	15.1	17.4	20.2	26.6	29.6
Chile	24.0	22.0	22.2	24.4	29.5
Colombia	15.9	16.9	20.8	23.4	26.3
Mexico	13.2	17.6	19.6	19.6	22.8
Venezuela	17.8	17.6	20.9	25.4	28.8
Average	17.6	18.6	21.4	24.3	27.5

Sources: Appendix C.

NOTES

1. The renewed focus on causes of economic growth in the 'new growth theory' and especially in the role of human capital, see for example Lucas (1988), was preceded in the 1960s when the human capital theory received much attention, promoted amongst others by Becker (1964), Harbison and Myers (1964), Schultz (1961) and Tinbergen and Bos (1965).
2. Most of the data on vital rates is obtained from the excellent book by Collver (1965).
3. See Díaz-Alejandro (1970, tables 1–14 and 1–15, pp. 37–38). Another indicator of the importance of immigration is that in 1914 30.3 per cent of the population were foreigners. This indicates that the relative importance of immigrants was much higher in Argentina than in the USA, where the ratio of foreigners in the total population reached a maximum of 14.4 per cent (in 1890 and 1910). See Díaz Alejandro (1970, p. 36).
4. An interesting thesis suggested by Collver (1965), which falls outside the scope of this study, is that the immigrants themselves played a major part in the change in reproductive behaviour in Brazil and especially Argentina.
5. The 1950 level of hours worked per year was quite similar in the different country groupings. It was somewhat lower in the advanced countries, with high levels in Japan, Germany and the Netherlands, and somewhat higher in the Asian developing countries. By 1990, this situation changed and differences are substantial – with levels around 2300 hours in the Asian countries and somewhat above 1600 hours in the advanced countries.
6. It should be noted that in many cases the only available information concerned the formal sector and no statistics were available regarding the informal and rural sector where people tend to work very long hours.
7. See the works of Denison, and in Latin America for example, Selowski, Elias and Langoni.
8. These averages relate to the whole of Latin America; our sample countries have a lower average (35 per cent) because the Southern Cone countries have much lower levels (especially Chile).
9. The female participation rates in this study coincide rather well with our estimates. However, it is necessary to be cautious with their mean because it apparently contains a calculation error.

5. New Standardised Estimates of Capital Stock for Latin America and the USA

INTRODUCTION

The lack of comparable estimates of fixed capital stocks in Latin American countries has hindered the analysis of economic development within the region, as well as comparisons with other developing and developed countries. This chapter tries to fill the gap by providing standardised estimates of gross and net stocks for Argentina, Brazil, Chile, Colombia, Mexico and Venezuela.

The estimates were generated by employing the 'Perpetual Inventory Method' (PIM) currently used by most OECD countries and, hence, the most appropriate in an international comparison. The analysis concentrates on the methodology and results for Latin America but also includes a comparison with the USA,[1] using the same methodology.

In spite of both the theoretical and practical difficulties associated with the use, estimation and meaning of capital stock estimates, they continue to be extensively employed and are useful for many kinds of economic analysis, such as growth accounting, productivity analysis, economic forecasting, studies of cyclical fluctuations and of the relationship between capital, output and labour and the role of technical progress.

In the past, significant efforts have been made to estimate capital stocks in many Latin American countries, and a review of these is presented in Appendix H. However, no official time series on capital stocks are prepared on a regular basis. Hence there have been estimates by a variety of independent researchers and institutes. This explains the great differences in methodology and coverage. These estimates may be useful for various types of analysis within each country, but are difficult to use in international comparisons because of differences in definitions and assumptions with respect to the different variables such as GDP, capital formation and its disaggregation, estimation of the initial stock, length of asset lives, retirement patterns (that is, distribution of service lives around the mean life), and differences in the relative prices of assets.

METHODOLOGY

There are basically two methods, each with its variations, for measuring capital stocks:

(a) direct measurement of the stock for a benchmark year, through different types of survey of physical assets, insured values, company book values, or stock exchange values;
(b) by cumulating historical series on past investment and deducting assets which are scrapped, written off or destroyed by war.

The second is widely known as the 'Perpetual Inventory Method' and was pioneered by Raymond Goldsmith (1951). In this chapter, annual fixed capital stock estimates are presented for the 1950–94 period using the Goldsmith method.[2] The attraction of the perpetual inventory model is based on its use of a methodology which facilitates international comparison. It produces more meaningful figures because all the hypotheses and calculations are transparent and consistent. It permits analysis of the structure and age distribution of the capital stock. It is now generally used in official estimates, sometimes in combination with direct estimates of the initial stock, for example Japanese statisticians use a post-war wealth survey benchmark.[3]

The capital assets considered in this study are the same as those included in gross fixed capital formation in the national accounts. Generally the countries examined in this study follow the United Nations classification (United Nations, 1968), where gross fixed capital formation is defined as outlays (purchases and own-account production) by industries, producers of government services, and producers of private non-profit services to households, for new durable goods (commodities) less net sales of similar second-hand and scrapped goods. Excluded are government outlays on durable goods for military use. In general, the goods included are durable (lasting more than one year), reproducible and tangible. Intangible assets like patents and other intellectual property are excluded, as are inventories, work in progress and non-reproducible assets like forests, land and mineral deposits.[4]

Capital formation is separated here into three asset types – residential structures, non-residential structures, and machinery and equipment. For each type fixed capital stocks have been estimated on the basis of past investment. Estimates are given for both gross and net fixed capital stocks. This makes it possible to differentiate between 'ex-post' and 'ex-ante' concepts of capital,[5] that is, between actual and expected contributions of capital to production. Here the 'ex-post' concept is used. Capital stocks are valued at constant 1980 prices. GDP and capital stocks were converted to international dollars, using the International Comparison Project (ICP) purchasing power parities (PPP), rather than exchange rates.

Separate PPPs were used for GDP, investment in residential structures, non-residential structures and machinery and equipment.

The perpetual inventory method estimates capital stock as a weighted sum of past investment flows. This involves estimation of a base year capital stock consisting of the sum of past investment during the assumed life-times of the different asset categories. The gross stock is calculated by adding investment during the year and subtracting assets that are scrapped. The net stock is obtained by adding investment during the year and deducting depreciation.

The objective of this chapter is to generate capital stocks for the 1950–94 period. To be able to use the perpetual inventory method, historical time series of gross fixed investment are needed over a long period of time, basically since 1900. This requirement was difficult to meet for Latin America since in many cases official series do not go further back than 1950.

The reliability of the stock estimates depends primarily on the accuracy of these basic data. Hence, Appendices B and D provide a detailed description of the sources and series used for each country. A set of three tables is provided for each country with long-term series (1900–1994) for GDP at constant 1980 national prices, GDP at constant 1980 international dollars, population, GDP per capita, gross total and disaggregated investment in national currencies and as a percentage of GDP. These appendices also contain an explanation of the estimation procedures applied to fill holes in the data base.

For most countries it was relatively easy to obtain information dating back to 1925 although, for example, finding data on investment in residential construction gave problems for the whole period in some countries. For 1900–1925 the basic series are mostly very rough estimates.

A working life of 50 years was assumed for residential structures, 40 years for other structures and 15 years for machinery and equipment, for all countries, over the whole period. These assumptions seem rather realistic for non-residential structures and machinery and equipment.

Several countries use asset life estimates which are close to the ones used here (for example the asset lives which the US Bureau of Economic Analysis uses in its estimation for the United States are practically the same, although the official United States estimates are more finely disaggregated). In the case of residential structures, the asset life of 50 years is probably rather low but it is practically impossible to obtain data on residential investment before 1900 in Latin America.[6] In order to be able to generate the initial total capital stock for 1950, data on capital formation in machinery and equipment was needed since 1935, in non-residential construction since 1910 and in residential construction since 1900.

A rectangular retirement pattern was assumed, that is, assets are completely scrapped after serving their respective lives (15, 40 and 50 years). These assumptions about the mortality function and the fixed nature of service life have been adopted for reasons of transparency and simplicity. Blades (1989) analyses these different assumptions in detail. In my model, the simultaneous exit mortality function was applied, which is also still in use in Canada, Japan and Norway. Simultaneous exit may be regarded as a limiting case of a bell-shaped function which Blades considers the only plausible candidate for a mortality function. In my approach all assets of a given vintage disappear simultaneously, but the results are not very different from the bell-shaped hypothesis.[7]

A major problem in this kind of research is the estimation of the length of life of capital assets. For developing countries, especially Latin American ones, these length-of-life assumptions may be critical as they are often not only related to technological and economic considerations but also to shortages of foreign exchange and the absence of regular repairs and maintenance because of budgetary constraints. Furthermore, the obsolescence of capital seems to be less significant than the collapse of the product market in determining utilisation rates. Future research should clarify the relative importance of these issues for Latin American capital stock estimates. Not much empirical information is available about service lives, especially in Latin America.[8] Changing service life assumptions affect the size of the capital stock and its rate of growth.[9]

One obvious question is whether average service lives remain constant over time as I assumed. The service life of a given type of asset almost certainly varies both between different users and from one period to another. When business conditions are favourable, assets will be used more intensively and discarded sooner. Relative price movements, maintenance levels, management efficiency and tax rates also have an effect. OECD concludes that there was 'little evidence of any secular tendency for given types of assets to be retained in production for longer or shorter periods' (OECD, 1993, p. 39). This does not, of course, mean that the average life of the aggregate capital stock remains constant because this is affected by changes in the structure of the stock.

For the calculation of net capital stock, one has to define a depreciation function for allocating the cost of the asset over its service life.[10] There exists a close relationship between replacement, service life and depreciation; see Jorgenson (1974) for theoretical aspects of replacement and its twin, the theory of depreciation. There is currently no agreement over this depreciation function, but in the literature two approaches stand out. The first is the straight-line pattern of depreciation, in which efficiency declines linearly over the lifetime of the capital good. A second method, also used quite often, is the so-called declining balance depreciation in which efficiency of the capital good declines geometrically.[11]

In order to obtain the net capital stock I chose the first method, assuming that the capital services are used up in equal instalments over time, that is, applying straight-line depreciation over the working life of the different types of assets. Not much attention is given in the literature on capital stock estimation to the moment depreciation starts. This assumption, however, is not without importance.[12] Very fast depreciation is often allowed for tax purposes in the developed countries, but is much less frequent in Latin America. After instalment machinery and equipment as well as structures need some time to start operating normally. Hulten (1990) presents a perpetual inventory model in which no first-year depreciation takes place, and Jorgenson and Sullivan (1981) also apply a depreciation lag. Thus, in this study, straight-line depreciation starts with a lag of one year. It has also been assumed that the scrap value of capital goods at the end of their economic life is zero, which is of course often not the case, but this treatment of obsolescence simplifies the calculation a great deal. This procedure is used in several OECD countries for estimation of net capital stock.

A model layout for capital stock estimation was developed to make all procedures transparent and to facilitate the replication of these results by other researchers (see Appendix E). Here I give the algebra involved in the procedures. In Table E.2 in Appendix E an example is presented of the procedure for estimating alternative benchmark capital stocks in non-residential structures as at 31 December 1949 in Argentina, a procedure which is the same for each country. The procedure is also the same for each category of investment and the only difference is that, in the case of residential capital stock the series starts in 1900, and in the case of machinery and equipment in 1935. The gross gross increment to capital stock in column 3 of Table E.2 is the result from the multiplying GDP at constant 1980 prices in column 1 and the ratio of total gross fixed investment in construction to GDP at constant prices in column 2. At the end of 1949 gross fixed capital stock in construction equals the sum of 1910–49 gross fixed investment or gross increments to capital stock as given at the bottom of column 3. The initial end-year gross capital stock was calculated as follows:

$$GGI_t^i = a_t^i * GDP_t \tag{5.1}$$

$$GK_b^i = \sum_{m=b-\theta^i+1}^{b} GGI_m^i \tag{5.2}$$

where:

GGI_t^i Gross increment to capital stock of asset i during period t

GDP_t Gross domestic product in t

GK_b^i Gross initial capital stock of asset i at b

a_t^i Ratio of total gross fixed investment of asset i to GDP at constant prices in t

b Initial year

θ^i Length of life of asset i

i Type of asset

t Time

Column 4 of Table E.2 presents the annual depreciation provision based upon straight-line depreciation which means that, in each year in which depreciation takes place, 1/40th of gross investment is depreciated. Column 5 gives the yearly components of depreciated capital formation remaining by the end of 1949, corresponding to 1/40th for 1910, 2/40th for 1911, and so on. End 1949 net stock consists of the sum of 1910–49 components of depreciated capital formation which equals the 1910–49 sum of column 5. Net mid-year capital stock was calculated as follows:

$$D_t^i = \frac{1}{\Theta} \sum_{m=t+1-\theta^i}^{t} GGI_m^i \qquad (5.3)$$

$$NK_b^i = \sum_{m=b-\theta^i+1}^{b} \frac{(m - b + \theta^i)}{\theta^i} * GGI_m^i \qquad (5.4)$$

where:

D_t^i Depreciation of asset i during t
NK_b^i Net initial capital stock of asset i at b

This procedure of benchmark year capital stock estimation can of course also be used to estimate the 1950–94 end-year net and gross capital stocks. Alternatively, the procedures which are detailed in Table E.3 of Appendix E can be applied. In this table capital stock estimates for the 1950–94 period are elaborated. In Table E.3, 1950 end-year gross capital stock (column 6) equals the benchmark end-year 1949 capital stock plus the gross gross increment in capital stock in 1950 as given in column 3 minus retirement of gross gross increment to capital stock of 40 years ago (column 4). The 1950 end-year net stock equals the 1949 stock plus the gross gross increment to capital stock (column 3) minus annual depreciation (column 7). The respective net and gross end-year capital stock series were calculated as follows:

$$GK_t^i = GK_{t-1}^i + GGI_t^i - GGI_{t-\theta}^i \quad (t > b) \qquad (5.5)$$

$$NK_t^i = NK_{t-1}^i + GGI_t^i - D^{it} \qquad (5.6)$$

where:

GK_{t}^i Gross capital stock of asset i at t
NK_{t}^i Net capital stock of asset i at t

Columns 10 and 11 of Table E.3 present average ages of gross and net capital stocks, respectively, and in columns 12 and 13 the end-year gross and net capital stock estimates are brought to a mid-year basis. Column 14 gives the average of mid-year net and gross capital stocks and the formulas for the calculation of average age and re-adjustment to mid-year[13] are given below. Finally, the formulas for total gross and net capital stock aggregation and total gross and net capital stock average age calculation are presented.

$$AAGK_t^i = \frac{\sum_{m=t-\theta^i+1}^{t} (t-m)*GGI_m^i}{GK_t^i} \tag{5.7}$$

$$AANK_t^i = \frac{\sum_{m=t-\theta^i+1}^{t} (\frac{m-t+\theta^i}{\theta^i})*(t-m)*GGI_m^i}{NK_t^i} \tag{5.8}$$

$$GMK_t^i = \frac{GK_{t-1}^i + GK_t^i}{2} \tag{5.9}$$

$$NMK_t^i = \frac{NK_{t-1}^i + NK_t^i}{2} \tag{5.10}$$

$$TGK_t = \sum_{i=1}^{n} GK_t^i \tag{5.11}$$

$$TNK_t = \sum_{i=1}^{n} NK_t^i \tag{5.12}$$

$$AAGK_t = \frac{\sum_{i=1}^{n} AAGK_t^i * GK_t^i}{TGK_t} \tag{5.13}$$

$$AANK_t = \frac{\sum_{i=1}^{n} AANK_t^i * NK_t^i}{TNK_t} \tag{5.14}$$

where:

$AAGK_t^i$:	Average age of gross capital stock of asset i in t
$AANK_t^i$:	Average age of net capital stock of asset i in t
GMK_t:	Gross capital stock, mid-year t
NMK_t:	Net capital stock, mid-year t
TGK_t:	Total gross capital stock in t
TNK_t:	Total net capital stock in t
$AAGK_t$:	Average age of total gross capital stock in t
$AANK_t$:	Average age of net capital stock in t
n:	Number of assets i

RESULTS

Appendix E presents a complete set of net and gross capital stock estimates for each country, that is, gross and net fixed tangible capital stocks by type of asset, 1950–94 at constant 1980 national prices as well as at constant 1980 international dollars. It also gives average age, average service lives and capital–output ratios for 1950–94 on the basis of national currencies and calculated on the basis of international dollars.

Previous Estimates

Appendix H contains a detailed analysis of previous capital stock estimates in Latin America. Table 5.1 presents a comparison of the national estimates with the standardized capital stock estimates of this chapter. The existing estimates have been elaborated for different time periods and we present those closest to our benchmark years. It is especially interesting to compare the national capital stock estimates with the standardised ones for the initial year. The standardised estimates were generated with the perpetual inventory method while many of the national estimates calculated the initial stock on the basis of direct estimation or used another methodology, for example the one developed by Harberger (1972).

For Argentina the Goldberg and Ianchivolici (1986) article is an excellent study which is also the only existing estimate completely based upon the perpetual inventory method. The differences with our standardised estimates come mainly from the different assumptions regarding service lives of assets which are higher than our standardised estimate. As a result the Secretaría de Planificación (1991) study, which is an update of Goldberg and Ianchivolici (1986), has higher fixed capital stock levels and lower growth rates than our estimate. The initial values of the IEERAL and ECLAC studies are quite high, especially the United Nations study (1959).

In the case of Brazil the estimates of Goldsmith (1986) and Langoni (1974) are worth consideration. The Goldsmith estimate is mainly based upon the study by Langoni which is one of the few dealing with the problem of fixed capital stock estimation in Brazil. However, his initial fixed stock estimate seems rather high and the falling capital–output ratio shows a tendency contrary to ours. Most of the other estimates also show relatively high initial capital stock estimates, much higher than the standardised estimates.

The movement of the capital–output ratio in the Haindl and Fuentes (1986) study for Chile coincides with ours. This is also largely the case in the Gutiérrez study.

In Colombia the estimates of Harberger (1972) coincide largely with ours in terms of both trend and level. The more recent estimates of Henao (1983) show much higher levels and a clear downward tendency of the capital–output ratio. The ECLAC (1957) study finds much higher initial levels. The Mexican estimates by the Banco de Mexico (1969) are very difficult to interpret because they lack a methodological explanation. In the case of Venezuela the Baptista (1991) estimates growth rates are similar to ours but the levels show important differences. The Banco Central de Venezuela (1968) estimate is very similar to ours, but not much is known about the methodology used.

Exchange Rates and Purchasing Power Parities

A crucial consideration in international comparisons is how to convert estimates in local currencies into a common currency, either using exchange rates or purchasing power parities (PPP).[14] The use of exchange rates as the conversion factor is the easiest and most direct way,[15] but at best the official exchange rate reflects the purchasing power of tradable goods and services. It does not include non-tradables and thus may give rise to distortions. These distortions may be small, as is probably the case between two very open economies such as the Netherlands and Belgium, but can be quite large in the case of low-income developing countries.

The aim of the present study is to make internationally comparable estimates. Therefore, purchasing power parities are needed for non-residential and residential construction and machinery and equipment. Capital stocks normally consist partly of tradables, especially machinery and equipment, which in Latin America are purchased mainly from abroad, and partly of non-tradables. It is for this reason that purchasing power parities are the most appropriate conversion factor. However, purchasing power parities are only available for a limited number of countries for a limited number of years.

Table 5.1 A Comparison of Standardised and National Estimates (on the basis of national currency capital–output ratios)

Argentina	Standardised estimates		Goldberg/ Ianchilovici (1986)		IEERAL (1986)	ECLAC (1954)	United Nations (1959)
	Gross	Net	Gross	Net	Net	Net	Net
1950	3.6	2.1			2.5	2.8	3.6
1973	3.5	2.3			2.3		
1980	4.1	2.7	4.2	2.7	2.8		
1984	4.6	2.9	4.9	3.2			
Brazil	Standardised estimates		Langoni (1974)		Goldsmith (1986)	ECLAC (1954)	United Nations (1959)
	Gross	Net	Net		Net	Net	Net
1950	1.4	0.9	2.6			2.6	1.8
1952	1.6	1.1	2.5		1.8		
1968	2.0	1.4	2.2		2.0		
1980	2.4	1.8			2.0		
Chile	Standardised estimates		Gutiérrez (1983)			Haindl/Fuentes (1986)	ECLAC (1954)
	Gross	Net	Net			Net	Net
1950	3.6	2.3	2.8				2.2
1973	3.9	2.4	2.8			3.0	
1980	3.6	2.1	2.4			2.6	
1984	4.2	2.4				3.0	
Colombia	Standardised estimates		Harberger (1972)			Henao (1983)	ECLAC (1957)
	Gross	Net	Net			Net	Net
1952	2.8	1.8	2.0			3.3	2.9
1967	2.7	1.6	1.9			2.7	
1973	2.4	1.5				2.2	
1980	2.4	1.5				2.2	
Mexico	Standardised estimates		Banco de Mexico (1969)			ECLAC (1954)	United Nations (1957b)
	Gross	Net	Net			Net	Net
1950	1.7	1.2	2.8			1.8	2.2
1967	2.2	1.6	2.3				
Venezuela	Standardised estimates		Banco Central de Venezuela (1986)		Baptista (1974)		
	Gross	Net	Net		Gross	Net	
1950	2.8	2.1	2.1		1.7	1.3	
1965	3.0	2.0	1.9		1.9	1.2	
1973	3.0	2.0			2.0	1.3	
1980	3.8	2.7			3.1	2.2	
1989	5.0	2.9			3.8	2.2	

Source: See Appendix H.

In Latin America the first efforts to estimate purchasing power parities date from the late 1940s, under the influence of the path-breaking study by Colin Clark

(1940). One of the earliest was an interesting, yet largely unknown, study conducted at the Inter-American Statistical Institute. Under the technical guidance of Simon Kuznets, Dominguez (1947) used PPPs to convert 1940 national income estimates into dollars. The national income data available at that time were not very reliable and the basket of goods compared in order to estimate a PPP consisted only of 12 items, all of them foodstuffs. Despite its shortcomings, the study provided a rough estimate of real income levels and gave an indication of the range of income disparities within Latin America and facilitated comparisons with the USA.

The first ECLAC estimates of real income in dollars were made for the 1945–52 period (ECLAC, 1954). However, the methodology was not very rigorous and was based partly on a 1950 United Nations study which calculated dollar estimates of real income on the basis of projections of exchange rates for a 'normal' period, and partly on arbitrary estimates by economists who were familiar with price levels and living standards in Latin America. The first systematic effort to calculate purchasing power figures in Latin America was the pioneering 1963 ECLAC study conducted by Stanley Braithwaite.

Towards the end of the 1960s, ECIEL,[16] a research programme of comparative studies on economic integration, initiated an international comparison project on the same lines as the ECLAC study. Finally, during the 1970s and the 1980s, ECLAC and ECIEL cooperated in the various phases of the International Comparison Project (ICP), which at the onset was a joint effort of the United Nations and the World Bank and, in later phases, involved the Statistical Office of the European Communities (EUROSTAT) and the Organisation for Economic Cooperation and Development (OECD).[17]

Table 5.2 presents the exchange rate and the purchasing power parities (PPPs) prepared during phase IV of the ICP project. I also give the adjusted exchange rates used in 1980 by ECLAC and the World Bank for conversion to dollars. For 1980, the benchmark year, I compare the PPPs used, which were supplied to us by Alan Heston, formerly with the ICP project, with the ones published by the United Nations/EUROSTAT (1987).

In this table the AH column includes also PPPs for Mexico which were not published in ICP IV. The AH results show that all countries, with the exception of Argentina, have much higher exchange rates than PPPs as can be seen in the lower panel which gives PPP–GDP exchange rate deviation indices. The range varies from 0.46 in Colombia to 1.41 in Argentina. The PPP–exchange rate deviation indices in the lower panel of Table 5.2 indicates that the AH results for 1980 are similar to those of ICP IV.

Table 5.2 Exchange Rates and GDP Purchasing Power Parities, 1980 (national currency units per dollar and ratio)

	Exchange rate	ICP IV	AH	ECLAC	World Bank
GDP purchasing power parities					
Argentina	1837	2709	2596	3334	4117
Brazil	52.7	30.6	32.4	50.9	51.0
Chile	39.0	28.8	26.5	41.7	44.7
Colombia	47.3	23.1	21.6	48.6	52.5
Mexico	23.0		13.4	25.4	30.8
Venezuela	4.3	3.6	3.1	5.0	9.7
PPP–exchange rate deviation indices					
Argentina		1.47	1.41	1.82	2.24
Brazil		0.58	0.61	0.96	0.97
Chile		0.74	0.68	1.07	1.15
Colombia		0.49	0.46	1.03	1.11
Mexico			0.58	1.10	1.34
Venezuela		0.84	0.73	1.17	1.09

Sources: Exchange rates from IMF, *International Financial Statistics*; ICP IV refers to the fourth phase of the International Comparison Project, see Kravis, Kenessey, Heston and Summers (1975) and Kravis, Heston and Summers (1978 and 1982) and United Nations/Eurostat (1987); AH refers to PPPs for Latin America which were kindly supplied by Alan Heston of the University of Pennsylvania and former director of the ICP project; ECLAC and World Bank refer to the adjusted exchange rates used by these organisations.

Table 5.3 shows PPPs for capital goods along with the resulting PPP–exchange rate deviation indices as estimated by ICP IV and the Alan Heston estimates. Here the results of the two estimates for 1980, ICP IV and AH, are given. Comparing the ICP IV and AH 1980 results, it becomes quite clear that the main difference occurred in the case of non-residential structures. It is because of these differences between exchange rates and PPPs that the appendices include capital stock estimates at both national and international prices. This gives the potential user the option of applying other PPPs or exchange rates than the ones used by us, without the need to go through the whole procedure of calculating the capital stock.

Standardised Estimates

By developing the model layout for capital stock estimation as described above, all procedures have been made transparent.[18] Also for each country a detailed description and explanation is given of all sources and series used in the preparation of the final 1980 constant price series.[19] In Figure 5.1 the results are presented in terms of capital output ratios, that is, capital per unit of output. The total capital stock refers to the sum of residential and non-residential fixed capital stock. The non-residential fixed capital stock consist of the sum of non-residential construction and machinery and equipment and reflects better the productive capacity of the fixed capital stock.

Table 5.3 Capital Formation PPP–Exchange Rate Deviation Indices, 1980 (national currency units per dollar and ratio)

	(ICP phase IV)			(Alan Heston)		
	Res.	N.R.	M&E	Res.	N.R.	M&E
PPPs for capital goods						
Argentina	4025	1389	3959	4057	4670	3899
Brazil	33.7	27.1	46.3	32.0	25.9	47.0
Chile	52.2	15.4	51.2	52.1	27.0	50.7
Colombia	20.1	17.6	53.6	19.6	22.3	54.8
Mexico				16.2	19.2	21.2
Venezuela	5.1	6.4	4.5	5.5	5.1	4.5
PPP–Exchange rate deviation indices for capital goods						
Argentina	2.19	0.76	2.15	2.21	2.54	2.12
Brazil	0.64	0.51	0.88	0.61	0.49	0.89
Chile	1.34	0.39	1.31	1.34	0.69	1.30
Colombia	0.42	0.37	1.13	0.41	0.47	1.16
Mexico				0.70	0.83	0.92
Venezuela	1.19	1.49	1.06	1.29	1.20	1.06

Notes: Res. = Residential
  N.R. = Non residential
  M&E = Machinery and equipment

Source: Same as Table 5.2.

The average age of the capital stock has been estimated by giving each vintage of capital formation a weight proportional to the number of years it formed part of the capital stock (which in the case of machinery and equipment is a minimum of 1 year and a maximum of 15 years). The average service life expectancy of the capital stock has been estimated by dividing the gross stock of a given year by the depreciation allowance in the same year. As straight-line depreciation was applied this gives a reasonable estimate of average service life.[20]

Table 5.4 presents a summary of the results with respect to average service life expectancy of the capital stock, that is, how long the assets remain, on average, in the capital stock. It shows that the weighted average service life fell in most countries (except for Brazil and Venezuela) from 1950–80 and remained relatively constant thereafter. As fixed asset lives for the separate assets were assumed, this shortening of lives is caused by changes in the composition of the capital stock, basically an increase for machinery and equipment and a decrease for residential structures (see also Tables 5.11 and 5.12).

In Table 5.5 the average age of the total, non-residential and residential gross capital stock is presented. This figure reflects a combination of changes in the composition of the capital stock as well as its growth rate. A faster rate of growth of the capital stock, without changes in its composition, leads to a greater share of newer vintages in the stock and a reduction of its average age. However, changes in the composition of the capital stock can also substantially affect the average age.

Table 5.4 Latin America: Weighted Average Service Life of Total and Non-Residential Fixed Capital Stock, 1950–94 (on the basis of international dollars)

	Total	N.R.	Res.	Total	N.R.	Res.
		1950			1973	
Argentina	38.6	29.4	50	34.3	26.7	50
Brazil	30.4	23.9	50	33.6	28.9	50
Chile	36.5	32.3	50	33.8	29.9	50
Colombia	39.3	35.3	50	37.5	32.9	50
Mexico	38.0	35.1	50	31.9	27.5	50
Venezuela	26.3	24.8	50	28.3	25.4	50
		1980			1994	
Argentina	33.3	25.7	50	32.4	23.5	50
Brazil	32.4	28.4	50	34.8	30.6	50
Chile	34.4	30.6	50	34.3	31.2	50
Colombia	36.5	32.1	50	35.6	31.0	50
Mexico	30.7	26.3	50	30.7	24.7	50
Venezuela	27.6	24.7	50	27.2	24.5	50

Source: Appendix E.

Table 5.5 shows only a relatively small reduction in average age in the 1950–80 period. As the composition of the capital stock did not change very much, on average, this largely reflects the acceleration in growth of the capital stock. In 1980–94, the combined effect of changing composition and falling capital stock growth causes a sharp increase in the stock's average age.

The changes in the level of total and non-residential gross fixed capital stock per capita relative to the United States were especially important during 1950–73 (Table 5.6). On average, there was an increase in per capita stocks relative to the United States from 1950–80 but thereafter the relative levels fell somewhat.

Figure 5.1 Latin America: Total and Non-Residential Capital Productivity, 1950–94 (ratio of GDP to gross fixed capital stock in constant prices)

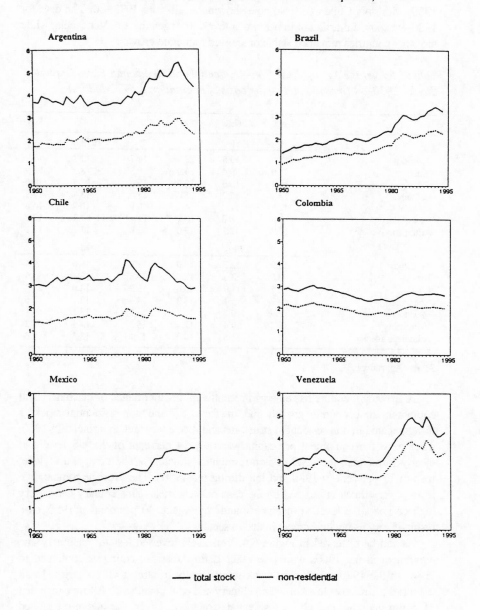

Source: Appendices B and E.

More detailed analysis of specific countries makes it clear that all countries (except Colombia) increased their comparative level from 1950–73 and even until 1980, with only Chile and Colombia showing a fall from 1973–80. The data for 1980–94 show a drastic fall in per capita levels in Argentina and Venezuela, while the other countries remained stable or showed moderate growth.

Table 5.5 Average Age of Total, Non-Residential and Residential Fixed Capital Stocks, 1950–94 (in years and on the basis of international 1980 dollars)

	Total	N.R.	Res.	Total	N.R.	Res.
	1950			1973		
Argentina	18.9	13.5	23.3	14.7	12.1	17.8
Brazil	11.9	9.4	15.9	9.8	8.5	12.9
Chile	16.4	15.6	18.9	15.0	13.5	19.0
Colombia	15.3	15.2	15.4	15.0	13.7	17.8
Mexico	11.8	11.1	14.1	10.9	10.9	10.8
Venezuela	8.8	8.0	15.3	11.4	11.3	12.2
Arithmetic average	13.9	12.1	17.0	12.8	11.7	15.1
	1980			1994		
Argentina	13.9	12.2	16.0	17.0	14.6	19.4
Brazil	9.5	8.6	12.2	13.8	13.1	15.6
Chile	16.5	14.9	20.8	15.7	14.0	21.7
Colombia	14.7	13.1	18.3	14.9	13.7	17.6
Mexico	10.9	10.7	11.6	13.5	13.1	14.1
Venezuela	10.7	10.4	12.1	15.5	14.1	21.3
Arithmetic average	12.7	11.6	15.2	15.1	13.8	18.3

Source: Appendix E.

A growing literature has emerged recently on the importance of machinery and equipment in economic growth and in Table 5.7 the non-residential stock is disaggregated in non-residential structures and machinery and equipment. In 1950, machinery and equipment per capita was only 14 per cent of the US level and clearly lower than the level of non-residential structures. The comparative level rose to 17 per cent in 1980 and fell during the 1980s. The average comparative level is very much influenced by the case of Venezuela. This country had a very high comparative level in machinery and equipment, 40 per cent in 1950, as a result of very heavy investment in the oil sector.

As can be observed in Figure 5.4, Venezuela invested less in machinery and equipment in the 1960s while the other Latin American countries continued to grow. In the 1970s machinery stock grew rapidly in almost all countries. In all countries the relative level of the machinery and equipment stock is lower than that of non-residential as well as residential structures. Given the above-mentioned importance of machinery in economic growth, through the incorporation of technical progress, this may have been an important limiting factor in post-war economic growth in Latin America (see also Chapter 6).

Table 5.6 Levels of Total and Residential Gross Fixed Capital Stock per Capita, 1950–94 (in 1980 international dollars)

	Total Capital Stock/per capita				Residential Capital Stock/per capita			
	1950	1973	1980	1994	1950	1973	1980	1994
Argentina	6,415	10,598	13,000	14,256	3,562	4,858	5,870	7,165
Brazil	1,235	4,419	7,517	10,740	483	1,318	1,978	3,153
Chile	6,096	8,809	8,953	11,392	1,881	2,444	2,451	2,621
Colombia	3,596	4,628	5,498	7,567	1,095	1,543	1,736	2,340
Mexico	2,231	6,593	9,181	12,748	500	1,821	2,615	4,580
Venezuela	5,132	9,568	12,833	12,067	579	1,824	2,518	2,360
USA	26,168	34,183	41,267	54,089	8,665	7,864	9,391	13,558
(as percentage of USA per capita level)								
Argentina	25	31	32	26	41	62	63	53
Brazil	5	13	18	20	6	17	21	23
Chile	23	26	22	21	22	31	26	19
Colombia	14	14	13	14	13	20	18	17
Mexico	9	19	22	24	6	23	28	34
Venezuela	20	28	31	22	7	23	27	17
Arithmetic average	16	22	23	21	16	29	30	27
USA	100	100	100	100	100	100	100	100

Source: Appendices A and E.

Figure 5.2 presents levels of per capita gross total fixed capital stock in the six Latin American countries. Here the impressive growth recorded in Brazil and Mexico in 1950–94 stands out. Argentina maintains its position as the country with the highest total capital stock per capita. Chile's relative position weakened considerably although capital stock started growing rapidly in the 1990s. Colombia experienced relatively slow growth.

The growth performance of Venezuela is impressive: starting from an already high level in 1950, its per capita stock grew initially very rapidly, reaching the highest level in Latin America in the late 1950s. After a spurt in growth in the 1970s, as a result of the oil crisis, Venezuela again had the highest per capita capital stock. However, the crisis of the 1980s hit Venezuela very hard and capital stock started to decline rapidly, and still continues to do so. Chile, Argentina and Colombia have all experienced rather steady growth.

Table 5.7 Levels of Gross Fixed Capital Stock per Capita of Non-Residential Structures and Machinery and Equipment, 1950–94 (in 1980 international dollars)

	Non-residential structure/per capita				M&E /per capita			
	1950	1973	1980	1994	1950	1973	1980	1994
Argentina	2,168	3,737	4,453	3,910	685	2,004	2,677	3,181
Brazil	346	2,067	3,716	6,037	406	1,035	1,823	1,531
Chile	3,494	4,908	5,098	6,807	721	1,385	1,405	1,901
Colombia	2,238	2,559	3,038	4,132	262	526	724	1,095
Mexico	1,483	3,086	3,965	4,946	248	1,685	2,602	3,223
Venezuela	2,362	4,743	5,955	6,086	2,191	3,001	4,359	3,621
USA	11,967	16,563	18,653	22,216	5,536	9,756	13,224	18,315
(as percentage of USA per capita level)								
Argentina	18	23	24	18	12	21	20	17
Brazil	3	12	20	27	7	11	14	8
Chile	29	30	27	31	13	14	11	10
Colombia	19	15	16	19	5	5	5	6
Mexico	12	19	21	22	4	17	20	18
Venezuela	20	29	32	27	40	31	33	20
Arithmetic average	17	21	23	24	14	16	17	13
USA	100	100	100	100	100	100	100	100

Source: Appendices A and E.

Another interesting point is the fact that all countries, with the exception of Venezuela, resumed growth in capital stock per capita in the 1990s. Venezuela has yet to recover from the crisis of the 1980s, which had a severe impact on all countries. As mentioned above, Colombia experienced steady growth but at a low rate, especially in the 1950s and the 1960s, and its total capital stock per capita ended at the lowest level in the Latin American sample. Figure 5.3 reflects level and growth of the residential fixed capital stock. In comparison with the other stock components the stock of dwellings grow at a smoother rate. One of the main reasons for this is the fact that the service life of dwellings is the longest (50 years) of all assets considered.

Figure 5.2 Total Gross Fixed Capital Stock per Capita, 1950–94 (1980 international dollars)

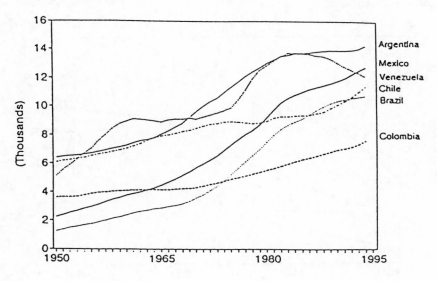

Source: Appendices A and E.

Figure 5.3 Residential Gross Fixed Capital Stock per Capita, 1950–94 (1980 international dollars)

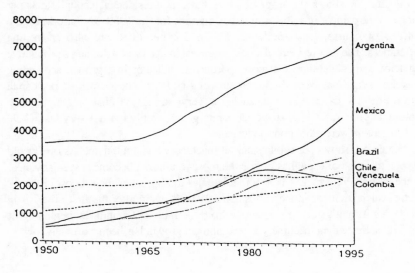

Source: Appendices A and E.

Figure 5.4 Non-Residential Gross Fixed Capital Stock per Capita, 1950–94 (1980 international dollars)

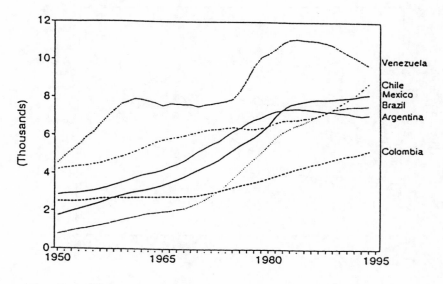

Source: Appendices A and E.

Figure 5.4 shows the level of gross fixed non-residential capital stock per capita in the sample of Latin American countries for the 1950–94 period. Figure 5.4. is, of course, very similar to Figure 5.2 but there are also interesting differences. The non-residential stock is the best indicator of a country's productive capacity, and is therefore the most appropriate indicator in a growth accounting exercise. Brazil has been the fastest growing country. The growth of per capita non-residential capital in Venezuela is very similar to that in Figure 5.2. Colombia's non-residential stock per capita grew steadily but not very fast. Chile and Argentina were other poor performers.

Figure 5.5 shows per capita stock of machinery and equipment. As one would expect, this type of capital asset was the most volatile, as becomes especially clear in the case of Venezuela where it is related to the big investment boost in the oil sector which occurred in the 1940s and 1950 and again after the first oil crisis in the 1970s. Brazil's stock grew rapidly from the mid-1960s until the beginning of the 1980s. Since then machinery and equipment growth has been extremely low.

*Figure 5.5 Gross Fixed Machinery and Equipment Capital Stock per Capita,
1950–94 (1980 international dollars)*

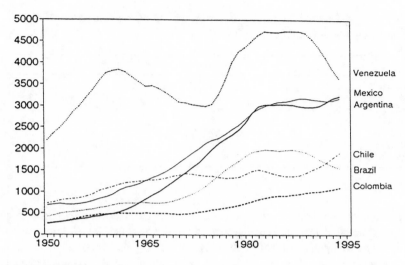

Source: Appendices A and E.

Tables 5.8 to 5.11 show these movements in more detail. Tables 5.8 and 5.9
give annual average compound growth rates for total and non-residential capital
stock in 1950–94.

*Table 5.8 Latin America: Total Gross Fixed Capital Stock, 1950–94 (annual
average compound growth rates)*

	1950–73	1973–80	1980–94
Argentina	3.9	4.6	2.1
Brazil	8.8	10.4	4.6
Chile	3.8	1.8	3.4
Colombia	4.0	4.7	4.3
Mexico	8.0	7.8	4.4
Venezuela	6.7	8.0	2.1
Arithmetic average	5.9	6.2	3.5

Source: Appendix E.

With respect to growth rates, the countries can be divided into two distinct
groups: the fast growers – Brazil, Mexico and Venezuela – and the slower growers
– Argentina, Chile and Colombia. Table 5.9 presents the growth rates for non-
residential capital stock which are somewhat higher than the growth rates for total
stock in four countries (Argentina, Brazil, Chile, and Venezuela) and lower in

Colombia and Mexico in the 1950–80 period. From 1980–94 the growth of non-residential capital stock was slower than that of total stock in most of the countries.

Table 5.9 Latin America: Gross Fixed Non-Residential Capital Stock, 1950–94 (annual average compound growth rates)

	1950–73	1973–80	1980–94
Argentina	4.8	4.8	1.4
Brazil	9.4	11.2	4.3
Chile	4.2	1.9	3.8
Colombia	3.8	5.1	4.3
Mexico	7.7	7.6	3.6
Venezuela	6.2	7.8	2.1
Arithmetic average	6.0	6.4	3.3

Source: Appendix E.

The relationship between the growth of net and gross stocks depends on the history of capital formation. When growth slows down as in 1980–94, gross stock will grow more rapidly than net stock. This is what happened in all the countries. The converse is true in periods of growth acceleration. Table 5.10 gives annual average compound growth rates for total net and gross capital stock for the 1950–94 period.

Table 5.10 Comparative Growth of Gross and Net Total Fixed Capital Stock, 1950–94 (annual average compound growth rates)

	1950–73		1973–80		1980–94	
	Gross	Net	Gross	Net	Gross	Net
Argentina	3.9	4.4	4.6	4.9	2.1	1.1
Brazil	8.8	9.2	10.4	10.5	4.6	3.6
Chile	3.8	4.0	1.8	0.9	3.4	3.6
Colombia	4.0	4.0	4.7	4.8	4.3	4.1
Mexico	8.0	8.0	7.8	7.5	4.4	3.8
Venezuela	6.7	6.2	8.0	8.7	2.1	0.6
Arithmetic average	5.9	6.0	6.2	6.2	3.5	2.8

Source: See Appendix E.

During 1950–80 net stock grew faster in Argentina and Brazil. The growth rates of both stocks were about the same in Colombia and Mexico, indicating a process of steady growth. For Chile and Venezuela, the period 1950–94 was not homogeneous as both had sub-periods of faster and slower growth in net stock compared to gross. In the case of some countries, especially Chile, the 1980–94 period should be divided into a crisis period in the 1980s and recuperation in the 1990s.

The changing composition and age structure of the capital stock gives an indication of the rate at which technical change has been embodied in the capital stock (Maddison, 1993). Table 5.11 gives an indication of changes in the composition of gross total capital stock, measured in international dollars, during the 1950–94 period. In all countries the share of machinery and equipment in the total capital stock increased from 1950 to 1980 (except in Brazil and Venezuela, which had very high shares) and stabilised or dropped slightly during 1980–94. The share of residential structures fell in Argentina, Brazil and Chile, and rose in Mexico and Venezuela. The share of non-residential structures increased in Brazil, Chile and Venezuela and fell in Argentina, Colombia and Mexico. Here I am interested in the effect on the growth rates of the different stocks. Growth rates expressed in international dollars may be different from those in national currencies, because the PPPs change the composition of the capital stock. The sign of the change in the growth rate will depend on these compositional changes.

Table 5.11 Latin America: Composition of Gross Total Fixed Capital Stock, 1950–94 (in 1980 international dollars and as a % of total capital stock)

	Dwellings				Non-residential structures				M&E			
	1950	1973	1980	1994	1950	1973	1980	1994	1950	1973	1980	1994
Argentina	55	46	45	50	34	35	34	27	11	19	21	22
Brazil	39	30	26	30	28	47	49	56	33	23	24	14
Chile	31	28	27	23	57	56	57	60	12	16	16	17
Colombia	31	33	32	31	62	55	55	55	7	11	13	14
Mexico	22	28	29	36	67	47	43	39	11	25	28	25
Venezuela	11	19	20	20	46	50	46	50	43	31	34	30
Arithmetic average	32	31	30	32	49	48	47	48	19	21	23	20

Source: Appendix E.

A comparison of Tables 5.11 and 5.12 shows that whether the measurement is performed in international dollars or national currencies makes a big difference to the composition of the capital stock. The difference was very notable in the cases of machinery and equipment in Chile and Colombia.

Table 5.12 Latin America: Composition of Gross Total Fixed Capital Stock, 1950–94 (on the basis of national currencies and as a % of total capital stock)

	Dwellings				Non-residential structures				M&E			
	1950	1973	1980	1994	1950	1973	1980	1994	1950	1973	1980	1994
Argentina	53	44	43	49	37	39	38	30	10	17	19	21
Brazil	35	29	26	30	21	37	39	48	44	34	35	22
Chile	43	38	38	33	41	42	41	44	16	21	21	23
Colombia	25	26	24	23	58	49	48	47	17	25	28	30
Mexico	19	24	24	31	68	47	44	40	13	29	32	29
Venezuela	13	21	22	22	48	51	47	51	39	28	31	27
Arithmetic average	31	30	30	31	46	44	43	43	23	26	28	25

Source: Appendix E.

Table 5.13 Latin America: Difference between Growth of Fixed Capital Stocks in National Currencies and International Dollars, 1950–94 (difference in annual average compound growth rates at constant prices)[a]

	1950–73		1973–80		1980–94	
	Gross	Net	Gross	Net	Gross	Net
Total capital stock						
Argentina	0.0	0.0	0.0	0.0	0.1	0.0
Brazil	0.4	0.4	0.0	0.0	0.4	0.5
Chile	0.0	0.2	0.2	0.1	0.2	-0.2
Colombia	-0.2	-0.2	-0.4	-0.4	-0.1	0.0
Mexico	0.0	0.0	0.0	0.0	0.1	0.1
Venezuela	0.1	0.1	0.0	0.1	0.0	0.0
Non-residential capital stock						
Argentina	0.1	0.1	0.1	0.1	0.1	0.1
Brazil	0.6	0.7	0.0	0.0	0.6	0.7
Chile	-0.1	0.0	0.1	0.0	0.0	-0.1
Colombia	-0.4	-0.3	-0.4	-0.3	-0.1	-0.1
Mexico	-0.1	-0.1	-0.1	0.0	0.0	0.0
Venezuela	0.0	0.1	0.1	0.1	0.0	0.1

Note: [a] Difference calculated as growth rate in international dollars minus growth rate in national currency.

Source: Appendix E.

Table 5.13 compares the growth of capital stock as measured in national currencies with measures in international dollars (the latter being the method I prefer). Argentina, Mexico and Venezuela show very small differences between the two growth rates, while the other countries show larger differences.

There are sometimes differences of over 10 per cent in the growth rates, especially in the 1980–94 period when growth was slow. For 1950–80 only Colombia showed differences of over 10 per cent with respect to non-residential capital stock. Brazil showed the largest absolute differences in total capital stock and in non-residential capital stock in 1950–73 and 1980–94, while Colombia presented the largest differences in 1973–80.

Table 5.14 presents the ratio of non-residential capital stock to total capital stock. This ratio can be seen as an indicator of the share of the productive capital stock (measured as the non-residential stock) in the total stock. The initial 1950 ratio of productive to total fixed capital was very low in Argentina where residential capital stock is more substantial than non-residential. The other countries had much higher productive capital stock participation levels. In 1994, at the end of the period under consideration, Argentina remains the country with the highest level of residential capital stock. The role of productive capital is more dominant in the other countries, of which Venezuela has the lowest residential capital stock levels.

Table 5.14 Latin America: Ratio of Non-Residential Fixed Capital Stock to Total Fixed Capital Stock, 1950–94 (on the basis of international dollars)

	1950 Gross	Net	1973 Gross	Net	1980 Gross	Net	1994 Gross	Net
Argentina	0.44	0.47	0.54	0.53	0.55	0.52	0.50	0.45
Brazil	0.61	0.60	0.70	0.70	0.74	0.73	0.71	0.68
Chile	0.69	0.67	0.72	0.72	0.73	0.72	0.77	0.78
Colombia	0.70	0.67	0.67	0.66	0.68	0.68	0.69	0.68
Mexico	0.78	0.77	0.72	0.69	0.72	0.68	0.64	0.59
Venezuela	0.89	0.89	0.81	0.78	0.80	0.78	0.80	0.79
Arithmetic average	0.68	0.68	0.69	0.68	0.70	0.69	0.68	0.66

Source: Appendix E.

The following tables present estimates of capital–output ratios. There are many forces that affect the development of the capital–output ratios, including technical progress, capital widening or deepening, demand and supply factors, the interest rate and so on. It is not the objective of this chapter to attempt to explain developments for six countries over a 44-year period. These estimates are included, however, because they are used quite intensively in economic forecasting, planning and econometric models.

In Tables 5.15 to 5.17, a comparison of capital–output ratios of total and non-residential capital stock is given for the 1950–94 period based on estimations in international dollars. It becomes clear from Table 5.15 that in 1950 the Latin American countries showed considerable variation in their gross capital–output ratios. Measured in national currencies, Argentina had the highest, and Brazil and

Mexico the lowest. In 1980 international dollars, Colombia had the highest level in 1950. This situation had changed at the end of the period under consideration. In national currencies, Argentina and Venezuela again had the highest level, and Colombia the lowest. In international dollars Brazil and Venezuela had the highest level, and Chile and Colombia the lowest. During the 1950–94 period, the capital–output ratios of Chile and Colombia have remained more or less stable while the ratios of the other countries have risen substantially.

Table 5.15 Total Fixed Gross Capital–Output Ratios, 1950–94 (in 1980 international dollars)

	1950	1973	1980	1994
Argentina	2.3	2.3	2.6	2.8
Brazil	1.2	1.8	2.2	3.3
Chile	2.8	3.0	2.8	2.5
Colombia	2.8	2.2	2.1	2.3
Mexico	1.2	1.7	1.9	2.6
Venezuela	2.1	2.1	2.8	3.1
Arithmetic average	2.1	2.2	2.4	2.8

Source: Appendix E.

The gross non-residential capital–output ratios (Table 5.16) show quite different, and much lower, ratios than the total fixed gross capital–output ratios of Table 5.15. In 1994 the gross total capital–output ratio of Brazil (the highest) was about 50 per cent higher than the ratio in Colombia (the lowest). With respect to gross non-residential capital–output ratios, in 1994 this spread was much wider (80 per cent), with Venezuela being the highest and Argentina the lowest. This difference in spread between total capital and non-residential capital–output ratios can be observed for the whole 1950–94 period.

Table 5.16 Non-Residential Fixed Gross Capital–Output Ratios, 1950–94 (in 1980 international dollars)

	1950	1973	1980	1994
Argentina	1.0	1.2	1.5	1.4
Brazil	0.7	1.3	1.6	2.3
Chile	1.9	2.1	2.0	1.9
Colombia	1.9	1.4	1.5	1.6
Mexico	0.9	1.2	1.3	1.7
Venezuela	1.8	1.7	2.2	2.5
Arithmetic average	1.4	1.5	1.7	1.9

Source: Appendix E.

Table 5.17 shows a comparison of gross and net capital-output ratios for the 1950–94 period. Table 5.13 showed that the comparison of the growth rates of capital stock in national currencies and international dollars does not yield very large differences.

Table 5.17 A Comparison of Gross and Net Total Capital–Output Ratios, 1950–94 (in 1980 international dollars)

| | 1950 | | 1973 | | 1980 | | 1994 | |
	Gross	Net	Gross	Net	Gross	Net	Gross	Net
Argentina	2.3	1.4	2.3	1.5	2.6	1.7	2.8	1.6
Brazil	1.2	0.8	1.8	1.3	2.2	1.7	3.3	2.2
Chile	2.8	1.7	3.0	1.9	2.8	1.6	2.5	1.5
Colombia	2.8	1.8	2.2	1.4	2.1	1.4	2.3	1.5
Mexico	1.2	0.9	1.7	1.2	1.9	1.3	2.6	1.7
Venezuela	2.1	1.5	2.1	1.4	2.8	1.9	3.1	1.8
Arithmetic average	2.1	1.4	2.2	1.5	2.4	1.6	2.8	1.7

Source: Appendix E.

CONCLUSIONS

This chapter presented a comprehensive set of standardised and hitherto unavailable capital stock estimates for six Latin American countries, employing the perpetual inventory method. These estimates can be used in the analysis of comparative economic performance, productivity growth, convergence and catch-up.

Total capital stock increased in all Latin American countries but at very different rates. In Brazil it grew by about 8 per cent between 1950–94, but only by some 3 per cent in Argentina and Chile. In 1950 Argentina had the highest level of total stock per capita, with Brazil by far the lowest. At the end of the period under consideration, Argentina remained the country with the highest level, while Colombia had the lowest. The non-residential stock level for the period as a whole was clearly highest in Venezuela, while Brazil made an impressive catch-up from the lowest level in 1950.

These trends are also true for the 'productive', that is, non-residential, capital stock. This stock grew slightly faster then total stock in the 1950–80 period, especially in the cases of Argentina and Brazil. When economic activity fell down sharply in the 1980s the growth rate of the 'productive' fixed capital stock became lower than the rate of the total stock.

It is also important to emphasise some points with respect to the composition of the stock. On the one hand, the relatively high level of the residential capital stock in Argentina and the corresponding somewhat lower level, in comparative perspective, of its productive capital stock. Venezuela is the extreme case on the other hand, presenting a relatively small stock of dwellings and the highest stock of machinery and equipment in our sample. This last fact is related to the very heavy investment in the oil sector over time. In the case of Brazil it is possible to observe rather high levels of machinery and equipment, especially initially in the 1950s, in the composition of the total capital stock.

Maddison (1993) found that the evidence for advanced capitalist countries did not confirm Kaldor's (1961) hypothesis of constant capital–output ratios over the long run in capitalist countries. The Latin American evidence also contradicts Kaldor's view and indicates increasing capital–output ratios in Argentina, Brazil, Mexico and Venezuela. Capital productivity remained almost constant in Chile and increased somewhat in Colombia. There are some small differences between the evidence for total as opposed to non-residential capital–output ratios (Argentina and Chile for example) but the general trend is clear. However, Maddison's evidence refers to a much longer period, for some countries since 1820. For Latin America the evidence is restricted to the relatively short, for this type of analysis, 1950–94 period.

NOTES

1. The investment estimates for the USA are taken from Maddison (1995) but the stock estimation procedure was adjusted slightly due to changes in the benchmark year and for the use of somewhat different asset service life assumptions.
2. The description of this model is based upon Michael Ward (1976a).
3. See Maddison (1991a), Appendix D.
4. See Derek Blades (1989), p. 3.
5. See Ward (1976a), pp. 19–20.
6. The official estimate of the US Department of Commerce (1993), uses a service life of 80 years for new, one- to four-unit structures and 65 years for new, five or more unit structures based upon estimates from Goldsmith and Lipsey (1963). Improvements to residential structures are assigned the following lives: additions and alterations are assumed to have lives one-half as long as those for new structures; and lives for residential major replacements are based on industry estimates for items replaced during the 1970s. Mobile homes are assigned a life of 20 years on the basis of trade association data. The resulting average service life is probably above our 50 years estimate but well below 80 years.
7. See Blades (1989, Figure 2, p. 25).
8. Well-known studies for the USA were made by Terborgh (1954) and Winfrey (1935). The main sources used by the OECD countries as described in OECD (1993) are: asset lives prescribed by tax authorities, company accounts, surveys, expert advice and other countries, estimates. Tax authorities in many countries specify the number of years over which the depreciation of assets may be deducted from profits before charging taxes. The estimation procedure for these asset lives is not very clear, Hibbert, Griffin and Walker (1977), note that tax lives in the United Kingdom are based on 'custom and practice rather than any scientific study on the longevity of assets'. However, about half of the OECD countries make use of tax life estimates in their capital stock estimation. Five countries use company accounts and industry studies. Japan is the only country for which large scale surveys are available; in the USA and the United Kingdom some small scale surveys have been carried out. In several countries, investigations are under way with respect to service lives; for

example, Canada, Italy, the Netherlands and Spain. Finally, most countries rely on expert advice and use other countries' estimates (at least to check their own estimates). The empirical material for OECD countries is abundant compared to what is available for Latin America (see Bernstein and Shah, 1993).

9. If service life assumptions are changed with respect to the whole period of capital stock estimation, this will cause the stock size to change but the effect on the growth rate will be limited to change in the stocks composition. Changes within the period of estimation can have substantial effects on growth rates.

10. Hudson and Matthews (1963) analyse three theoretical variants of calculating depreciation charges over the working life of the asset: reducing, constant or increasing depreciation. The authors indicate that increasing depreciation over the asset's life is a rather unreal example, because it obviously implies that net services will continue to increase throughout the asset's life until the asset is ready for scrapping. They also discuss diminishing-balance and straight-line depreciation. With respect to the latter they observe: 'A pattern of gradually diminishing periodic net services could arise in practice as a result, say, of the need for increasing maintenance expenses in the later years of the asset's life' (Hudson and Matthews, 1963, p. 234).

11. The specification of the depreciation function is especially relevant for tax deduction purposes. The imposed tax system asset lives have, therefore, a direct effect on depreciation. Hulten and Wykoff (1980) conclude in a study on the USA that economic depreciation and tax depreciation are interrelated.

12. Depreciation represents a decline in efficiency and here we have assumed that efficiency decline is constant over time. For calculating convenience this assumption has to be expressed in discrete time for which we use the normal year period. We have assumed that the stock is at its maximum efficiency during the first period and starts declining by a fixed proportion in the subsequent periods (see Jorgenson 1974 and Jorgenson and Sullivan 1981). This assumption can have a sizable effect on the levels of the net capital stock. To give an example: assuming constant investment (100) and a working life of four years, means that the gross stock will be 400 at the end of the period. The net stock with immediate depreciation will amount to 150 (75 + 50 + 25) and with lagged depreciation will be 250 (100 + 75 + 50 + 25). The difference will vary according to investment flows and, again, will depend especially on working life assumptions, being lower with longer lives.

13. The calculation procedure comes from Ward (1976a, p. 58) who calls this the approximate method.

14. I use the 1980 international dollar which represents the same purchasing power parity over total GDP as the US dollar, but with a purchasing power over subaggregates and over detailed categories determined by average international prices rather than by US relative prices.

15. The exchange rates normally used are the annual average (rf) series of the IMF, published in *International Financial Statistics*.

16. Spanish acronym standing for: Programa de Estudios Conjuntos sobre la Integración Económica Latinoamericana.

17. Unfortunately the Latin American countries did not participate in the last phases of the ICP, which makes it impossible to change the benchmark to a more recent year.

18. For an example of this layout see Appendix E and for a complete description see the pages above.

19. See Appendices B and D.

20. See Maddison (1982, p. 216).

6. Explaining Latin American Post-War Development – The Growth Accounts

There have been relatively few growth accounting studies for Latin America.[1] One of the problems in comparing these is the great variety of methodologies used. The heterogeneity is especially evident in the case of capital stock estimation, but GDP and employment measures also differ widely. A major contribution of the present study is the use of a standardised approach applied both to Latin American and other countries with which Latin America is compared.

STARTING POINT AND COMPARATIVE PERFORMANCE

Table 6.1 presents comparative levels of economic performance between 1950 and 1994 in 16 countries and averages for regional groups. 1950 was for many countries a new dynamic starting point after two world wars and the Great Depression. In the post-war period many European and Asian countries started growing and converging much faster. This convergence process was much weaker in Latin America.

In 1950, per capita real income in Latin America was three times as high as that of developing Asia, a bit higher than the Iberian level and about a third of that of the United States. Within Latin America, real per capita income ranged in 1950 from around 40 per cent of the United States' level in Argentina and Venezuela, 30 per cent in Chile and Mexico and 19 and 15 per cent in Colombia and Brazil, respectively.

This picture had changed totally by 1994 when per capita real income in Latin America was about 30 per cent lower than in developing Asia, about two thirds of the Iberian level, around a quarter to a third of that in the United States and the other advanced countries. However, within Latin America, some convergence can be observed with levels of per capita GDP ranging from 35 per cent of the United States level for Argentina to 22 per cent in Colombia.

Latin American labour productivity (GDP per hour worked) was 3.5 times as high as developing Asia in 1950. Venezuela and Argentina had the highest level at around 40 per cent of the United States, Chile and Mexico about 30 per cent and Colombia and Brazil around 20 per cent. In 1994, labour productivity in Latin

Table 6.1 Comparative Levels of Economic Performance of 16 Countries Between 1950 and 1994 (USA = 100)

	GDP per capita		GDP per hour worked		Labour input per capita		Years of education per capita	
	1950	1994	1950	1994	1950	1994	1950	1994
Argentina	41	35	38	39	107	90	45	61
Brazil	15	23	17	24	89	92	18	37
Chile	33	31	30	34	109	94	43	63
Colombia	19	22	20	25	99	88	24	54
Mexico	27	33	30	40	90	84	19	49
Venezuela	38	27	42	34	90	79	18	61
Arithmetic average	29	29	29	33	97	88	28	54
Korea	8	46	9	33	90	141	30	86
Taiwan	8	47	7	36	106	132	32	98
Arithmetic average	8	46	8	34	98	136	31	92
Portugal	16	37	15	36	109	102	22	54
Spain	25	51	21	75	122	69	42	62
Arithmetic average	21	44	18	56	116	85	32	58
France	44	72	37	92	120	79	85	88
Germany	37	76	29	86	130	88	92	67
Japan	17	81	14	64	122	128	81	82
Netherlands	53	71	45	92	119	77	72	74
UK	62	69	54	82	115	85	96	78
Arithmetic average	43	74	36	83	121	91	85	78

	Total land area per capita		Merchandise exports per capita		Gross NR. capital stock per employee	
	1950	1994	1950	1994	1950	1994
Argentina	214	224	102	23	16	19
Brazil	99	108	38	14	4	20
Chile	72	61	68	42	25	23
Colombia	88	59	49	12	15	14
Mexico	92	52	28	20	10	22
Venezuela	110	52	275	37	27	26
Arithmetic average	113	93	93	25	16	21
Korea	7	6	2	110	5	48
Taiwan	5	3	14	97	6	24
Arithmetic average	6	5	8	103	5	36
Portugal	22	34	33	91	10	26
Spain	51	56	21	95	34	40
Arithmetic average	37	45	27	93	22	33
France	33	38	109	207	45	97
Germany	10	13	59	326	29	103
Japan	5	5	15	162	21	128
Netherlands	8	8	207	516	45	89
UK	12	15	186	178	30	64
Arithmetic average	13	16	115	278	34	96

Source: Latin America from Appendices A, B, C, E and F. Other countries from Maddison (1995), updated to 1994 using his sources, and OECD and FAO sources. Capital stocks estimated by the author.

America is the same as in the Asian developing countries, which is surprising given that average per capita income in the Latin American countries is 30 per cent lower than in Asia. However, only about 35 per cent of the population is employed in Latin America compared with almost 50 per cent in the Asian countries. Annual hours worked were less than 2000 hours per person employed, compared to over 2300 in Asia. Latin American labour productivity in 1994 was 33 per cent of the level in the United States, 40 per cent of that in the advanced capitalist countries and 59 per cent of the Iberian countries (see Maddison, 1995).

An element of growth that continues to receive much attention in the literature is the role of human capital, that is the increase of a country's productive potential through education and training. Table 6.1 shows that in 1950 the levels for Latin America, the Iberian Peninsula and the Asian countries were very similar (around 30 per cent of the US level). Although all countries show impressive growth in years of education, by 1994 the Latin American level is less than two thirds of the Asian level.

With respect to natural resources, the Latin American advantage was, and still is, overwhelming. A comparison of levels of total land area per capita in 1950 shows Latin American endowments above the level of the United States (the best endowed developed country among those considered), and well over ten times the natural resource endowment of our two South-East Asian countries. Moreover, this measure does not include mineral resources, which most probably would amplify the differences. With respect to the physical reproducible capital stock, Latin America's position relative to the United States improved slightly from an average of 16 per cent per capita in 1950 to around 21 per cent in 1994.

Latin American export performance has also been poor. From a relatively strong position in 1950, Latin America became the worst performer in 1994, indicating an important comparative loss of growth potential to realise efficiency gains through specialisation.

THE 1950–94 GROWTH ACCOUNTS

The objective of this book is to analyse economic development in Latin America in the twentieth century. In this chapter growth accounts are presented which constitute a useful framework for assembling quantitative 'facts' and qualified hypotheses about growth causality in a coherent way (Maddison, 1987). The growth accounts start in 1950 as data inadequacy prevents systematic analysis of previous periods for Latin America. Growth accounting exercises are important because they can serve many different purposes – explaining differences in growth rates and levels between countries, illuminating processes of convergence and divergence, assessing the role of technical progress and calculating potential output losses. The results with respect to the most traditional explanatory factors, that is changes in the quantity and quality of labour inputs and changes in the quantity and quality of capital inputs are presented. I also include natural resources as an explanatory factor.

In order to explain in more detail the complex developments which have occurred since 1950, measures of total factor productivity have been prepared which differ from the traditional labour productivity indicator presented in Chapter 3. Increases in different factor inputs are measured in terms of average annual compound growth rates. Labour input is derived by multiplying employment and annual hours per person. The quantity and quality effects are weighted by the relevant factor shares to show the contribution of augmented labour input.[2]

The average annual compound growth rates of the gross capital stock and of the quality of the capital stock (vintage effect) were also weighted by the respective factor shares to give the augmented capital input. The sum of augmented capital and labour input, and the growth rate of the natural resources input weighted by 0.1, gives the augmented joint factor input, which is an indicator of the impact of factor inputs on economic growth.

A very important element of the analytical framework is its transparency. The appendices present all the basic series, giving the reader the opportunity to follow each step in the reasoning and test alternative hypotheses, because in this kind of research, large judgmental elements are inevitable.

Labour Input

Labour input was estimated in terms of hours worked rather than employment because average annual hours worked per employee year vary substantially between countries and over time.[3] Average annual hours in 1994 were around 2500 in Korea, compared to about 1400 in the Netherlands. Within Latin America the variation is much lower.

It is important to adjust for changes in the quality of labour input. In this study, this is represented by changes in the level of education of the population aged between 15 and 64 years. Our estimate consists of equivalent years of education per person. The quality effect of labour results from the growth of equivalent years of education, and is based on the assumption that a 1 per cent increase in education causes a 0.5 proportionate gain in labour quality.[4]

Table 6.2 shows the growth rates of the labour force and employment, respectively. The labour force is related, much more than employment, to demographic forces, and in the post-war period many countries in Latin America entered the initial phase of demographic transition, with its characteristics of still high birth rates, and falling mortality rates. During 1950–73, the labour force grew somewhat more rapidly than employment. In the period from 1973–80, employment growth accelerated and both employment and the labour force grew at approximately the same rate. This situation changed in the crisis period since 1980, when in all countries (except Mexico) employment grew more slowly than the labour force, with unemployment growing especially fast in Colombia and Venezuela.

Table 6.2 Latin America: Labour Force (LF) and Employment (EMP), 1950–94 (annual average compound growth rates)

| | 1950–73 | | 1973–80 | | 1980–94 | |
	L.F.	EMP.	L.F.	EMP.	L.F.	EMP.
Argentina	1.4	1.4	0.9	1.0	1.8	1.6
Brazil	2.8	2.8	3.8	3.8	2.7	2.4
Chile	1.3	1.1	1.9	2.0	3.1	2.9
Colombia	2.5	2.4	3.5	3.5	3.0	2.4
Mexico	2.6	2.4	3.6	3.7	2.2	2.6
Venezuela	3.3	3.3	5.0	4.8	3.2	2.7
Arithmetic average	2.3	2.2	3.1	3.1	2.7	2.4

Source: Appendix C.

Table 4.7 of Chapter 4 showed a downward trend in working hours per person per year for the 1950–94 period in all countries, with an average decline of about 10 per cent. The range of decline varied from 122 hours for Mexico to 348 hours in the case of Colombia.

Chapter 4 highlighted the importance of the increasing average educational level in the post-war period as a crucial element in raising the quality of labour and labour productivity. The type of work an individual can do and the efficiency with which he or she performs is determined to a large degree by the level of educational attainment.

Table 6.3 presents the increase in the level of formal education of the population, measured in years. For growth accounting purposes, primary education has been given a weight of 1, secondary education a weight of 1.4 and higher education a weight of 2. These weights were applied to the whole sample and are the same as used by Maddison (1995). Maddison based his weights on Psacharopoulos' (1984) evidence on the relative earnings associated with different levels of education.

In all Latin American countries, the average level of education increased rapidly from 1950 to 1994, primary education was the first to increase, ultimately followed by secondary and higher education. The differences in levels of education are still very considerable, ranging in 1994 from 6.7 years in Brazil to 11.4 in Chile. Many authors consider the educational level of the labour force, instead of the total population, as the relevant measure for the quality of labour adjustment. Unfortunately, information regarding educational level for the whole 1950–94 period is not available in most countries in Latin America.[5]

Table 6.3 Latin America: Level of Education of the Population Aged 15–64 (weighted years of formal education)

	1950	1973	1980	1989	1994
Argentina	5.12	7.63	8.63	10.07	10.97
Brazil	1.98	3.64	4.69	5.89	6.69
Chile	4.85	7.41	8.50	10.25	11.38
Colombia	2.66	4.92	5.85	8.16	9.82
Mexico	2.16	4.46	6.48	7.86	8.75
Venezuela	2.02	4.42	6.19	8.99	11.06
Arithmetic average	3.13	5.41	6.72	8.54	9.78

Sources: Appendix C and applying the following weights; 1 for primary education, 1.4 for secondary education and 2 for higher education.

Table 6.4 summarises the main trends in labour quantity and quality growth in Latin America. Employment in Latin America also grew fast but annual hours per person declined steadily during the whole period. Labour quality, which is reflected in educational level, shows a steady increase over the whole period.

In Table 6.4 the quantitative and qualitative changes in labour inputs are presented separately. No uniform trend can be distinguished from this table. Comparing the 1950–73 and 1973–80 periods, all countries, except Argentina and Brazil, showed slow to marked acceleration in the incorporation of labour. In 1980–89, four countries experienced a slowdown (Brazil, Colombia, Mexico and Venezuela), while in the case of Chile the trend was acceleration. In the 1989–94 period, most countries increased the rate of incorporation of labour, with the exception of Brazil and Chile. However, in the case of Chile labour quantity incorporation was maintained at a comparatively high level.

Reproducible Capital Input

An important element in growth accounting from a comparative perspective is the availability of reliable measures of capital stock. In Chapter 4 comparable capital stock estimates were generated using the perpetual inventory method. With respect to quality improvement in successive vintages of the capital stock, representing technical progress in physical investment, modest assumptions were made regarding the embodiment in non-residential structures and machinery and equipment (see also the section on capital and investment in this chapter).

It is interesting to see that capital productivity, presented in Table 6.5, behaves quite different from labour productivity. Table 3.4 in Chapter 3 shows that labour productivity growth is generally positive: long-run growth is about 2.4 per cent annually and only 1980–89 shows negative growth. Table 6.5 shows that capital productivity growth in the Latin American countries has been negative for large periods. On average, capital productivity fell over the 1950–89 period and only

1989–94 shows increasing capital productivity. However, on a country-by-country comparison large differences can be observed, as well as between periods in particular countries.

Table 6.4 Rate of Growth of Labour Inputs, 1950–94 (annual average compound growth rates)

	Labour quantity				Labour quality			
	1950–73	1973–80	1980–89	1989–94	1950–73	1973–80	1980–89	1989–94
Argentina	1.32	0.82	1.06	1.39	0.87	0.88	0.86	0.86
Brazil	2.90	3.01	2.11	1.54	1.33	1.83	1.27	1.28
Chile	0.55	1.85	3.17	3.10	0.93	0.99	1.05	1.05
Colombia	2.03	3.02	1.95	2.12	1.35	1.24	1.87	1.87
Mexico	2.22	3.66	2.46	2.60	1.59	2.70	1.08	1.08
Venezuela	2.87	5.01	1.83	3.39	1.80	1.01	1.35	0.27
Arithmetic average	1.98	2.90	2.10	2.36	1.31	1.44	1.25	1.07

Source: Appendix C.

The quantity and quality increases of capital are presented in Table 6.6 below[6]. On the quality side the average growth rates were 0.7 per cent during the 1950–73 period, 0.9 per cent in 1973–80, 0.8 per cent in 1980–89, and 0.6 per cent in 1989–94. The combined effect of quantity and quality growth makes clear that especially in 1950–80, capital inputs grew at a very high pace. Since then, growth has been much slower.

Table 6.5 Capital Productivity Growth, 1950–94 (annual average compound growth rates)

	1950–73	1973–80	1980–89	1989–94
Argentina	0.03	-0.44	-1.21	0.91
Brazil	-1.46	-0.88	-1.03	-0.29
Chile	-0.25	0.29	0.20	0.34
Colombia	0.84	-0.06	-0.49	0.08
Mexico	-1.52	-0.40	-1.21	1.39
Venezuela	0.03	-1.12	-1.13	0.92
Arithmetic average	-0.39	-0.44	-0.81	0.56

Source: Appendices B and E.

The results with respect to quantity increases were discussed in detail in Chapter 5. During 1950–73, Argentina, Chile and Colombia witnessed the slowest growth, and fastest growth occurred in Brazil, Mexico and Venezuela. During the 1973–80 period, capital stock growth showed no signs of slowing down (except in Chile). However, in the 1980–94 period, growth rates decelerated drastically in all countries, with the exception of Chile and Colombia.

Table 6.6 Rate of Growth of Capital Inputs, 1950–94 (annual average compound growth rates)

	Capital quantity				Capital quality			
	1950–73	1973–80	1980–89	1989–94	1950–73	1973–80	1980–89	1989–94
Argentina	3.59	4.56	2.11	1.74	0.75	1.10	0.88	0.34
Brazil	8.50	10.35	4.99	2.25	0.74	1.06	0.44	-0.02
Chile	3.85	1.87	2.42	4.75	0.62	0.48	0.86	1.23
Colombia	4.25	5.17	4.63	3.89	0.64	0.92	0.95	0.74
Mexico	8.14	7.85	4.57	3.70	0.61	0.86	0.63	0.52
Venezuela	6.68	8.04	2.94	0.37	0.58	0.93	0.73	0.47
Arithmetic average	5.84	6.31	3.61	2.78	0.66	0.89	0.75	0.55

Source: Appendix E.

Land

Land was used as a proxy indicator of natural resource endowment for the countries, using respective weights of 1 for arable and permanent crop land, 0.3 for permanent pasture and 0.1 for forest land. The factor share used for weighting land was 0.10 for all countries (see next section). Table 6.7 shows clearly that the movement of the agricultural frontier has slowed down since 1950. In some cases land has been increasingly diverted from agricultural uses since 1973.

Table 6.7 Latin America: Movement of the Agricultural Frontier – Expansion of Area of Land in Use for Agriculture (annual average compound growth rate)

	1950–73	1973–80	1980–94
Argentina	0.77	0.11	0.01
Brazil	2.07	1.37	0.50
Chile	0.87	0.75	-0.93
Colombia	0.00	-0.09	0.88
Mexico	0.36	0.99	-0.70
Venezuela	0.67	-0.01	0.00
Arithmetic average	0.79	0.52	-0.04

Source: FAO (various issues).

Factor Shares

Factor shares are necessary for calculating total factor productivity, as each factor input has to be weighted by its respective factor share. The factor weights used in growth accounting affect the results of the exercises substantially, because rather big differences exist in growth rates of labour and capital stocks. The three main components of GDP are fixed capital consumption, compensation of employees and operating surplus. This last component must be divided between capital, labour and land income.

In Latin America an important part of the operating surplus, much more than in the advanced countries, consists of labour compensation for the self-employed and these earnings have to be attributed to labour's share. The total capital share has been disaggregated into the capital shares of its three components, residential and non-residential capital and machinery and equipment. In some growth-accounting exercises, the individual items in the capital stock are weighted at their total stock value. However, the service flow per unit of capital in machinery and equipment is much higher than from a unit of residential capital. Therefore, the components of the capital stock have been weighted by their asset life, and the resulting disaggregated capital stock shares were multiplied by the national accounts total capital share. For the standardised capital shares the disaggregation of Maddison (1991a) has been used. For land income, used as a proxy for natural resource endowment, it was impossible to obtain estimates for all countries and a 10 per cent share was assumed for the whole period based on national accounts estimates available for some years in the case of Argentina and Mexico. Table 6.8 presents the resulting shares of capital, labour and natural resources in GDP for the six Latin American countries.

However, several authors have expressed their preference for constant factor shares (for example Maddison, 1987) and the sensitivity of the results was tested by using alternatively a set of standardised factor shares, with similar weights as used in Maddison (1991a), constant over time for all countries, as presented in Table 6.9. In general, the standardised factor shares will generate somewhat lower factor input growth as a result of a slightly lower standardised capital share combined with the fact that the capital stock generally grows faster than labour input.

Table 6.8 Capital, Labour and Natural Resource Shares in GDP, 1950–94 (percentage of GDP)

	1950–73	1973–80	1980–89	1989–94	1950–73	1973–80	1980–89	1989–94
	Argentina				Brazil			
Labour	52.9	49.7	37.8	36.0	70.1	56.8	56.7	57.6
Residential capital	11.8	11.4	14.9	16.3	3.1	4.6	4.9	5.6
Non-res. structures	12.1	12.5	14.5	13.5	4.4	8.2	9.6	11.0
M&E	13.2	16.5	22.7	24.2	12.5	20.4	18.8	15.7
Total capital	37.1	40.3	52.2	54.0	19.9	33.2	33.3	32.4
Natural resources	10.0	10.0	10.0	10.0	10.0	10.0	10.0	10.0
Total	100	100	100	100	100	100	100	100
	Chile				Colombia			
Labour	5.9	54.4	54.4	55.6	53.3	53.6	52.2	49.3
Residential capital	14.7	13.2	12.5	11.4	9.4	5.1	4.8	5.0
Non-res. structures	12.1	11.4	12.4	12.3	18.8	12.4	12.3	13.0
M&E	11.2	11.0	10.7	10.8	8.5	18.9	20.7	22.7
Total capital	38.1	35.6	35.6	34.4	36.7	36.4	37.8	40.7
Natural resources	10.0	10.0	10.0	10.0	10.0	10.0	10.0	10.0
Total	100	100	100	100	100	100	100	100
	Mexico				Venezuela			
Labour	42.7	54.3	41.6	35.5	63.0	51.5	48.3	43.4
Residential capital	6.1	4.6	6.9	9.0	2.9	4.5	4.8	5.5
Non-res. structures	16.7	10.8	14.4	15.9	9.2	12.7	13.2	15.9
M&E	24.5	20.4	27.1	29.6	15.0	21.3	23.7	25.2
Total capital	47.3	35.7	48.4	54.5	27.0	38.5	41.7	46.6
Natural resources	10.0	10.0	10.0	10.0	10.0	10.0	10.0	10.0
Total	100	100	100	100	100	100	100	100

Source: Estimated by the author on the basis of national account and census information.

Table 6.9 Standardised Capital, Labour and Natural Resource Shares in GDP, 1950–94 (percentage of GDP)

	1950–73	1973–80	1980–89	1989–94
Labour	60.0	60.0	60.0	60.0
Residential capital	7.5	7.5	7.5	7.5
Non-residential structures	10.0	10.0	10.0	10.0
M&E	12.5	12.5	12.5	12.5
Total capital	30.0	30.0	30.0	30.0
Natural resources	10.0	10.0	10.0	10.0
Total	100	100	100	100

Source: Estimated by the author.

Table 6.10 Basic Indicators of Growth Performance, 1950–94 (annual average compound growth rates)

	1950–73	1973–80	1980–89	1989–94	1950–73	1973–80	1980–89	1989–94
	Argentina				Brazil			
Population	1.69	1.58	1.49	1.25	2.89	2.36	2.07	1.77
GDP	3.99	3.04	-1.02	6.09	6.91	7.18	2.26	0.90
Employment	1.41	0.98	1.72	1.25	2.78	3.81	2.67	1.86
Hours per employee	-0.08	-0.16	-0.65	0.14	0.11	-0.77	-0.55	-0.31
Education	0.87	0.88	0.86	0.86	1.33	1.83	1.27	1.28
M&E	6.71	5.84	3.11	1.52	7.44	10.76	2.05	-2.66
Residential capital	3.07	4.36	2.92	2.75	7.48	8.48	6.17	4.06
Non-res. struct	4.12	4.16	0.50	0.40	11.21	11.31	6.54	3.81
Capital quality	0.75	1.10	0.88	0.34	0.74	1.06	0.44	-0.02
Natural resources	0.77	0.11	0.03	-0.03	2.07	1.37	0.49	0.52
	Chile				Colombia			
Population	2.18	1.57	1.62	1.67	2.85	2.20	2.01	1.71
GDP	3.58	2.84	2.95	6.38	5.12	4.97	3.31	4.27
Employment	1.09	1.97	2.93	2.86	2.39	3.49	2.48	2.16
Hours per employee	-0.54	-0.12	0.23	0.23	-0.35	-0.45	-0.52	-0.04
Education	0.93	0.99	1.05	1.05	1.35	1.24	1.87	1.87
M&E	5.13	2.25	1.91	7.60	6.16	7.08	5.16	4.37
Residential capital	3.35	1.61	1.58	3.12	4.39	3.93	3.93	4.42
Non-res. struct.	3.77	1.91	3.40	4.60	3.45	4.74	4.64	3.33
Capital quality	0.62	0.48	0.68	1.23	0.64	0.92	0.95	0.74
Natural resources	0.87	0.75	-1.53	0.14	0.00	-0.09	1.33	0.07
	Mexico				Venezuela			
Population	3.06	2.84	2.13	1.86	3.79	3.58	2.61	2.36
GDP	6.50	6.43	1.36	2.99	6.44	4.10	-0.01	3.61
Employment	2.42	3.73	2.41	2.87	3.33	4.77	2.39	3.28
Hours per employee	-0.19	-0.07	0.04	-0.26	-0.45	0.23	-0.55	0.11
Education	1.59	2.70	1.08	1.08	1.80	1.01	1.35	0.27
M&E	12.29	9.30	3.21	3.62	5.22	9.43	3.18	-3.20
Residential capital	9.03	8.30	6.00	6.57	9.03	8.46	2.72	0.84
Non-res. struct.	6.40	6.59	4.70	1.81	6.91	7.01	2.87	2.34
Capital quality	0.61	0.86	0.63	0.52	0.58	0.93	0.73	0.47
Natural resources	0.36	0.99	-1.05	-0.06	0.67	-0.01	0.02	-0.04

Source: Appendices A, B, C and E.

Results

The core of the causal analysis is presented in Tables 6.10–6.12 stating the basic indicators of growth performance and the sources of growth. Tables 6.11 and 6.12 on sources of GDP growth have been generated weighting the basic indicators of Table 6.10 by their respective factor shares. Table 6.11 represents the specific factor weights, either in time as per country, as presented in Table 6.8 and in Table 6.12 the standardised shares of Table 6.9 were employed.

Table 6.11 Sources of GDP Growth with Country-Specific Factor Shares, 1950–94 (annual average percentage point contribution to growth rates)

	1950–73	1973–80	1980–89	1989–94	1950–73	1973–80	1980–89	1989–94
	Argentina				Brazil			
GDP	3.99	3.04	-1.02	6.09	6.91	7.18	2.26	0.90
Employment	0.74	0.49	0.65	0.45	1.95	2.17	1.52	1.07
Hours per employee	-0.04	-0.08	-0.24	0.05	0.08	-0.44	-0.31	-0.18
Education	0.46	0.44	0.33	0.31	0.93	1.04	0.72	0.74
M&E	0.52	0.75	0.48	0.42	1.06	2.11	0.94	0.35
Residential capital	0.47	0.52	0.31	0.28	0.26	0.47.	0.25	0.13
Non-res. structures	0.48	0.57	0.31	0.24	0.38	0.85	0.48	0.25
Capital quality	0.28	0.44	0.46	0.18	0.15	0.35	0.15	-0.01
Natural resources	0.08	0.01	0.00	0.00	0.21	0.14	0.05	0.05
Total factor input	2.98	3.14	2.29	1.93	5.01	6.68	3.78	2.40
Doubly augmented total factor productivity	1.00	-0.10	-3.31	4.16	1.90	0.50	-1.53	-1.50
	Chile				Colombia			
GDP	3.58	2.84	2.95	6.38	5.12	4.97	3.31	4.27
Employment	0.56	1.07	1.59	1.59	1.27	1.87	1.29	1.07
Hours per employee	-0.28	-0.07	0.13	0.13	-0.19	-0.24	-0.27	-0.02
Education	0.48	0.54	0.57	0.58	0.72	0.67	0.97	0.92
M&E	0.61	0.30	0.38	0.75	0.36	0.98	0.96	0.88
Residential capital	0.37	0.16	0.19	0.34	0.40	0.26	0.22	0.20
Non-res. structures	0.48	0.21	0.29	0.55	0.80	0.64	0.57	0.50
Capital quality	0.23	0.17	0.24	0.42	0.24	0.34	0.36	0.30
Natural resources	0.09	0.07	-0.15	0.01	0.00	-0.01	0.13	0.01
Total factor input	2.56	2.45	3.24	4.38	3.60	4.50	4.24	3.86
Doubly augmented total factor productivity	1.03	0.39	-0.29	2.01	1.53	0.47	-0.92	0.41
	Mexico				Venezuela			
GDP	6.50	6.43	1.36	2.99	6.44	4.10	-0.01	3.61
Employment	1.03	2.03	1.00	1.02	2.10	2.46	1.16	1.42
Hours per employee	-0.08	-0.04	0.02	-0.09	-0.28	0.12	-0.27	0.05
Education	0.68	1.47	0.45	0.38	1.13	0.52	0.65	0.12
M&E	1.99	1.60	1.24	1.10	1.00	1.71	0.70	0.09
Residential capital	0.50	0.36	0.31	0.33	0.19	0.36	0.14	0.02
Non-res. structures	1.36	0.84	0.66	0.59	0.61	1.02	0.39	0.06
Capital quality	0.29	0.31	0.30	0.28	0.16	0.36	0.30	0.22
Natural resources	0.04	0.10	-0.10	-0.01	0.07	0.00	0.00	0.00
Total factor input	5.81	6.66	3.88	3.60	4.98	6.55	3.07	1.97
Doubly augmented total factor productivity	0.70	-0.24	-2.52	-0.62	1.46	-2.45	-3.08	1.64

Source: Tables 6.8 and 6.10.

Table 6.12 Sources of GDP Growth, Standardised Factor Shares, 1950–94 (annual average percentage point contribution to growth rates)

	1950–73	1973–80	1980–89	1989–94	1950–73	1973–80	1980–89	1989–94
	Argentina				Brazil			
GDP	3.99	3.04	-1.02	6.09	6.91	7.18	2.26	0.90
Employment	0.84	0.59	1.03	0.75	1.67	2.29	1.60	1.11
Hours per employee	-0.05	-0.09	-0.39	0.08	0.07	-0.46	-0.33	-0.19
Education	0.52	0.53	0.52	0.52	0.80	1.10	0.76	0.77
M&E	0.49	0.57	0.26	0.22	1.06	1.29	0.62	0.28
Residential capital	0.30	0.34	0.16	0.13	0.64	0.78	0.37	0.17
Non-res. structures	0.40	0.46	0.21	0.17	0.85	1.03	0.50	0.23
Capital quality	0.17	0.25	0.20	0.08	0.17	0.24	0.10	0.00
Natural resources	0.08	0.01	0.00	0.00	0.21	0.14	0.05	0.05
Total factor input	2.75	2.65	1.99	1.95	5.46	6.40	3.69	2.42
Doubly augmented total factor productivity	1.24	0.39	-3.01	4.15	1.46	0.78	-1.43	-1.52
	Chile				Colombia			
GDP	3.58	2.84	2.95	6.38	5.12	4.97	3.31	4.27
Employment	0.65	1.18	1.76	1.71	1.43	2.10	1.49	1.30
Hours per employee	-0.32	-0.07	0.14	0.14	-0.21	-0.27	-0.31	-0.02
Education	0.56	0.59	0.63	0.63	0.81	0.75	1.12	1.12
M&E	0.48	0.23	0.30	0.59	0.53	0.65	0.58	0.49
Residential capital	0.29	0.14	0.18	0.36	0.32	0.39	0.35	0.29
Non-res. structures	0.38	0.19	0.24	0.48	0.42	0.52	0.46	0.39
Capital quality	0.14	0.11	0.15	0.28	0.14	0.21	0.21	0.17
Natural resources	0.09	0.07	-0.15	0.01	0.00	-0.01	0.13	0.01
Total factor input	2.27	2.44	3.25	4.20	3.45	4.32	4.03	3.73
Doubly augmented total factor productivity	1.22	0.40	-0.30	2.18	1.68	0.65	-0.72	0.53
	Mexico				Venezuela			
GDP	6.50	6.43	1.36	2.99	6.44	4.10	-0.01	3.61
Employment	1.45	2.24	1.45	1.72	2.00	2.86	1.43	1.97
Hours per employee	-0.12	-0.04	0.03	-0.16	-0.27	0.14	-0.33	0.06
Education	0.95	1.62	0.65	0.65	1.08	0.60	0.81	0.16
M&E	1.02	0.98	0.57	0.46	0.83	1.00	0.37	0.05
Residential capital	0.61	0.59	0.34	0.28	0.50	0.60	0.22	0.03
Non-res. structures	0.81	0.78	0.46	0.37	0.67	0.80	0.29	0.04
Capital quality	0.14	0.19	0.14	0.12	0.13	0.21	0.16	0.11
Natural resources	0.04	0.10	-0.10	-0.01	0.07	0.00	0.00	0.00
Total factor input	4.90	6.47	3.53	3.43	5.01	6.23	2.96	2.40
Doubly augmented total factor productivity	1.60	0.04	-2.17	-0.45	1.43	-2.13	-2.96	1.20

Source: Tables 6.9 and 6.10.

The results indicate that the growth accounts are a useful framework in the quantitative interpretation of economic growth in Latin America in the post-war period. The degree of explanation of the exercise over a 44-year period shows positive results for the countries as a group, though for individual countries the degree to which growth is explained leads in some periods for some countries to overexplanation. It was also possible to compare Latin America's relative stance in a comparative perspective. The main results of the growth accounting exercise are presented in Tables 6.10–6.15 and Figures 6.1–6.5.

The interpretation of total factor productivity is still a matter of debate; here, a step-by step approach has been followed, starting with measurement of total factor productivity, including quantities of factor inputs and doubly augmented total factor productivity, which includes also the quality improvement of the factor inputs. The doubly augmented total factor productivity which finally remains can be considered as an approximate measure of the effect of disembodied technical progress on long term growth, but it is also includes other measured influences, especially changes in capacity utilisation rates, statistical and other errors.

The finally remaining 'residual' includes advances of knowledge, it also picks up the net error (positive or negative) in the other estimates as well as the net contribution of other sources of growth for which no estimation was attempted (Denison, 1967). I will return to this subject in the next section on growth causality in Latin America.

Table 6.13 resumes the explanatory power of the growth components presented in the causal analysis of Tables 6.10, 6.11 and 6.12. Two variants of total factor productivity are expressed as a percentage of GDP, in order to give an idea of the order of magnitude of the role of factor inputs and TFP in the growth performance of Latin America. I have left out the period 1980–89, showing highly negative total factor productivity growth caused by the significant difference between actual and potential output in this period, see also below. The degree of explanation varies significantly across countries and, within each country, between periods.

Table 6.13 Explanatory Power of Total Factor Productivity in Growth, 1950–94 (by sub-period, in percentages of GDP growth)

	Total factor productivity (TFP)			Doubly augmented total factor productivity (DATFP)		
	1950–73	1973–80	1989–94	1950–73	1973–80	1989–94
Argentina	50	39	78	33	13	68
Brazil	38	31	-77	24	13	-162
Chile	59	41	49	39	17	34
Colombia	51	32	43	33	13	13
Mexico	42	29	10	25	1	-15
Venezuela	42	-32	41	23	-52	33
Arithmetic average Latin America	47	23	24	30	1	-5

Source: Tables 6.10 and 6.12.

Table 6.14 shows the results in terms of growth rates of two measures of total factor productivity growth; total factor productivity without capital and labour augmentation and doubly augmented total factor productivity.

Table 6.14 GDP and Total Factor Productivity based on Standardised Factor Shares, 1950–94 (average annual compound growth rates)

	1950–73	1973–80	1980–89	1989–94
		GDP		
Argentina	3.99	3.04	-1.02	6.09
Brazil	6.91	7.18	2.26	0.90
Chile	3.58	2.84	2.95	6.38
Colombia	5.12	4.97	3.31	4.27
Mexico	6.50	6.43	1.36	2.99
Venezuela	6.44	4.10	-0.01	3.61
Arithmetic average Latin America	5.43	4.76	1.48	4.04
		TFP		
Argentina	2.01	1.18	-2.29	4.74
Brazil	2.63	2.25	-0.52	-0.70
Chile	2.10	1.17	0.32	3.10
Colombia	2.63	1.60	0.75	1.83
Mexico	2.73	1.88	-1.49	0.31
Venezuela	2.71	-1.31	-1.99	1.46
Arithmetic average Latin America	2.47	1.13	-0.87	1.79
		DATFP		
Argentina	1.31	0.40	-3.00	4.15
Brazil	1.66	0.92	-1.38	-1.46
Chile	1.40	0.47	-0.46	2.19
Colombia	1.68	0.64	-0.58	0.54
Mexico	1.63	0.06	-2.27	-0.45
Venezuela	1.50	-2.13	-2.96	1.20
Arithmetic average Latin America	1.53	0.06	-1.78	1.03

Source: Appendix B and Tables 6.10 and 6.12.

In the 1980–89 period the Latin American economies experienced a severe crisis due to the large debt accumulated in the 1970s and a deterioration in the international capital and goods markets. The fall in demand caused a movement away from the production possibilities frontier and resulted in the under-utilisation of installed capacity (see also Chapter 7 for a more detailed treatment of policy in this period[7]). Jorgenson (1990) concluded that the aggregate production model used for analysing economic growth is appropriate for studying long-term growth trends. However, the results for Latin America in the shorter run and especially in the period of crisis of the 1980s have to be treated with caution. The negative growth of total factor productivity can be attributed partly to demand-side distortions which cause economic growth to decline. The debt crisis of the 1980s caused economic growth to stagnate in Latin America. Negative total factor productivity growth has to be attributed in part to this difference between potential and actual growth. In Table 6.14 this is reflected in the very low average GDP growth rate of 1.48 per cent for the 1980–89 period and in the negative total factor productivity.

When comparing the results of growth accounting exercises, one must be aware that the residual may differ, depending of the factors included in its calculation. Very often a total factor productivity without quality augmentation is what is presented in this kind of study. Figure 6.1 presents this estimate for the Latin American countries. Figures 6.2 and 6.3 include the quality effects of labour and capital respectively. Figure 6.4 presents doubly augmented total factor productivity growth including both capital and labour quality effects.

Figure 6.1, presenting total factor productivity growth without quality augmentation, shows that only two countries, Colombia and Chile, experienced continuous total factor productivity growth over the whole 1950–94 period. Argentina was consistently the lowest ranking country over the whole period despite its rapid recuperation in 1989–94. Venezuela was the only country to experience a significant fall in the 1973–80 period. In 1980–89, Brazil, Mexico, Venezuela and Argentina all showed falling total factor productivity. All countries, with the exception of Brazil, witnessed positive total factor productivity growth in the 1989–94 period.

Figure 6.2, presenting labour-augmented total factor productivity growth, shows some interesting differences with respect to Table 6.1. Colombia scores higher than all other countries for the whole period. At the lower end, Argentina managed to leave Mexico and Venezuela behind in the 1989–94 period.

In Venezuela the fall in total factor productivity growth started in 1973. Also Mexico and Argentina had experienced negative labour-augmented total factor productivity growth, although to a lower degree than Venezuela, in 1973–80.

In Figure 6.3 quality improvement through embodiment of capital quality is taken into account. It is similar to the figures presented above. Mexico is the country with the lowest overall total factor productivity growth, if capital and labour augmentation are taken into account. In general, it is possible to conclude that only Colombia maintained a relatively stable total factor productivity growth over the whole period, while the other Latin American countries experienced major setbacks in one or more periods. Finally, Figure 6.4 presents doubly augmented total factor productivity growth in Latin America.

When analysing total factor productivity in a comparative perspective at least two striking results become clear.[8] First, the similarity of total factor productivity growth rates between Asia and the advanced and Iberian countries, especially in the 1950–80 period. From 1980 onwards Asian total factor productivity growth rates are much higher than in Iberia and the advanced countries. Latin America's total factor productivity growth rates are much lower than those of Asia or the other countries of our sample.

Figure 6.1 Latin America: Total Factor Productivity without Augmentation, 1950–94 (index 1950 = 100)

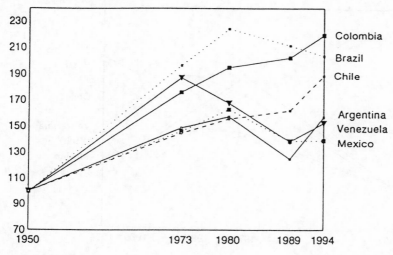

Source: Table 6.12.

Figure 6.2 Latin America: Labour-Augmented Total Factor Productivity, 1950–94 (index 1950 = 100)

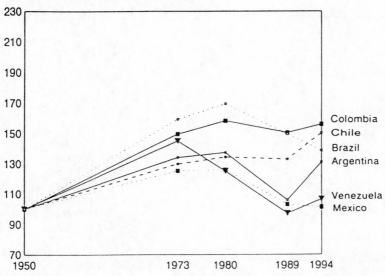

Source: Table 6.12.

Figure 6.3 Latin America: Capital-Augmented Total Factor Productivity,
1950–94 (index 1950 = 100)

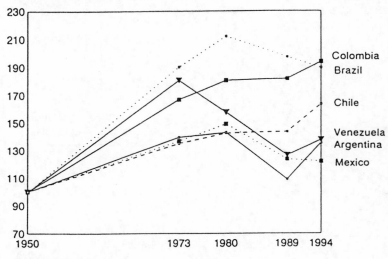

Figure 6.4 Latin America: Doubly-Augmented Total Factor Productivity,
1950–94 (index 1950 = 100)

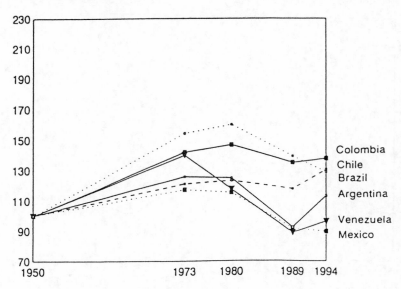

The second striking result is, the relatively small differences in total factor productivity growth, measured as a percentage of GDP growth, between Latin America and the Asian group for the 1950–80 period, both as regards total factor productivity and doubly augmented total factor productivity. In very general terms, there is less than a 10 percentage point difference between the Latin American and Asian group (Asia being higher) along with a difference of equal magnitude, or somewhat higher, between Asia and the advanced countries.

Table 6.15 International Comparison: GDP and Total Factor Productivity, 1950–94 (average annual compound growth rates and % of GDP)

	1950–73	1973–80	1980–89	1989–94
	Arithmetic averages:			
	GDP			
Latin America	5.4	4.8	1.5	4.0
Asia	8.4	7.7	8.0	6.9
Iberian countries	5.8	2.7	2.7	1.8
Advanced countries	5.3	2.2	2.6	1.8
	TFP			
Latin America	2.5	1.1	-0.9	1.8
Asia	4.4	1.6	3.9	3.4
Iberian countries	4.1	1.1	1.3	0.8
Advanced countries	3.5	1.0	1.3	1.1
	DATFP			
Latin America	1.5	0.1	-1.8	1.0
Asia	2.9	-0.1	2.5	2.0
Iberian countries	2.9	0.0	-0.2	0.1
Advanced countries	2.8	0.3	0.6	0.8
	Explanatory Power of Total Factor Productivity (as % of GDP):			
	TFP			
Latin America	46	23	-60	45
Asia	52	21	48	50
Iberian countries	71	41	48	44
Advanced countries	66	45	50	61
	DATFP			
Latin America	28	2	-120	25
Asia	35	-2	31	29
Iberian countries	50	0	-7	6
Advanced countries	53	14	23	41

Source: See note 7.

Krugman (1994) generated a lively debate about the Asian growth performance by asserting that:

> Asian growth seems to be driven by extraordinary growth in inputs like labour and capital rather than by gains in efficiency. (p. 70)

He considered in particular Singapore, using the data of Young (1994), showing that total factor productivity was zero. However, my data show that although factor accumulation explains a great part of the growth performance in Asia (see Table 6.15), total factor productivity also played an important role.[9]

Latin America's 'lost decade' of the 1980s caused the residual to become highly negative, indicating that total factor productivity growth was negative. This was not, however, the case in the Asian or the developed countries (although doubly augmented total factor productivity was also negative in some periods in those countries), since their total factor productivity remained positive, albeit with declining growth rates.

Figure 6.5 Doubly-Augmented Total Factor Productivity: An International Comparison, 1950–94 [10] (index 1950 = 100)

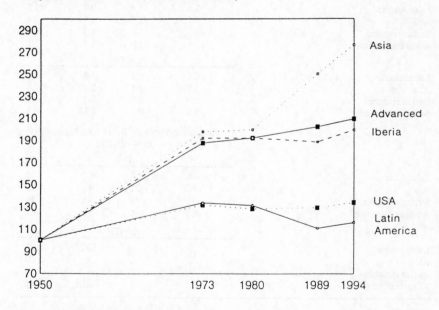

Source: Table 6.13, Maddison (1995) and see note 7.

Figure 6.5 indicates clearly that Latin America's performance has been worse than all the other regions of our sample. Total factor productivity grew at an annual 2.5 per cent between 1950–73, falling to 1 per cent from 1973–80, and then became sharply negative in the 1980s (some recovery occurred in the 1989–94 period). It shows a widening gap between Latin America and the other groups of countries for the whole period since 1950. Interestingly, Figure 6.5 shows that Latin America's performance was nearest to that of the United States.

GROWTH CAUSALITY IN LATIN AMERICA

In this and the following sections, some aspects of growth causality will be discussed. First I analyse some of the proximate causes of growth, and then look at ultimate causes of growth in the last section of this chapter. Through growth accounting it is possible to identify and quantify the proximate causes of growth but no light is shed on the ultimate causes of growth.

A major shortcoming of the growth accounts is that interactions among the sources are not taken into account. The proximate sources of growth are probably not as independent as is assumed in growth accounting. Abramovitz (1993) traced one line of dependence, namely the dependence of tangible and human capital accumulation on the pace and character of technological progress.

As Abramovitz (1993) stated:

> Standard growth accounting is based on the notion that the several proximate sources of growth that it identifies operate independently of one another. The implication of this assumption is that the contributions attributable to each can be added up. And if the contributions of every substantial source other than technological progress has been estimated, whatever of growth is left over – that is, not accounted for by the sum of the measured sources – is the presumptive contribution of technological progress. (p. 220)

Maddison (1991a) stressed that:

> The most difficult problem at the proximate level is analysing the role of technical progress, which interacts in myriad ways with other items in the growth accounts. Hence technical progress must be treated separately from other elements of proximate causality, because it is almost as difficult to quantify satisfactorily as are the elements of ultimate causality. (p. 11)

A new line of reasoning, with inverted causality from capital accumulation to technical progress, is emphasised in the new growth theories. In the last decade the general theme of interdependence has become imbedded in those new theories of economic growth.

In the past decades the literature on technology has increasingly moved away from the neo-classical framework, where knowledge is assumed to be completely exogenous and equally accessible to all firms as in the case of a public good.

Recent models of technological change focus on the process in which the firm searches for new techniques in an environment characterised by incomplete information. Such models also point more clearly in the direction of ultimate causes, such as institutional and organisational factors, which determine the pace of technological change.

These factors bear much resemblance to what Abramovitz referred to as the social capability of a society to adopt, and adapt to, new technology. The search for such ultimate causes is one of the major challenges in the study of comparative productivity levels (Van Ark, 1993). In previous chapters I have analysed in detail two of the most important proximate sources of growth: human resources and physical capital. In this section I will return to them shortly to analyse some factors directly related to growth accounting.

Capital and Investment

One of the most important factors explaining Latin America's economic performance is without doubt its investment and capital stock formation. In Chapter 5 standardised estimates of capital stock were generated and analysed, and in this section, I will concentrate on the importance of capital stocks in growth accounting and the role of investment in Latin America's development process.

Growth accounting only becomes possible if reliable estimates of the flow of services from physical capital are available. Making an analogy with labour, one would like to know the amount of machine hours used in production during the period of reference. However, the lack of available data normally does not permit this procedure, so I used the general accepted proxy for this calculation, that is, the estimation of the capital stock based upon the 'perpetual inventory model' developed by Raymond Goldsmith (1951).[11]

The capital stock was disaggregated into machinery and equipment, structures and dwellings with service lives of 15, 40 and 50 years, respectively. The 'perpetual inventory model' provides an indication of productive capacity. It includes all capital assets, but some of these may be temporarily idle while others may have been withdrawn from production and held in reserve in case they may be needed to meet an unexpected rise in demand. Therefore, this model will not produce estimates of the 'utilised' stock.

The service lives used in this method refer to the total length of time from the initial installation of assets to the moment when they are finally scrapped. Clearly these lives may include periods when some assets are not being used to produce anything. In this study, capital stock estimates are basically used to explain Latin America's performance in comparison with other regions in the 1950–94 period (see Table 6.16). Therefore capital has been used in the 'ex-post' sense, that is, in its observable role as a factor input in the production process. This notion should be distinguished from the one in which capital is used as an indicator of net worth which embodies potential economic services and has the capacity to generate future income. The present net worth of a capital asset, which is related to its future earning potential, progressively declines as it gets older, even though the annual real value of its services may remain unchanged over time.

To estimate capital-augmented total factor productivity one needs to augment the capital stock. The rates of vintage improvement chosen here are rather low, 1.5 per cent for machinery and equipment and a 0.5 per cent for structures. Following Maddison (1991a) no vintage improvement was used for dwellings. This capital embodiment effect is not a 'catch-all' effect of technical progress (as suggested initially by Solow), because a portion of technical progress is embodied in the labour force and consists of organisational and other improvements. This quality effect is the result of three forces; embodied technical progress, changes in the average age of the stock, and changes in its composition. If the average age of the capital stock goes down, this raises the embodiment effect as newer vintages will have more weight in the total capital stock.

Table 6.16 Explanatory Power of Capital in Growth, 1950–94 (by subperiods, in percentages)

	Quantity of capital			Quality of capital		
	1950–73	1973–80	1980–94	1950–73	1973–80	1980–94
Argentina	30	45	40	4	8	11
Brazil	37	43	68	2	3	4
Chile	32	20	23	4	4	5
Colombia	25	31	36	3	4	5
Mexico	38	37	66	2	3	7
Venezuela	31	59	48	2	5	11
Arithmetic average Latin America	32	39	47	3	5	7

Source: Table 6.12.

The idea of embodying technical progress in the form of quality improvement in successive vintages of capital was first put forward by Robert Solow (1962). The basic argument is that physical investment is the prime vehicle by which technical progress is realised. The debate is about whether technical progress is due primarily to improvements in the design of new capital ('embodiment'), or is mainly 'disembodied' and thus independent of the rate of capital formation (Hulten, 1992).

This point, also known as the Solow–Salter vintage argument (Maddison, 1972), leads to the inclusion in growth accounting exercises of an adjustment for differences in vintages of capital. Denison (1993) formulates it as follows:

It was argued that when advances in knowledge permit later vintages of capital goods to have higher marginal product than capital with the same production cost in earlier vintages, the quantity of capital should be counted as increasing proportionally, thus transferring part of the contribution of advances in knowledge to capital. (p. 48)

Denison (1993) suggests that 'this procedure divorces cause from effect'. A strong argument is that it defies measurement, like a capital stock series that equates different vintages by their marginal product. Maddison (1991a) finds Solow's basic point extraordinarily illuminating and inclusion of a modest element of technical progress in the analysis does help explain the nature of the growth process, and clarifies the impact of changes in the age of capital in a way that is not possible outside the vintage context.

It has been argued that existing differences in technology between advanced countries are increasingly related to differences in work practice and shop-floor organisation, these being typically features of disembodied rather than embodied technological change (Van Ark, 1993). However, in the case of the Latin American countries the difference between their capital stock and that of the technological leader is still very substantial and it seems reasonable to assume that technological advance in Latin America will take place, at least partially, through the embodiment of technology in the capital stock.

The age of capital is the basic argument for the inclusion of a vintage element and our analysis shows a secular trend of a falling average age of the capital stock for all countries (except Brazil). Direct measurement of the vintage effect is very difficult but the empirical information on age gives us a clue as to the importance of this effect. However, the age effect is only one factor in the embodiment effect. A recent article by Hulten (1992) shows that the failure to adjust capital explicitly for quality changes diverts the quality effects into the conventional total-factor-productivity residual. Hulten found that approximately 20 per cent of the residual growth of quality-adjusted output could be attributed to embodied technical change. This estimate is based on the American economy, using data obtained from the US Bureau of Labor Statistics (1983) and Gordon (1990).

Employment

Table 6.17 provides an indication of the importance of labour inputs in the economic performance of Latin America. On average for the 1950–94 period the quantity of labour 'explains' a quarter of economic growth, while quality of labour explains an additional 15 per cent. The quality effect of labour has been estimated with respect to the segment of the population aged 15–64, but in Chapter 4 an additional exercise was carried out comparing the results for the population with some available estimates concerning the work force.

Table 4.11 provided a comparison between the educational level of the population and the labour force for some countries over the 1951–92 period. On average the labour force had a somewhat higher level of education (2.5 per cent).

The difference was small in primary education (0.8 per cent) but substantial in higher education (23.6 per cent). On the basis of the somewhat scanty evidence of Table 4.11, there is no discernible trend towards change in the differences of level in time. This fact, together with the lack of systematic information on the educational level of the labour force, obliged us to adopt the educational level of the population as the measure for quality improvement. In terms of my model for explaining economic growth, this approach probably does not introduce a large error. In level accounting exercises this factor obviously assumes greater importance (see Van Ark, 1993 and Pilat, 1994).

Table 6.17 Explanatory Power of Labour in Growth, 1950–94 (percentage of GDP growth)

| | Quantity of labour | | | Quality of labour | | |
	1950–73	1973–80	1980–94	1950–73	1973–80	1980–94
Argentina	20	16	48	13	17	35
Brazil	25	25	65	12	15	43
Chile	9	39	45	15	21	15
Colombia	24	37	33	16	15	31
Mexico	21	34	78	15	25	33
Venezuela	27	73	113	17	15	45
Arithmetic average Latin America	21	37	64	15	18	34

Source: Table 6.12.

Some Remarks on Ultimate Causes

The breakdown of economic growth gives an indication regarding the costs of increasing the growth rate of output. However, growth accounting can only explain part of the process of economic growth, it does not take into consideration other factors such as economic policy, the national and international environments and non-economic factors such as natural disasters and war. These belong to the realm of what is now generally termed the ultimate causes of growth, in contrast to the proximate causes of growth analysed earlier.

The study of ultimate causality involves giving consideration to institutions, ideologies, pressures of socioeconomic interest groups, historical accidents, and economic policy at the national level (Maddison, 1995). The ultimate sources of Latin American economic performance are less clearly identified than its proximate causes. In Chapter 2, I have analysed some of the topics included in the realm of ultimate sources; institutional set-up, social capabilities and path dependency.

In the next chapter, economic policy, probably the single most important ultimate cause in Latin America's economic performance, will be analysed in some detail for the post-war period, with some consideration also of the international economic context. The growth accounting results presented here fit in rather well with the nature of the policy problems experienced, for example, in the 1970s and 1980s. In Chapter 2 some possible historical causes of political and policy instability in Latin America were discussed.

Some of the ultimate sources of economic growth in Latin America have recently been discussed in the context of the concept of path dependency. Path dependency has been defined as the incapacity of a society to leave a certain development path due to some specific factor. Factors identified include the institutional set-up, historical events, social capability and technological congruence.

Finally, it is again important to stress the interdependency of growth factors, either in the proximate or the ultimate sphere, or in combination. As Abramovitz (1993) emphasised, the growth accounting framework, even in its extended version, is not able to specify the interrelationship that exists between the different factors.

NOTES

1. Among the first authors were Bruton (1967), Correa (1970) and Langoni (1974). More recently Cavallo and Mundlak (1982), De Gregorio (1991), Coeymans (1992) and Elías (1992) have worked on growth accounting in Latin America.
2. The country-specific factor shares were estimated by the author on the basis of national accounts and population censuses, especially adjusting for own account workers.
3. See Chapter 4 for a more elaborate treatment, with respect to data sources and estimation procedures, of human capital.
4. See Maddison (1972 and 1987), Denison (1967) and Psacharopoulos (1984) for the rationale of the education adjustment.
5. See Table 4.11 of Chapter 4 for a comparison of the educational level of the total population with that of the labour force.
6. See the section on capital and investment (pp. 120–122) for a discussion of the quality aspect in capital stock estimation and the actual vintages used in the calculation.
7. One of the authors who treated this theme is Ffrench-Davis, see for example Ffrench-Davis (1994).
8. The growth accounting exercise presented here for the six Latin American countries was also done for the whole sample group of 16 countries. This thesis is about Latin American economic development so I do not present the whole data base for all countries but these are available upon request by the author. Most of the data with respect to GDP and employment come from Maddison (1995) and were updated by me using the same sources. If necessary I used national sources or data bases of international organisations such as OECD, IMF, World Bank or United Nations. The capital stock estimates necessary for this exercise come from Maddison (1993) for the advanced countries, and were updated to 1994 by me, using the same methodology as in the case of the Latin American countries. I prepared specific estimates, again using the same methodology, for the Asian and Iberian countries.
9. The results of Young (1995), which is an updated version of Young (1994), presenting slightly higher total factor productivity growth estimates, coincide to a great extent with the results of this study. His estimates of total factor productivity growth for Korea and Taiwan for the

1960–90 period are 1.7 and 2.6 per cent respectively. My estimates for the 1950–94 period are 1.7 and 3.0 per cent, respectively.
10. The advanced countries group includes the USA, although this country is also presented separately.
11. See Chapter 5 for a more detailed treatment of capital stock estimation and its limitations.

7. Performance and Policy in Latin America

INTRODUCTION

Performance and policy are related and Latin America is a region where policy regimes have changed dramatically in the twentieth century. This chapter concentrates on the second half of the century and relates the results obtained in the productivity analysis of the previous chapters to the policy regimes adopted.

Chapter 3 analysed in some detail the events of the first half of the century, namely the breakdown of the liberal world order and Latin America's policy reaction. Of particular relevance was the period of recovery after the Great Depression and the subsequent world war in which Latin America adopted a more inward-looking policy regime of industrialisation through import substitution, though this was to a certain extent forced on it by the circumstances. The strong recovery process, both in terms of GDP growth and, especially, in labour productivity, had repercussions on the policy regime adopted in the second half of the twentieth century. The policy of industrialisation through import substitution remained in place long after World War II, and in some countries even until the debt crisis of the early 1980s. Since then almost all Latin American countries have drastically altered their development strategy, placing greater emphasis on neo-liberal policies and export-oriented policies.

During the twentieth century, Latin America faced two major economic crises: the Great Depression of the 1930s and the 'lost decade' of the 1980s. Through analysis of just a few economic indicators, total GDP, GDP per capita and labour productivity, it becomes clear that the crisis of the 1980s, which continued partly in the 1990s, was more profound for Latin America than the Great Depression. On the other hand, our international comparison shows that Latin America's relative performance in the 1930s was much more favourable than that of the other countries in the sample. This was in marked contrast to the current situation which has obliged Latin America to adopt a more outward orientation.

A comparison of trends in levels of GDP per capita in Latin America, as compared to the United States, shows striking results. Its relative position *vis-à-vis* the United States improved during the 1929–38 period. The results were quite different in 1980–94, when Latin America's performance was disastrous compared to the United States and the rest of the world. The results with respect to the development of labour productivity in Latin America also speak for themselves:

whereas labour productivity rose by 0.9 per cent per annum from 1929–38, it fell by an average 0.6 per cent per annum between 1980–89.

The situation facing Latin America today is totally different from the one it faced in the 1930s, when inward orientation yielded results in terms of growth performance. The post-war experience and especially the crisis of the 1980s demonstrates that Latin America now stands at the crossroads, and that the process of modernising its productive system, its institutions and policies can no longer be delayed (see also ECLAC, 1990c).

THE POST-WAR GOLDEN AGE (1950–73)

For the world economy, 1950–73 was a period of unparalleled prosperity with the OECD countries in our sample growing at 5.3 per cent, almost three times the rate of the period 1913–50. The Iberian countries grew by 5.8 per cent, compared with a mere 1.4 per cent between 1913–50, while the Asian countries grew by 7.7 per cent, 3.5 times faster than in the period 1913–50. The Latin American countries grew by 5.4 per cent, compared with about 3.8 per cent during 1913–50. In 1950, per capita real income in Latin America countries was three times higher than that of developing Asia, a bit higher than the Iberian countries and about half of that of the six advanced countries. Within Latin America, real income per capita ranged from around 35 per cent of the US level in Argentina, Chile and Venezuela, to 27 per cent in Mexico and 19 and 15 per cent respectively for Colombia and Brazil.

In 1950, the international economy embarked on an expansion that was to continue unabated until 1973, when the first oil crisis erupted. Moreover, the growth in world output was the highest ever recorded. Latin America also achieved an expansion during this quarter century that probably outstripped regional growth in any previous 25 year period. Furthermore, the rate of growth in regional output between 1950 and 1973 exceeded both the rate of growth in world gross domestic product and the rate of output growth of the United States. However, there was a fundamental contrast between the growth performance of Latin America and that of much of the rest of the world.

In effect, while the expansion of world commerce, and especially of advanced countries' trade, was appreciably more intense than the growth in world output, the growth of Latin America's exports was significantly less than the growth of its gross domestic product and, during the final third of this period, considerably less than one half the rate of increase of its imports. And whereas the unprecedented expansion of the advanced countries was achieved with an exceptional degree of price stability, in Latin America the acceleration of growth was accompanied, in a good number of countries, by sustained price instability.

While mildly expansionary monetary and fiscal policies, in combination with large devaluations, promoted the strong recovery of Latin American economies from the Great Depression, expansionary monetary and fiscal policies continued to be pursued or even intensified over the course of the 1950s and 1960s, that is, long after output had returned to, or approached, its potential. Moreover, in a number of countries money supply growth far exceeded the potential rate of growth of output.

The evolution of the Latin American economies thus continued to diverge considerably from that of other developing economies; but in this historical instance the departure entailed the progressive build-up of macroeconomic disequilibria (Bianchi and Nohara, 1988). Income growth resulting from the expansion of primary exports led to a rise in demand for manufactured consumer goods and their inputs in Latin America. This demand had increasingly been satisfied by domestic production that enjoyed the 'natural protection' provided by transportation costs, complemented in some cases by tariff protection prior to World War II. The foreign exchange scarcity created by the fall in primary exports during the Great Depression and limited access to foreign goods during World War II subsequently boosted import substitution. Only after the war, however, did import substitution become a doctrine, guiding policy making in much of Latin America.

Although there was some variation across the range of countries, the policies pursued by the respective governments to promote industrialisation in the early post-war era were broadly similar. Under these policies, the production of import substitutes was encouraged through the exclusion of foreign competition, the allocation of foreign exchange, bank credit, essential inputs at preferential rates, and exemption from, or remission of, certain taxes and duties. At the same time the production of traditional exports was discouraged by unfavourable exchange rates, export taxes and pricing policies (Lin, 1988).

Although average nominal protection gradually increased in the course of the 1950s, the average tariff was still rather low in a number of Latin American countries in 1950. However, between the mid-1950s and the mid-1960s tariffs soared to reach extremely high protective levels. It becomes clear that the rates of effective protection came rather close to those of nominal protection. As a rule, effective protection rates were lowest, or even negative, for commodities, including importables as well as traditional exports, and highest for manufactured consumer importables.

Argentina

The government of Juan Perón (1943–55) established a populist tradition which was based on favouring import substitution industrialisation, high manufacturing wages, price controls, a squeeze on the agricultural sector, and antagonism towards the export orientation of the old landowning oligarchy, increases in public-sector employment, hostility to foreign capital and nationalisation of foreign assets. Díaz-Alejandro (1970) concluded that Argentina's economic history, especially since

1943, is a dramatic example of the dangers arising in the development process when a balance between the production of exportables, importables, and home goods is neglected. The paradox of post-war Argentine experience is that, if there had been less discrimination against exports, manufacturing expansion would have been greater.

Brazil

In the post-war period, Brazil continued the policy of industrialisation which had begun before World War II, and which was given an extra boost during the war, as was the case in many other Latin American countries. President Vargas who returned to power in 1951, on this occasion through elections, initiated a growth-oriented strategy. In response to greater international competition after the war, Brazil reintroduced exchange controls, imposed a system of multiple exchange rates and increased tariff protection, particularly favouring the domestic production of consumer goods. With the military threatening to take power, Vargas committed suicide in 1954.

Again, in 1956–61, this time under Juscelino Kubitschek, there was a new surge of industrialisation. Massive state investment occurred in electric power and transport, and in the capital and intermediate goods industries. The private sector was given high protection in the consumer goods industries, but low or negative effective protection in capital goods (which was partly compensated by direct government subsidies). Multiple exchange rates were also used. Liberal policies towards foreign capital were adopted, and in response direct foreign investment in manufacturing rose very rapidly. In 1969, the most recent surge of industrial expansion began. This period, which effectively ended in 1976, was marked by rapid growth and in fact is known as the 'Brazilian miracle' (Griffin, 1989).

Chile

In the 1950s, Chile continued the industrialisation through the import substitution strategy already started a decade before, in the wake of the Great Depression and the collapse of the nitrate market, after the replacement of natural nitrate by a synthetic substitute. However, this development model began to encounter problems, such as a stagnated agriculture, and the emphasis on import substitution hindered the development of new exports, severely restricting external trade options and the management of the balance of payments. The instability of traditional export prices was transmitted to the domestic economy through recurrent balance-of-payments shocks (Ffrench-Davis and Muñoz, 1992). The increasing price instability drove policy makers to the conclusion that new economic strategies were needed. A first attempt was based on the recommendations of the Klein-Saks mission which marked the return to more orthodox short-term economic policies, with maximum priority accorded to price stabilisation and proposals for a gradual liberalisation of the Chilean economy. However, as inflation was stopped it triggered the worst short-term recession since the Great Depression and provoked a public outcry (Mamalakis, 1976).

During the presidency of Alessandri (1958–64), the reform of the economic system was tackled in a more comprehensive fashion. The private sector was seen as the engine of growth and was supported by an active fiscal policy in the Keynesian tradition but the government also took an active role as entrepreneur through the creation of new public enterprises. This required a broader scope for the market, prices and competition, especially from external sources. However, great importance was given to stabilisation in the short run based on: a fixed nominal exchange rate, the elimination of 'inflationary' Central Bank financing of the fiscal deficit, wage and salaries increases in line with productivity increases and the promotion of domestic and foreign investment (Ffrench-Davis, 1973). This programme enjoyed considerable though temporary success, especially in the reduction of inflation[1] but around the half-way mark of Alessandri's presidency a balance of payments crisis occurred, caused by the rapid increase in imports, especially of consumer goods, while exports grew at a slower pace, which obliged the government to devalue, close the economy and reintroduce exchange controls while the inflation surfaced.

The strategy of the Frei administration was based upon a three point programme: First, a gradual stabilisation programme; second, an industrial modernisation programme, and third, a programme of structural and social change including agrarian reform and the first steps towards the nationalisation of the copper mines. The role of the state in production was reinforced, and protection increased to promote domestic production of electronic and other durable consumer goods. However, it became clear that the system's low capacity to convert internal and external resources into physical, human, and institutional capital remained the main bottleneck to growth and economic independence. Another crucial element was that during Frei's government the antagonism felt between the country's principal social and political actors became more and more evident.

The Allende administration attempted to achieve within three years what Chile's previous presidents had failed to achieve in almost a hundred years: maximum growth and economic independence through a revolutionary but bloodless redistribution of income. The policy of nationalising foreign mining interests, takeover of private banks, industry and transnational firms caused a great redistribution of income and power. Public sector salaries and wages were raised and the expansion of demand quickly affected sales and production, which rose sharply in 1971. But the expansionary fiscal and monetary policies, combined with sluggishness of production due to labour disputes, accelerated inflation. During 1973 output started to fall, inflation continued to rise, the external sector deficit reduced external reserves, black markets transactions increased, all of these developments together with domestic economic opposition and the foreign economic embargo caused the economy to enter into a state of near chaos (Dornbusch and Edwards, 1990).

Colombia

Monetary policy was expansionary during the 1950–73 period, with a little less than 20 per cent average annual growth in money supply. Throughout this period also the size of the state did not expand appreciably. During the 1950s and through the mid 1960s, the peso was chronically overvalued from the viewpoint of competitiveness of non-coffee exports, effectively constraining export diversification. The country's success in increasing exports during the 1967–75 period was based on an outward-looking policy that was in part the result of significant domestic inducements to export promotion. The most important element of the new policies was the introduction of a crawling peg-exchange rate system and a package of export incentives, including fiscal incentives, concessionary credits for export-related activities from the Export Promotion Fund and an expanded and more effective import–export regime (Plan Vallejo). The new policies represented an attempt to compensate for the distortions in relative prices generated by the import-substitution effort. Together with the favourable development of world trade, this shift in policy emphasis brought about impressive results (Thomas, 1985).

Mexico

The period from the beginnings of the 1950s until the 1970s is often referred to as the period of stabilising development because it was one of steady GDP growth, while at the same time the price level stayed relatively stable (Hofman, 1982). However, beneath the surface a number of problems were brewing: (a) levels of unemployment and underemployment[2] were high and rising; (b) the balance of payments was steadily worsening; (c) there were major sectoral disequilibria; (d) inadequate and deteriorating fiscal revenues.

Venezuela

Venezuela experienced rather high total GDP growth coupled with price stability during the period under consideration. Until 1958 the economy grew fast as a result of an expansive public expenditures policy based upon the revenues of oil exports, Venezuela's major export product. In 1958, when oil prices fell some 25 per cent, influenced by the reopening of the Suez canal, the development of new oil fields in the Middle East and a world recession, the administration opted for development on the basis of import substitution.

STRUCTURAL PROBLEMS STILL CONCEALED (1973–80)

For the world economy, 1973–80 saw the departure from the uniform tendency of very high growth experienced during the previous period. The OECD countries as a whole experienced a sharp slowdown, GDP per capita growth rates being less than a half as in the previous period. However Latin America and Asian developing countries continued growing. The period 1973–80 showed a uniform tendency in all Latin American countries to falling population growth. All our sample countries are now in a more advanced stage of demographic transition, in which the fertility rates also start falling. During this period Latin America's GDP per capita continued to grow rather fast compared to the United States and its comparative level reached 34 per cent in 1980, the highest level of the entire twentieth century. However, when this is compared with other areas, Latin America's performance is not as good as first appears. Asian developing countries more than doubled their income level, while the other OECD countries also markedly improved their position relative to the United States.

In Latin America the drastic changes which occurred in the world economic system at the beginning of the 1970s, such as the demise of the Bretton Woods fixed exchange rate mechanism (1971) and the action of the OPEC price cartel, did not have the same effect on policy making as in the developed countries, where a sharp change in economic policy occurred. The new disturbance was simply a new variation on a familiar theme, and was not regarded as a razor's edge situation, calling for drastic policy change (Maddison, 1989).

Many Latin American countries delayed pursuing stabilisation policies while relying on expanded external borrowing to sustain a higher rate of domestic demand. These policies provided for stronger growth of the economy in 1974–75, but they also resulted in the persistence of inflationary trends and the continuation of large current account deficits. For Latin American countries whose exports were dominated by primary commodities, the upsurge of inflationary pressures in the world economy did not constitute a serious problem as long as their export prices rose. In fact, the market prices of non-oil primary commodities continued to surge in 1974, in line with the jump in oil prices, thus enabling many Latin American countries to realise large gains in export receipts.

Moreover, to business enterprises in many of these countries, having domestic finances that had been constricted by the persistence of inflation, the increased availability of external credit after the first oil shock appeared as a blessing. The real interest costs of these credits was negative or relatively low. This explains why, after the first oil shock, many governments in Latin America condoned or encouraged the expanded use of external credit in order to sustain a high rate of investment and imports. It also explains why, in countries such as Brazil and Mexico, the growth of real wages and real private consumption was not restrained, thus contributing to the persistence of inflationary pressures and balance of payments difficulties (Lin, 1988).

In the 1960s and especially in the early 1970s several countries implemented trade policies combining import protection with export promotion. However, the intensity of policy reform fluctuated over time because of the lack of social consensus. In many countries of Latin America, the rural landed class and organised urban labour had considerable, but opposing, political influence, with the import substituting industrialists occupying a middle ground. Policy conflicts often occurred between these groups, resulting in frequent shifts of political alliances and economic policies (Lin, 1988).

The combination of biased macroeconomic policies and compensatory sectoral subsidies with unlimited access to international capital markets led to economic growth in the 1973–80 period. Eventually it created pervasive imbalances, including stagnation of exports, overproduction of non-traded goods and services, uncommonly large resource gaps, unparalleled excess external debt and rampant domestic price instability (Bianchi and Nohara, 1988). During this period several countries experimented with neo-conservative economic policies, that is, the marriage of monetarist views concerning economic stabilisation and radical conservative approaches. Both ingredients were present in varying degrees in the economic plans of Chile after 1973 and Argentina after 1976, both put into practice by strong military governments (Foxley, 1983).

Argentina

Argentina's GDP growth was among the slowest of the countries in our sample. During the first years of the period under consideration, Juan Perón tried to repeat the policies of his previous administration, with an expansionary monetary and fiscal policy, and wage increases combined with price control. His successor, Isabel Perón, first made a stabilisation effort to deal with the huge budget deficit, but under pressure from union interests, large wage increases were granted. In early 1976, in the midst of a severe economic social and political crisis, the armed forces once again took power in Argentina. The economic objectives of the new government were to correct the basic macroeconomic disequilibria and to change the course of the inward-oriented development strategy, which had been followed since the Great Depression (Ramos, 1986).

This neo-conservative experiment started with a substantial devaluation, reduction in real wages and the government deficit, deregulation of prices and abolition of subsidies, followed by a tight monetary policy, gradual tariff reduction and liberalisation of exchange controls. There was a notable improvement in the balance-of-payments situation, but inflation slowed down only partially. A second period was characterised by the ready availability of foreign capital and the extensive use of such capital to reduce inflation. The exchange rate was used principally to control inflation, and tariffs were lowered. What progress there was in this phase was at the expense of an increasingly artificial exchange rate. The neo-conservative policies took four years to bring down the average annual rate of inflation from 443 to 101 per cent, but also depressed economic activity, caused widespread bankruptcies, led to a large trade deficit in 1980 and permitted large-scale capital flight by Argentineans who correctly foresaw that they would unlikely be able to continue buying US dollars so cheaply (Maddison, 1985).

Brazil

Brazil relaxed its export promotion drive and shifted its trade policies in favour of a renewed inward orientation. This took the form of increased import control, widespread tariff increases, and the establishment of a prohibitive prior deposit system. The country also became dependent on external borrowing when its terms of trade worsened drastically. However, Brazil's creditworthiness was very high because of the creditors' continued belief in its development potential and also, of course, because of the great liquidity in the international capital markets due to the first oil shock.

The Brazilian approach to policy in 1973–80 was rather eclectic and growth oriented. It avoided the deflationary shocks imposed by extreme neo-conservatism in Chile and Argentina, its expansionism was never as wild as that of the Lopez Portillo administration in Mexico, and the policy course was very much steadier than in Argentina. The political regime was a stable military autocracy which was somewhat liberalised in the 1980s. The government intervened actively to control economic activity with very high levels of public investment, effective control of wage rates, exchange controls, and various devices to manipulate exports and imports. It also followed a rather consistent crawling peg policy for most of the period, without episodes of extreme overvaluation. Brazil is also notable in Latin America for its export diversification into manufactures and a wide variety of new primary products like soybeans and iron ore.

Chile

Two overriding concerns marked the economic policy of the Chilean junta upon its assumption of power at the end of 1973: (1) the unavoidable need to restore basic macroeconomic equilibria, and (2) the intention to instil dynamism in an economy whose performance in recent decades was considered quite unsatisfactory. The main objective of the first period (1973–76) was to restore market mechanisms in an economy with extended controls and severe imbalances. The initial policy mix sought to: (a) free virtually all prices; (b) devalue the exchange rate sharply with the purpose of narrowing the deficit in the balance of payments; (c) control wages by demobilising labour unions and by changing the wage adjustment system (from looking backward to looking forward); (d) follow a restrictive monetary policy to reduce the fiscal deficit. During the second period of the Chilean neo-conservative experiment, the price stabilisation strategy was modified as inflation was still advancing at 250 per cent per year. Emphasis was not placed on monetary and wage restrictions, but rather on controlling expectations and exerting downward pressure on domestic prices via foreign competition and real exchange appreciation.

Foxley (1983) summarises the economic results for Chile in the 1973–80 period as follows: the rate of inflation decreased; after a deep recession GDP reached pre-recession levels; the fiscal deficit was eliminated; there was an accumulation of reserves, and nontraditional exports expanded rapidly. At the same time, a low investment rate, a significant deficit in the trade balance, increasing external indebtedness, high unemployment, real wage reduction, and a deterioration in the distribution of income, consumption, and basic social services were among the negative factors.

Colombia

Activism in export promotion in Colombia diminished significantly after the mid-1970s, partly on account of the increase in foreign-exchange earnings that accompanied the commodity price boom of 1976–79. Rapid increases in external demand for Colombian agriculture products were the most significant development of this period, with the demands for coffee and illegal drugs leading other exports (Thomas, 1985). These revenues were used to reduce the debt and to build up reserves (World Bank, 1991).

Mexico

Mexico had an excellent growth record during 1973–80, the best of the Latin American countries in our sample. This can be attributed partly to the stability of the political system and to a greater socioeconomic consensus than in the rest of Latin America about appropriate policies to follow. It also can be explained by the booming government revenues from oil exports after the first oil shock and heavy foreign borrowing to finance expanded public consumption and investment, and subsidies on basic private consumer items. In Mexico, import controls were tightened and tariffs increased while the exchange rate became increasingly overvalued.

Venezuela

The oil crisis, together with the increase in public expenditures and private consumption, caused a rapid rise in GDP and imports. Inflation was on the rise but for Latin American standards was still very low. In the latter part of the 1970s the expansionary monetary and fiscal policies caused bottlenecks in domestic production and caused GDP growth to fall and inflation to rise. Severe balance-of-payments problems and a rapid increase in the foreign debt were also features of the economy.

THE LOST DECADE (1980–89) AND THE FIRST SIGNS OF RECOVERY (1989–94)

The period since 1980 has witnessed a broad range of economic performance and policy shifts. It also showed a diverging economic performance between Latin America and the rest of the world. The years since 1980 can be divided into the crisis period (1980–89) for Latin America and the subsequent period of recovery. As can be seen in Table 3.2 most Latin American countries experienced this recovery as Argentina and Chile grew almost 5 per cent per capita, Colombia 2.5 per cent and Mexico and Venezuela over 1 per cent. The most notable exception, however, was Brazil which had negative growth per capita of about 1 per cent a year.

During 1980–89 the world economy recovered to some degree from the slow growth of the previous period, with the exception of Latin America. Total GDP of the OECD countries grew on average 2.5 per cent a year compared to around 2 per cent in 1973–80. The Asian developing countries continued to grow at the same or somewhat higher growth rates. Latin American growth performance was abysmal, as per capita income fell by 0.5 per cent a year.

In 1989 GDP per capita in Latin America had fallen, on average, to the lowest relative levels of the twentieth century, from a level of 32 per cent of the United States in 1980 to 24 per cent in 1989. Argentina experienced the biggest decline from being a rather prosperous country in 1900 (ranking sixth among our 16 countries) to being one of the poorest in Latin America in 1989 (ranking fifteenth).

Between 1980 and 1989 Latin America experienced its deepest and most prolonged economic crisis since the ill-fated years of the Great Depression. Indeed, so much ground was lost that from the standpoint of economic welfare, the 1980s turned out to be truly a lost decade. On average GDP per capita fell from 4392 to 3727 constant 1980 international dollars with heavy per capita income losses in Argentina, Venezuela and, to a lesser degree, Mexico, virtual stability in Brazil and (recently) some improvement in Chile and Colombia.

Another disturbing characteristic of the crisis was the generalised and simultaneous deterioration of virtually all main economic indicators. Many countries have not only experienced a decline in the level or in the rate of growth of total output but also a deterioration in the employment situation and decreases in real wages. Inflationary processes intensified enormously and became more widespread.

The period 1989–94 can be looked at in different ways. From the growth perspective it was disastrous. But it was also a period in which Latin America prepared itself for a change in development strategy. The growth figures for the 1989–94 period of Tables 3.1 and 3.2 show that although a great effort is still needed, important progress was made in Latin America in the last decade.

Argentina

Argentina is one of a number of countries which went through a major crisis and several failures of orthodox and heterodox stabilisation programmes during the 1980s until finally at the beginning of the 1990s the programme introduced by Domingo Cavallo under the presidency of Carlos Menem led to the stabilisation of the Argentine economy. After negative growth of 2.5 per cent per capita in 1980–94 the Argentine economy has grown rapidly since then, recording about 4.8 per cent per capita growth for the 1989–94 period.

The Menem government introduced a fiscal reform in 1990 which included centralisation of expenditure-related decisions. It put public enterprises under the direct authority of the minister of economic affairs in order to exercise tighter control over their financial management. The reform also included improved tax administration and tax simplification.

One of the most important and controversial elements of the stabilisation plan was the anchoring of the exchange rate. Under the 'Convertibility Law', the Central Bank is obliged to meet any demand for US dollars at the rate of 10.000 australes to the dollar, that is, the exchange rate could not rise above this level unless Congress passed another bill allowing it to do so. The second provision required that the Central Bank's monetary liabilities must at all times be less than the external assets making up its reserves; the purpose of this provision was to ensure that the currency would have backing and to limit money creation via domestic credit. These measures meant establishing a fixed exchange-rate system under which fluctuations in the primary money supply would be closely linked to the balance of payments.

Significant steps have been taken in the field of trade liberalisation as exports taxes were eliminated and overall tariffs were reduced to 0–20 per cent range. The government also initiated an ambitious process of privatisations and many public enterprises have been sold. Argentina entered the 'Mercado Común del Sur' (MERCOSUR) together with Brazil, Paraguay and Uruguay, in order to promote intra-regional trade and establish a common external tariff between the members and the rest of the world. Trade between these countries has risen considerably recently.

Argentina was strongly affected by the 'tequila effect' of the Mexican crisis. After four years of growth, unparalleled in recent history, the economy fell into a recession in 1995, with open unemployment reaching record levels of close to 20 per cent. The country experienced a deficit in the capital account after receiving annually 10 billion US dollars in previous years. Argentina's banking sector, at great risk after the Mexico crisis and the resulting removal of around 8 billion US dollars, experienced great liquidity problems and embarked on a major restructuring process reducing significantly the number of banks and financial institutions operating in the country. However, there are some signs of improvement in the major economic indicators and the Menem government has also reached an agreement with the United Kingdom about oil exploitation of the disputed 'Islas Malvinas' or Falkland Islands. At the beginning of 1996 the bulk of the capital that left the country after 20 December 1994 has returned; however, the economy is growing at much lower rates than before the crisis. The country's annual inflation rate has fallen to less than 2 per cent, the lowest it has been in the last 50 years.

Brazil

Brazil experienced a major growth crisis at the beginning of the 1980s, but during the middle of the decade growth rates went up again and the pressure for structural reform became less acute. However, Brazilian growth performance at the end of the 1980s and in the 1990s has been very bad. Inflation, which did not subside after the first oil shock, accelerated sharply in 1979 when wage adjustments were changed from once to twice a year, at a time when the economy was subjected to renewed import costs and balance-of-payments pressures (Dornbusch and Simonsen, 1987). In Brazil, no major fiscal reform has taken place although in the field of trade liberalisation some measures have been taken, such as tariff reduction. Nonetheless, the Brazilian economy has not been, until now, opened up to the world. The privatisation process was set into motion and some enterprises have been sold, but recently privatisations have slowed down.

The Brazilian government's latest attempt at stabilisation (the eighth in nearly a decade) – the *Real* Plan – has also been the most successful, having reduced inflation from a monthly 50 per cent in June 1994 to about 22 per cent for the whole of 1995, the lowest rate in the last two decades. Nonetheless, some difficulties have arisen which could hamper efforts to consolidate this process, such as emerging inflationary pressures, a significant increase in demand, the risk of a return to indexation, a somewhat overvalued exchange rate and problems in controlling liquidity. Unlike previous stabilisation plans, the *Real* Plan was notable for its transparency with regard to the measures contemplated and the timetable for their implementation: price freezes, intervention in labour contracts and all other types of drastic or unexpected action were explicitly ruled out. The plan was carried out in three stages, which were announced and described ahead of time in December 1993. The first stage involved fiscal adjustment to balance the budget in 1994, for which purpose mandatory allocations of taxes and social security contributions were reduced in order to provide greater flexibility in the use of fiscal resources.

The second stage, launched in March 1994, sought to coordinate the economy's prices. To that end, a basic indexing instrument was created, the unit of real value (URV), whose level was adjusted daily. In order to avoid the traumatic situations caused by previous plans the authorities eschewed the use of punitive measures opting instead, and only in the case of highly sensitive items in the family budget, for negotiation and persuasion.

The third stage of the plan was initiated in July 1994, with the introduction of a new currency, the *real*, the sixth since 1986. A new monetary regime was established; the old currency still in circulation was replaced at the rate of one real for one URV, or 2,750 cruzeiros reales, the value as of 30 June 1994. Furthermore, the plan specified mechanisms for the issuance of the new currency, under which the Central Bank would be required to maintain international reserves in an amount equivalent to the value of reales in circulation, at the selling rate of one real per dollar. The plan also placed quarterly limits on the monetary base.

Since the plan does not call for strict convertibility, the Central Bank will not make any commitment to purchase foreign exchange. In addition, the plan limits public-sector financing. With regard to monetary policy, the Central Bank has replaced the automatic buy-back of public securities with standard rediscount operations.

Under the Real stabilisation programme, the Brazilian economy started growing again after the economic and political instability of the late 1980s and early 1990s. The government of President Cardoso is embarked on an ambitious plan of restructuring the Brazilian economy, including major privatisations and reorganisation of the central and local state apparatus, the judiciary and the financial system. However, the maintenance of the stabilisation programme is the priority, and due to a worsening of the trade balance the government opted for an increase in tariffs on motor vehicles and electronic goods, and maintained a tight monetary policy with high interest rates and an increasing budget deficit. Capital flows have increased recently as Brazil received 28 billion US dollars in 1995, partly in foreign direct investment but also a substantial part of a short-term nature attracted by the high internal interest rates. At the same time 1995 showed an all-time record in exports, with a substantial share of industrial exports.

Chile

At the beginning of the 1980s the Chilean economy was growing rapidly and the key instrument in the modified price-stabilisation strategy remained the exchange rate. Early in 1982 the Chilean economy went into a nosedive. The continued build-up of imbalances in the foregoing period, especially the increased disparity between domestic and international prices and persistently high real rates of interests, led to a very sharp fall in output. Increased imports and the resulting loss in international reserves caused an automatic adjustment and aggregate demand fell drastically. Because of the crisis the government was obliged to take drastic steps and sharply restrictive policies aimed at deflating the economy and avoiding devaluation were implemented. These policies proved ineffective and unnecessarily costly. A massive devaluation was eventually inevitable, generating great uncertainty and causing a massive exit of the dollar. Output fell 14 per cent in 1982 and unemployment reached unprecedented levels (Ramos, 1986).

The adjustment programme started in 1983 was less drastic than the previous programmes, and included a restrictive monetary and fiscal policy combined with devaluations. In late 1982, Chile put into effect a 'crawling peg' exchange-rate system based on mini-devaluations. The policy of uniform import tariffs was basically continued but the base rate was raised to 20 per cent in March 1983 and to 35 per cent in September 1984, and was only lowered to 15 per cent in 1988. The economy started growing again in the context of macroeconomic stability, although there was a very high level of foreign indebtedness, see UNCTAD (1992) and ECLAC (1989). The 1980s ended with the Chilean economy experiencing fast growth, close to full utilisation of its productive capacity, and with relatively moderate levels of inflation.

The privatisation programme in Chile started around 1974, earlier than in any other country in Latin America.[3] In the 1982 crisis, the privatisations programme experienced a reversal and the government took over 50 banks and firms from the 'grupos'. Many of these – plus some others – were sold off again in the second half of the 1980s. The democratic government that assumed office in 1990 respected the sales and embarked on a limited privatisation programme.

Chile has become the showcase of the Latin American economies, growing rapidly since 1984 and in the 1990s. The 1989–94 per capita growth rate was close to 5 per cent. Inflation fell to 8 per cent, the lowest rate in more than three decades. The export-led growth also boosted other sectors of the economy such as construction, telecommunications and other services. The economic restructuring initiated two decades ago has brought about very important changes in economic strategy and the institutional framework. After initially applying rather drastic neo-liberal policies and institutional change, the economic policy makers opted for a more pragmatic approach, including an active macroeconomic policy stance, which has yielded very good results. However, there have been some disappointing results with respect to the distribution of these gains, as the latest equity report shows a decrease of several points of the GDP share of the lowest deciles, together with an increase in the share of the highest decile.

The country has become a major foreign direct investor in Latin America, investing around 10 billion US dollars abroad in the last 5 years, especially in Argentina and Peru, but also increasingly in Bolivia, Brazil and Colombia. Most of the investments were channelled towards the energy and industrial sector.

Colombia

In the late 1970s Colombia started a public investment boom in order to counteract any recession the fall in coffee prices might engender. This boom involved foreign borrowing. The move could be regarded as a sensible countercyclical policy, and for a while the country was able to afford it. However, in 1981 coffee prices collapsed, and gradually Colombia's Keynesian strategy got out of hand, especially in 1983, when a serious recession resulted. Colombia continued its policy of stimulating the domestic economy by fiscal and monetary expansion into 1984, running up ever larger public-sector and current-account deficits, supporting the policy by a fall in reserves and heavy borrowing.

In 1984 Colombia undertook an orthodox adjustment programme, involving fiscal discipline and substantial depreciation; this programme was so successful that by 1986–88 the current account was roughly in balance (World Bank, 1991). Although fiscal reform started in Colombia much earlier than in many other countries the government found it necessary to introduce new fiscal reforms in 1991 and 1992. Also big steps have been taken in the field of trade liberalisation in the late 1980s and the early 1990s. The objective was to change Colombia from a regulated and closed economy to a more open and flexible one, more responsive to market forces. The average tariff, which was close to 100 per cent at the beginning of the 1980s, was reduced to less than 10 per cent in the 1990s. Currency exchange controls were loosened and the market was given a greater role in determining the exchange rate. There were few privatisations in Colombia also because government intervention in the productive process had been limited.

Colombia was beset by major economic and political turmoil in the 1990s although the country continued growing at a stable and rather high rate. The country also became increasingly interesting for foreign investors mainly because of its abundant natural resources and – at least in the Latin American context – a relatively stable economy. Colombia is stepping up its oil production after bringing on stream several new oil fields in the eastern part of the country.

Mexico

In Mexico, a country which enjoyed the benefits of increased oil revenues in the late 1970s, the ongoing inflation accelerated sharply in 1982 and 1983, when declining oil revenues and expanded external deficits compelled the authorities to resort increasingly to deficit financing and sharp exchange rate depreciations. At the beginning of 1982, the exchange crisis preannounced the debt moratorium that was to come. In August 1982, the debt crisis broke out as the Minister of Finance flew to Washington to announce that Mexico could not meet its obligations.

The Mexican government had already started in 1983 an ambitious programme of privatisations, and has since then sold over a thousand state-owned enterprises, leaving less than a hundred in government hands. Mexico initiated around 1986 a rather successful stabilisation and reform programme which consisted of a drastic fiscal reform, a cautious exchange rate policy, a plan to deregulate, modernise and open the economy, and a social programme which was the result of concerted social agreement.[4]

Until 1989, the objectives were basically stabilisation and structural adjustment, and as inflation went down growth again became a major objective. However, growth was moderate at an average of 1.1 per cent per capita for 1989–94. The current account and trade balance started showing deficits from the late 1980s onwards and capital flows into Mexico were increasing.

The North American Free Trade Agreement (NAFTA), whose members are Canada, Mexico and the United States, was implemented in 1994. Early in the same year, the country was shocked by the insurgency in the province of Chiapas of the Ejército Zapatista de Liberación Nacional (EZLN).[5] Several hundreds of people died, and the year was characterised by political unrest due to the campaign for the upcoming elections, in which several political candidates were murdered. Mexico's dominant political party for the major part of the twentieth century is facing great problems, and has lost elections in several states.

At the end of 1994, the newly elected government devalued the peso by 15.3 per cent and after losing 5 billion US dollars in international reserves in two days, the peso was allowed to float freely. The Mexican devaluation caused a major crisis of confidence in business circles, which spread rapidly to the whole of Latin America; indeed several observers foresaw the coming of a major crisis. However, this did not occur, although several countries, particularly Argentina, were severely affected by the crisis. The Mexican economy went into a recession: GDP per capita fell over 8 per cent in 1995 and inflation soared to around 50 per cent.

The Mexican crisis was caused by the financing, through large capital inflows, of high and unsustainable current account deficits. The high level of capital inflows was partly due to the very positive evaluation of Mexico by the international financial community, the reforms undertaken and sheers overconfidence. The Mexican crisis emphasised the importance of sound macroeconomic policy with respect to a sustainable deficit in the current account and the level and composition of capital inflows (short- and long-term or speculative and direct investment).

Venezuela

The debt crisis also hit Venezuela hard, its economy having experienced five consecutive years of negative GDP per capita growth at the beginning of the 1980s, with GDP per capita falling over 8 per cent in 1983. In the second part of the 1980s the country recovered somewhat, although in 1989 the country implemented a severe adjustment and stabilisation programme designed to reduce macroeconomic imbalances that caused GDP to fall by almost 8 per cent and led to severe social unrest. However, after the relaxation of the adjustment programme, the first part of the 1990s showed a strong recovery with annual per capita GDP growth over 5 per cent, also influenced by the higher oil prices prompted by the Gulf War.

Economic, social and political instability continued, however, causing wide fluctuations in economic performance. The recession which started in 1993, was aggravated in 1994, fuelled by a crisis in the financial system, and the Government opted to reverse the liberalisation policy adopted in 1989. Among the many problems facing Venezuela are the consistently big budget deficits and the continued delay of necessary fiscal and tax reforms.

Some measures have been taken in the field of trade liberalisation, in particular those concerning elimination of quantitative restrictions; and also the privatisation process has begun. Venezuela has become the country with one of the highest rates of inflation of all Latin American countries, with price increases of over 50 per cent in the last years. The country's stabilisation process was affected by serious political and social problems aggravated by inconsistencies in its economic policies, especially with respect to economic restructuring and modernisation, the role of the private and public sectors, and exchange rate and prices policies.

NOTES

1. Inflation was on average less than 5 per cent during 1960–62, compared with an average of around 40 per cent during the 1950s and about 30 per cent in the remainder of the 1960s (Ffrench-Davis, 1973, Table 29, p. 242).
2. Underemployment refers to persons working part-time but wanting to work more and persons earning salaries below a certain minimum, for example, the minimum salary.
3. Some of the privatisations in the 1970s consisted of returning enterprises seized by the Unidad Popular to their owners, and some involved selling banks and firms to the private sector.
4. Since 1987, government, business associations and labour unions have agreed to coordinate economic policies in so-called pacts whose names reflect their emphasis. The names changed from 'Economic Solidarity Pact' to 'Pact for Stability and Economic Growth', then 'Stability, Competitiveness and Employment Pact', and finally, to 'Alliance for Economic Recovery'.

5. The Zapatist National Liberation Army can be compared to Emiliano Zapata's movement which, during the Mexican Revolution, fought against the system of land tenure and bad living conditions of the people in Mexico's south and obtained the incorporation of land reform in the 1917 Constitution (Hofman, 1982).

8. Conclusions

This book analyses Latin America's economic development in the twentieth century in a comparative historical perspective. On the one hand, emphasis is placed on measurable supply-side evidence through the comparative use of growth accounts. This involved examination of the systematic quantification of output, human and physical capital, the role of diffusion and adaptation of technical progress and its potential in economic growth and catch-up.

On the other hand, there is considerable emphasis on the historical and institutional context in which economic development took place, as well as the role of policy. After the lost decade of the 1980s, the region is reaching a consensus on new types of domestic policy weapons needed to achieve macroeconomic stability. There is also consensus on the need for a more outward-looking strategy. The need for structural and institutional reform is recognised, although there is a wide spectrum of opinion with respect to its implementation.

Several of Latin America's most pressing problems are rooted in its history. Throughout this study, elements like macroeconomic instability, institutional deficiencies and unequal distribution of income and wealth have been identified as factors in Latin America's relatively poor performance. These have offset the region's enormous comparative advantage in natural resources.

Latin America has the world's most unequal income distribution, and there is evidence that this situation has not improved during the last half century. The region's leading economic performer in recent years, Chile, has an impressive record in reducing poverty, but income distribution has not improved and there are slightly increasing Gini coefficients. The recurrence of financial crises and their effects on economic activity show that history keeps repeating itself. Latin America is still characterised by high inflation rates.

Latin America's GDP per capita level relative to the United States remained almost stable during the first 80 years of the twentieth century, but deteriorated steadily during the 'lost decade' of the 1980s. The relative position of the Asian countries in our sample worsened during the first half of the twentieth century, but improved dramatically from 1950 onwards. The relative position of the European countries and Japan deteriorated during 1900–1950 but improved gradually during the second half of the twentieth century, as these countries reduced the gap with the United States.

The growth phases identified in this study are somewhat different from those in most other regions. If one looks both at performance and policy, four phases can be identified in the twentieth century. The first phase, which ended in 1929, was a rather prosperous period of stable growth. At that time world trade was the main engine. Average population and GDP growth were very similar in 1900–1913 and 1913–29. From 1929 to 1950, the world experienced crisis and war but Latin America was relatively sheltered and its growth rates faltered less than those of most countries. Its fast recovery in the 1930s initiated a growth process, which gave great emphasis to import substitution. This emphasis in policy was adventitious and induced by the world crisis, but from 1950 onwards import substitution became the main development strategy in most Latin American countries. This emphasis only ended with the debt crisis of the early 1980s.

The first oil crisis that finished the golden age of expansion of the advanced European countries also affected Latin America, and 1973 was therefore adopted as an additional benchmark. From 1980 onwards, through the crisis of the 'lost decade', Latin America began to adopt neo-liberal policies and, especially, a more outward looking economic orientation.

The results with respect to joint factor inputs and total factor productivity growth are among the most interesting of this study. Total factor productivity provides an approximate measure of technical progress, and suggests a rather weak process of incorporation of technical progress in Latin America. Latin America's performance in terms of total factor productivity shows that total factor productivity growth is a less important source of growth than in other regions. It shows also a steady tendency to deteriorate, only in the 1990s does one observe an incipient improvement of total factor productivity growth. From 1950 to 1973, when GDP grew quickly, total factor productivity growth was correspondingly high, although much lower than in other regions. From 1973 to 1980, when GDP growth remained fast, total factor productivity growth slowed down drastically. In the 1980s, during the 'lost decade', total factor productivity became negative.

These developments with respect to total factor productivity in the post-war period are related to growing macro- and microeconomic misallocations in Latin America. Macroeconomic misallocations became manifest with the debt crisis at the beginning of the 1980s, when the combination of internal and external factors caused a deep recession, generating highly negative total factor productivity growth. However, microeconomic misallocations related to the strategy of industrialisation through import substitution and heavy state intervention had been building up for a very long period. High levels of allocative and technical inefficiency at the micro level can explain the fact that the 1980s crisis in Latin America has been so profound. The implementation of a vast programme of structural reforms implicates a rather long transition period with a relatively poor economic performance.

In the Asian countries, total factor productivity played a more important role than in Latin America, although the contribution was on average only 10 per cent higher. Technical progress during the 1950–73 period accounted for around 40 per cent of growth in Taiwan and about 30 per cent in Korea. During 1973–80 these countries increased their factor input (especially capital) and total factor productivity growth faltered. They did better after 1980.

Total factor productivity's role was more important in the advanced countries than in the developing ones and negative estimates are rarely found. This can partly be explained by better resource allocation but is also due to structural differences with respect to factor inputs. Labour input growth in particular was much smaller in developed countries than in developing ones. First, there is a very clear difference in the role of labour input, which is increasing rapidly in the developing countries (although in many cases not fast enough to keep pace with demographic trends), while it has virtually come to a halt in the advanced European countries. Second, employment is growing quite fast over the whole range of developing countries but working hours showed markedly different trends. In Latin America there was a clear downward trend and in Asia they increased substantially. On the quality side, educational levels showed systematic improvement in all countries. Education grew fastest in Asia, at a moderate rate in Latin America and the Iberian countries, and at a much lower rate in the developed countries.

Recently, the human capital dimension to economic growth has returned to the centre of attention, and indeed the human capital factor is a very important source of growth. The quality of labour input is affected by many factors such as education, health and nutrition, as well as social norms and values. Widespread schooling, good health care and nutrition early in a country's development have a positive effect on economic performance. It is recognised that the quality and flexibility of labour supply is important, but the deregulation of the labour market was not, until recently, a priority of the reform programme in most countries in Latin America.

One of the major contributions of the present study is the generation of comparable measures of capital stock disaggregated into machinery and equipment, productive structures, and dwellings, using a similar methodology, the perpetual inventory method. In our analysis, we have included the effect of natural resources, measured as the amount of land in use. Latin America saw an increase in cropped area (especially in Brazil), while in other parts of the world land in use either remained stable (as in Asia) or declined as in the advanced capitalist group.

For a comparison of the standardised capital stock estimates presented in Chapter 6 and the national estimates, see Appendix G, which gives details of the history of capital stock and national wealth estimation in Latin America in the twentieth century. Given the great differences between the national and the standardised estimates in assumptions and methodology, it was concluded that the latter estimates are the most appropriate for international comparisons of capital–output ratios, growth performance and the role of technical progress.

This study therefore presents a new comprehensive set of standardised capital stock estimates for the six Latin American countries, employing the perpetual inventory method. Total capital stock increased in all Latin American countries. While in Brazil it grew at about 8 per cent during 1950–94, the corresponding growth was just over 3 per cent in Argentina and Chile. These variations can also be seen when looking at the 'productive', non-residential capital stock.

Capital–output ratios increased in Argentina, Brazil, Mexico and Venezuela, indicating a fall in capital productivity. Capital productivity remained almost constant in Chile and increased somewhat in Colombia. There are some small differences between total or non-residential capital–output ratios (Argentina and Chile for example) but the general trend is clear. The estimates in this study are presented in national currencies and international dollars, and the analysis indicates that the difference between the two estimates is not that big as regards the growth rates, but is more substantial as regards the level of the capital stocks.

There exists a growing consensus among Latin American leaders and policy makers with respect to economic policy (see Williamson, 1990 and Edwards, 1995). First, it is almost universally recognised that macroeconomic adjustment and stabilisation is a precondition for sustainable economic growth, and in this respect inflation should be controlled and government spending brought into line with tax revenues. Second, it has become clear that Latin American leaders and policy makers are increasingly convinced that an outward-looking strategy is essential for the achievement of rapid growth. This means export-oriented policies, lower tariff barriers for imports, and also new approaches with respect to foreign capital and foreign direct investment. The strategy reflects the view that regional economic integration, within the process of opening up to the world, will play an important role in the region's future. Third, each country has to adopt structural reforms in its economy, such as privatisation and deregulation, and so on. Structural measures are also needed with respect to equity and poverty. In order for the reforms to advance, there exists consensus that the political sustainability of the process should go hand in hand with measures directed at reducing poverty and inequality. Fourth, the role of the state has been reformulated, putting less emphasis on its role in production and more on creating institutions conducive to modernisation and growth.

There is still considerable disagreement on some issues (see Edwards, 1995 and Moguillansky, 1995). First, the need for regulation and control of the financial system. There is a growing conviction that the financial system in many Latin American countries is rather weak and unable to meet the growing and diversified need for new financial instruments. Empirical analysis reveals that liberalisation and deregulation did not automatically increase the savings rate to the level of investment required to secure economic growth, for example increases in external savings correlate negatively with internal savings, and sometimes they promote capital outflow. The institutional framework of the financial system, the relationship between savings and investment, the improvement in width and depth of the financial market, all remain important and controversial issues in Latin America. A second problem is the sequencing and speed of trade reform, financial liberalisation and the opening of the capital account, on which a growing literature has emerged. Elimination of export bias and import liberalisation is one of the controversial sequencing issues. Most analysts agree that trade reform should precede the liberalisation of the capital account.

The liberalisation of the capital account is in itself controversial. Recent developments in Mexico have once more highlighted the importance of this issue. It seems increasingly clear that the unconditional liberalisation of capital flows of all sorts, speculative and short-term, brings considerable risks. Keeping speculative capital under control, while encouraging long-term investment, seems recommendable but difficult to implement (Ffrench-Davis and Griffith-Jones, 1995).

There is a need to improve export promotion schemes or other sectoral policies with incentives for industry, agriculture or technological development. This subject is perhaps one of the most controversial, and not only in Latin America. In Latin America the debate has a highly ideological content, while in many other regions the problem is dealt with more pragmatically.

The privatisation strategy and the regulation of the private sector, such as energy, telecommunications and infrastructure, is also a major issue. In some countries privatisation is well advanced, although there are major exceptions, such as Brazil, Colombia and Venezuela. However, it is important to distinguish between markets which are self-regulating, through competition or contestability, and markets which are not. An important task facing many countries is to regulate those privatised sectors, such as utilities and the financial sector, which are difficult to be made self-regulating.

APPENDICES

Appendix A. Population

In this appendix population estimates, on a mid-year basis, are presented for the 1820–1995 period. The pre-1950 data come from the sources mentioned in Maddison (1995) linked with the data from CELADE (1995) latest estimates for the post-war period. In the case of Mexico INEGI (1985) was used for yearly estimates between 1900 and 1921 and the 1922–49 series was used to link 1921 with 1950. For 1950–80 CELADE gives 5-yearly estimates which were interpolated, and the 1980–95 figures come from the yearly estimates of CELADE.

Table A.1 Latin American Population, Six Countries, 1820–1995 (in thousands at mid year)

	Argentina	Brazil	Chile	Colombia	Mexico	Venezuela
1820	534	4,507	885	1,206	6,587	718
1850	1,100	7,234	1,443	2,065	7,662	1,324
1870	1,796	9,797	1,943	2,392	9,219	1,653
1890	3,376	14,199	2,651	3,369	11,729	2,224
1900	4,693	17,984	2,974	3,998	13,607	2,542
1901	4,873	18,367	3,011	4,079	13,755	2,576
1902	5,060	18,759	3,048	4,162	13,904	2,609
1903	5,254	19,159	3,086	4,247	14,055	2,643
1904	5,455	19,568	3,124	4,334	14,208	2,690
1905	5,664	19,985	3,163	4,422	14,363	2,706
1906	5,881	20,411	3,202	4,512	14,591	2,720
1907	6,107	20,846	3,242	4,604	14,676	2,741
1908	6,341	21,291	3,282	4,697	14,836	2,761
1909	6,584	21,745	3,323	4,793	14,997	2,780
1910	6,836	22,209	3,364	4,890	15,000	2,805
1911	7,098	22,682	3,406	4,990	14,990	2,834
1912	7,370	23,166	3,448	5,091	14,980	2,856
1913	7,653	23,660	3,491	5,195	14,970	2,874
1914	7,885	24,152	3,537	5,330	14,960	2,899
1915	8,072	24,655	3,584	5,468	14,950	2,918
1916	8,226	25,168	3,631	5,609	14,940	2,929
1917	8,374	25,692	3,679	5,754	14,930	2,944
1918	8,518	26,226	3,728	5,903	14,920	2,958
1919	8,672	26,772	3,777	6,056	14,910	2,973
1920	8,861	27,329	3,827	6,213	14,900	2,992
1921	9,092	27,898	3,877	6,374	14,895	3,008
1922	9,368	28,478	3,928	6,539	15,114	3,025
1923	9,707	29,071	3,980	6,709	15,358	3,049
1924	10,054	29,675	4,033	6,882	15,605	3,077
1925	10,358	30,293	4,086	7,061	15,857	3,114
1926	10,652	30,923	4,140	7,243	16,112	3,152
1927	10,965	31,567	4,195	7,431	16,372	3,185
1928	11,282	32,224	4,250	7,624	16,635	3,221
1929	11,592	32,894	4,306	7,821	16,903	3,259
1930	11,896	33,568	4,370	7,914	17,176	3,300
1931	12,167	34,255	4,434	8,009	17,473	3,336
1932	12,402	34,957	4,500	8,104	17,776	3,368
1933	12,623	35,673	4,567	8,201	18,085	3,401
1934	12,834	36,404	4,634	8,299	18,398	3,431
1935	13,044	37,150	4,703	8,398	18,717	3,465
1936	13,260	37,911	4,773	8,498	19,040	3,510
1937	13,490	38,687	4,843	8,599	19,370	3,565
1938	13,724	39,480	4,915	8,702	19,705	3,623
1939	13,984	40,489	5,003	8,935	20,047	3,699
1940	14,169	41,524	5,093	9,174	20,393	3,784
1941	14,402	42,585	5,184	9,419	20,955	3,858
1942	14,638	43,673	5,277	9,671	21,532	3,943
1943	14,877	44,790	5,371	9,930	22,125	4,020
1944	15,130	45,934	5,467	10,196	22,734	4,114

Table A.1 (continued)

	Argentina	Brazil	Chile	Colombia	Mexico	Venezuela
1945	15,390	47,108	5,565	10,469	23,361	4,223
1946	15,654	48,312	5,665	10,749	24,004	4,347
1947	15,942	49,547	5,767	11,036	24,665	4,486
1948	16,307	50,813	5,870	11,332	25,345	4,656
1949	16,737	52,112	5,975	11,635	26,043	4,843
1950	17,150	53,444	6,082	11,946	27,737	5,094
1951	17,492	55,155	6,213	12,288	28,495	5,219
1952	17,840	56,922	6,346	12,641	29,273	5,437
1953	18,196	58,744	6,482	13,003	30,073	5,664
1954	18,558	60,626	6,622	13,376	30,894	5,901
1955	18,928	62,567	6,764	13,759	31,738	6,230
1956	19,254	64,455	6,925	14,170	32,717	6,398
1957	19,586	66,400	7,090	14,593	33,726	6,657
1958	19,923	68,404	7,258	15,028	34,767	6,928
1959	20,267	70,468	7,431	15,477	35,839	7,209
1960	20,616	72,594	7,608	15,939	36,945	7,579
1961	20,939	74,796	7,792	16,422	38,110	7,775
1962	21,267	77,065	7,980	16,920	39,311	8,058
1963	21,601	79,402	8,173	17,433	40,551	8,351
1964	21,939	81,811	8,370	17,961	41,829	8,655
1965	22,283	84,292	8,572	18,506	43,148	9,094
1966	22,609	86,486	8,749	19,045	44,544	9,275
1967	22,940	88,737	8,930	19,599	45,986	9,591
1968	23,276	91,046	9,115	20,169	47,474	9,917
1969	23,616	93,416	9,304	20,756	49,010	10,255
1970	23,962	95,847	9,496	21,360	50,596	10,721
1971	24,366	98,169	9,659	21,823	52,193	10,987
1972	24,776	100,547	9,824	22,295	53,840	11,385
1973	25,193	102,982	9,992	22,778	55,539	11,796
1974	25,618	105,477	10,163	23,272	57,291	12,223
1975	26,049	108,032	10,337	23,776	59,099	12,734
1976	26,449	110,562	10,494	24,302	60,704	13,105
1977	26,856	113,150	10,654	24,840	62,352	13,561
1978	27,269	115,800	10,816	25,389	64,045	14,032
1979	27,688	118,511	10,980	25,951	65,784	14,519
1980	28,114	121,286	11,147	26,525	67,570	15,091
1981	28,546	124,010	11,319	27,105	69,188	15,515
1982	28,987	126,768	11,493	27,699	70,776	15,917
1983	29,432	129,538	11,672	28,298	72,344	16,311
1984	29,879	132,303	11,856	28,895	73,904	16,713
1985	30,325	135,042	12,047	29,481	75,465	17,137
1986	30,771	137,751	12,247	30,054	77,023	17,590
1987	31,221	140,445	12,454	30,619	78,571	18,061
1988	31,670	143,127	12,667	31,180	80,117	18,542
1989	32,114	145,803	12,883	31,739	81,666	19,025
1990	32,546	148,477	13,100	32,300	83,226	19,502
1991	32,965	151,152	13,320	32,863	84,803	19,972
1992	33,374	153,824	13,545	33,426	86,391	20,441
1993	33,778	156,491	13,771	33,987	87,983	20,909
1994	34,180	159,147	13,994	34,546	89,570	21,377
1995	34,587	161,790	14,210	35,101	91,145	21,844

Appendix B. GDP Indices (1950 = 100) and Levels of Total and Per Capita GDP

As the output measure gross domestic product (GDP) at market prices was used because it is the most easily available aggregate for comparative purposes and also widely used in growth accounting (see Maddison, 1987 for a comparison of different output measures used in growth accounting studies). The output measure as well as the capital formation measure are actually under scrutiny because of the so-called 'productivity paradox', that is, the seeming paradox contradiction between the perception that technological change has accelerated in the recent decade and the observed fact that productivity growth has not recovered its average post World War II level (see OECD, 1991a).

For all countries a detailed description is given of the sources used for the construction of the GDP series. For 1950 onwards, if not otherwise specified, the series used for Latin America are derived from currently collected official estimates by ECLAC corresponding to the most recent revision of the United Nations System of National Accounts (SNA).

For the years before 1950 the estimates have nearly all been made retrospectively and the underlying data are less complete. Nevertheless, most of the historical estimates are based upon substantial statistical research by distinguished scholars, and in some cases emanate from the governmental statistical service responsible for making the more recent official estimates. But the estimates for the first half of the twentieth century are obviously not as comparable as those for 1950 onwards, and in some cases may well be substantially revised when further research is done.

In order to compare levels of output, capital and income per capita, or productivity in different countries, it is useful to have a unit which expresses the comparative value of their currencies better than exchange rates. The latter reflect purchasing power over tradeable goods and services, and are subject to a good deal of fluctuations as a result of capital movements.

In this study the results of the United Nations ICP IV were used which generated purchasing power parities (PPP) for GDP and the different types of capital formation.[1] The PPPs were expressed in 'international dollars' obtained by applying a common set of prices, representative of the world price structure, to the quantities of the commodities and services entering into each country's final expenditure on GDP. The PPPs for Latin America were provided by Alan Heston of the University of Pennsylvania and former director of the ICP. These PPPs differ somewhat from the ones published in United Nations/EUROSTAT (1987) which contained some computational errors.

Table B.1 presents a comparison of the exchange rate and the purchasing power parities (PPPs) prepared during different phases of the ICP project from 1970–85. I also give the adjusted exchange rates used in 1980 by ECLAC and World Bank for conversion to dollars. For 1980, our benchmark year, I compare the PPPs used, provided to us by Alan Heston, with the ones published by the United Nations/EUROSTAT (1987).

The results are presented in 1980 constant international dollars while the base year in Summers and Heston (1991) is 1985. Also enclosed are the PPPs for Mexico which were originally not published. The AH results show that all countries, with the exception of Argentina which has a lower exchange rate, have much higher exchange rates than PPPs as can be seen in the column which gives the total GDP/PPP exchange rate deviation index. The range goes from 0.46 in Colombia to 1.41 in Argentina. This implies that for all countries, except Argentina, a conversion from national currencies to international dollars gives higher GDPs than in the case of conversion with the exchange rate.

The PPP–exchange rate deviation index in the lower part of Table B.1 indicates, in spite of the scanty evidence, that the AH results for 1980 are similar to those of ICP IV. At the same time the comparison of these results with previous phases of the ICP shows that the PPPs are rather stable in time. Somewhat an exception are the 1985 Summers and Heston estimates which are on average somewhat lower than previous ones.

SOURCES

Argentina

The source for 1900–1950 is Banco Central de la República Argentina (1976). From 1970–94, ECLAC estimates based upon official statistics were used, taking into account the following considerations.

In 1987 the Central Bank of Argentina, in cooperation with the Buenos Aires office of ECLAC, initiated a project regarding the revision of the national accounts, income distribution and input–output matrix. The final report[2] presented an extensive description of the methodology applied in the elaboration of the new series. The results were the updating of the current and constant series, by sector and expenditure, an estimation of factor shares[3] and a base year change from 1970 to 1986. The increase in GDP level of 43.2 per cent occurred mainly in the manufacturing and construction sector. Much of the increase was due to improved

Table B.1 Exchange Rates and Purchasing Power Parities with Respect to the International Dollar for GDP, 1970–85 (national currency units per international dollar)

	1970	1973	1975	1980	1985
			Exchange rate		
Argentina				1837	8753
Brazil			8.2	52.7	39230
Chile				39.0	245
Colombia	18.4	23.8	30.9	47.3	2992
Mexico			12.5	23.0	2250
Venezuela				4.3	14.5

	ICP I	ICP II	ICP III	ICP IV	AH	World Bank	ECLAC	S&H
				GDP purchasing power parities				
Argentina				2709	2596	4117	3334	5689
Brazil			5.2	30.6	32.4	.51.0	50.9	8045
Chile				28.8	26.5	44.7	41.7	90.7
Colombia	7.3	9.5	10.8	23.1	21.6	52.5	48.6	101.7
Mexico			7.4		13.4	30.8	25.4	900
Venezuela				3.6	3.1	9.7	5.0	7.0
				PPP/exchange rate deviation index				
Argentina				1.47	1.41	2.24	1.82	0.65
Brazil			0.63	0.58	0.61	0.97	0.96	0.46
Chile				0.74	0.68	1.15	1.07	0.37
Colombia	0.40	0.40	0.35	0.49	0.46	1.11	1.03	0.34
Mexico			0.59		0.58	1.34	1.10	0.40
Venezuela				0.84	0.73	1.09	1.17	0.48

Source: Table 5.2

statistical sources, for example, industrial and household surveys, and better coverage of the informal sector.

Afterwards, the Banco Central de la República Argentina (1993) published new series, based upon the 1991 revision, but once again revised. In this last revision, much less detailed, the increase of GDP was reduced from 43.2 to 35.5 per cent and the greater part of this reduction occurred in the construction sector, while the level of output in the industrial sector increased even more.

Several problems had to be addressed in order to be able to include these new estimates in our series. Backwards, the revision influenced both the level and the growth of the long-run series. As it was not reasonable to include all the differences in 1980 I decided, after extensive consultations with Argentine national accounts experts who had participated in the latest revision and some in previous ones, to distribute half of the increase in GDP as a level adjustment for the 1900–1980 period and to treat the other half of the increase as a linear augmentation of the growth rate over the 1961–1980 period. The basic argument for this distribution was that the national accounts before 1961 were considered rather reliable and it did not seem reasonable to increase the level of Argentina's GDP for the whole period by the whole of the 35 per cent. For 1980–94 I used the revised GDP estimates.

Brazil

Total GDP for 1900–1920 from Haddad (1975); for 1920–50 from Zerkowsky and De Gusmao Veloso (1982).

Chile

Total GDP for 1900–1908 from Maddison (1989); for 1908–25 from Ballesteros and Davis (1965); for 1925–40 ECLAC (1951); and for 1940–50 ECLAC (1972). An official revision of the national accounts for the base year 1986 was published in 1994.[4] The most important results were an increase in the level of capital formation in machinery and equipment and non-residential construction. Total GDP level estimates were somewhat lower due basically to changes in the sectorial composition.

Colombia

Total GDP for 1900–1925 from Maddison (1989) using his benchmarks for 1900, 1913 and 1929, with interpolation for the years in between, 1925–50 from ECLAC (1972).

Mexico

Total GDP, 1900–1950 from Banco de México (1986b). The period 1911–20 was interpolated on the basis of the 1910 and 1921 data.

Venezuela

Total GDP for the period 1900–1950 was based upon Baptista (1991) which is the most complete statistical source available on Venezuela's quantitative economic history.

Table B.2 Latin American GDP Indices, Six Countries, 1900–1994 (1950 = 100)

	Argentina	Brazil	Chile	Colombia	Mexico	Venezuela
1900	15.1	9.8	24.9	13.2	27.6	5.6
1901	16.4	10.9	25.7	13.8	29.9	5.5
1902	16.1	11.7	26.6	14.3	27.8	6.0
1903	18.4	11.8	27.5	14.9	30.9	6.5
1904	20.3	11.8	28.4	15.6	31.5	6.3
1905	23.0	12.1	29.4	16.2	34.7	6.2
1906	24.2	12.6	30.4	16.9	34.4	5.8
1907	24.7	14.4	31.4	17.6	36.4	5.8
1908	27.1	13.0	32.5	18.3	36.3	6.2
1909	28.5	14.3	33.0	19.1	37.4	6.4
1910	30.5	15.4	35.7	19.9	37.7	6.6
1911	31.1	15.4	35.4	20.8	38.0	7.1
1912	33.6	17.1	39.3	21.6	38.2	7.3
1913	34.0	17.3	39.8	22.5	38.5	8.5
1914	30.5	17.5	37.1	23.4	38.7	7.4
1915	30.6	17.3	34.4	24.3	39.0	7.6
1916	29.7	18.1	40.9	25.2	39.3	7.2
1917	27.3	19.1	44.2	26.2	39.5	8.4
1918	32.3	19.5	44.2	27.2	39.8	8.4
1919	33.5	20.6	35.0	28.3	40.1	7.8
1920	36.0	22.7	39.9	29.4	40.3	9.4
1921	36.9	23.1	34.4	30.5	40.6	9.8
1922	39.8	25.6	36.8	31.7	41.5	10.0
1923	44.2	27.8	45.8	32.9	43.0	11.6
1924	47.7	27.9	49.9	34.2	42.3	13.4
1925	47.5	28.3	50.5	35.5	44.9	17.3
1926	49.8	28.9	49.2	38.9	47.6	21.0
1927	53.3	31.6	47.2	42.4	45.5	23.5
1928	56.6	36.0	57.3	45.5	45.8	26.3
1929	59.2	35.9	62.8	47.1	44.0	29.9
1930	56.8	34.4	59.0	46.7	41.3	30.4
1931	52.8	33.3	44.5	46.0	42.6	24.6
1932	51.1	34.2	44.0	49.0	36.3	23.5
1933	53.5	38.6	52.1	51.8	40.4	25.8
1934	57.7	42.0	59.3	55.1	43.1	27.5
1935	60.2	44.0	60.4	56.4	46.3	29.5
1936	60.7	49.3	62.7	59.4	50.0	32.4
1937	65.1	51.2	67.4	60.3	51.6	37.2
1938	65.3	53.8	66.3	63.5	52.5	40.2
1939	67.8	55.9	68.3	68.2	55.3	42.6
1940	68.9	56.6	71.3	69.7	56.1	41.0
1941	72.5	61.1	71.4	70.8	61.5	40.3
1942	73.3	57.7	75.3	71.0	65.0	35.2
1943	72.8	62.4	78.5	71.3	67.4	38.4
1944	81.0	65.3	79.6	76.1	72.9	47.4
1945	78.4	67.1	86.8	79.6	75.2	57.6
1946	85.4	75.4	92.2	86.9	80.1	69.2
1947	94.9	78.7	86.0	90.3	82.9	82.7
1948	100.1	85.9	96.0	93.1	86.3	92.1

Table B.2 (continued)

	Argentina	Brazil	Chile	Colombia	Mexico	Venezuela
1949	98.8	93.4	95.4	98.2	91.0	97.7
1950	100.0	100.0	100.0	100.0	100.0	100.0
1951	103.9	106.2	104.3	103.1	107.5	111.7
1952	98.6	114.5	110.3	109.6	110.7	119.8
1953	103.9	118.1	116.0	116.3	116.7	127.2
1954	108.2	131.2	116.5	124.3	123.1	139.5
1955	115.8	138.4	116.4	129.2	132.8	151.8
1956	119.0	142.9	117.0	134.4	139.9	167.9
1957	125.2	154.5	129.3	137.4	150.4	187.4
1958	132.8	166.3	132.8	140.8	157.4	189.9
1959	124.3	175.1	132.1	151.0	164.2	204.8
1960	134.0	192.0	140.8	157.4	176.4	207.7
1961	143.6	212.2	147.6	165.4	185.1	218.1
1962	142.3	221.9	154.5	174.4	193.8	238.1
1963	140.0	224.9	164.3	180.1	209.2	254.5
1964	155.5	233.8	168.0	191.2	233.7	279.2
1965	171.1	240.3	169.3	198.1	248.9	295.7
1966	173.4	249.5	188.2	208.5	266.1	302.5
1967	179.4	261.5	194.3	217.1	282.8	314.7
1968	188.5	290.8	201.3	230.0	305.8	331.4
1969	206.1	319.7	208.8	244.0	325.1	345.2
1970	218.8	327.5	213.1	259.2	347.6	371.6
1971	228.7	364.7	232.1	274.6	362.1	383.0
1972	235.1	408.2	229.3	295.7	392.9	395.5
1973	245.8	465.2	224.8	315.6	425.9	420.2
1974	261.0	503.1	227.0	333.1	451.9	445.7
1975	261.3	529.1	196.8	341.4	477.3	472.8
1976	263.3	583.4	203.2	357.6	497.5	514.2
1977	282.1	612.2	220.0	372.5	514.7	548.8
1978	275.1	642.6	237.0	404.0	557.1	560.5
1979	296.5	686.1	253.9	425.7	608.1	568.0
1980	303.1	755.9	273.5	443.1	658.7	556.7
1981	286.7	723.8	291.8	453.2	716.5	555.1
1982	277.6	729.8	252.6	457.5	712.0	558.8
1983	289.0	708.4	243.8	464.7	682.2	527.5
1984	294.8	746.7	258.7	480.3	706.8	520.3
1985	274.3	805.3	267.7	495.2	725.1	521.3
1986	293.9	865.6	282.7	524.1	697.9	555.3
1987	301.3	896.1	301.3	552.2	710.8	575.1
1988	295.4	895.6	323.3	574.6	719.7	608.6
1989	274.7	923.9	355.2	594.3	749.9	556.5
1990	271.1	882.9	366.8	619.7	787.9	592.5
1991	299.5	885.9	393.4	632.1	821.2	650.1
1992	330.4	878.6	436.9	657.7	851.0	689.5
1993	351.0	915.4	464.3	691.7	867.6	686.7
1994	381.0	970.3	484.0	733.4	905.9	664.3

Table B.3 Levels of Latin American GDP, Six Countries, 1900–1994 (national currencies in 1980 constant prices)

	Argentina (million australes)	Brazil (thousand cruzeiros)	Chile (million pesos)	Colombia (million pesos)	Mexico (million pesos)	Venezuela (million bolívares)
1900	1,917	161,934	95,016	47,060	187,004	2,551
1901	2,079	180,932	98,229	49,035	203,230	2,509
1902	2,037	193,597	101,551	51,093	188,739	2,729
1903	2,329	194,501	104,985	53,237	209,877	2,950
1904	2,577	195,406	108,535	55,471	213,567	2,880
1905	2,919	199,929	112,205	57,799	235,756	2,846
1906	3,066	208,976	115,999	60,225	233,093	2,656
1907	3,131	237,925	119,922	62,752	246,770	2,654
1908	3,437	214,404	123,977	65,386	246,395	2,839
1909	3,607	237,020	125,990	68,130	253,636	2,938
1910	3,869	254,209	136,346	70,989	255,893	3,033
1911	3,939	255,114	135,195	73,968	257,615	3,246
1912	4,261	282,253	150,153	77,073	259,350	3,356
1913	4,305	286,777	151,879	80,307	261,095	3,875
1914	3,859	290,395	141,523	83,407	262,853	3,388
1915	3,879	286,777	131,456	86,626	264,622	3,491
1916	3,768	299,442	155,906	89,970	266,404	3,296
1917	3,463	315,726	168,562	93,443	268,197	3,845
1918	4,097	322,058	168,850	97,049	270,002	3,820
1919	4,248	341,056	133,469	100,795	271,820	3,570
1920	4,557	375,433	152,454	104,686	273,650	4,286
1921	4,674	381,613	131,168	108,726	275,492	4,459
1922	5,048	423,328	140,373	112,923	281,911	4,584
1923	5,604	460,408	174,603	117,282	291,596	5,289
1924	6,041	461,953	190,424	121,809	286,831	6,128
1925	6,015	468,133	192,725	126,510	304,670	7,919
1926	6,305	477,403	187,808	138,589	322,949	9,578
1927	6,753	522,207	180,192	151,073	308,743	10,743
1928	7,171	596,367	218,592	162,169	310,657	12,030
1929	7,501	594,822	239,810	168,006	298,642	13,641
1930	7,191	568,557	225,300	166,561	279,923	13,886
1931	6,692	551,562	169,690	163,903	289,201	11,225
1932	6,470	565,467	167,819	174,768	246,061	10,751
1933	6,774	638,082	198,657	184,593	273,863	11,762
1934	7,309	695,246	226,182	196,209	292,345	12,555
1935	7,627	727,691	230,431	201,006	314,013	13,463
1936	7,690	815,756	239,196	211,640	339,135	14,788
1937	8,248	846,656	257,394	214,935	350,360	16,968
1938	8,273	889,915	253,038	226,320	356,038	18,347
1939	8,590	925,450	260,708	242,965	375,180	19,454
1940	8,729	936,265	272,118	248,224	380,353	18,699
1941	9,185	1,010,425	272,423	252,385	417,400	18,393
1942	9,287	954,805	287,473	252,905	440,819	16,083
1943	9,223	1,032,055	299,472	253,945	457,144	17,554
1944	10,262	1,079,949	303,743	271,110	494,460	21,656
1945	9,933	1,110,849	331,301	283,825	509,994	26,321
1946	10,820	1,248,354	351,740	309,516	543,506	31,583

Table B.3 (continued)

	Argentina (million australes)	Brazil (thousand cruzeiros)	Chile (million pesos)	Colombia (million pesos)	Mexico (million pesos)	Venezuela (million bolívares)
1947	12,023	1,302,428	328,250	321,697	562,225	37,780
1948	12,682	1,421,393	366,282	331,664	585,391	42,058
1949	12,517	1,544,992	364,045	349,991	617,478	44,631
1950	12,669	1,654,687	381,637	356,359	678,580	45,659
1951	13,161	1,757,506	398,110	367,446	729,585	50,986
1952	12,498	1,894,044	420,888	390,639	751,441	54,700
1953	13,161	1,954,403	442,853	414,389	792,059	58,083
1954	13,704	2,171,698	444,683	443,041	835,207	63,676
1955	14,672	2,289,503	444,073	460,363	901,244	69,330
1956	15,080	2,364,016	446,616	479,043	949,418	76,652
1957	15,861	2,556,751	493,494	489,717	1,020,705	85,553
1958	16,829	2,751,567	506,917	501,751	1,067,789	86,690
1959	15,742	2,896,846	504,200	538,020	1,113,943	93,513
1960	16,982	3,176,998	537,404	560,970	1,197,080	94,830
1961	18,188	3,510,849	563,105	589,524	1,256,095	99,583
1962	18,032	3,671,115	589,789	621,426	1,314,783	108,700
1963	17,735	3,720,651	627,100	641,854	1,419,816	116,184
1964	19,707	3,868,428	641,053	681,446	1,585,837	127,466
1965	21,673	3,976,659	646,235	705,973	1,688,675	135,009
1966	21,974	4,128,651	718,298	742,943	1,805,725	138,111
1967	22,723	4,327,622	741,618	773,663	1,918,943	143,683
1968	23,876	4,811,233	768,166	819,565	2,075,061	151,317
1969	26,106	5,289,316	796,751	869,579	2,206,284	157,627
1970	27,715	5,419,200	813,135	923,561	2,358,990	169,677
1971	28,970	6,033,900	885,953	978,612	2,457,397	174,888
1972	29,791	6,754,300	875,205	1,053,663	2,665,977	180,585
1973	31,136	7,697,800	857,832	1,124,501	2,890,162	191,881
1974	33,062	8,325,500	866,191	1,186,949	3,066,771	203,516
1975	33,110	8,755,700	751,212	1,216,738	3,238,851	215,865
1976	33,353	9,653,700	775,358	1,274,270	3,376,136	234,798
1977	35,745	10,130,100	839,453	1,327,260	3,492,367	250,582
1978	34,848	10,633,500	904,525	1,439,678	3,780,483	255,940
1979	37,571	11,352,300	969,008	1,517,120	4,126,581	259,358
1980	38,400	12,508,000	1,043,920	1,579,130	4,470,077	254,201
1981	36,318	11,976,000	1,113,619	1,615,166	4,862,219	253,434
1982	35,171	12,076,000	964,151	1,630,403	4,831,689	255,163
1983	36,617	11,722,000	930,511	1,656,064	4,628,937	240,830
1984	37,350	12,355,000	987,196	1,711,554	4,796,050	237,570
1985	34,754	13,325,000	1,021,550	1,764,734	4,920,430	238,029
1986	37,237	14,323,000	1,078,718	1,867,513	4,735,721	253,525
1987	38,179	14,828,000	1,149,852	1,967,779	4,823,604	262,606
1988	37,432	14,819,000	1,233,921	2,047,753	4,883,679	277,893
1989	34,809	15,288,000	1,355,756	2,117,665	5,088,710	254,078
1990	34,343	14,610,000	1,399,930	2,208,343	5,346,622	270,512
1991	37,949	14,659,367	1,501,538	2,252,546	5,572,369	296,832
1992	41,857	14,538,692	1,667,315	2,343,659	5,774,572	314,821
1993	44,473	15,147,556	1,771,909	2,465,036	5,887,206	313,554
1994	48,264	16,055,367	1,847,183	2,613,490	6,147,145	303,301

Table B.4 Levels of Latin American GDP, Six Countries, 1900–1994 (million 1980 international dollars)

	Argentina	Brazil	Chile	Colombia	Mexico	Venezuela
1900	7,076	5,292	3,299	2,037	13,955	707
1901	7,675	5,913	3,411	2,123	15,166	695
1902	7,520	6,327	3,526	2,212	14,085	756
1903	8,596	6,356	3,645	2,305	15,662	817
1904	9,513	6,386	3,769	2,401	15,938	798
1905	10,775	6,534	3,896	2,502	17,594	788
1906	11,317	6,829	4,028	2,607	17,395	736
1907	11,556	7,775	4,164	2,717	18,416	735
1908	12,688	7,007	4,305	2,831	18,388	786
1909	13,315	7,746	4,375	2,949	18,928	814
1910	14,283	8,307	4,734	3,073	19,096	840
1911	14,540	8,337	4,694	3,202	19,225	899
1912	15,728	9,224	5,214	3,336	19,354	930
1913	15,891	9,372	5,274	3,476	19,485	1,074
1914	14,246	9,490	4,914	3,611	19,616	938
1915	14,321	9,372	4,564	3,750	19,748	967
1916	13,908	9,786	5,413	3,895	19,881	913
1917	12,782	10,318	5,853	4,045	20,015	1,065
1918	15,125	10,525	5,863	4,201	20,149	1,058
1919	15,681	11,146	4,634	4,363	20,285	989
1920	16,822	12,269	5,294	4,532	20,422	1,187
1921	17,252	12,471	4,554	4,707	20,559	1,235
1922	18,632	13,834	4,874	4,888	21,038	1,270
1923	20,685	15,046	6,063	5,077	21,761	1,465
1924	22,299	15,096	6,612	5,273	21,405	1,698
1925	22,205	15,298	6,692	5,477	22,737	2,194
1926	23,276	15,601	6,521	6,000	24,101	2,653
1927	24,927	17,066	6,257	6,540	23,041	2,976
1928	26,471	19,489	7,590	7,020	23,183	3,332
1929	27,691	19,439	8,327	7,273	22,287	3,779
1930	26,545	18,580	7,823	7,210	20,890	3,847
1931	24,703	18,025	5,892	7,095	21,582	3,109
1932	23,884	18,479	5,827	7,566	18,363	2,978
1933	25,007	20,852	6,898	7,991	20,438	3,258
1934	26,981	22,720	7,854	8,494	21,817	3,478
1935	28,154	23,781	8,001	8,702	23,434	3,729
1936	28,388	26,659	8,305	9,162	25,309	4,096
1937	30,445	27,668	8,937	9,305	26,146	4,700
1938	30,539	29,082	8,786	9,797	26,570	5,082
1939	31,708	30,243	9,052	10,518	27,999	5,389
1940	32,223	30,597	9,449	10,746	28,385	5,180
1941	33,907	33,020	9,459	10,926	31,149	5,095
1942	34,280	31,203	9,982	10,948	32,897	4,455
1943	34,047	33,727	10,398	10,993	34,115	4,863
1944	37,882	35,292	10,547	11,736	36,900	5,999
1945	36,666	36,302	11,504	12,287	38,059	7,291
1946	39,940	40,796	12,213	13,399	40,560	8,749
1947	44,382	42,563	11,398	13,926	41,957	10,465
1948	46,814	46,451	12,718	14,358	43,686	11,651

Table B.4 (continued)

	Argentina	Brazil	Chile	Colombia	Mexico	Venezuela
1949	46,207	50,490	12,640	15,151	46,080	12,363
1950	46,768	54,075	13,251	15,427	50,640	12,648
1951	48,582	57,435	13,823	15,907	54,447	14,124
1952	46,136	61,897	14,614	16,911	56,078	15,152
1953	48,582	63,869	15,377	17,939	59,109	16,089
1954	50,588	70,971	15,440	19,179	62,329	17,639
1955	54,161	74,820	15,419	19,929	67,257	19,205
1956	55,665	77,255	15,507	20,738	70,852	21,233
1957	58,551	83,554	17,135	21,200	76,172	23,699
1958	62,124	89,920	17,601	21,721	79,686	24,014
1959	58,111	94,668	17,507	23,291	83,130	25,904
1960	62,687	103,823	18,660	24,284	89,334	26,269
1961	67,139	114,734	19,552	25,521	93,738	27,585
1962	66,564	119,971	20,479	26,902	98,118	30,111
1963	65,468	121,590	21,774	27,786	105,956	32,184
1964	72,747	126,419	22,259	29,500	118,346	35,309
1965	80,002	129,956	22,439	30,562	126,020	37,399
1966	81,116	134,923	24,941	32,162	134,756	38,258
1967	83,880	141,426	25,751	33,492	143,205	39,801
1968	88,135	157,230	26,672	35,479	154,855	41,916
1969	96,369	172,853	27,665	37,644	164,648	43,664
1970	102,306	177,098	28,234	39,981	176,044	47,002
1971	106,941	197,186	30,762	42,364	183,388	48,445
1972	109,970	220,729	30,389	45,613	198,953	50,024
1973	114,935	251,562	29,786	48,680	215,684	53,153
1974	122,044	272,075	30,076	51,383	228,864	56,376
1975	122,223	286,134	26,084	52,673	241,705	59,796
1976	123,118	315,480	26,922	55,163	251,950	65,041
1977	131,951	331,049	29,148	57,457	260,624	69,413
1978	128,638	347,500	31,407	62,324	282,126	70,898
1979	138,688	370,990	33,646	65,676	307,954	71,844
1980	141,750	408,758	36,247	68,361	333,588	70,416
1981	134,065	391,373	38,667	69,921	362,852	70,203
1982	129,831	394,641	33,477	70,580	360,574	70,682
1983	135,170	383,072	32,309	71,691	345,443	66,712
1984	137,873	403,758	34,278	74,093	357,914	65,809
1985	128,289	435,458	35,470	76,395	367,196	65,936
1986	137,457	468,072	37,455	80,845	353,412	70,229
1987	140,932	484,575	39,925	85,185	359,970	72,744
1988	138,175	484,281	42,844	88,647	364,454	76,979
1989	128,493	499,608	47,075	91,674	379,754	70,382
1990	126,774	477,451	48,609	95,599	399,002	74,934
1991	140,083	479,064	52,137	97,513	415,848	82,225
1992	154,511	475,121	57,893	101,457	430,938	87,208
1993	164,169	495,018	61,525	106,712	439,344	86,857
1994	178,163	524,685	64,138	113,138	458,742	84,017

Table B.5 Levels of GDP per Capita in Latin America, Six Countries, 1900–1994 (1980 international dollars)

	Argentina	Brazil	Chile	Colombia	Mexico	Venezuela
1900	1,508	294	1,109	510	1,026	278
1901	1,575	322	1,133	520	1,103	270
1902	1,486	337	1,157	531	1,013	290
1903	1,636	332	1,181	543	1,114	309
1904	1,744	326	1,206	554	1,122	297
1905	1,902	327	1,232	566	1,225	291
1906	1,924	335	1,258	578	1,192	270
1907	1,892	373	1,284	590	1,255	268
1908	2,001	329	1,312	603	1,239	285
1909	2,022	356	1,316	615	1,262	293
1910	2,089	374	1,407	628	1,273	300
1911	2,048	368	1,378	642	1,283	317
1912	2,134	398	1,512	655	1,292	325
1913	2,076	396	1,511	669	1,302	374
1914	1,807	393	1,389	677	1,311	324
1915	1,774	380	1,274	686	1,321	331
1916	1,691	389	1,491	694	1,331	312
1917	1,526	402	1,591	703	1,341	362
1918	1,776	401	1,573	712	1,350	358
1919	1,808	416	1,227	720	1,361	333
1920	1,898	449	1,383	729	1,371	397
1921	1,898	447	1,175	738	1,380	411
1922	1,989	486	1,241	748	1,392	420
1923	2,131	518	1,523	757	1,417	481
1924	2,218	509	1,640	766	1,372	552
1925	2,144	505	1,638	776	1,434	704
1926	2,185	505	1,575	828	1,496	842
1927	2,273	541	1,492	880	1,407	934
1928	2,346	605	1,786	921	1,394	1,035
1929	2,389	591	1,934	930	1,319	1,159
1930	2,231	554	1,790	911	1,216	1,166
1931	2,030	526	1,329	886	1,235	932
1932	1,926	529	1,295	934	1,033	884
1933	1,981	585	1,510	974	1,130	958
1934	2,102	624	1,695	1,024	1,186	1,014
1935	2,158	640	1,701	1,036	1,252	1,076
1936	2,141	703	1,740	1,078	1,329	1,167
1937	2,257	715	1,845	1,082	1,350	1,318
1938	2,225	737	1,788	1,126	1,348	1,403
1939	2,267	747	1,809	1,177	1,397	1,457
1940	2,274	737	1,855	1,171	1,392	1,369
1941	2,354	775	1,825	1,160	1,487	1,321
1942	2,342	714	1,892	1,132	1,528	1,130
1943	2,289	753	1,936	1,107	1,542	1,210
1944	2,504	768	1,929	1,151	1,623	1,458
1945	2,382	771	2,067	1,174	1,629	1,727
1946	2,551	844	2,156	1,247	1,690	2,013
1947	2,784	859	1,977	1,262	1,701	2,333
1948	2,871	914	2,167	1,267	1,724	2,502

Table B.5 (continued)

	Argentina	Brazil	Chile	Colombia	Mexico	Venezuela
1949	2,761	969	2,116	1,302	1,769	2,553
1950	2,727	1,012	2,179	1,291	1,826	2,483
1951	2,777	1,041	2,225	1,294	1,911	2,706
1952	2,586	1,087	2,303	1,338	1,916	2,787
1953	2,670	1,087	2,372	1,380	1,966	2,841
1954	2,726	1,171	2,332	1,434	2,018	2,989
1955	2,861	1,196	2,280	1,448	2,119	3,083
1956	2,891	1,199	2,239	1,464	2,166	3,319
1957	2,989	1,258	2,417	1,453	2,259	3,560
1958	3,118	1,315	2,425	1,445	2,292	3,466
1959	2,867	1,343	2,356	1,505	2,320	3,593
1960	3,041	1,430	2,453	1,524	2,418	3,466
1961	3,206	1,534	2,509	1,554	2,460	3,548
1962	3,130	1,557	2,566	1,590	2,496	3,737
1963	3,031	1,531	2,664	1,594	2,613	3,854
1964	3,316	1,545	2,659	1,642	2,829	4,080
1965	3,590	1,542	2,618	1,651	2,921	4,112
1966	3,588	1,560	2,851	1,689	3,025	4,125
1967	3,657	1,594	2,884	1,709	3,114	4,150
1968	3,787	1,727	2,926	1,759	3,262	4,227
1969	4,081	1,850	2,974	1,814	3,359	4,258
1970	4,269	1,848	2,973	1,872	3,479	4,384
1971	4,389	2,009	3,185	1,941	3,514	4,409
1972	4,439	2,195	3,093	2,046	3,695	4,394
1973	4,562	2,443	2,981	2,137	3,883	4,506
1974	4,764	2,579	2,959	2,208	3,995	4,612
1975	4,692	2,649	2,523	2,215	4,090	4,696
1976	4,655	2,853	2,565	2,270	4,150	4,963
1977	4,913	2,926	2,736	2,313	4,180	5,119
1978	4,717	3,001	2,904	2,455	4,405	5,053
1979	5,009	3,130	3,064	2,531	4,681	4,948
1980	5,042	3,370	3,252	2,577	4,937	4,666
1981	4,696	3,156	3,416	2,580	5,244	4,525
1982	4,479	3,113	2,913	2,548	5,095	4,441
1983	4,593	2,957	2,768	2,533	4,775	4,090
1984	4,614	3,052	2,891	2,564	4,843	3,938
1985	4,230	3,225	2,944	2,591	4,866	3,848
1986	4,467	3,398	3,058	2,690	4,588	3,993
1987	4,514	3,450	3,206	2,782	4,581	4,028
1988	4,363	3,384	3,382	2,843	4,549	4,152
1989	4,001	3,427	3,654	2,888	4,650	3,699
1990	3,895	3,216	3,711	2,960	4,794	3,842
1991	4,249	3,169	3,914	2,967	4,904	4,117
1992	4,630	3,089	4,274	3,035	4,988	4,266
1993	4,860	3,163	4,468	3,140	4,994	4,154
1994	5,213	3,297	4,583	3,275	5,122	3,930

NOTES

1. See Chapter 6 for a more extensive analysis of exchange rates and purchasing power parities. I used the results of ICP IV for 1980 because Latin America did not participate in the following rounds. Mexico now participates as an OECD member with the OECD secretariat and EUROSTAT. There exist good prospects that Latin America will participate in the next round of ICP as many countries expressed their interest, especially the MERCOSUR and Andean Pact countries. ECLAC will coordinate the ICP work with the substantive and financial assistance of World Bank and OECD.
2. Banco Central de la República Argentina (1991) is only available in mimeographed form and was never published officially.
3. Of which no official estimates were available since 1973.
4. Banco Central de Chile (1994).

Appendix C. Activity Rates, Employment, Education and Labour Productivity

In order to analyse the labour market in Latin America some basic quantification is necessary. There are many institutes working on this theme, some regional like the former PREALC. The basic value added of this appendix is its presentation of series since 1950, estimates on hours worked and the human capital estimates. The appendix presents a complete description of the sources for each country. First, a general source note is given which presents the databases and other general information we used in common for all countries. Then, in specific source notes, the sources and procedures are detailed if they are different from the one described in the general source note. It should be noted that the basic tables have as benchmark years: 1950, 1960, 1970, 1980 and 1990. This is the case because the information with respect to activity rates, labour force and employment normally comes from population censuses which are only available on a decade basis. These benchmarks are used in this appendix although the text often presents a periodisation with benchmarks in 1950, 1973, 1980, 1989 and 1994. If not otherwise indicated, the data for 1973, 1989 and 1994 have been estimated by intra- and extrapolation.

SOURCE NOTE

Table C.1

Male and female activity rates for 1950–80 from ECLAC (1985). These activity rates were calculated on the basis of population censuses and household surveys. However, the population figures of CELADE are adjusted for undercounting, especially for males, in the censuses. This adjustment causes small changes in total activity rates. We used ECLAC's sex-specific activity rates for the respective population and calculated the total activity rate. For 1990 I used population censuses when available. For Brazil and Colombia CELADE (1992) was used.

Table C.2

The employment rates for 1950–80 come from the Projections Center of ECLAC and are based upon population censuses. The 1990 estimate was elaborated by the author using population censuses. For Brazil IBGE (1990) was used and in the case of Colombia the 1985 census (DANE, 1986), updated to 1990 and ECLAC (1992). The updating to 1994 was done with the employment information of the household surveys of the countries available at the employment data base of the Statistics and Projections Division of ECLAC. Unemployment rates were assumed equal for both sexes.

Table C.3

Annual hours per person employed were calculated on the basis of the number of days worked per year and the average number of hours worked per day. Number of days worked during the year on the basis of public and statutory holidays from ILO (1982) and estimated for missing years. Half day Saturday working was assumed in 1950 and 1960 in the cases of Argentina, Brazil, Colombia and Mexico, and only in 1950 in the cases of Chile and Venezuela and a free Saturday onwards. Time lost through industrial disputes from ILO, *Yearbook of Labour Statistics*, various issues. Annual hours data from ILO, *Yearbook of Labour Statistics*, various issues, and other sources. In the case of Brazil the 1960 and 1970 estimate from Bonelli (1976), with 1959 and 1969 estimates for manufacturing. The estimates for 1980 and 1990 were based upon IBGE, *Anuario Estadístico do Brasil*, various issues, and IBGE, *Recenseamento Geral do Brasil*, 1970 and 1980. The Chile 1960 and 1970 estimates were on the basis of information from Instituto de Economía, *Ocupación y Desocupación*, Universidad de Chile, Santiago (various issues) and INE, *Muestra Nacional de Hogares*, Santiago, 1966 and 1971. In the case of Colombia, 1950 from DANE (1956), *Anuario General de Estadística Colombia. 1956*, p. 412, figures for 1956 and 1980 and 1990 were estimates. Mexico for 1950–90, Instituto Nacional de Estadística, *Encuesta Anual de Trabajo y Salarios Nacionales*, various issues. The 1950 and 1960 figures for Venezuela are estimates. The 1994 estimates were from ILO (1995) in the case of Chile and Mexico; the remainder were estimated by the author.

Table C.5

The 1950–80 sectoral employment data were provided by ECLAC's Projections Center. For 1990 national census and country sources were used as follows: Argentina's1990 sectoral employment from PREALC (1993); the 1990 sectoral employment in Brazil from IBGE (1990) which represents the 1988 estimate; the

Chilean 1990 sectoral employment from García (1992); Colombia's 1990 sectoral employment was estimated on the basis of Junguito (1990) and ECLAC (1992); the Mexican 1990 sectoral employment data was from INEGI (1992); the 1990 sectoral employment in Venezuela was from OCEI (1990).

Table C.6

The estimates for average years of formal education of the population between 15 and 64 years were made on the basis of the population censuses of the countries. In many cases the information of the census had to be adjusted which generally (for specifics see the country notes) has been done as follows: in the cases where the census presented only data of the educational level of 15 years and older, the information from previous censuses was used to estimate the cohort 65–75 and the census was adjusted with this information. If information within the 50–64 group was insufficient we tried to apply the same procedures. We adjusted for differences in the number of years particulary in primary and secondary education. The first six years were considered primary education and the second six years secondary education. If, for example, Argentina has seven years of primary education and five years of secondary, then we considered the seventh year of primary as the first year of secondary and so on.

In case the census was not available from national sources, the World Bank database on capital stock, which was kindly provided to us by the World Bank, or the estimates of Maddison (1989) were used as indicated in the country source notes. In Table C.9 of this appendix, the Maddison (1989) and the World Bank data with respect to formal years of education are presented. In the case of the World Bank data the extremely low (in comparison with Maddison's (1989) and my data) level of secondary education draws the attention. This becomes extreme, for example, in the case of Argentina, where formal educational experience in higher education exceeds the experience in secondary education, implying that Argentina's brilliant youngsters jump directly from primary to higher education.

Argentina's 1950 estimate was obtained from Maddison (1989) using as the linkage year 1980, for which we had estimates in common. Total years of education in 1990 was estimated by using the World Bank database 1980–87 growth rate. The disaggregation of years of education was obtained on the basis of retropolation, in the case of 1950, or extrapolation, in 1990 of the available distribution. Brazil's 1950–70 estimates are based upon Langoni (1974). The 1990 estimate was based upon the 1980 population census, containing the educational level of the population aged 25–64 and IBGE (1992) which contained information about educational level of the population aged 15–24.

The estimates for Chile in 1950, 1980 and 1990 were based on intrapolation of the census information of 1952, 1982 and 1992. In 1952 the group with special education was distributed over secondary and higher education and not, as in the case of Maddison (1989), completely to higher education. The level of education from 1962 onwards was given for total population over 15. In order to obtain population figures for the age group 15–64 previous population censuses were used to subtract the educational level of the cohort over 64. The Colombian estimates for 1950–80 were based on intrapolation of the census information of 1951, 1964, 1973 and 1985. Special adjustments were made using cohorts of previous population censuses to estimate the educational level of the 60–64 age group. For 1990 the 1980–87 growth rate of the World Bank database was used. The 1950 estimate for Mexico was obtained from Maddison (1989) using as the linkage year 1980 for which we had estimates in common. For 1960–80 an adjustment was made, using cohorts from other censuses to estimate the educational level over 65, to obtain the educational level 15–64. In the case of Venezuela for 1960–80 the estimates for 1961, 1971 and 1981 were retropolated. The distribution with respect to educational level for 1971 was obtained through cohort analysis of the available censuses. For 1990 the 1980–87 growth rate of the World Bank database was used.

Table C.1 Latin America: Total Female and Male Activity Rates, Six Countries, 1950–94 (economic active population divided by total population)

	Argentina	Brazil	Chile	Colombia	Mexico	Venezuela
Total						
1950	40.91	33.30	37.64	32.54	32.02	32.92
1960	39.09	32.13	32.57	29.51	29.15	31.19
1970	38.89	31.56	30.47	29.11	27.94	28.49
1973	38.11	32.92	30.80	30.23	28.59	29.67
1980	36.34	36.33	31.57	33.04	30.19	32.61
1989	36.79	37.13	32.96	34.13	30.37	33.29
1990	37.83	39.08	36.43	36.81	30.82	34.93
1994	38.45	40.24	38.58	38.43	31.08	35.91
Female						
1950	16.33	10.04	17.91	10.31	8.30	10.39
1960	15.87	11.18	14.18	9.90	10.28	8.25
1970	19.09	12.77	13.38	12.04	11.13	11.27
1973	19.08	14.46	13.90	12.95	11.42	12.70
1980	19.06	19.33	15.19	15.34	12.11	16.78
1989	19.57	20.39	16.80	16.41	12.73	17.76
1990	20.80	23.07	21.24	19.20	14.31	20.29
1994	21.54	24.76	24.29	21.00	15.30	21.89
Male						
1950	64.10	56.54	57.77	55.07	55.77	54.88
1960	61.59	53.00	51.38	49.36	48.12	51.91
1970	58.56	50.30	48.02	46.36	44.73	45.28
1973	57.17	51.20	48.13	47.69	45.78	46.10
1980	54.07	53.34	48.39	50.95	48.32	48.05
1989	54.49	53.88	49.44	52.04	48.09	48.43
1990	55.47	55.14	51.98	54.68	47.55	49.33
1994	56.04	55.88	53.49	56.25	47.24	49.86

Source: The values for 1973 and 1989 are intrapolations. 1994 was extrapolated using the 1980–90 growth rate.

Table C.2 Latin American Employment, Six Countries, 1913–94 (thousand persons engaged at mid-year)

	Argentina	Brazil	Chile	Colombia	Mexico	Venezuela
1913	3,201	11,302	1,323	2,099	5,521	529
1950	6,821	17,657	2,256	3,844	8,766	1,571
1960	7,849	23,138	2,354	4,516	10,600	2,066
1970	9,132	29,643	2,729	5,968	13,599	2,902
1973	9,402	33,164	2,894	6,616	15,180	3,338
1980	10,065	43,091	3,318	8,413	19,622	4,626
1989	11,731	54,646	4,303	10,487	24,318	5,722
1990	11,932	56,108	4,429	10,747	24,905	5,859
1994	12,483	59,908	4,954	11,670	28,018	6,724

Table C.3 Latin America: Annual Hours per Person Employed, Six Countries, 1950–94

	Argentina	Brazil	Chile	Colombia	Mexico	Venezuela
1950	2,034	2,042	2,212	2,323	2,154	2,179
1960	2,073	2,134	2,031	2,218	2,150	2,024
1970	2,006	2,145	1,962	2,170	2,066	1,951
1973	1,996	2,096	1,955	2,141	2,061	1,965
1980	1,974	1,985	1,938	2,074	2,051	1,997
1989	1,862	1,889	1,979	1,979	2,059	1,900
1990	1,850	1,879	1,984	1,969	2,060	1,889
1994	1,875	1,860	2,002	1,975	2,032	1,910

Table C.4 Latin America: Total Hours Worked, Six Countries, 1950–94 (billion)

	Argentina	Brazil	Chile	Colombia	Mexico	Venezuela
1950	13,871	36,053	4,991	8,930	18,878	3,423
1960	16,271	49,367	4,781	10,017	22,785	4,181
1970	18,322	63,571	5,354	12,950	28,090	5,662
1973	18,766	69,512	5,658	14,165	31,286	6,559
1980	19,868	85,517	6,432	17,445	40,239	9,238
1989	21,843	103,226	8,516	20,754	50,071	10,872
1990	22,068	105,428	8,788	21,159	51,295	11,069
1994	23,406	111,429	9,918	23,049	56,943	12,842

Source: Appendix Tables C.2 and C.3

Table C.5 *Latin America: Sectoral Employment, Six Countries, 1950–94*
(thousand persons employed at mid-year)

	Argentina	Brazil	Chile	Colombia	Mexico	Venezuela
Agriculture						
1950	1,723	10,606	722	2,164	5,338	710
1960	1,589	12,687	705	2,317	5,247	728
1970	1,483	13,437	636	2,477	5,684	747
1973	1,429	14,199	626	2,577	6,032	782
1980	1,333	13,078	540	2,524	7,221	731
1989	1,464	13,527	709	3,004	6,076	780
1990	1,480	13,578	731	3,063	5,960	786
1994	1,508	13,243	822	3,258	5,645	845
Industry						
1950	2,141	3,116	684	700	1,464	315
1960	2,807	4,146	704	867	2,258	457
1970	3,130	6,619	920	1,301	3,549	716
1973	3,182	7,911	1,011	1,498	4,211	851
1980	3,654	12,596	984	2,204	5,239	1,341
1989	3,033	13,226	1,031	2,501	6,542	1,364
1990	2,971	13,298	1,036	2,536	6,705	1,367
1994	2,673	13,056	1,054	2,642	7,568	1,438
Services						
1950	2,957	3,935	850	980	1,963	546
1960	3,453	6,304	945	1,332	3,095	881
1970	4,519	9,587	1,173	2,190	4,365	1,439
1973	4,791	11,055	1,257	2,541	4,937	1,705
1980	5,078	17,417	1,794	3,685	7,162	2,554
1989	7,233	27,893	2,563	4,982	11,701	3,578
1990	7,481	29,232	2,662	5,148	12,240	3,706
1994	8,302	33,610	3,078	5,770	14,804	4,441
Total						
1950	6,821	17,657	2,256	3,844	8,765	1,571
1960	7,849	23,137	2,354	4,516	10,600	2,066
1970	9,132	29,643	2,729	5,968	13,598	2,902
1973	9,402	33,165	2,894	6,616	15,180	3,338
1980	10,065	43,091	3,318	8,413	19,622	4,626
1989	11,730	54,646	4,303	10,487	24,319	5,722
1990	11,932	56,108	4,429	10,747	24,905	5,859
1994	12,483	59,909	4,954	11,670	28,017	6,724

Table C.6 Latin America: Average Years of Formal Education of Population Aged 15–64, Six Countries, 1950–94

	Argentina	Brazil	Chile	Colombia	Mexico	Venezuela
Total						
1950	4.72	1.83	4.46	2.45	2.07	1.93
1960	5.09	2.09	5.16	3.05	2.66	2.38
1970	6.41	2.92	6.13	4.05	3.51	3.51
1973	6.87	3.23	6.45	4.40	3.81	3.94
1980	7.41	4.22	7.34	5.07	5.72	5.51
1989	8.37	5.25	8.65	6.90	6.77	7.75
1990	8.49	5.38	8.82	7.15	6.91	8.06
1994	8.97	5.93	9.48	8.20	7.45	9.39
Primary						
1950	3.86	1.53	3.65	2.04	1.88	1.74
1960	4.00	1.73	4.00	2.37	2.33	2.10
1970	4.69	2.23	4.42	2.98	2.93	2.84
1973	4.92	2.41	4.55	3.19	3.14	3.11
1980	4.97	3.22	4.91	3.45	4.17	4.11
1989	5.09	3.87	5.30	4.29	4.60	5.23
1990	5.10	3.95	5.35	4.39	4.65	5.37
1994	5.15	4.29	5.54	4.83	4.86	5.98
Secondary						
1950	0.77	0.25	0.70	0.34	0.16	0.16
1960	0.96	0.30	1.03	0.54	0.29	0.23
1970	1.49	0.58	1.43	0.92	0.49	0.59
1973	1.68	0.69	1.55	1.06	0.56	0.74
1980	2.04	0.88	2.12	1.40	1.32	1.20
1989	2.65	1.23	2.93	2.27	1.83	2.16
1990	2.73	1.28	3.04	2.40	1.90	2.30
1994	3.01	1.48	3.45	2.93	2.16	2.90
Higher						
1950	0.09	0.05	0.11	0.07	0.03	0.03
1960	0.13	0.06	0.13	0.14	0.04	0.05
1970	0.23	0.11	0.28	0.15	0.09	0.08
1973	0.27	0.13	0.35	0.15	0.11	0.09
1980	0.40	0.12	0.31	0.22	0.23	0.20
1989	0.63	0.15	0.42	0.34	0.34	0.36
1990	0.66	0.15	0.43	0.36	0.36	0.39
1994	0.81	0.16	0.49	0.44	0.43	0.51

Table C.7 Latin American Labour Productivity, GDP per Person Employed, Six Countries, 1950–94 (in 1980 international dollars)

	Argentina	Brazil	Chile	Colombia	Mexico	Venezuela
1950	8,519	3,062	5,875	4,013	5,777	8,050
1960	7,986	4,487	7,926	5,378	8,428	12,716
1970	11,203	5,974	10,346	6,699	12,946	16,196
1973	12,224	7,585	10,292	7,358	14,208	15,924
1980	14,084	9,486	10,924	8,126	17,001	15,222
1989	11,428	7,162	10,940	8,742	15,616	12,300
1990	10,625	8,510	10,976	8,895	16,021	12,790
1994	14,272	8,758	12,947	9,695	16,373	12,496

Source: Appendix Tables B.3 and C.2.

Table C.8 Latin American Labour Productivity, GDP per Hour Worked, Six Countries, 1950–94 (in 1980 international dollars)

	Argentina	Brazil	Chile	Colombia	Mexico	Venezuela
1950	3.37	1.50	2.66	1.73	2.68	3.69
1960	3.85	2.10	3.90	2.42	3.92	6.28
1970	5.58	2.79	5.27	3.09	6.27	8.30
1973	6.12	3.62	5.26	3.44	6.89	8.10
1980	7.13	4.78	5.64	3.92	8.29	7.62
1989	5.88	4.84	5.53	4.42	7.58	6.47
1990	5.74	4.53	5.53	4.52	7.78	6.77
1994	7.61	4.71	6.47	4.91	8.06	6.54

Source: Appendix Tables B.3 and C.3.

Table C.9 Latin America: Average Years of Formal Educational Experience of Population Aged 15–64 in 1950 and 1980, Five Countries

	Total	Primary	Secondary	Higher
Argentina				
1950	4.60	4.15	0.42	0.03
1980	7.21	5.00	1.74	0.47
Brazil				
1950	1.83	1.36	0.42	0.05
1980	3.94	2.52	1.31	0.11
Chile				
1950	4.88	3.59	1.16	0.13
1980	7.57	4.38	2.77	0.42
Colombia				
1950	3.61	2.95	0.56	0.10
1980	6.66	3.47	2.77	0.42
Mexico				
1950	2.30	1.61	0.65	0.04
1980	4.94	2.87	1.95	0.12

Source: Maddison (1989).

Appendix D. Total and Disaggregated Gross Investment, 1900–1994

Estimates for total and disaggregated capital formation are the essential building blocks for the construction of capital stock estimates using the 'perpetual inventory method'. Tables D.1 to D.8 present total and disaggregated gross fixed investment for the 1900–1994 period, in national currencies as well as a percentage of GDP. For all countries a detailed description is given of the sources used for the construction of the series which consist of total capital formation, capital formation in machinery and equipment and capital formation in residential and non-residential structures. For 1950 onwards, if not otherwise specified, the series used for Latin America are derived from currently collected official estimates by ECLAC corresponding to the most recent revision of the United Nations System of National Accounts (SNA).

These official estimates since 1950 apply especially to GDP and in many cases total capital formation estimates. In the case of disaggregated capital formation the official series in Latin America often only start in the 1970s and for residential capital formation sometimes no official estimates were available. As already indicated in Appendix B, for years before 1950, the estimates have nearly all been made retrospectively and the underlying data are less complete. Nevertheless, most of the historical estimates are based upon substantial statistical research by distinguished scholars. But the estimates for the first half of the twentieth century are obviously not as comparable as those for 1950 onwards, and in some cases may well be substantially revised when further research is done. This applies especially for the data before 1925 in the case of disaggregated capital formation.

SOURCES

Argentina[1]

The source for 1900–1950 including GDP, total fixed capital formation and fixed capital formation in machinery and equipment is Banco Central de la República Argentina (1976). Fixed capital formation in residential structures for 1900–1955 is from ECLAC (1958). For 1955–70 fixed capital formation was estimated at 46 per cent of fixed capital formation in non-residential structures, which is the average residential/non-residential structures ratio for 1955 and 1970. From 1970–94, ECLAC estimates based upon official statistics were used, taking into account the following considerations. In 1987 the Central Bank of Argentina, in cooperation with the Buenos Aires office of ECLAC, initiated a project regarding the revision of the national accounts, income distribution and input–output matrix. The final report[2] presented an extensive description of the methodology applied in the elaboration of the new series. The results were the updating of the current and constant series, by sector and expenditure, an estimation of factor shares[3] and a base year change from 1970 to 1986. The increase in the GDP level of 43.2 per cent occurred mainly in the manufacturing and construction sector, and expenditure-wise in fixed capital formation in private construction (114 per cent) and machinery and equipment (64 per cent). Much of the increase was due to improved statistical sources, for example, industrial and household surveys, and better coverage of the informal sector. Afterwards, the Banco Central de la República de Argentina (1993) published new series, based upon the 1991 revision, but once again revised. Expenditure-wise capital formation grew less than in the former revision.

Several problems had to be addressed in order to be able to include these new estimates in our series. Backwards, the revision influenced both the level and the growth of the long-run series. From 1980 onwards only gross total capital formation was presented, so estimates had to be made for fixed capital formation. As it was not reasonable to include all the difference in 1980 I decided, after extensive consultations with Argentine national accounts experts, who had participated in the latest revision and some in previous ones, to distribute half of the increase in GDP and fixed capital formation as a level adjustment for the 1900–1980 period and to treat the other half of the increase as a linear augmentation of the growth rate over the 1961–80 period. The basic argument for this distribution was that the national accounts before 1961 were considered rather reliable and it did not seem reasonable to increase the level of Argentina's GDP for the whole period by the whole of the 35 per cent. For 1980–94 we used the revised GDP estimates.

In order to be able to reach the needed level of disaggregation in capital formation, available in the 1991 revision, but not in the April 1993 revision, the following procedure was applied. The new (1993) revision contained a major change in methodology with respect to the estimation of capital formation in residential construction. I used therefore the unchanged 1991 estimates for machinery and equipment. Also public capital formation was unchanged, assumed to be non-residential, so I had to disaggregate private capital formation in residential and non-residential capital formation. A level increase of private non-residential capital formation of 50 per cent was assumed. This resulted in level increase of 64 per cent in machinery and equipment, 85 per cent in residential and

22 per cent in non-residential capital formation. Half of this level increase was applied to increase the level of the 1900–1980 series and the remainder half consisted of a linear augmentation of the growth rate over the 1961–80 period. For the 1980–94 period capital formation was disaggregated using these growth rates. Comparing the results of disaggregated fixed capital formation series with total capital formation of the new 1993 series and the stock variations estimate available from the old series leads to an upward adjustment of 10 per cent of the components of capital formation and the resulting increase in stocks distribution fitted rather well with the older series, as well as with fluctuations of the economy.

Brazil

Total capital formation for 1900–1925 is calculated as the sum of capital formation in machinery and equipment and capital formation in residential and non-residential construction. For 1925–50 ECLAC (1951) was used to calculate a capital coefficient as the ratio of capital goods and the sum of agricultural and industrial production with an adjustment for differences in base year. The figures for capital formation in machinery and equipment for 1900–1925 are from Villela and Suzigan (1977), table 133, p. 363 using a quantum index of industrial capital goods imports, for 1925–49 from ECLAC (1951), using index of imports of other capital goods; and for 1949–69 from Langoni (1974), based upon an unpublished study of the Getúlio Vargas Foundation (1970). The figures for capital formation in non-residential structures for 1900–1925 are based upon Villela and Suzigan (1977, p. 359), using a combined quantum index of domestic cement consumption and domestic rolled-steel consumption. The figures for capital formation in residential structures for 1900–1920 are from Villela and Suzigan (1977, p. 359), using a quantum index of domestic cement consumption and 1920–85 was based upon IBGE, *Brasil, Censo Demográfico*, 1920, 1940, 1950, 1970, 1980. For the 1985 data the national household survey of IBGE was used. On the basis of the census and household survey information a stock of housing was estimated. Gross investment was calculated on the basis of the yearly increase of the housing stock plus the depreciation. With these data an index of investment in residential structures was calculated with base year 1974. For 1974, Borges and Vasconcellos (1974), estimated capital formation in residential structures at 20 per cent of total capital formation. For 1985–92 capital formation in residential structures was estimated as 39 per cent of capital formation in non-residential structures.

Chile

Total capital formation for 1900–1904 and 1916–19 was estimated at three times capital formation in machinery and equipment, and for 1905–15 it was estimated at two times capital formation in machinery and equipment. Total capital formation for 1920–22 was estimated at 9 per cent of GDP and for 1923–24 at 14 per cent of GDP, for 1925–40 ECLAC (1951) (adjusted for 1925–31 to 2/3) and for 1940–50 ECLAC (1972). Capital formation in machinery and equipment for 1900–1940, using a quantum index of imports of capital goods from ECLAC (1951) (adjusting the 1900–1931 level by 2/3 to avoid extremely high estimates caused by linking problems) and for 1940–50, CORFO (1963). Capital formation in residential structures for 1920–25 was estimated applying the index of total capital formation and for 1925–28 using the 1928 ratio of capital formation in residential structures to total capital formation. For 1928–40 ECLAC (1951) was used; for 1940–54 CORFO (1957); for 1954–60, CORFO (1963); for 1960–75 ODEPLAN (1976). For 1974–82, ECLAC was used, based upon official estimates and for 1982–92 Banco Central de Chile, *Boletín Mensual*, various issues. In the case of Chile a revision of the national accounts for the base year 1986 took place in the early 1990s. The most important results are an increase of capital formation in machinery and equipment and non-residential construction.

Colombia

Total GDP for 1900–1925 is from Maddison (1989) using his benchmarks for 1900, 1913 and 1929, and interpolating the years in between, and for 1925–50 from ECLAC (1972). Total capital formation for 1900–1909 was estimated constant at 10 per cent of GDP, for 1910–24 at 18 per cent of GDP based upon the periodisation and description of McGreevey (1985), and for 1925–50 from ECLAC (1972). Capital formation in machinery and equipment for 1900–1925 was estimated at 33 per cent of total capital formation and for 1925–50 from ECLAC (1957). Capital formation in residential structures from 1900–1925 was estimated at 25 per cent of capital formation in non-residential structures and for 1925–50 from ECLAC (1957). For 1950–70, it was estimated at 28 per cent of capital formation in non-residential structures.

Mexico

Total capital formation for 1900–1910 and for 1920–25 was estimated at 10 per cent of GDP. For the period 1911–20 we have assumed that no capital formation occurred, that is, capital formation in this period was offset by war destruction caused by the Mexican Revolution. For total capital formation from 1925–39, ECLAC (1951) was used to calculate a capital coefficient as the ratio total of available capital goods (see table 6, p. 414) and national production (table 3A, p. 404) and for 1939–60 from Banco de Mexico (1986a). Capital formation in machinery and equipment for 1920–25 was calculated applying the ratio of 1925 and for 1925–39 using ECLAC (1951), based upon imports of other capital goods (see table 6, p. 414). The figures for 1939–50 were from the World Bank (1953), and for 1950–60 from Banco de Mexico (1969). Capital formation in non-residential structures for 1900–1929 were assumed to move as total capital formation, the figures for 1929–70 are from INEGI (1985) using an index of the total housing stock adjusted for the changing weight of brick houses in total housing stock.

Venezuela

Capital formation estimates were based upon Baptista (1991) which is the most complete statistical historical source available on Venezuela's quantitative economic history. Total capital formation was estimated as follows: 1900–1909 at 10 per cent of GDP, with 3.1 per cent in residential and non-residential structures each, and 3.7 per cent in machinery and equipment; 1910–19 at 15 per cent of GDP, with 4.7 per cent in residential and non-residential construction and 5.6 per cent in machinery and equipment on the basis of the growth figures of Baptista (1991) and the description of Venezuela's economic development in Quero Morales (1978) and Brito Figueroa (1966) which both indicate that the period 1900–1909 was one of stagnation and that during 1910–19 foreign investment increased especially in the oil sector (63 per cent of total capital formation in industry came from foreign investment, see Brito Figueroa, 1966, p. 398). Total and disaggregated capital formation from 1920–50 is based upon Baptista (1991, Cuadro IV-1, p. 149). For 1950–76, the figures are from Banco Central de Venezuela (1978, p. 177).

*Table D.1 Latin America: Gross Total Fixed Investment, Six Countries,
1900–1994 (constant 1980 national prices)*

	Argentina (thousand australes)	Brazil (million cruzeiros)	Chile (million pesos)	Colombia (million pesos)	Mexico (million pesos)	Venezuela (million bolívares)
1900	318,869	26,187	12,880	4,706	18,907	255
1901	331,235	26,185	15,224	4,903	20,548	251
1902	327,113	18,491	19,371	5,109	19,082	273
1903	358,362	21,147	19,886	5,324	21,220	295
1904	518,461	23,728	25,760	5,547	21,593	288
1905	801,693	33,675	22,583	5,780	23,836	285
1906	958,601	37,901	36,544	6,022	23,567	266
1907	1,183,723	52,330	41,576	6,275	24,950	265
1908	1,009,662	52,898	43,929	6,539	24,912	284
1909	1,137,848	54,392	29,332	6,813	25,644	294
1910	1,360,311	65,337	27,769	12,778	25,872	455
1911	1,339,833	80,830	44,753	13,314	0	487
1912	1,092,371	107,437	44,186	13,873	0	503
1913	1,107,796	91,538	42,950	14,455	0	581
1914	686,538	39,161	31,976	15,013	0	508
1915	412,216	19,847	14,769	15,593	0	524
1916	364,744	23,348	27,331	16,195	0	494
1917	275,652	20,654	36,965	16,820	0	577
1918	278,046	19,235	26,687	17,469	0	573
1919	325,118	40,112	27,846	18,143	0	536
1920	603,297	61,349	15,403	18,843	27,667	553
1921	697,841	60,666	13,252	19,571	27,854	706
1922	819,245	53,935	14,182	20,326	28,503	645
1923	1,131,731	64,229	26,461	21,111	29,482	888
1924	1,214,307	86,677	28,858	21,926	29,000	1,451
1925	1,222,817	110,147	43,810	23,957	36,952	2,620
1926	1,206,063	93,486	63,010	29,896	31,850	3,682
1927	1,385,310	91,396	42,999	36,085	28,639	3,570
1928	1,646,336	97,380	44,503	42,773	29,346	3,158
1929	1,883,426	113,489	63,470	36,933	32,588	4,061
1930	1,585,833	61,082	64,990	24,057	26,336	3,428
1931	970,568	26,399	31,335	19,814	18,058	1,816
1932	680,687	27,067	16,017	23,408	11,060	1,258
1933	760,471	44,302	19,449	22,909	16,582	2,076
1934	1,007,667	57,348	25,421	23,358	22,414	2,198
1935	991,977	71,106	37,297	26,702	27,697	1,927
1936	1,042,506	78,640	41,416	29,397	28,779	3,067
1937	1,398,474	105,919	46,559	34,138	38,538	3,993
1938	1,540,090	100,927	52,197	34,887	20,890	4,922
1939	1,291,298	91,470	44,559	39,828	27,044	5,089
1940	1,132,795	76,386	50,943	38,281	35,308	4,125
1941	1,135,587	74,721	50,309	36,684	43,072	3,041
1942	1,062,053	52,594	39,951	32,242	37,318	2,677
1943	1,031,470	62,799	42,911	34,188	37,350	2,926
1944	1,185,585	92,065	48,195	37,233	46,994	5,010
1945	1,176,144	99,829	50,943	46,416	67,509	7,211
1946	1,463,631	98,654	70,602	54,851	89,993	9,795

Table D.1 (continued)

	Argentina (thousand australes)	Brazil (million cruzeiros)	Chile (million pesos)	Colombia (million pesos)	Mexico (million pesos)	Venezuela (million bolívares)
1947	2,323,034	235,526	77,578	66,181	101,421	12,845
1948	2,322,236	199,158	68,911	64,733	96,143	15,836
1949	1,950,311	241,019	78,846	49,411	87,604	16,373
1950	1,959,353	310,611	72,716	57,047	100,638	14,502
1951	2,410,316	380,546	82,651	56,636	127,610	15,422
1952	2,145,958	409,003	86,667	61,019	132,307	19,363
1953	2,120,041	345,337	87,513	82,566	127,545	21,260
1954	2,035,378	375,723	84,765	96,108	132,379	24,285
1955	2,361,937	354,019	98,082	101,582	149,319	22,926
1956	2,513,985	381,511	93,431	96,396	173,320	24,854
1957	2,755,881	432,636	106,960	72,276	187,775	26,422
1958	3,002,960	458,199	105,269	68,716	176,758	26,196
1959	2,377,487	517,524	90,683	73,840	179,131	26,951
1960	3,592,148	538,746	117,529	86,970	205,852	20,993
1961	4,188,247	566,238	119,040	94,358	207,555	17,856
1962	3,852,110	583,601	133,646	94,708	218,773	18,643
1963	3,297,120	567,202	153,375	87,135	243,945	19,136
1964	3,695,795	581,189	144,635	98,042	293,610	23,006
1965	3,898,929	566,238	135,895	92,588	315,182	24,694
1966	4,067,647	680,064	140,265	105,406	343,114	25,223
1967	4,312,835	692,604	143,266	114,666	390,132	26,067
1968	4,898,295	842,122	156,816	130,468	427,579	29,799
1969	5,937,388	1,019,131	164,727	142,819	459,119	32,078
1970	6,310,089	1,114,600	175,361	160,105	497,179	31,508
1971	6,891,500	1,285,600	171,294	167,885	488,666	35,347
1972	7,037,744	1,500,600	136,878	164,577	548,467	40,640
1973	6,595,551	1,815,500	128,630	178,890	629,341	44,455
1974	6,931,004	2,056,200	142,438	194,422	679,070	43,356
1975	7,015,796	2,256,400	111,818	186,974	741,988	54,473
1976	7,825,806	2,414,900	95,517	204,759	745,319	69,984
1977	9,557,860	2,386,600	114,088	206,201	695,276	90,249
1978	8,419,729	2,500,000	133,672	225,476	800,774	93,843
1979	9,081,094	2,597,100	153,504	234,059	962,921	75,034
1980	9,619,295	2,947,000	194,537	264,894	1,106,758	64,145
1981	8,197,575	2,589,000	230,491	281,500	1,286,376	66,070
1982	6,571,945	2,413,000	136,520	289,830	1,070,371	63,604
1983	6,595,427	2,019,000	113,958	293,252	767,667	46,850
1984	6,424,684	2,015,000	143,519	296,899	817,006	38,012
1985	5,505,986	2,191,000	161,269	281,398	881,160	40,501
1986	6,135,219	2,687,000	165,168	302,900	777,198	44,087
1987	7,021,012	2,650,000	201,031	305,371	776,246	44,317
1988	6,706,316	2,519,000	229,482	338,568	821,117	48,247
1989	5,234,993	2,549,000	284,174	320,840	873,599	35,944
1990	4,714,846	2,269,000	289,322	310,111	988,265	33,789
1991	5,899,822	2,196,000	283,096	290,968	1,070,379	45,796
1992	7,723,865	1,996,000	356,663	327,096	1,186,485	58,263
1993	8,799,094	2,192,000	419,860	435,544	1,171,780	54,786
1994	10,400,469	2,466,000	434,451	493,906	1,267,019	40,870

Table D.2 Latin America: Gross Fixed Investment in Machinery and Equipment, Six Countries, 1900–1994 (constant 1980 national prices)

	Argentina (thousand australes)	Brazil (million cruzeiros)	Chile (million pesos)	Colombia (million pesos)	Mexico (million pesos)	Venezuela (million bolívares)
1900	30,536	22,791	4,293	1,569	0	95
1901	25,938	22,783	5,075	1,634	0	93
1902	36,094	12,715	6,457	1,703	0	102
1903	48,925	15,242	6,629	1,775	0	110
1904	81,039	16,566	8,587	1,849	0	107
1905	86,803	24,989	11,291	1,927	0	106
1906	120,289	26,513	18,272	2,007	0	99
1907	129,553	37,303	20,788	2,092	0	99
1908	102,105	38,667	21,964	2,180	0	106
1909	119,123	41,274	14,666	2,271	0	109
1910	136,346	47,612	13,884	4,259	0	170
1911	138,611	61,610	22,376	4,438	0	181
1912	162,765	82,348	22,093	4,624	0	188
1913	176,489	61,209	21,475	4,818	0	217
1914	116,996	25,430	15,988	5,004	0	189
1915	87,627	10,108	7,384	5,198	0	195
1916	89,548	12,916	9,110	5,398	0	184
1917	71,021	12,836	12,322	5,606	0	215
1918	62,924	14,801	8,896	5,823	0	213
1919	83,647	25,912	9,282	6,048	0	200
1920	136,072	43,360	7,943	6,281	6,465	257
1921	151,099	50,460	9,376	6,524	6,509	301
1922	135,180	36,702	10,141	6,775	6,660	305
1923	196,114	47,892	13,275	7,037	6,889	399
1924	246,206	60,568	16,108	7,308	6,776	622
1925	288,887	83,912	15,834	8,520	8,635	982
1926	313,796	63,475	22,935	10,350	7,775	1,459
1927	315,854	58,394	15,310	14,375	7,138	1,355
1928	381,454	67,164	15,748	17,511	7,624	1,339
1929	421,116	84,058	22,574	13,904	7,999	1,594
1930	302,954	46,170	22,995	5,907	6,569	1,442
1931	201,397	16,603	10,871	3,189	4,327	767
1932	130,033	16,021	2,769	2,980	2,134	546
1933	144,855	24,695	2,718	4,025	2,855	808
1934	176,420	31,484	5,152	5,645	3,892	920
1935	226,855	46,974	9,943	5,698	5,043	931
1936	242,020	45,771	11,888	7,318	5,430	1,327
1937	348,242	64,646	12,880	9,775	6,557	1,918
1938	384,062	66,708	14,219	10,350	3,772	2,273
1939	279,692	49,694	11,515	10,820	4,774	2,502
1940	248,539	34,047	13,292	8,207	5,857	2,159
1941	229,874	36,742	12,837	7,684	7,198	1,620
1942	185,752	23,569	10,427	2,875	4,051	1,243
1943	158,991	29,846	10,722	2,718	4,314	1,073
1944	160,432	45,676	9,333	4,652	6,429	2,040
1945	164,274	50,219	11,042	11,604	13,799	3,231
1946	276,467	83,577	16,280	17,668	16,625	4,349

Table D.2 (continued)

	Argentina (thousand australes)	Brazil (million cruzeiros)	Chile (million pesos)	Colombia (million pesos)	Mexico (million pesos)	Venezuela (million bolívares)
1947	706,091	135,416	23,510	26,084	19,442	6,610
1948	575,509	115,934	21,727	20,857	19,376	8,543
1949	343,096	137,460	25,772	17,041	16,686	7,900
1950	324,912	151,929	23,731	22,582	18,097	6,619
1951	500,381	216,559	28,404	24,914	23,958	5,319
1952	436,574	212,701	29,510	26,769	23,153	8,538
1953	413,066	123,955	26,436	40,712	24,964	9,698
1954	392,077	164,469	23,362	44,670	24,293	11,451
1955	528,087	137,460	29,264	47,002	28,104	9,964
1956	591,894	147,106	34,183	42,388	31,765	9,573
1957	646,465	180,868	45,495	23,698	35,128	11,496
1958	662,417	182,797	45,618	22,779	32,136	11,767
1959	533,124	220,418	31,847	22,631	33,545	12,832
1960	1,012,516	211,254	40,085	34,488	36,919	8,327
1961	1,268,583	219,936	48,663	36,853	82,823	7,559
1962	1,176,214	228,135	46,142	34,981	87,299	8,819
1963	945,815	224,759	40,552	32,534	97,344	8,422
1964	1,086,203	227,170	44,323	39,152	117,162	9,588
1965	1,154,111	215,595	38,676	34,603	125,771	9,753
1966	1,186,988	286,013	47,868	41,186	136,917	9,768
1967	1,231,262	279,260	49,971	36,872	155,679	9,211
1968	1,364,647	345,337	57,137	44,487	170,622	10,361
1969	1,646,348	419,614	56,165	49,613	183,207	11,789
1970	1,735,159	463,500	59,310	63,371	198,395	11,409
1971	1,923,174	553,100	53,699	70,195	194,684	13,187
1972	2,062,034	637,000	41,246	69,333	219,624	15,054
1973	2,047,341	771,400	46,019	68,846	256,874	16,758
1974	2,052,797	917,100	43,211	76,039	284,541	17,360
1975	1,945,225	1,025,000	43,908	75,803	317,039	23,342
1976	2,068,574	1,058,300	38,572	87,087	305,320	30,359
1977	2,941,236	959,000	53,283	83,915	268,912	41,256
1978	2,276,889	983,800	64,994	98,764	317,253	41,296
1979	2,737,406	1,024,600	74,369	108,925	412,392	29,022
1980	3,096,194	1,120,700	90,001	121,830	485,720	25,918
1981	3,367,910	874,000	104,663	127,728	579,675	28,749
1982	2,403,583	739,100	56,844	130,322	409,180	29,043
1983	2,701,008	587,000	38,991	127,494	255,205	19,018
1984	2,898,643	600,000	44,901	124,717	284,491	18,187
1985	2,390,729	692,000	51,859	102,791	329,424	22,360
1986	2,713,125	920,000	50,095	113,742	280,329	24,977
1987	3,111,747	870,000	68,508	133,176	269,902	24,617
1988	2,902,700	794,000	82,679	144,646	321,096	27,418
1989	2,385,729	772,000	108,575	142,875	357,709	20,245
1990	2,220,375	665,000	108,706	146,864	434,832	15,086
1991	2,313,505	646,000	101,549	129,709	499,674	21,565
1992	3,028,884	549,000	141,891	153,420	574,165	26,895
1993	3,450,630	674,000	172,223	204,286	540,104	23,347
1994	4,078,701	876,200	180,663	231,660	584,002	17,417

Table D.3 Latin America: Gross Fixed Investment in Residential Structures, Six
Countries, 1900–1994 (constant 1980 national prices)

	Argentina (thousand australes)	Brazil (million cruzeiros)	Chile (million pesos)	Colombia (million pesos)	Mexico (million pesos)	Venezuela (million bolivares)
1900	247,063	1,459	2,582	784	1,891	80
1901	245,226	1,460	4,364	817	2,055	79
1902	225,012	2,301	5,553	852	1,908	86
1903	218,478	2,497	5,701	887	2,122	93
1904	238,284	3,678	7,384	925	2,159	90
1905	384,480	5,071	4,855	963	2,384	89
1906	485,143	7,055	7,857	1,004	2,357	83
1907	694,024	7,016	8,939	1,046	2,495	83
1908	677,485	7,744	9,445	1,090	2,491	89
1909	672,380	7,897	6,306	1,136	2,564	92
1910	856,351	10,339	5,970	2,130	2,587	143
1911	849,612	10,515	9,622	2,219	0	153
1912	652,574	14,361	9,500	2,312	0	158
1913	654,004	18,208	9,234	2,409	0	182
1914	287,900	7,075	6,875	2,502	0	159
1915	147,626	5,670	3,175	2,599	0	164
1916	124,144	6,645	7,835	2,699	0	155
1917	98,009	3,858	10,597	2,803	0	181
1918	120,877	2,023	7,650	2,911	0	180
1919	142,113	7,764	7,983	3,024	0	168
1920	306,277	6,770	3,208	3,141	2,949	144
1921	352,219	6,140	1,667	3,262	2,248	152
1922	469,216	12,507	1,738	3,388	2,648	153
1923	706,479	8,742	5,670	3,518	2,761	173
1924	677,893	12,413	5,482	3,654	3,137	187
1925	621,334	16,460	12,021	2,304	2,990	219
1926	517,404	17,937	17,289	3,213	2,898	245
1927	576,822	19,224	11,798	4,142	3,377	273
1928	676,668	18,971	12,211	5,531	3,086	329
1929	845,325	19,283	13,680	6,078	2,994	363
1930	752,829	10,000	10,603	4,311	3,276	389
1931	506,378	6,000	4,700	3,930	3,586	325
1932	356,915	7,000	6,057	4,924	3,924	324
1933	341,805	14,000	7,894	6,205	4,295	335
1934	442,877	21,350	14,145	5,574	4,701	361
1935	338,538	21,579	15,135	6,380	5,145	403
1936	293,413	24,677	13,073	6,667	5,630	402
1937	402,652	27,720	15,645	8,311	6,162	458
1938	434,301	26,615	14,339	8,118	6,744	482
1939	456,761	29,505	18,247	10,526	7,900	516
1940	410,615	30,543	20,819	10,450	6,874	516
1941	490,452	27,678	20,598	9,673	7,579	520
1942	541,702	25,944	18,137	10,008	8,356	453
1943	574,576	27,725	22,110	10,634	9,212	486
1944	646,244	32,109	25,391	9,763	10,156	578
1945	636,239	33,757	19,748	9,984	11,197	684
1946	704,029	10,000	35,156	10,955	12,345	789

Table D.3 (continued)

	Argentina (thousand australes)	Brazil (million cruzeiros)	Chile (million pesos)	Colombia (million pesos)	Mexico (million pesos)	Venezuela (million bolivares)
1947	737,515	49,076	27,145	12,915	13,610	937
1948	811,838	45,375	25,065	14,568	15,005	1,021
1949	799,996	51,788	24,013	12,754	16,543	1,072
1950	908,213	67,656	26,099	13,786	18,238	1,164
1951	917,606	75,056	25,360	12,689	18,765	2,499
1952	908,213	85,378	26,118	13,700	20,535	2,844
1953	838,382	93,821	30,735	16,741	22,472	3,952
1954	883,711	92,815	34,339	20,575	24,592	3,225
1955	958,647	96,078	39,318	21,832	26,911	3,246
1956	1,005,567	102,830	25,868	21,603	29,449	4,045
1957	1,103,504	109,549	19,982	19,431	32,227	3,473
1958	1,223,282	118,070	18,629	18,375	35,266	5,003
1959	964,184	126,177	25,627	20,484	38,592	2,927
1960	1,354,067	136,749	32,577	20,993	42,232	2,818
1961	1,535,081	144,307	27,637	17,252	48,764	2,231
1962	1,413,104	149,380	38,058	17,918	53,670	3,122
1963	1,244,965	148,578	45,469	16,380	59,070	3,462
1964	1,388,293	154,576	37,209	17,667	65,014	4,539
1965	1,466,593	156,673	39,525	17,396	71,555	5,384
1966	1,545,005	171,591	40,760	19,266	78,755	5,755
1967	1,658,669	180,143	38,444	23,338	86,680	5,585
1968	1,908,657	206,233	44,157	25,794	95,401	5,961
1969	2,327,030	237,727	50,101	27,962	105,000	5,946
1970	2,692,252	255,560	49,020	29,921	115,565	6,519
1971	2,685,340	285,914	56,740	29,120	142,727	7,940
1972	2,560,080	326,220	47,554	26,229	148,696	9,495
1973	2,419,476	380,166	39,448	34,477	152,304	10,633
1974	2,740,898	411,240	45,006	34,117	149,498	9,839
1975	3,479,417	441,877	33,752	29,369	175,814	10,814
1976	3,355,967	481,732	27,229	31,344	194,237	13,032
1977	3,012,400	507,238	27,498	35,083	186,692	14,332
1978	3,054,126	537,855	23,545	40,724	173,841	15,600
1979	3,361,661	560,090	32,061	36,469	190,016	16,655
1980	3,472,979	636,185	45,414	35,695	198,510	15,243
1981	3,047,975	613,828	43,103	37,981	214,240	12,582
1982	2,580,584	610,906	27,705	39,328	217,557	9,090
1983	2,383,802	554,065	22,662	47,064	204,734	6,748
1984	2,452,109	558,594	22,246	47,405	215,051	4,983
1985	2,242,132	590,972	29,813	49,129	232,479	4,591
1986	2,469,233	689,130	35,410	52,712	228,704	4,664
1987	2,827,810	694,200	40,236	57,066	238,828	4,665
1988	2,757,813	672,750	47,921	55,273	235,924	4,390
1989	2,071,202	693,030	58,088	55,273	262,825	3,465
1990	1,817,076	625,560	58,907	51,299	319,491	2,234
1991	2,618,598	604,500	66,032	60,319	367,133	2,422
1992	3,436,159	564,330	79,462	71,182	421,865	3,225
1993	3,923,568	592,020	93,541	94,782	396,839	3,159
1994	4,648,330	620,022	96,792	107,482	429,093	2,357

Table D.4 Latin America: Gross Fixed Investment in Non-Residential Structures,
Six Countries, 1900–1994 (constant 1980 national prices)

	Argentina (thousand australes)	Brazil (million cruzeiros)	Chile (million pesos)	Colombia (million pesos)	Mexico (million pesos)	Venezuela (million bolivares)
1900	41,270	1,938	6,005	2,353	0	80
1901	60,071	1,942	5,785	2,452	0	79
1902	66,008	3,475	7,361	2,555	0	86
1903	90,958	3,408	7,557	2,662	0	93
1904	199,138	3,484	9,789	2,774	0	90
1905	330,410	3,615	6,436	2,890	0	89
1906	353,168	4,333	10,415	3,011	0	83
1907	360,147	8,010	11,849	3,138	0	83
1908	230,072	6,487	12,520	3,269	0	89
1909	346,345	5,221	8,359	3,407	0	92
1910	367,614	7,386	7,914	6,389	0	143
1911	351,610	8,705	12,755	6,657	0	153
1912	277,032	10,728	12,593	6,937	0	158
1913	277,304	12,121	12,241	7,228	0	182
1914	281,642	6,655	9,113	7,507	0	159
1915	176,963	4,069	4,209	7,796	0	164
1916	151,052	3,787	10,386	8,097	0	155
1917	106,623	3,960	14,047	8,410	0	181
1918	94,245	2,411	10,141	8,734	0	180
1919	99,359	6,436	10,582	9,072	0	168
1920	160,948	11,219	4,252	9,422	18,253	151
1921	194,523	4,067	2,209	9,785	19,097	254
1922	214,849	4,727	2,304	10,163	19,194	187
1923	229,138	7,594	7,516	10,555	19,832	316
1924	290,208	13,697	7,267	10,963	19,086	642
1925	312,597	9,775	15,956	13,132	25,328	1,420
1926	374,863	12,073	22,786	16,333	21,177	1,979
1927	492,634	13,777	15,891	17,569	18,124	1,942
1928	588,213	11,246	16,545	19,730	18,636	1,491
1929	616,985	10,148	27,216	16,951	21,596	2,104
1930	530,050	4,911	31,391	13,839	16,491	1,597
1931	262,793	3,796	15,765	12,696	10,144	723
1932	193,739	4,046	7,191	15,505	5,002	388
1933	273,811	5,606	8,838	12,679	9,432	933
1934	388,371	4,513	6,125	12,139	13,821	917
1935	426,583	2,553	12,219	14,625	17,510	592
1936	507,073	8,192	16,454	15,412	17,719	1,338
1937	647,580	13,553	18,035	16,052	25,819	1,616
1938	721,728	7,604	23,639	16,419	10,374	2,167
1939	554,845	12,270	14,798	18,482	14,370	2,071
1940	473,641	11,796	16,832	19,624	22,576	1,451
1941	415,261	10,301	16,874	19,327	28,295	902
1942	334,599	3,082	11,387	19,359	24,911	982
1943	297,903	5,228	10,079	20,836	23,823	1,367
1944	378,909	14,279	13,472	22,818	30,408	2,392
1945	375,630	15,853	20,154	24,828	42,513	3,296
1946	483,136	5,077	19,166	26,229	61,024	4,657

Table D.4 (continued)

	Argentina (thousand australes)	Brazil (million cruzeiros)	Chile (million pesos)	Colombia (million pesos)	Mexico (million pesos)	Venezuela (million bolivares)
1947	879,427	51,034	26,923	27,182	68,369	5,298
1948	934,889	37,848	22,119	29,308	61,762	6,272
1949	807,220	51,771	29,061	19,616	54,376	7,401
1950	726,228	91,026	22,886	20,679	64,303	6,718
1951	992,329	88,931	28,887	19,033	84,887	7,604
1952	801,171	110,924	31,039	20,550	88,618	7,980
1953	868,593	127,562	30,342	25,112	80,109	7,610
1954	759,589	118,438	27,063	30,862	83,495	9,609
1955	875,203	120,481	29,499	32,748	94,304	9,715
1956	916,524	131,575	33,381	32,405	112,107	11,237
1957	1,005,911	142,219	41,483	29,147	120,420	11,453
1958	1,117,260	157,332	41,022	27,562	109,356	9,425
1959	880,179	170,929	33,210	30,726	106,995	11,192
1960	1,225,565	190,742	44,867	31,489	126,702	9,848
1961	1,384,583	201,995	42,741	40,254	75,969	8,067
1962	1,262,792	206,086	49,446	41,809	77,804	6,701
1963	1,106,340	193,865	67,353	38,221	87,531	7,251
1964	1,221,299	199,443	63,102	41,223	111,434	8,879
1965	1,278,225	193,970	57,694	40,590	117,856	9,556
1966	1,335,654	222,460	51,636	44,954	127,442	9,699
1967	1,422,904	233,201	54,851	54,456	147,774	11,271
1968	1,624,991	290,551	55,522	60,187	161,557	13,477
1969	1,964,011	361,790	58,461	65,244	170,911	14,343
1970	1,882,678	395,540	67,030	66,814	183,219	13,580
1971	2,282,986	446,586	60,855	68,569	151,256	14,220
1972	2,415,629	537,380	48,078	69,016	180,147	16,090
1973	2,128,734	663,934	43,163	75,567	220,163	17,065
1974	2,137,309	727,860	54,221	84,266	245,031	16,157
1975	1,591,154	789,523	34,158	81,802	249,136	20,317
1976	2,401,265	874,868	29,715	86,328	245,762	26,593
1977	3,604,225	920,362	33,307	87,203	239,672	34,662
1978	3,088,715	978,345	45,134	85,988	309,680	36,947
1979	2,982,027	1,012,410	47,073	88,665	360,512	29,358
1980	3,050,122	1,190,115	59,122	107,369	422,528	22,984
1981	1,781,690	1,101,172	82,724	115,791	492,461	24,738
1982	1,587,778	1,062,994	51,972	120,181	443,634	25,471
1983	1,510,616	877,935	52,306	118,694	307,728	21,083
1984	1,073,932	856,406	76,371	124,778	317,464	14,842
1985	873,125	908,028	79,597	129,479	319,257	13,550
1986	952,861	1,077,870	79,663	136,447	268,165	14,445
1987	1,081,455	1,085,800	92,287	115,128	267,516	15,036
1988	1,045,803	1,052,250	98,882	138,649	264,097	16,440
1989	778,062	1,083,970	117,512	122,692	253,065	12,234
1990	677,396	978,440	121,709	111,948	233,942	16,469
1991	967,719	945,500	115,515	100,940	203,572	21,809
1992	1,258,822	882,670	135,311	102,495	190,455	28,143
1993	1,424,896	925,980	154,096	136,477	234,837	28,279
1994	1,673,438	969,778	156,997	154,764	253,924	21,096

Table D.5 Latin America: Gross Total Fixed Investment, Six Countries, 1900–1994 (as percentage of GDP at constant 1980 national currencies)

	Argentina	Brazil	Chile	Colombia	Mexico	Venezuela
1900	16.6	16.2	13.6	10.0	10.1	10.0
1901	15.9	14.5	15.5	10.0	10.1	10.0
1902	16.1	9.6	19.1	10.0	10.1	10.0
1903	15.4	10.9	18.9	10.0	10.1	10.0
1904	20.1	12.1	23.7	10.0	10.1	10.0
1905	27.5	16.8	20.1	10.0	10.1	10.0
1906	31.3	18.1	31.5	10.0	10.1	10.0
1907	37.8	22.0	34.7	10.0	10.1	10.0
1908	29.4	24.7	35.4	10.0	10.1	10.0
1909	31.5	22.9	23.3	10.0	10.1	10.0
1910	35.2	25.7	20.4	18.0	10.1	15.0
1911	34.0	31.7	33.1	18.0	0.0	15.0
1912	25.6	38.1	29.4	18.0	0.0	15.0
1913	25.7	31.9	28.3	18.0	0.0	15.0
1914	17.8	13.5	22.6	18.0	0.0	15.0
1915	10.6	6.9	11.2	18.0	0.0	15.0
1916	9.7	7.8	17.5	18.0	0.0	15.0
1917	8.0	6.5	21.9	18.0	0.0	15.0
1918	6.8	6.0	15.8	18.0	0.0	15.0
1919	7.7	11.8	20.9	18.0	0.0	15.0
1920	13.2	16.3	10.1	18.0	10.1	12.9
1921	14.9	15.9	10.1	18.0	10.1	15.8
1922	16.2	12.7	10.1	18.0	10.1	14.1
1923	20.2	14.0	15.2	18.0	10.1	16.8
1924	20.1	18.8	15.2	18.0	10.1	23.7
1925	20.3	23.5	22.7	18.9	12.1	33.1
1926	19.1	19.6	33.6	21.6	9.9	38.4
1927	20.5	17.5	23.9	23.9	9.3	33.2
1928	23.0	16.3	20.4	26.4	9.4	26.2
1929	25.1	19.1	26.5	22.0	10.9	29.8
1930	22.1	10.7	28.8	14.4	9.4	24.7
1931	14.5	4.8	18.5	12.1	6.2	16.2
1932	10.5	4.8	9.5	13.4	4.5	11.7
1933	11.2	6.9	9.8	12.4	6.1	17.7
1934	13.8	8.2	11.2	11.9	7.7	17.5
1935	13.0	9.8	16.2	13.3	8.8	14.3
1936	13.6	9.6	17.3	13.9	8.5	20.7
1937	17.0	12.5	18.1	15.9	11.0	23.5
1938	18.6	11.3	20.6	15.4	5.9	26.8
1939	15.0	9.9	17.1	16.4	7.2	26.2
1940	13.0	8.2	18.7	15.4	9.3	22.1
1941	12.4	7.4	18.5	14.5	10.3	16.5
1942	11.4	5.5	13.9	12.7	8.5	16.6
1943	11.2	6.1	14.3	13.5	8.2	16.7
1944	11.6	8.5	15.9	13.7	9.5	23.1
1945	11.8	9.0	15.4	16.4	13.2	27.4
1946	13.5	7.9	20.1	17.7	16.6	31.0
1947	19.3	18.1	23.6	20.6	18.0	34.0
1948	18.3	14.0	18.8	19.5	16.4	37.7

Table D.5 (continued)

	Argentina	Brazil	Chile	Colombia	Mexico	Venezuela
1949	15.6	15.6	21.7	14.1	14.2	36.7
1950	15.5	18.8	19.1	16.0	14.8	31.8
1951	18.3	21.7	20.8	15.4	17.5	30.2
1952	17.2	21.6	20.6	15.6	17.6	35.4
1953	16.1	17.7	19.8	19.9	16.1	36.6
1954	14.9	17.3	19.1	21.7	15.8	38.1
1955	16.1	15.5	22.1	22.1	16.6	33.1
1956	16.7	16.1	20.9	20.1	18.3	32.4
1957	17.4	16.9	21.7	14.8	18.4	30.9
1958	17.8	16.7	20.8	13.7	16.6	30.2
1959	15.1	17.9	18.0	13.7	16.1	28.8
1960	21.2	17.0	21.9	15.5	17.2	22.1
1961	23.0	16.1	21.1	16.0	16.5	17.9
1962	21.4	15.9	22.7	15.2	16.6	17.2
1963	18.6	15.2	24.5	13.6	17.2	16.5
1964	18.8	15.0	22.6	14.4	18.5	18.0
1965	18.0	14.2	21.0	13.1	18.7	18.3
1966	18.5	16.5	19.5	14.2	19.0	18.3
1967	19.0	16.0	19.3	14.8	20.3	18.1
1968	20.5	17.5	20.4	15.9	20.6	19.7
1969	22.7	19.3	20.7	16.4	20.8	20.4
1970	22.8	20.6	21.6	17.3	21.1	18.6
1971	23.8	21.3	19.3	17.2	19.9	20.2
1972	23.6	22.2	15.6	15.6	20.6	22.5
1973	21.2	23.6	15.0	15.9	21.8	23.2
1974	21.0	24.7	16.4	16.4	22.1	21.3
1975	21.2	25.8	14.9	15.4	22.9	25.2
1976	23.5	25.0	12.3	16.1	22.1	29.8
1977	26.7	23.6	13.6	15.5	19.9	36.0
1978	24.2	23.5	14.8	15.7	21.2	36.7
1979	24.2	22.9	15.8	15.4	23.3	28.9
1980	25.1	23.6	18.6	16.8	24.8	25.2
1981	22.6	21.6	20.7	17.4	26.5	26.1
1982	18.7	20.0	14.2	17.8	22.2	24.9
1983	18.1	17.2	12.2	17.7	16.6	19.5
1984	17.4	16.3	14.5	17.3	17.0	16.0
1985	15.9	16.4	15.8	15.9	17.9	17.0
1986	16.5	18.8	15.3	16.2	16.4	17.4
1987	18.4	17.9	17.5	15.5	16.1	16.9
1988	18.0	17.0	18.6	16.5	16.8	17.4
1989	14.9	16.7	21.0	15.2	17.3	14.1
1990	13.5	15.5	20.7	14.0	18.7	12.5
1991	15.5	15.0	18.9	12.9	19.6	15.4
1992	18.6	13.7	21.4	14.0	21.1	18.5
1993	20.0	14.5	23.7	17.6	20.7	17.5
1994	22.1	15.4	23.5	18.9	21.7	13.5

Table D.6 Latin America: Gross Fixed Investment in Machinery and Equipment, Six Countries, 1900–1994 (as percentage of GDP at constant 1980 national currencies)

	Argentina	Brazil	Chile	Colombia	Mexico	Venezuela
1900	1.6	14.1	4.5	3.3	0.0	3.7
1901	1.2	12.6	5.2	3.3	0.0	3.7
1902	1.8	6.6	6.4	3.3	0.0	3.7
1903	2.1	7.8	6.3	3.3	0.0	3.7
1904	3.1	8.5	7.9	3.3	0.0	3.7
1905	3.0	12.5	10.1	3.3	0.0	3.7
1906	3.9	12.7	15.8	3.3	0.0	3.7
1907	4.1	15.7	17.3	3.3	0.0	3.7
1908	3.0	18.0	17.7	3.3	0.0	3.7
1909	3.3	17.4	11.6	3.3	0.0	3.7
1910	3.5	18.7	10.2	6.0	0.0	5.6
1911	3.5	24.2	16.6	6.0	0.0	5.6
1912	3.8	29.2	14.7	6.0	0.0	5.6
1913	4.1	21.3	14.1	6.0	0.0	5.6
1914	3.0	8.8	11.3	6.0	0.0	5.6
1915	2.3	3.5	5.6	6.0	0.0	5.6
1916	2.4	4.3	5.8	6.0	0.0	5.6
1917	2.1	4.1	7.3	6.0	0.0	5.6
1918	1.5	4.6	5.3	6.0	0.0	5.6
1919	2.0	7.6	7.0	6.0	0.0	5.6
1920	3.0	11.5	5.2	6.0	2.4	6.0
1921	3.2	13.2	7.1	6.0	2.4	6.7
1922	2.7	8.7	7.2	6.0	2.4	6.6
1923	3.5	10.4	7.6	6.0	2.4	7.6
1924	4.1	13.1	8.5	6.0	2.4	10.1
1925	4.8	17.9	8.2	6.7	2.8	12.4
1926	5.0	13.3	12.2	7.5	2.4	15.2
1927	4.7	11.2	8.5	9.5	2.3	12.6
1928	5.3	11.3	7.2	10.8	2.5	11.1
1929	5.6	14.1	9.4	8.3	2.7	11.7
1930	4.2	8.1	10.2	3.5	2.3	10.4
1931	3.0	3.0	6.4	1.9	1.5	6.8
1932	2.0	2.8	1.7	1.7	0.9	5.1
1933	2.1	3.9	1.4	2.2	1.0	6.9
1934	2.4	4.5	2.3	2.9	1.3	7.3
1935	3.0	6.5	4.3	2.8	1.6	6.9
1936	3.1	5.6	5.0	3.5	1.6	9.0
1937	4.2	7.6	5.0	4.5	1.9	11.3
1938	4.6	7.5	5.6	4.6	1.1	12.4
1939	3.3	5.4	4.4	4.5	1.3	12.9
1940	2.8	3.6	4.9	3.3	1.5	11.5
1941	2.5	3.6	4.7	3.0	1.7	8.8
1942	2.0	2.5	3.6	1.1	0.9	7.7
1943	1.7	2.9	3.6	1.1	0.9	6.1
1944	1.6	4.2	3.1	1.7	1.3	9.4
1945	1.7	4.5	3.3	4.1	2.7	12.3
1946	2.6	6.7	4.6	5.7	3.1	13.8

Table D.6 (continued)

	Argentina	Brazil	Chile	Colombia	Mexico	Venezuela
1947	5.9	10.4	7.2	8.1	3.5	17.5
1948	4.5	8.2	5.9	6.3	3.3	20.3
1949	2.7	8.9	7.1	4.9	2.7	17.7
1950	2.6	9.2	6.2	6.3	2.7	14.5
1951	3.8	12.3	7.1	6.8	3.3	10.4
1952	3.5	11.2	7.0	6.9	3.1	15.6
1953	3.1	6.3	6.0	9.8	3.2	16.7
1954	2.9	7.6	5.3	10.1	2.9	18.0
1955	3.6	6.0	6.6	10.2	3.1	14.4
1956	3.9	6.2	7.7	8.8	3.3	12.5
1957	4.1	7.1	9.2	4.8	3.4	13.4
1958	3.9	6.6	9.0	4.5	3.0	13.6
1959	3.4	7.6	6.3	4.2	3.0	13.7
1960	6.0	6.6	7.5	6.1	3.1	8.8
1961	7.0	6.3	8.6	6.3	6.6	7.6
1962	6.5	6.2	7.8	5.6	6.6	8.1
1963	5.3	6.0	6.5	5.1	6.9	7.2
1964	5.5	5.9	6.9	5.7	7.4	7.5
1965	5.3	5.4	6.0	4.9	7.4	7.2
1966	5.4	6.9	6.7	5.5	7.6	7.1
1967	5.4	6.5	6.7	4.8	8.1	6.4
1968	5.7	7.2	7.4	5.4	8.2	6.8
1969	6.3	7.9	7.0	5.7	8.3	7.5
1970	6.3	8.6	7.3	6.9	8.4	6.7
1971	6.6	9.2	6.1	7.2	7.9	7.5
1972	6.9	9.4	4.7	6.6	8.2	8.3
1973	6.6	10.0	5.4	6.1	8.9	8.7
1974	6.2	11.0	5.0	6.4	9.3	8.5
1975	5.9	11.7	5.8	6.2	9.8	10.8
1976	6.2	11.0	5.0	6.8	9.0	12.9
1977	8.2	9.5	6.3	6.3	7.7	16.5
1978	6.5	9.3	7.2	6.9	8.4	16.1
1979	7.3	9.0	7.7	7.2	10.0	11.2
1980	8.1	9.0	8.6	7.7	10.9	10.2
1981	9.3	7.3	9.4	7.9	11.9	11.3
1982	6.9	6.1	5.9	8.0	8.5	11.4
1983	7.4	5.0	4.2	7.7	5.5	7.9
1984	7.8	4.9	4.5	7.3	5.9	7.7
1985	6.9	5.2	5.1	5.8	6.7	9.4
1986	7.3	6.4	4.6	6.1	5.9	9.9
1987	8.2	5.9	6.0	6.8	5.6	9.4
1988	7.8	5.4	6.7	7.1	6.6	9.9
1989	6.8	5.0	8.0	6.7	7.1	8.0
1990	6.3	4.6	7.8	6.7	8.2	5.6
1991	6.1	4.4	6.8	5.8	9.1	7.3
1992	7.3	3.8	8.5	6.5	10.2	8.5
1993	7.8	4.5	9.7	8.3	9.6	7.4
1994	8.7	5.5	9.8	8.9	10.0	5.7

Table D.7 Latin America: Gross Fixed Investment in Residential Structures, Six Countries, 1900–1994 (as percentage of GDP at constant 1980 national currencies)

	Argentina	Brazil	Chile	Colombia	Mexico	Venezuela
1900	12.9	0.9	2.7	1.7	1.0	3.1
1901	11.8	0.8	4.4	1.7	1.0	3.1
1902	11.0	1.2	5.5	1.7	1.0	3.1
1903	9.4	1.3	5.4	1.7	1.0	3.1
1904	9.2	1.9	6.8	1.7	1.0	3.1
1905	13.2	2.5	4.3	1.7	1.0	3.1
1906	15.8	3.4	6.8	1.7	1.0	3.1
1907	22.2	2.9	7.5	1.7	1.0	3.1
1908	19.7	3.6	7.6	1.7	1.0	3.1
1909	18.6	3.3	5.0	1.7	1.0	3.1
1910	22.1	4.1	4.4	3.0	1.0	4.7
1911	21.6	4.1	7.1	3.0	0.0	4.7
1912	15.3	5.1	6.3	3.0	0.0	4.7
1913	15.2	6.3	6.1	3.0	0.0	4.7
1914	7.5	2.4	4.9	3.0	0.0	4.7
1915	3.8	2.0	2.4	3.0	0.0	4.7
1916	3.3	2.2	5.0	3.0	0.0	4.7
1917	2.8	1.2	6.3	3.0	0.0	4.7
1918	3.0	0.6	4.5	3.0	0.0	4.7
1919	3.3	2.3	6.0	3.0	0.0	4.7
1920	6.7	1.8	2.1	3.0	1.1	3.4
1921	7.5	1.6	1.3	3.0	0.8	3.4
1922	9.3	3.0	1.2	3.0	0.9	3.3
1923	12.6	1.9	3.2	3.0	0.9	3.3
1924	11.2	2.7	2.9	3.0	1.1	3.1
1925	10.3	3.5	6.2	1.8	1.0	2.8
1926	8.2	3.8	9.2	2.3	0.9	2.6
1927	8.5	3.7	6.5	2.7	1.1	2.5
1928	9.4	3.2	5.6	3.4	1.0	2.7
1929	11.3	3.2	5.7	3.6	1.0	2.7
1930	10.5	1.8	4.7	2.6	1.2	2.8
1931	7.6	1.1	2.8	2.4	1.2	2.9
1932	5.5	1.2	3.6	2.8	1.6	3.0
1933	5.0	2.2	4.0	3.4	1.6	2.9
1934	6.1	3.1	6.3	2.8	1.6	2.9
1935	4.4	3.0	6.6	3.2	1.6	3.0
1936	3.8	3.0	5.5	3.2	1.7	2.7
1937	4.9	3.3	6.1	3.9	1.8	2.7
1938	5.2	3.0	5.7	3.6	1.9	2.6
1939	5.3	3.2	7.0	4.3	2.1	2.7
1940	4.7	3.3	7.7	4.2	1.8	2.8
1941	5.3	2.7	7.6	3.8	1.8	2.8
1942	5.8	2.7	6.3	4.0	1.9	2.8
1943	6.2	2.7	7.4	4.2	2.0	2.8
1944	6.3	3.0	8.4	3.6	2.1	2.7
1945	6.4	3.0	6.0	3.5	2.2	2.6
1946	6.5	0.8	10.0	3.5	2.3	2.5

Table D.7 (continued)

	Argentina	Brazil	Chile	Colombia	Mexico	Venezuela
1947	6.1	3.8	8.3	4.0	2.4	2.5
1948	6.4	3.2	6.8	4.4	2.6	2.4
1949	6.4	3.4	6.6	3.6	2.7	2.4
1950	7.2	4.1	6.8	3.9	2.7	2.6
1951	7.0	4.3	6.4	3.5	2.6	4.9
1952	7.3	4.5	6.2	3.5	2.7	5.2
1953	6.4	4.8	6.9	4.0	2.8	6.8
1954	6.4	4.3	7.7	4.6	2.9	5.1
1955	6.5	4.2	8.9	4.7	3.0	4.7
1956	6.7	4.3	5.8	4.5	3.1	5.3
1957	7.0	4.3	4.0	4.0	3.2	4.1
1958	7.3	4.3	3.7	3.7	3.3	5.8
1959	6.1	4.4	5.1	3.8	3.5	3.1
1960	8.0	4.3	6.1	3.7	3.5	3.0
1961	8.4	4.1	4.9	2.9	3.9	2.2
1962	7.8	4.1	6.5	2.9	4.1	2.9
1963	7.0	4.0	7.3	2.6	4.2	3.0
1964	7.0	4.0	5.8	2.6	4.1	3.6
1965	6.8	3.9	6.1	2.5	4.2	4.0
1966	7.0	4.2	5.7	2.6	4.4	4.2
1967	7.3	4.2	5.2	3.0	4.5	3.9
1968	8.0	4.3	5.7	3.1	4.6	3.9
1969	8.9	4.5	6.3	3.2	4.8	3.8
1970	9.7	4.7	6.0	3.2	4.9	3.8
1971	9.3	4.7	6.4	3.0	5.8	4.5
1972	8.6	4.8	5.4	2.5	5.6	5.3
1973	7.8	4.9	4.6	3.1	5.3	5.5
1974	8.3	4.9	5.2	2.9	4.9	4.8
1975	10.5	5.0	4.5	2.4	5.4	5.0
1976	10.1	5.0	3.5	2.5	5.8	5.6
1977	8.4	5.0	3.3	2.6	5.3	5.7
1978	8.8	5.1	2.6	2.8	4.6	6.1
1979	8.9	4.9	3.3	2.4	4.6	6.4
1980	9.0	5.1	4.4	2.3	4.4	6.0
1981	8.4	5.1	3.9	2.4	4.4	5.0
1982	7.4	5.1	2.9	2.4	4.5	3.6
1983	6.6	4.7	2.4	2.8	4.4	2.8
1984	6.6	4.5	2.3	2.8	4.5	2.1
1985	6.5	4.4	2.9	2.8	4.7	1.9
1986	6.7	4.8	3.3	2.8	4.8	1.8
1987	7.4	4.7	3.5	2.9	5.0	1.8
1988	7.4	4.5	3.9	2.7	4.8	1.6
1989	5.9	4.5	4.3	2.6	5.2	1.4
1990	5.2	4.3	4.2	2.3	6.1	0.8
1991	6.9	4.1	4.4	2.7	6.7	0.8
1992	8.3	3.9	4.8	3.0	7.5	1.0
1993	8.9	3.9	5.3	3.8	7.0	1.0
1994	9.9	3.9	5.2	4.1	7.3	0.8

Table D.8 Latin America: Gross Fixed Investment in Non-Residential Structures, Six Countries, 1900–1994 (as percentage of GDP at constant 1980 national currencies)

	Argentina	Brazil	Chile	Colombia	Mexico	Venezuela
1900	2.2	1.2	6.3	5.0	0.0	3.1
1901	2.9	1.1	5.9	5.0	0.0	3.1
1902	3.2	1.8	7.2	5.0	0.0	3.1
1903	3.9	1.8	7.2	5.0	0.0	3.1
1904	7.7	1.8	9.0	5.0	0.0	3.1
1905	11.3	1.8	5.7	5.0	0.0	3.1
1906	11.5	2.1	9.0	5.0	0.0	3.1
1907	11.5	3.4	9.9	5.0	0.0	3.1
1908	6.7	3.0	10.1	5.0	0.0	3.1
1909	9.6	2.2	6.6	5.0	0.0	3.1
1910	9.5	2.9	5.8	9.0	0.0	4.7
1911	8.9	3.4	9.4	9.0	0.0	4.7
1912	6.5	3.8	8.4	9.0	0.0	4.7
1913	6.4	4.2	8.1	9.0	0.0	4.7
1914	7.3	2.3	6.4	9.0	0.0	4.7
1915	4.6	1.4	3.2	9.0	0.0	4.7
1916	4.0	1.3	6.7	9.0	0.0	4.7
1917	3.1	1.3	8.3	9.0	0.0	4.7
1918	2.3	0.7	6.0	9.0	0.0	4.7
1919	2.3	1.9	7.9	9.0	0.0	4.7
1920	3.5	3.0	2.8	9.0	6.7	3.5
1921	4.2	1.1	1.7	9.0	6.9	5.7
1922	4.3	1.1	1.6	9.0	6.8	4.1
1923	4.1	1.6	4.3	9.0	6.8	6.0
1924	4.8	3.0	3.8	9.0	6.7	10.5
1925	5.2	2.1	8.3	10.4	8.3	17.9
1926	5.9	2.5	12.1	11.8	6.6	20.7
1927	7.3	2.6	8.8	11.6	5.9	18.1
1928	8.2	1.9	7.6	12.2	6.0	12.4
1929	8.2	1.7	11.3	10.1	7.2	15.4
1930	7.4	0.9	13.9	8.3	5.9	11.5
1931	3.9	0.7	9.3	7.7	3.5	6.4
1932	3.0	0.7	4.3	8.9	2.0	3.6
1933	4.0	0.9	4.4	6.9	3.4	7.9
1934	5.3	0.6	2.7	6.2	4.7	7.3
1935	5.6	0.4	5.3	7.3	5.6	4.4
1936	6.6	1.0	6.9	7.3	5.2	9.0
1937	7.9	1.6	7.0	7.5	7.4	9.5
1938	8.7	0.9	9.3	7.3	2.9	11.8
1939	6.5	1.3	5.7	7.6	3.8	10.6
1940	5.4	1.3	6.2	7.9	5.9	7.8
1941	4.5	1.0	6.2	7.7	6.8	4.9
1942	3.6	0.3	4.0	7.7	5.7	6.1
1943	3.2	0.5	3.4	8.2	5.2	7.8
1944	3.7	1.3	4.4	8.4	6.1	11.0
1945	3.8	1.4	6.1	8.7	8.3	12.5
1946	4.5	0.4	5.4	8.5	11.2	14.7

Table D.8 (continued)

	Argentina	Brazil	Chile	Colombia	Mexico	Venezuela
1947	7.3	3.9	8.2	8.4	12.2	14.0
1948	7.4	2.7	6.0	8.8	10.6	14.9
1949	6.4	3.4	8.0	5.6	8.8	16.6
1950	5.7	5.5	6.0	5.8	9.5	14.7
1951	7.5	5.1	7.3	5.2	11.6	14.9
1952	6.4	5.9	7.4	5.3	11.8	14.6
1953	6.6	6.5	6.9	6.1	10.1	13.1
1954	5.5	5.5	6.1	7.0	10.0	15.1
1955	6.0	5.3	6.6	7.1	10.5	14.0
1956	6.1	5.6	7.5	6.8	11.8	14.7
1957	6.3	5.6	8.4	6.0	11.8	13.4
1958	6.6	5.7	8.1	5.5	10.2	10.9
1959	5.6	5.9	6.6	5.7	9.6	12.0
1960	7.2	6.0	8.3	5.6	10.6	10.4
1961	7.6	5.8	7.6	6.8	6.0	8.1
1962	7.0	5.6	8.4	6.7	5.9	6.2
1963	6.2	5.2	10.7	6.0	6.2	6.2
1964	6.2	5.2	9.8	6.0	7.0	7.0
1965	5.9	4.9	8.9	5.7	7.0	7.1
1966	6.1	5.4	7.2	6.1	7.1	7.0
1967	6.3	5.4	7.4	7.0	7.7	7.8
1968	6.8	6.0	7.2	7.3	7.8	8.9
1969	7.5	6.8	7.3	7.5	7.7	9.1
1970	6.8	7.3	8.2	7.2	7.8	8.0
1971	7.9	7.4	6.9	7.0	6.2	8.1
1972	8.1	8.0	5.5	6.6	6.8	8.9
1973	6.8	8.6	5.0	6.7	7.6	8.9
1974	6.5	8.7	6.3	7.1	8.0	7.9
1975	4.8	9.0	4.5	6.7	7.7	9.4
1976	7.2	9.1	3.8	6.8	7.3	11.3
1977	10.1	9.1	4.0	6.6	6.9	13.8
1978	8.9	9.2	5.0	6.0	8.2	14.4
1979	7.9	8.9	4.9	5.8	8.7	11.3
1980	7.9	9.5	5.7	6.8	9.5	9.0
1981	4.9	9.2	7.4	7.2	10.1	9.8
1982	4.5	8.8	5.4	7.4	9.2	10.0
1983	4.2	7.5	5.6	7.2	6.6	8.8
1984	2.9	6.9	7.7	7.3	6.6	6.2
1985	2.5	6.8	7.8	7.3	6.5	5.7
1986	2.6	7.5	7.4	7.3	5.7	5.7
1987	2.8	7.3	8.0	5.9	5.5	5.7
1988	2.8	7.1	8.0	6.8	5.4	5.9
1989	2.2	7.1	8.7	5.8	5.0	4.8
1990	1.9	6.7	8.7	5.1	4.4	6.1
1991	2.5	6.5	7.7	4.5	3.7	7.3
1992	3.0	6.1	8.1	4.4	3.4	8.9
1993	3.2	6.1	8.7	5.5	4.2	9.0
1994	3.6	6.1	8.5	5.9	4.3	7.0

NOTES

1. The source note is the same as in Appendix B but includes also the disaggregation of capital formation.
2. Banco Central de la República de Argentina (1991) is only available in mimeographed form and was never published officially.
3. Of which no official estimates were available since 1973.

Appendix E. Standardised Estimates of Capital Stock

This appendix presents standardised gross and net fixed capital stock estimates, starting with the estimation of the initial capital stock and subsequently the yearly additions to the gross and net stocks. It gives the potential user the possibility to check on our assumptions and eventually replicate the capital stock estimates using different assumptions about, for example, service lives.

In the second part of this appendix a set of four tables for each of the Latin American countries and the USA is presented, giving gross and net fixed tangible reproducible capital stocks for 1950–94 in national currencies and 1980 international dollars. It also presents, again on the basis of estimates in national currencies and 1980 international dollars, average ages, average service lives and capital–output ratios for 1950–94. As indicated in Chapter 6 the capital stocks have been generated applying the perpetual inventory method which estimates capital stocks as a weighted sum of past investment flows. The detailed sources used for the calculation of the investment series used in the capital stock estimation are given in Appendix D.

A very crucial element in international comparisons is how to convert estimates in local currencies into estimates expressed in a common currency, either existing, for example the US dollar, or fictitious such as the concept of the constant 1980 international dollar.[1] The use of exchange rates as the conversion factor is the easiest and most direct way,[2] but the official exchange rate basically reflects the purchasing power of tradable goods and services and does not include the non-tradables, and thus may give rise to distortions. See Chapter 6 for a detailed description of real income estimation in Latin America.

In Table E.1 the disaggregated PPPs with respect to capital formation are presented with the resulting PPP–exchange rate deviation index as estimated by various phases of ICP which is still the only source for this kind of disaggregated information. Here the results for the two estimates for 1980, ICP IV and AH are given, and these PPPs are also analysed for the 1970–80 period since for 1985 we do not dispose of the disaggregation. Comparing the ICP IV and AH 1980 results it becomes directly clear that the main difference occurred in the case of non-residential structures. In this case the results for ICP IV are not very reliable as a major transcription error occurred.

In analysing the PPPs of the components of gross investment in time the pattern is obviously not as uniform as in the case of total GDP, but the deviation index of machinery and equipment is higher in all cases. Non-residential structures PPPs are generally lower. In the case of Colombia, with five observations, the first three (1970, 1973 and 1975) are almost identical, and also the 1980 estimates show a fairly stable tendency. In the case of Brazil the estimates for 1975 and 1980 are rather similar, as is the case in Mexico although with somewhat higher differences.

It is in the light of all the abovementioned that this appendix shows capital stock estimates both in national currencies and at international prices, therefore giving the potential user the option to apply other PPPs or exchange rates than the ones used by us, without having to go through the whole procedure of calculating the capital stock. The application of these disaggregated PPPs has, as shown in Chapter 6, a great impact on the capital stock levels. Tables E.2 and E.3 give a step-by-step explanation of the procedures used to calculate the capital stock using as an example non-residential stock estimation in Argentina.

Table E.1 Capital Formation PPPs–Exchange Rate Deviation Index, 1970–80 (national currency units per international dollar)

	Argentina	Brazil	Chile	Colombia	Mexico	Venezuela
PPPs of capital formation						
1970 (ICP phase I)						
Res.				4.3		
N.R.				4.5		
M&E				21.6		
1973 (ICP phase II)						
Res.				5.2		
N.R.				5.5		
M&E				32.5		
1975 (ICP phase III)						
Res.		4.6		8.3	6.6	
N.R.		5.4		7.4	5.9	
M&E		7.6		4.3	17.0	
1980 (ICP phase IV)						
Res.	4025	33.7	52.2	20.1		5.1
N.R.	1389	27.1	15.4	17.6		6.4
M&E	3959	46.3	51.2	53.6		4.55
1980 (Alan Heston)						
Res.	4057	32.0	52.1	19.6	16.2	5.5
N.R.	4670	25.9	27.0	22.3	19.2	5.1
M&E	3899	47.0	50.7	54.8	21.2	4.5
PPP–Exchange rate deviation index						
1970 (ICP phase I)						
Res.				0.23		
N.R.				0.25		
M&E				1.18		
1973 (ICP phase II)						
Res.				0.22		
N.R.				0.23		
M&E				1.36		
1975 (ICP phase III)						
Res.		0.56		0.27	0.53	
N.R.		0.66		0.24	0.47	
M&E		0.93		1.38	1.34	
1980 (ICP phase IV)						
Res.	2.19	0.64	1.34	0.42		1.19
N.R.	0.76	0.51	0.39	0.37		1.49
M&E	2.15	0.88	1.31	1.13		1.06
1980 (Alan Heston)						
Res.	2.21	0.61	1.34	0.41	0.70	1.29
N.R.	2.54	0.49	0.69	0.47	0.83	1.20
M&E	2.12	0.89	1.30	1.16	0.92	1.06

Notes: Res. = Residential; N.R. = Non-residential; M&E = Machinery and equipment.

Source: Table 5.2.

Table E.2 Argentina: Procedure for Estimating Alternative Benchmark of the Stocks of Non-Residential Structures at 31 December 1949

	GDP (1980 australes) (1)	Ratio of total gross fixed capital formation to GDP at constant prices (2)	Gross gross increment to capital stock in course of year specified (3)	Annual straight-line depreciation provision (equals 1/40th of figure in column 3 (4)	Yearly components of depreciated capital formation remaining by end 1949 (5)	Index of vintage effect (assuming steady technical progress of 1 per cent per annum) (6)
1910	3,869	9.5	368	9	9	1,00
1911	3,939	8.9	352	9	18	1,01
1912	4,261	6.5	277	7	21	1,02
1913	4,305	6.4	277	7	28	1,03
1914	3,859	7.3	282	7	35	1,04
1915	3,879	4.6	177	4	27	1,05
1916	3,768	4.0	151	4	26	1,06
1917	3,463	3.1	107	3	21	1,07
1918	4,097	2.3	94	2	21	1,08
1919	4,248	2.3	99	2	25	1,09
1920	4,557	3.5	161	4	44	1,10
1921	4,674	4.2	195	5	58	1,12
1922	5,048	4.3	215	5	70	1,13
1923	5,604	4.1	229	6	80	1,14
1924	6,041	4.8	290	7	109	1,15
1925	6,015	5.2	313	8	125	1,16
1926	6,305	5.9	375	9	159	1,17
1927	6,753	7.3	493	12	222	1,18
1928	7,171	8.2	588	15	279	1,20
1929	7,501	8.2	617	15	308	1,21
1930	7,191	7.4	530	13	278	1,22
1931	6,692	3.9	263	7	145	1,23
1932	6,470	3.0	194	5	111	1,24
1933	6,774	4.0	274	7	164	1,26
1934	7,309	5.3	388	10	243	1,27
1935	7,627	5.6	427	11	277	1,28
1936	7,690	6.6	507	13	342	1,30
1937	8,248	7.9	648	16	453	1,31
1938	8,273	8.7	722	18	523	1,32
1939	8,590	6.5	555	14	416	1,33
1940	8,729	5.4	474	12	367	1,35
1941	9,185	4.5	415	10	332	1,36
1942	9,287	3.6	335	8	276	1,37
1943	9,223	3.2	298	7	253	1,39
1944	10,262	3.7	379	9	332	1,40
1945	9,933	3.8	376	9	338	1,42
1946	10,820	4.5	483	12	447	1,43
1947	12,023	7.3	879	22	835	1,45
1948	12,682	7.4	935	23	912	1,46
1949	12,517	6.4	807	20	807	1,47
Total			15546	389	9539	

Table E.3 Argentina: Procedure for Estimating Alternative Variants of 1950–94 Estimates of the Stock of Non-Residential Structures

	(1)	(2)	(3)	(4)	(5)	(6)	(7)	(8)	(9)	(10)	(11)	(12)	(13)	(14)	(15)	(16)
1949	12517	6.4	807	368	359	15546	389	338	9539	16.46	10.52	15725	9708	12716	0.8	1.2
1950	12669	5.7	726	352	641	15904	398	595	9877	16.16	10.55	16225	10174	13199	0.8	1.2
1951	13161	7.5	992	277	524	16545	414	388	10471	15.68	10.28	16807	10665	13736	0.9	1.3
1952	12498	6.4	801	277	591	17069	427	442	10859	15.55	10.21	17365	11080	14222	0.8	1.3
1953	13161	6.6	869	282	478	17660	442	318	11301	15.40	10.14	17899	11460	14680	0.8	1.3
1954	13704	5.5	760	177	698	18138	453	422	11619	15.38	10.14	18487	11830	15159	0.8	1.3
1955	14672	6.0	875	151	765	18837	471	446	12041	15.43	10.11	19219	12263	15741	0.8	1.3
1956	15080	6.1	917	107	899	19602	490	516	12486	15.52	10.12	20052	12744	16398	0.8	1.3
1957	15861	6.3	1006	94	1023	20501	513	605	13002	15.63	10.20	21013	13304	17159	0.8	1.3
1958	16829	6.6	1117	99	781	21524	538	342	13607	15.71	10.31	21915	13778	17846	0.8	1.2
1959	15742	5.6	880	161	1065	22305	558	668	13949	15.99	10.48	22837	14283	18560	0.9	1.4
1960	16982	7.2	1226	195	1190	23370	584	800	14617	15.98	10.32	23965	15017	19491	0.8	1.3
1961	18188	7.6	1385	215	1048	24560	614	649	15417	15.89	10.12	25084	15741	20413	0.8	1.3
1962	18032	7.0	1263	229	877	25608	640	466	16066	15.90	10.07	26046	16299	21173	0.9	1.4
1963	17735	6.2	1106	290	931	26485	662	559	16532	16.03	10.14	26951	16812	21881	0.9	1.5
1964	19707	6.2	1221	313	966	27416	685	593	17091	16.06	10.15	27899	17388	22643	0.9	1.4
1965	21673	5.9	1278	375	961	28382	710	626	17684	16.08	10.17	28862	17997	23430	0.8	1.3
1966	21974	6.1	1336	493	930	29342	734	689	18310	16.04	10.27	29808	18655	24231	0.8	1.3
1967	22723	6.3	1423	588	1037	30273	757	868	18999	15.90	10.26	30791	19434	25112	0.8	1.3
1968	23876	6.8	1625	617	1347	31310	783	1181	19868	15.62	10.11	31983	20458	26221	0.8	1.3
1969	26106	7.5	1964	530	1353	32657	816	1066	21049	15.22	9.96	33333	21582	27457	0.8	1.2
1970	27715	6.8	1883	263	2020	34009	850	1433	22115	14.99	9.95	35019	22832	28925	0.8	1.2
1971	28970	7.9	2283	194	2222	36029	901	1515	23548	14.86	9.79	37140	24305	30723	0.8	1.2
1972	29791	8.1	2416	274	1855	38251	956	1172	25063	14.79	9.64	39179	25649	32414	0.8	1.2
1973	31136	6.8	2129	388	1749	40106	1003	1135	26235	14.83	9.64	40981	26803	33892	0.8	1.3
1974	33062	6.5	2137	427	1165	41855	1046	545	27370	14.84	9.59	42437	27642	35040	0.8	1.2
1975	33110	4.8	1591	507	1894	43020	1075	1326	27915	15.04	9.83	43967	28578	36272	0.8	1.3
1976	33353	7.2	2401	648	2957	44914	1123	2481	29240	14.96	9.80	46392	30481	38437	0.9	1.3
1977	35745	10.1	3604			47871			31722	14.49	9.49				0.9	1.3

Table E.3 (continued)

	(1)	(2)	(3)	(4)	(5)	(6)	(7)	(8)	(9)	(10)	(11)	(12)	(13)	(14)	(15)	(16)
1978	34848	8.9	3089	722	2367	50238	1197	1892	33614	14.24	9.34	49054	32668	40861	0.9	1.4
1979	37571	7.9	2982	555	2427	52665	1256	1726	35340	14.16	9.38	51451	34477	42964	0.9	1.4
1980	38400	7.9	3050	474	2576	55241	1317	1734	37073	14.16	9.39	53953	36207	45080	0.9	1.4
1981	36318	4.9	1782	415	1366	56608	1381	401	37474	14.52	9.79	55924	37274	46599	1.0	1.5
1982	35171	4.5	1588	335	1253	57861	1415	173	37647	14.97	10.14	57234	37560	47397	1.1	1.6
1983	36617	4.1	1511	298	1213	59073	1447	64	37711	15.47	10.53	58467	37679	48073	1.0	1.6
1984	37350	2.9	1074	379	695	59769	1477	-403	37308	16.03	11.07	59421	37509	48465	1.0	1.6
1985	34754	2.5	873	376	497	60266	1494	-621	36687	16.65	11.56	60017	36997	48507	1.1	1.7
1986	37237	2.6	953	483	470	60736	1507	-554	36133	17.20	12.04	60501	36410	48455	1.0	1.6
1987	38179	2.8	1081	879	202	60938	1518	-437	35696	17.57	12.34	60837	35914	48376	0.9	1.6
1988	37432	2.7	1020	935	85	61023	1523	-504	35192	17.93	12.76	60980	35444	48212	0.9	1.6
1989	34809	2.2	762	807	-45	60977	1526	-764	34429	18.42	13.22	61000	34811	47905	1.0	1.8
1990	34343	1.8	625	726	-102	60876	1524	-900	33529	18.97	13.76	60927	33979	47453	1.0	1.8
1991	37949	2.5	938	992	-54	60822	1522	-584	32945	19.33	14.06	60849	33237	47043	0.9	1.6
1992	41857	3.0	1245	801	443	61265	1521	-276	32669	19.67	14.27	61043	32807	46925	0.8	1.5
1993	44473	3.2	1435	869	566	61831	1532	-97	32572	19.93	14.36	61548	32621	47084	0.7	1.4
1994	48264	3.6	1736	760	976	62807	1546	190	32762	20.13	14.32	62319	32667	47493	0.7	1.3

Note:
(1) GDP (1980 australes)
(2) Ratio of total gross fixed capital formation to GDP at constant prices
(3) Gross Gross increment to capital stock in course of year specified
(4) Retirements
(5) Increment to gross capital stock in year specified (col.3–4)
(6) End-year gross stock equals benchmark stock
(see table AR1)+ col.5
(7) Annual depreciation
(8) Increment to net capital stock equals col.3–7
(9) End-year net stock equals benchmark stock
(see table AR1 + col.8)
(10) End-year gross stock average age
(11) End-year net stock average age
(12) Mid-year gross capital stock
(13) Mid-year net capital stock
(14) Average of mid-year gross and net stocks
(15) Capital–output ratios net
(16) Capital–output ratios gross

210

Table E.4 Argentina 1. Gross and Net Fixed Tangible Reproducible Capital Stocks by Type of Asset, 1950–94 (constant 1980 australes)

| | Gross stocks | | | | |
| | | Non-residential | | | |
Mid-year	Total	Total	M&E	Structures	Res.
1950	45,084	20,304	4,579	15,725	24,781
1951	46,429	20,982	4,757	16,225	25,447
1952	47,863	21,737	4,930	16,807	26,125
1953	49,131	22,354	4,989	17,365	26,777
1954	50,369	22,959	5,060	17,899	27,409
1955	51,762	23,743	5,256	18,487	28,019
1956	53,362	24,796	5,577	19,219	28,567
1957	55,071	26,040	5,988	20,052	29,031
1958	56,992	27,483	6,470	21,013	29,509
1959	58,751	28,823	6,908	21,915	29,928
1960	60,679	30,356	7,519	22,837	30,323
1961	63,318	32,404	8,439	23,965	30,914
1962	65,891	34,254	9,170	25,084	31,637
1963	67,949	35,636	9,590	26,046	32,313
1964	70,256	37,097	10,147	26,951	33,159
1965	73,200	38,832	10,933	27,899	34,368
1966	76,291	40,553	11,691	28,862	35,738
1967	79,468	42,239	12,431	29,808	37,229
1968	82,999	44,096	13,305	30,791	38,903
1969	87,280	46,391	14,408	31,983	40,890
1970	92,146	48,971	15,638	33,333	43,175
1971	97,461	51,927	16,907	35,019	45,535
1972	103,168	55,421	18,281	37,140	47,747
1973	108,508	58,860	19,681	39,179	49,649
1974	113,651	62,114	21,133	40,981	51,537
1975	118,794	64,797	22,360	42,437	53,997
1976	124,038	67,193	23,226	43,967	56,845
1977	130,383	70,901	24,508	46,392	59,482
1978	136,999	75,110	26,056	49,054	61,889
1979	143,335	78,999	27,548	51,451	64,336
1980	150,251	83,297	29,344	53,953	66,954
1981	156,915	87,330	31,406	55,924	69,585
1982	162,284	90,317	33,082	57,234	71,968
1983	166,904	92,804	34,337	58,467	74,100
1984	171,178	95,052	35,631	59,421	76,126
1985	174,685	96,602	36,585	60,017	78,083
1986	177,931	97,809	37,308	60,501	80,122
1987	181,487	99,064	38,228	60,837	82,423
1988	184,887	100,124	39,144	60,980	84,763
1989	187,353	100,677	39,677	61,000	86,676
1990	188,891	100,797	39,870	60,927	88,094
1991	190,608	100,857	40,009	60,849	89,751
1992	193,369	101,166	40,122	61,043	92,203
1993	197,614	102,296	40,748	61,548	95,318
1994	203,506	104,412	42,093	62,319	99,094

Table E.4 (continued)

| | | Net stocks | | | |
| | | Non-residential | | | |
Mid-year	Total	Total	M&E	Structures	Res.
1950	26,089	12,374	2,666	9,708	13,715
1951	27,079	12,947	2,773	10,174	14,132
1952	28,126	13,590	2,925	10,665	14,536
1953	28,987	14,101	3,021	11,080	14,887
1954	29,763	14,551	3,091	11,460	15,212
1955	30,629	15,043	3,214	11,830	15,585
1956	31,694	15,687	3,423	12,263	16,007
1957	32,905	16,415	3,671	12,744	16,490
1958	34,303	17,230	3,926	13,304	17,073
1959	35,447	17,870	4,092	13,778	17,577
1960	36,824	18,687	4,405	14,283	18,137
1961	39,036	20,061	5,044	15,017	18,975
1962	41,276	21,445	5,704	15,741	19,831
1963	42,980	22,452	6,153	16,299	20,527
1964	44,539	23,342	6,530	16,812	21,198
1965	46,323	24,361	6,974	17,388	21,962
1966	48,193	25,413	7,415	17,997	22,780
1967	50,168	26,500	7,845	18,655	23,667
1968	52,455	27,748	8,314	19,434	24,707
1969	55,438	29,391	8,933	20,458	26,046
1970	58,983	31,245	9,663	21,582	27,738
1971	62,845	33,281	10,450	22,832	29,563
1972	66,896	35,621	11,315	24,305	31,276
1973	70,611	37,800	12,151	25,649	32,810
1974	74,089	39,692	12,889	26,803	34,398
1975	77,599	41,122	13,479	27,642	36,477
1976	81,388	42,573	13,996	28,578	38,815
1977	86,295	45,433	14,952	30,481	40,862
1978	91,301	48,595	15,927	32,668	42,706
1979	95,850	51,174	16,697	34,477	44,676
1980	100,791	53,984	17,778	36,207	46,806
1981	105,055	56,327	19,053	37,274	48,728
1982	107,556	57,406	19,845	37,560	50,150
1983	109,064	57,871	20,192	37,679	51,193
1984	110,341	58,212	20,703	37,509	52,129
1985	110,923	57,970	20,972	36,997	52,954
1986	111,243	57,495	21,085	36,410	53,748
1987	112,219	57,425	21,510	35,914	54,794
1988	113,281	57,377	21,933	35,444	55,904
1989	113,285	56,717	21,907	34,811	56,567
1990	112,118	55,433	21,454	33,979	56,686
1991	111,209	54,178	20,941	33,237	57,031
1992	111,904	53,700	20,892	32,807	58,204
1993	114,107	54,073	21,452	32,621	60,034
1994	117,768	55,255	22,588	32,667	62,513

Table E.5 Argentina 2. Gross and Net Fixed Tangible Reproducible Capital Stocks by Type of Asset, 1950–94 (constant million 1980 international dollars)

| | Gross stocks | | | | |
| | | Non-residential | | | |
Mid-year	Total	Total	M&E	Structures	Res.
1950	106,498	45,416	11,744	33,672	61,081
1951	109,668	46,943	12,201	34,742	62,725
1952	113,031	48,635	12,645	35,990	64,395
1953	115,981	49,980	12,796	37,184	66,001
1954	118,867	51,306	12,977	38,329	67,561
1955	122,132	53,068	13,480	39,588	69,064
1956	125,871	55,458	14,303	41,155	70,413
1957	129,854	58,295	15,358	42,938	71,559
1958	134,326	61,590	16,594	44,996	72,736
1959	138,413	64,645	17,718	46,927	73,769
1960	142,928	68,186	19,283	48,903	74,742
1961	149,160	72,960	21,643	51,317	76,200
1962	155,214	77,232	23,518	53,713	77,982
1963	160,018	80,370	24,596	55,774	79,648
1964	165,466	83,734	26,024	57,710	81,732
1965	172,495	87,781	28,040	59,741	84,714
1966	179,878	91,788	29,984	61,804	88,090
1967	187,477	95,712	31,884	63,828	91,765
1968	195,949	100,058	34,123	65,934	95,892
1969	206,226	105,439	36,952	68,487	100,788
1970	217,907	111,485	40,108	71,377	106,421
1971	230,589	118,352	43,363	74,988	112,237
1972	244,106	126,416	46,886	79,530	117,689
1973	256,750	134,372	50,477	83,895	122,377
1974	268,987	141,956	54,202	87,754	127,031
1975	281,316	148,220	57,347	90,873	133,096
1976	293,834	153,717	59,569	94,148	140,117
1977	308,817	162,200	62,858	99,342	146,617
1978	324,419	171,870	66,829	105,042	152,549
1979	339,408	180,828	70,653	110,175	158,580
1980	355,826	190,793	75,261	115,532	165,034
1981	371,820	200,302	80,548	119,753	171,518
1982	384,798	207,407	84,848	122,558	177,391
1983	395,912	213,264	88,065	125,198	182,648
1984	406,267	218,626	91,385	127,241	187,641
1985	414,813	222,349	93,832	128,518	192,464
1986	422,730	225,239	95,685	129,553	197,491
1987	431,479	228,317	98,044	130,273	203,162
1988	439,904	230,974	100,395	130,580	208,929
1989	446,030	232,385	101,763	130,622	213,645
1990	449,864	232,723	102,258	130,465	217,141
1991	454,136	232,911	102,612	130,298	221,225
1992	460,888	233,620	102,904	130,715	227,268
1993	471,252	236,304	104,508	131,796	234,948
1994	485,659	241,405	107,958	133,447	244,254

Table E.5 (continued)

		Net stocks			
		Non-residential			
Mid-year	Total	Total	M&E	Structures	Res.
1950	61,431	27,626	6,838	20,788	33,805
1951	63,733	28,899	7,113	21,786	34,834
1952	66,168	30,339	7,501	22,838	35,830
1953	68,168	31,474	7,748	23,726	36,694
1954	69,963	32,467	7,927	24,539	37,497
1955	71,989	33,574	8,242	25,331	38,416
1956	74,495	35,040	8,780	26,260	39,455
1957	77,350	36,704	9,414	27,289	40,646
1958	80,641	38,558	10,069	28,489	42,083
1959	83,323	39,999	10,496	29,503	43,324
1960	86,587	41,881	11,297	30,584	44,706
1961	91,864	45,093	12,936	32,156	46,772
1962	97,218	48,337	14,629	33,708	48,881
1963	101,281	50,684	15,782	34,902	50,597
1964	104,997	52,748	16,748	35,999	52,250
1965	109,253	55,119	17,886	37,233	54,134
1966	113,708	57,557	19,019	38,538	56,151
1967	118,405	60,067	20,121	39,946	58,337
1968	123,837	62,938	21,324	41,614	60,899
1969	130,920	66,719	22,911	43,808	64,201
1970	139,370	70,998	24,784	46,215	68,371
1971	148,562	75,692	26,801	48,890	72,870
1972	158,157	81,067	29,021	52,046	77,090
1973	166,962	86,088	31,165	54,923	80,873
1974	175,237	90,451	33,058	57,394	84,786
1975	183,674	93,763	34,571	59,192	89,911
1976	192,763	97,090	35,895	61,195	95,674
1977	204,339	103,619	38,349	65,271	100,720
1978	216,067	110,803	40,850	69,953	105,264
1979	226,772	116,652	42,825	73,827	110,120
1980	238,498	123,126	45,595	77,531	115,372
1981	248,791	128,683	48,867	79,816	120,108
1982	254,943	131,329	50,899	80,430	123,614
1983	258,656	132,471	51,788	80,683	126,185
1984	261,910	133,418	53,098	80,320	128,492
1985	263,537	133,013	53,789	79,224	130,524
1986	264,526	132,045	54,078	77,966	132,481
1987	267,134	132,074	55,169	76,905	135,060
1988	269,947	132,151	56,253	75,898	137,796
1989	270,158	130,727	56,186	74,541	139,431
1990	267,508	127,784	55,023	72,761	139,724
1991	265,455	124,881	53,708	71,172	140,575
1992	267,302	123,836	53,584	70,252	143,466
1993	272,848	124,872	55,019	69,852	147,976
1994	281,971	127,884	57,932	69,952	154,087

Table E.6 Argentina 3. Capital Stock: Average Ages, Average Service Lives and Capital–Output Ratios, 1950–94 (on the basis of national currencies at constant 1980 prices)

Mid-year	Average age capital stock				Average service life capital stock		Capital–output ratios			
	Total		Non-residential		Total	Non-residential	Total		Non-residential	
	Gross	Net	Gross	Net			Gross	Net	Gross	Net
1950	19.18	12.01	14.17	9.16	38,69	29,73	3,6	2,1	1,6	1,0
1951	18.91	11.72	13.75	8.93	39,07	30,35	3,5	2,1	1,6	1,0
1952	18.83	11.58	13.63	8.88	38,65	29,81	3,8	2,3	1,7	1,1
1953	18.80	11.49	13.51	8.87	38,64	29,89	3,7	2,2	1,7	1,1
1954	18.81	11.43	13.50	8.92	38,72	30,00	3,7	2,2	1,7	1,1
1955	18.68	11.30	13.51	8.88	38,94	30,50	3,5	2,1	1,6	1,0
1956	18.49	11.18	13.54	8.85	38,79	30,53	3,5	2,1	1,6	1,0
1957	18.16	11.07	13.58	8.87	38,58	30,58	3,5	2,1	1,6	1,0
1958	17.82	10.97	13.63	8.93	38,38	30,47	3,4	2,0	1,6	1,0
1959	17.72	11.04	13.88	9.08	37,60	29,81	3,7	2,3	1,8	1,1
1960	17.19	10.77	13.75	8.80	37,92	30,38	3,6	2,2	1,8	1,1
1961	16.59	10.45	13.50	8.46	37,53	30,07	3,5	2,1	1,8	1,1
1962	16.25	10.31	13.36	8.34	36,53	28,94	3,7	2,3	1,9	1,2
1963	16.09	10.36	13.41	8.40	36,10	28,61	3,8	2,4	2,0	1,3
1964	16.03	10.34	13.38	8.39	36,44	28,87	3,6	2,3	1,9	1,2
1965	16.03	10.31	13.34	8.39	36,28	28,65	3,4	2,1	1,8	1,1
1966	16.03	10.32	13.26	8.46	35,92	28,22	3,5	2,2	1,8	1,2
1967	16.00	10.27	13.12	8.46	35,81	28,06	3,5	2,2	1,9	1,2
1968	15.86	10.13	12.88	8.34	35,78	27,97	3,5	2,2	1,8	1,2
1969	15.60	9.91	12.54	8.19	35,91	28,03	3,3	2,1	1,8	1,1
1970	15.31	9.73	12.32	8.14	35,59	27,63	3,3	2,1	1,8	1,1
1971	15.07	9.53	12.19	7.99	35,56	27,73	3,4	2,2	1,8	1,1
1972	14.87	9.39	12.11	7.86	35,27	27,62	3,5	2,2	1,9	1,2
1973	14.70	9.36	12.12	7.84	34,70	27,22	3,5	2,3	1,9	1,2
1974	14.54	9.32	12.13	7.80	34,51	27,00	3,4	2,2	1,9	1,2
1975	14.42	9.34	12.25	7.97	34,09	26,28	3,6	2,3	2,0	1,2
1976	14.28	9.31	12.19	7.98	34,22	26,39	3,7	2,4	2,0	1,3
1977	13.97	9.16	11.81	7.72	34,68	27,15	3,6	2,4	2,0	1,3
1978	13.82	9.17	11.69	7.68	34,13	26,63	3,9	2,6	2,2	1,4
1979	13.65	9.19	11.62	7.70	34,11	26,68	3,8	2,6	2,1	1,4
1980	13.52	9.19	11.59	7.67	34,04	26,67	3,9	2,6	2,2	1,4
1981	13.64	9.37	11.74	7.85	33,55	26,19	4,3	2,9	2,4	1,6
1982	13.95	9.66	12.08	8.12	32,93	25,56	4,6	3,1	2,6	1,6
1983	14.28	9.94	12.41	8.37	32,84	25,49	4,6	3,0	2,5	1,6
1984	14.59	10.26	12.74	8.68	32,59	25,20	4,6	3,0	2,5	1,6
1985	15.01	10.61	13.17	9.01	32,31	24,85	5,0	3,2	2,8	1,7
1986	15.37	10.90	13.51	9.29	32,38	24,81	4,8	3,0	2,6	1,5
1987	15.60	11.06	13.68	9.40	32,41	24,73	4,8	2,9	2,6	1,5
1988	15.85	11.30	13.88	9.63	32,26	24,48	4,9	3,0	2,7	1,5
1989	16.24	11.65	14.22	9.93	32,02	24,22	5,4	3,3	2,9	1,6
1990	16.72	12.08	14.65	10.32	31,97	24,12	5,5	3,3	2,9	1,6
1991	17.03	12.31	14.93	10.52	32,17	24,12	5,0	2,9	2,7	1,4
1992	17.21	12.35	15.10	10.55	32,46	24,18	4,6	2,7	2,4	1,3
1993	17.28	12.27	15.18	10.44	32,92	24,52	4,4	2,6	2,3	1,2
1994	17.23	12.03	15.15	10.17	33,13	24,56	4,2	2,4	2,2	1,1

Table E.7 Argentina 4. Capital Stock: Average Ages, Average Service Lives and Capital–Output Ratios, 1950–94 (on the basis of constant 1980 international dollars)

Mid-year	Average age capital stock				Average service life capital stock		Capital–output ratios			
	Total		Non-residential		Total	Non-residential	Total		Non-residential	
	Gross	Net	Gross	Net			Gross	Net	Gross	Net
1950	19.27	12.05	13.88	8.96	37.40	28.58	2.3	1.3	1.0	0.6
1951	19.01	11.76	13.46	8.72	37.43	29.20	2.3	1.3	1.0	0.6
1952	18.94	11.62	13.34	8.68	37.27	28.65	2.4	1.4	1.1	0.7
1953	18.92	11.53	13.23	8.68	38.26	28.71	2.4	1.4	1.0	0.6
1954	18.93	11.47	13.22	8.74	38.36	28.85	2.3	1.4	1.0	0.6
1955	18.79	11.33	13.23	8.69	38.58	29.35	2.3	1.3	1.0	0.6
1956	18.59	11.20	13.25	8.66	38.42	29.39	2.3	1.3	1.0	0.6
1957	18.24	11.08	13.29	8.67	38.18	29.43	2.2	1.3	1.0	0.6
1958	17.88	10.97	13.33	8.73	37.96	29.31	2.2	1.3	1.0	0.6
1959	17.75	11.04	13.58	8.87	37.16	28.66	2.4	1.4	1.1	0.7
1960	17.20	10.76	13.43	8.58	37.48	29.25	2.3	1.4	1.1	0.7
1961	16.57	10.42	13.17	8.23	37.06	28.94	2.2	1.4	1.1	0.7
1962	16.21	10.29	13.01	8.10	36.02	27.78	2.3	1.5	1.2	0.7
1963	16.03	10.33	13.05	8.17	35.58	27.45	2.4	1.5	1.2	0.8
1964	15.97	10.31	13.01	8.16	35.93	27.74	2.3	1.4	1.2	0.7
1965	15.97	10.28	12.97	8.16	35.76	27.52	2.2	1.4	1.1	0.7
1966	15.97	10.28	12.89	8.22	35.39	27.08	2.2	1.4	1.1	0.7
1967	15.94	10.23	12.76	8.22	35.28	26.93	2.2	1.4	1.1	0.7
1968	15.81	10.09	12.53	8.11	35.25	26.84	2.2	1.4	1.1	0.7
1969	15.55	9.86	12.20	7.96	35.36	26.90	2.1	1.4	1.1	0.7
1970	15.26	9.68	11.99	7.90	35.04	26.51	2.1	1.4	1.1	0.7
1971	15.02	9.48	11.86	7.76	34.98	26.58	2.2	1.4	1.1	0.7
1972	14.82	9.34	11.78	7.64	34.67	26.47	2.2	1.4	1.1	0.7
1973	14.64	9.31	11.78	7.61	34.11	26.09	2.2	1.5	1.2	0.7
1974	14.46	9.26	11.80	7.58	33.91	25.89	2.2	1.4	1.2	0.7
1975	14.33	9.28	11.91	7.74	33.50	25.18	2.3	1.5	1.2	0.8
1976	14.19	9.25	11.86	7.75	33.61	25.26	2.4	1.6	1.2	0.8
1977	13.89	9.11	11.49	7.50	34.05	26.01	2.3	1.5	1.2	0.8
1978	13.74	9.12	11.38	7.47	33.51	25.51	2.5	1.7	1.3	0.9
1979	13.57	9.14	11.32	7.49	33.49	25.56	2.4	1.6	1.3	0.8
1980	13.44	9.15	11.28	7.46	33.42	25.56	2.5	1.7	1.3	0.9
1981	13.54	9.31	11.41	7.61	32.95	25.13	2.8	1.9	1.5	1.0
1982	13.84	9.59	11.74	7.88	32.32	24.49	3.0	2.0	1.6	1.0
1983	14.16	9.87	12.05	8.11	32.23	24.43	2.9	1.9	1.6	1.0
1984	14.46	10.17	12.36	8.40	31.99	24.16	2.9	1.9	1.6	1.0
1985	14.87	10.52	12.77	8.72	31.70	23.80	3.2	2.1	1.7	1.0
1986	15.22	10.80	13.09	8.97	31.78	23.77	3.1	1.9	1.6	1.0
1987	15.44	10.96	13.24	9.06	31.82	23.70	3.1	1.9	1.6	0.9
1988	15.69	11.19	13.43	9.27	31.67	23.47	3.2	2.0	1.7	1.0
1989	16.07	11.53	13.76	9.56	31.43	23.21	3.5	2.1	1.8	1.0
1990	16.55	11.95	14.17	9.93	31.38	23.11	3.5	2.1	1.8	1.0
1991	16.86	12.18	14.44	10.12	31.59	23.11	3.2	1.9	1.7	0.9
1992	17.03	12.22	14.60	10.14	31.87	23.16	3.0	1.7	1.5	0.8
1993	17.09	12.13	14.66	10.01	32.35	23.50	2.9	1.7	1.4	0.8
1994	17.02	11.88	14.60	9.72	32.57	23.54	2.7	1.6	1.4	0.7

Table E.8 Brazil 1. Gross and Net Fixed Tangible Reproducible Capital Stocks by Type of Asset, 1950–94 (constant 1980 cruzeiros)

		Gross stocks			
		Non-residential			
Mid-year	Total	Total	M&E	Structures	Res.
1950	2,325	1,498	1.019	480	827
1951	2,615	1,718	1.157	562	897
1952	2,943	1,968	1.316	652	975
1953	3,240	2,178	1.419	760	1.062
1954	3,530	2,378	1.505	873	1.152
1955	3,844	2,601	1.614	987	1.242
1956	4,166	2,830	1.721	1.109	1.336
1957	4,532	3,097	1.855	1.243	1.435
1958	4,940	3,399	2.010	1.389	1.541
1959	5,378	3,722	2.173	1.549	1.656
1960	5,840	4,062	2.341	1.721	1.778
1961	6,308	4,400	2.490	1.910	1.908
1962	6,756	4,714	2.605	2.109	2.042
1963	7,184	5,008	2.705	2.303	2.175
1964	7,608	5,294	2.805	2.489	2.314
1965	8,019	5,555	2.881	2.674	2.463
1966	8,441	5,819	2.948	2.871	2.621
1967	8,894	6,102	3.016	3.086	2.792
1968	9,478	6,495	3.160	3.336	2.982
1969	10,248	7,049	3.398	3.651	3.199
1970	11,150	7,711	3.689	4.022	3.439
1971	12,197	8,494	4.055	4.439	3.703
1972	13,412	9,413	4.486	4.927	4.000
1973	14,873	10,531	5.008	5.523	4.342
1974	16,592	11,864	5.651	6.214	4.727
1975	18,514	13,375	6.406	6.969	5.140
1976	20,612	15,028	7.232	7.796	5.584
1977	22,759	16,699	8.017	8.682	6.060
1978	24,946	18,383	8.762	9.621	6.563
1979	27,240	20,146	9.540	10.607	7.093
1980	29,764	22,087	10.391	11.696	7.677
1981	32,262	23,968	11.138	12.830	8.294
1982	34,467	25,567	11.662	13.906	8.900
1983	36,356	26,884	12.012	14.872	9.472
1984	37,963	27,953	12.223	15.729	10.010
1985	39,588	29,024	12.428	16.597	10.564
1986	41,483	30,302	12.726	17.577	11.181
1987	43,499	31,653	13.026	18.628	11.846
1988	45,308	32,806	13.153	19.653	12.502
1989	46,925	33,768	13.092	20.676	13.157
1990	48,262	34,475	12.840	21.636	13.786
1991	49,349	34,977	12.470	22.507	14.372
1992	50,346	35,417	12.097	23.320	14.929
1993	51,336	35,858	11.755	24.103	15.479
1994	52,498	36,441	11.511	24.931	16.057

Table E.8 (continued)

		Net stocks			
			Non-residential		
Mid-year	Total	Total	M&E	Structures	Res.
1950	1.560	983	659	325	577
1951	1.809	1.177	775	402	632
1952	2.095	1.401	913	488	694
1953	2.348	1.584	993	591	764
1954	2.574	1.738	1.043	695	836
1955	2.793	1.886	1.093	792	908
1956	3.004	2.022	1.128	894	982
1957	3.242	2.180	1.177	1.003	1.062
1958	3.503	2.357	1.236	1.121	1.147
1959	3.792	2.554	1.303	1.250	1.238
1960	4.103	2.767	1.374	1.392	1.336
1961	4.421	2.979	1.434	1.546	1.441
1962	4.744	3.194	1.492	1.702	1.550
1963	5.052	3.393	1.544	1.849	1.658
1964	5.344	3.578	1.590	1.988	1.766
1965	5.622	3.747	1.624	2.122	1.876
1966	5.937	3.947	1.683	2.264	1.990
1967	6.303	4.189	1.769	2.419	2.114
1968	6.736	4.485	1.881	2.604	2.251
1969	7.313	4.899	2.052	2.847	2.414
1970	7.998	5.401	2.267	3.134	2.596
1971	8.782	5.984	2.530	3.454	2.798
1972	9.720	6.690	2.854	3.835	3.030
1973	10.876	7.572	3.260	4.313	3.303
1974	12.253	8.640	3.770	4.870	3.612
1975	13.782	9.838	4.364	5.474	3.944
1976	15.414	11.110	4.979	6.131	4.303
1977	17.026	12.339	5.505	6.834	4.686
1978	18.596	13.509	5.942	7.566	5.087
1979	20.189	14.683	6.362	8.321	5.505
1980	21.917	15.956	6.799	9.157	5.961
1981	23.547	17.114	7.104	10.010	6.433
1982	24.818	17.939	7.168	10.771	6.879
1983	25.731	18.447	7.053	11.394	7.284
1984	26.386	18.735	6.846	11.889	7.651
1985	27.080	19.055	6.677	12.378	8.025
1986	28.065	19.611	6.655	12.956	8.454
1987	29.222	20.299	6.701	13.598	8.922
1988	30.235	20.866	6.665	14.201	9.369
1989	31.151	21.349	6.571	14.778	9.802
1990	31.907	21.709	6.417	15.292	10.198
1991	32.482	21.946	6.233	15.713	10.537
1992	32.932	22.100	6.038	16.062	10.833
1993	33.353	22.242	5.860	16.381	11.111
1994	33.975	22.566	5.836	16.730	11.409

Table E.9 Brazil 2. Gross and Net Fixed Tangible Reproducible Capital Stocks by Type of Asset, 1950–94 (constant million 1980 international dollars)

| | Gross stocks | | | | |
| | | Non-residential | | | |
Mid-year	Total	Total	M&E	Structures	Res.
1950	65,995	40.163	21.676	18.488	25.832
1951	74,271	46.254	24.609	21.645	28.016
1952	83,587	53.123	28.001	25.122	30.464
1953	92,651	59.462	30.185	29.277	33.189
1954	101,680	65.671	32.015	33.655	36.009
1955	111,213	72.389	34.336	38.053	38.824
1956	121,111	79.369	36.611	42.758	41.742
1957	132,183	87.343	39.458	47.885	44.841
1958	144,459	96.293	42.759	53.534	48.167
1959	157,672	105.934	46.245	59.689	51.739
1960	171,697	116.135	49.817	66.318	55.562
1961	186,199	126.572	52.980	73.591	59.628
1962	200,530	136.703	55.417	81.285	63.828
1963	214,290	146.316	57.562	88.754	67.974
1964	227,913	155.597	59.674	95.923	72.316
1965	241,337	164.357	61.305	103.052	76.980
1966	255,293	173.376	62.721	110.655	81.917
1967	270,354	183.105	64.168	118.937	87.249
1968	288,973	195.779	67.232	128.547	93.194
1969	312,984	213.006	72.301	140.705	99.978
1970	340,950	233.492	78.484	155.008	107.458
1971	373,056	257.339	86.271	171.067	115.717
1972	410,310	285.320	95.443	189.877	124.991
1973	455,092	319.396	106.557	212.839	135.696
1974	507,425	359.694	120.230	239.463	147.731
1975	565,474	404.865	136.299	268.566	160.610
1976	628,809	454.305	153.874	300.430	174.504
1977	694,548	505.173	170.568	334.604	189.376
1978	762,310	557.202	186.418	370.783	205.109
1979	833,404	611.738	202.977	408.761	221.666
1980	911,727	671.827	221.089	450.738	239.900
1981	990,619	731.437	236.973	494.464	259.182
1982	1,062,143	784.028	248.120	535.908	278.115
1983	1,124,721	828.731	255.583	573.148	295.990
1984	1,179,087	866.265	260.072	606.192	312.823
1985	1,234,147	904.033	264.422	639.611	330.114
1986	1,297,529	948.136	270.756	677.380	349.393
1987	1,365,223	995.034	277.138	717.896	370.189
1988	1,427,938	1.037.239	279.857	757.382	390.698
1989	1,486,534	1.075.373	278.554	796.819	411.162
1990	1,537,815	1.106.989	273.181	833.808	430.826
1991	1,581,847	1.132.716	265.313	867.403	449.131
1992	1,622,614	1.156.096	257.390	898.706	466.518
1993	1,662,694	1.178.991	250.113	928.877	483.703
1994	1,707,462	1.205.693	244.905	960.788	501.769

Table E.9 (continued)

Mid-year	Net stocks				
		Non-residential			
	Total	Total	M&E	Structures	Res.
1950	44,547	26.521	14.014	12.506	18.026
1951	51,736	31.996	16.490	15.507	19.739
1952	59,913	38.227	19.416	18.812	21.686
1953	67,781	43.905	21.130	22.775	23.876
1954	75,093	48.964	22.186	26.778	26.129
1955	82,160	53.800	23.264	30.536	28.360
1956	89,130	58.439	24.002	34.437	30.692
1957	96,865	63.689	25.050	38.639	33.175
1958	105,333	69.498	26.289	43.209	35.835
1959	114,607	75.919	27.728	48.191	38.688
1960	124,662	82.901	29.237	53.664	41.761
1961	135,113	90.072	30.503	59.569	45.042
1962	145,763	97.325	31.738	65.588	48.438
1963	155,936	104.119	32.861	71.258	51.817
1964	165,638	110.444	33.831	76.613	55.194
1965	174,965	116.354	34.563	81.791	58.611
1966	185,247	123.047	35.813	87.234	62.201
1967	196,946	130.888	37.645	93.243	66.058
1968	210,719	140.369	40.012	100.357	70.350
1969	228,800	153.376	43.667	109.709	75.423
1970	250,153	169.022	48.242	120.780	81.131
1971	274,395	186.952	53.825	133.127	87.443
1972	303,233	208.540	60.734	147.806	94.693
1973	338,787	235.557	69.354	166.203	103.231
1974	380,791	267.909	80.213	187.696	112.882
1975	427,060	303.802	92.858	210.944	123.258
1976	476,708	342.231	105.934	236.296	134.477
1977	526,950	380.511	117.137	263.374	146.439
1978	577,006	418.024	126.434	291.591	158.982
1979	628,083	456.049	135.372	320.677	172.035
1980	683,850	497.556	144.662	352.894	186.293
1981	737,942	536.916	151.143	385.773	201.027
1982	782,593	567.614	152.506	415.108	214.979
1983	816,798	589.178	150.072	439.106	227.620
1984	842,938	603.853	145.661	458.192	239.085
1985	869,890	619.099	142.067	477.032	250.791
1986	905,082	640.892	141.588	499.304	264.190
1987	945,454	666.637	142.580	524.057	278.817
1988	981,882	689.110	141.806	547.304	292.772
1989	1,015,635	709.337	139.809	569.528	306.298
1990	1,044,547	725.870	136.526	589.344	318.678
1991	1,067,440	738.165	132.608	605.557	329.275
1992	1,085,997	747.479	128.458	619.021	338.518
1993	1,103,217	756.006	124.691	631.315	347.211
1994	1,125,451	768.913	124.174	644.739	356.538

Table E.10 Brazil 3. Capital Stock: Average Ages, Average Service Lives and Capital–Output Ratios, 1950–94 (on the basis of national currencies at constant 1980 prices)

Mid-year	Average age capital stock				Average service life capital stock		Capital–output ratios			
	Total		Non-residential		Total	Non-residential	Total		Non-residential	
	Gross	Net	Gross	Net			Gross	Net	Gross	Net
1950	11.06	6.85	8.43	4.69	26.84	21.10	1.4	0.9	0.9	0.6
1951	10.37	6.34	7.72	4.30	27.29	21.80	1.5	1.0	1.0	0.7
1952	9.78	6.07	7.14	4.22	26.65	21.35	1.6	1.1	1.0	0.7
1953	9.54	6.11	6.94	4.41	25.81	20.52	1.7	1.2	1.1	0.8
1954	9.40	6.14	6.91	4.56	26.50	21.28	1.6	1.2	1.1	0.8
1955	9.44	6.28	7.10	4.80	26.41	21.26	1.7	1.2	1.1	0.8
1956	9.47	6.40	7.29	5.02	26.57	21.48	1.8	1.3	1.2	0.9
1957	9.49	6.48	7.47	5.17	26.95	21.95	1.8	1.3	1.2	0.9
1958	9.54	6.52	7.67	5.25	26.89	21.96	1.8	1.3	1.2	0.9
1959	9.52	6.53	7.76	5.29	26.98	22.13	1.9	1.3	1.3	0.9
1960	9.51	6.57	7.85	5.36	26.88	22.09	1.8	1.3	1.3	0.9
1961	9.53	6.64	7.97	5.46	26.85	22.08	1.8	1.3	1.3	0.8
1962	9.53	6.72	8.03	5.56	26.77	22.01	1.8	1.3	1.3	0.9
1963	9.58	6.86	8.18	5.71	26.96	22.21	1.9	1.4	1.3	0.9
1964	9.68	7.01	8.28	5.87	27.07	22.26	2.0	1.4	1.4	0.9
1965	9.85	7.21	8.45	6.08	27.18	22.30	2.0	1.4	1.4	0.9
1966	9.88	7.31	8.43	6.18	27.57	22.62	2.0	1.4	1.4	1.0
1967	9.95	7.43	8.45	6.31	27.87	22.84	2.1	1.5	1.4	1.0
1968	9.99	7.44	8.48	6.32	28.84	23.81	2.0	1.4	1.4	0.9
1969	9.90	7.36	8.39	6.25	29.09	24.10	1.9	1.4	1.3	0.9
1970	9.86	7.29	8.36	6.18	29.29	24.39	2.1	1.5	1.4	1.0
1971	9.78	7.17	8.30	6.06	29.43	24.61	2.0	1.5	1.4	1.0
1972	9.62	7.02	8.18	5.93	29.46	24.74	2.0	1.4	1.4	1.0
1973	9.41	6.83	8.00	5.77	29.74	25.11	1.9	1.4	1.4	1.0
1974	9.20	6.64	7.82	5.60	29.64	25.15	2.0	1.5	1.4	1.0
1975	9.04	6.53	7.71	5.52	29.45	25.11	2.1	1.6	1.5	1.1
1976	8.92	6.47	7.65	5.49	29.11	24.88	2.1	1.6	1.6	1.2
1977	8.92	6.49	7.71	5.56	28.62	24.47	2.2	1.7	1.6	1.2
1978	8.97	6.57	7.83	5.67	28.54	24.45	2.3	1.7	1.7	1.3
1979	9.07	6.65	7.97	5.78	28.45	24.41	2.4	1.8	1.8	1.3
1980	9.14	6.69	8.10	5.84	28.61	24.60	2.4	1.8	1.8	1.3
1981	9.37	6.88	8.36	6.06	28.07	24.08	2.7	2.0	2.0	1.4
1982	9.67	7.12	8.71	6.33	28.01	24.01	2.9	2.1	2.1	1.5
1983	10.08	7.45	9.16	6.68	27.79	23.78	3.1	2.2	2.3	1.6
1984	10.47	7.78	9.59	7.02	27.94	23.89	3.1	2.1	2.3	1.5
1985	10.82	8.03	9.97	7.27	28.27	24.15	3.0	2.0	2.2	1.4
1986	11.05	8.15	10.23	7.38	28.75	24.57	2.9	2.0	2.1	1.4
1987	11.28	8.31	10.47	7.53	28.80	24.58	2.9	2.0	2.1	1.4
1988	11.55	8.50	10.75	7.71	28.87	24.60	3.1	2.0	2.2	1.4
1989	11.82	8.70	11.01	7.89	29.12	24.76	3.1	2.0	2.2	1.4
1990	12.12	8.97	11.30	8.16	29.28	24.85	3.3	2.2	2.4	1.5
1991	12.45	9.24	11.59	8.41	29.73	25.22	3.4	2.2	2.4	1.5
1992	12.82	9.56	11.93	8.71	30.15	25.59	3.5	2.3	2.4	1.5
1993	13.16	9.82	12.22	8.95	30.67	26.02	3.4	2.2	2.4	1.5
1994	13.43	10.01	12.45	9.10	31.24	26.55	3.3	2.1	2.3	1.4

Table E.11 Brazil 4. Capital Stock: Average Ages, Average Service Lives and Capital–Output Ratios, 1950–94 (on the basis of constant 1980 international dollars)

Mid-year	Average age capital stock				Average service life capital stock		Capital–output ratios			
	Total		Non-residential		Total	Non-residential	Total		Non-residential	
	Gross	Net	Gross	Net			Gross	Net	Gross	Net
1950	11.93	7.37	9.41	5.22	30.42	23.87	1.2	0.8	0.7	0.5
1951	11.18	6.80	8.57	4.74	30.73	24.48	1.3	0.9	0.8	0.6
1952	10.50	6.48	7.86	4.58	30.17	24.14	1.4	1.0	0.9	0.6
1953	10.13	6.41	7.50	4.68	29.47	23.48	1.5	1.1	0.9	0.7
1954	9.92	6.40	7.39	4.80	30.09	24.27	1.4	1.1	0.9	0.7
1955	9.89	6.50	7.52	5.02	30.02	24.31	1.5	1.1	1.0	0.7
1956	9.86	6.60	7.65	5.22	30.21	24.60	1.6	1.2	1.0	0.8
1957	9.84	6.68	7.78	5.39	30.56	25.09	1.6	1.2	1.0	0.8
1958	9.85	6.71	7.94	5.47	30.53	25.16	1.6	1.2	1.1	0.8
1959	9.80	6.74	8.00	5.54	30.62	25.35	1.7	1.2	1.1	0.8
1960	9.74	6.78	8.04	5.63	30.55	25.36	1.7	1.2	1.1	0.8
1961	9.75	6.86	8.15	5.75	30.55	25.43	1.6	1.2	1.1	0.8
1962	9.74	6.95	8.24	5.88	30.50	25.42	1.7	1.2	1.1	0.8
1963	9.79	7.10	8.40	6.05	30.65	25.63	1.8	1.3	1.2	0.9
1964	9.90	7.27	8.52	6.24	30.77	25.71	1.8	1.3	1.2	0.9
1965	10.08	7.48	8.72	6.49	30.89	25.80	1.9	1.3	1.3	0.9
1966	10.14	7.60	8.76	6.62	31.31	26.19	1.9	1.4	1.3	0.9
1967	10.24	7.74	8.82	6.77	31.62	26.47	1.9	1.4	1.3	0.9
1968	10.30	7.76	8.87	6.81	32.57	27.47	1.8	1.3	1.2	0.9
1969	10.22	7.70	8.81	6.76	32.87	27.84	1.8	1.3	1.2	0.9
1970	10.20	7.64	8.81	6.70	33.06	28.13	1.9	1.4	1.3	1.0
1971	10.14	7.53	8.78	6.59	33.19	28.35	1.9	1.4	1.3	0.9
1972	10.00	7.39	8.68	6.46	33.27	28.52	1.9	1.4	1.3	0.9
1973	9.80	7.20	8.51	6.29	33.57	28.93	1.8	1.3	1.3	0.9
1974	9.61	7.01	8.35	6.11	33.45	28.95	1.9	1.4	1.3	1.0
1975	9.46	6.90	8.26	6.02	33.24	28.87	2.0	1.5	1.4	1.1
1976	9.36	6.83	8.21	5.98	32.91	28.63	2.0	1.5	1.4	1.1
1977	9.34	6.83	8.25	6.01	32.44	28.24	2.1	1.6	1.5	1.1
1978	9.38	6.89	8.35	6.10	32.36	28.22	2.2	1.7	1.6	1.2
1979	9.46	6.96	8.48	6.20	32.24	28.16	2.2	1.7	1.6	1.2
1980	9.52	6.98	8.58	6.25	32.44	28.39	2.2	1.7	1.6	1.2
1981	9.72	7.16	8.82	6.45	31.89	27.87	2.5	1.9	1.9	1.4
1982	10.01	7.38	9.15	6.70	31.81	27.81	2.7	2.0	2.0	1.4
1983	10.41	7.70	9.60	7.04	31.55	27.55	2.9	2.1	2.2	1.5
1984	10.79	8.03	10.03	7.40	31.68	27.67	2.9	2.1	2.1	1.5
1985	11.14	8.28	10.41	7.66	32.00	27.96	2.8	2.0	2.1	1.4
1986	11.39	8.42	10.69	7.81	32.50	28.43	2.8	1.9	2.0	1.4
1987	11.62	8.59	10.94	7.98	32.54	28.45	2.8	2.0	2.1	1.4
1988	11.90	8.79	11.25	8.18	32.61	28.50	2.9	2.0	2.1	1.4
1989	12.18	9.00	11.53	8.38	32.86	28.71	3.0	2.0	2.2	1.4
1990	12.50	9.28	11.84	8.66	32.97	28.81	3.2	2.2	2.3	1.5
1991	12.84	9.56	12.17	8.93	33.38	29.19	3.3	2.2	2.4	1.5
1992	13.22	9.88	12.53	9.24	33.73	29.53	3.4	2.3	2.4	1.6
1993	13.57	10.15	12.85	9.49	34.19	29.97	3.4	2.2	2.4	1.5
1994	13.87	10.35	13.12	9.68	34.69	30.47	3.3	2.1	2.3	1.5

Table E.12 Chile 1. Gross and Net Fixed Tangible Reproducible Capital Stocks by Type of Asset, 1950–94 (constant 1980 pesos)

		Gross stocks			
		Non-residential			
Mid-year	Total	Total	M&E	Structures	Res.
1950	1,392,179	796.211	222.280	573.931	595.968
1951	1,445,139	826.915	237.432	589.483	618.225
1952	1,499,782	860.777	254.005	606.772	639.005
1953	1,555,279	893.475	268.429	625.046	661.804
1954	1,611,331	923.533	280.461	643.072	687.798
1955	1,677,570	959.063	294.371	664.692	718.507
1956	1,746,609	1.001.865	313.030	688.835	744.744
1957	1,814,558	1.055.288	341.237	714.051	759.270
1958	1,888,813	1.119.429	376.219	743.209	769.384
1959	1,958,525	1.174.888	404.924	769.964	783.637
1960	2,038,889	1.232.288	430.703	801.586	806.601
1961	2,132,486	1.303.575	461.416	842.159	828.912
1962	2,227,117	1.374.919	488.923	885.996	852.198
1963	2,333,732	1.449.137	509.652	939.486	884.595
1964	2,443,541	1.525.661	528.340	997.321	917.880
1965	2,542,417	1.591.195	545.088	1.046.107	951.222
1966	2,629,553	1.643.694	562.293	1.081.401	985.860
1967	2,713,807	1.697.561	582.255	1.115.306	1.016.246
1968	2,810,534	1.762.110	607.836	1.154.275	1.048.423
1969	2,916,709	1.828.973	639.588	1.189.386	1.087.736
1970	3,025,541	1.893.839	671.012	1.222.827	1.131.702
1971	3,141,129	1.958.984	695.793	1.263.192	1.182.145
1972	3,242,196	2.009.606	703.426	1.306.180	1.232.590
1973	3,317,676	2.045.289	701.503	1.343.786	1.272.387
1974	3,401,420	2.092.382	707.386	1.384.997	1.309.038
1975	3,474,659	2.134.993	714.979	1.420.014	1.339.665
1976	3,504,961	2.149.460	711.845	1.437.614	1.355.501
1977	3,530,573	2.162.252	710.371	1.451.881	1.368.321
1978	3,578,265	2.196.427	726.163	1.470.264	1.381.838
1979	3,647,251	2.250.555	753.406	1.497.149	1.396.696
1980	3,751,815	2.328.523	794.092	1.534.432	1.423.292
1981	3,896,551	2.436.653	848.151	1.588.501	1.459.899
1982	4,011,628	2.521.703	879.985	1.641.718	1.489.925
1983	4,065,605	2.557.472	874.348	1.683.124	1.508.132
1984	4,114,898	2.595.331	859.643	1.735.687	1.519.567
1985	4,178,102	2.647.145	850.286	1.796.859	1.530.957
1986	4,251,052	2.701.587	844.758	1.856.829	1.549.465
1987	4,349,276	2.776.346	856.587	1.919.759	1.572.929
1988	4,481,386	2.879.370	888.548	1.990.823	1.602.016
1989	4,651,716	3.012.989	939.559	2.073.430	1.638.727
1990	4,849,398	3.171.707	1.004.641	2.167.066	1.677.691
1991	5,047,772	3.328.320	1.068.528	2.259.792	1.719.453
1992	5,272,394	3.499.562	1.144.320	2.355.241	1.772.832
1993	5,550,702	3.711.493	1.242.238	2.469.254	1.839.210
1994	5,855,723	3.945.098	1.348.999	2.596.098	1.910.626

Table E.12 (continued)

Mid-year	Total	Non-residential			Res.
		Total	M&E	Structures	
1950	862,635	472.214	134.211	338.004	390.421
1951	899,232	495.001	145.459	349.542	404.231
1952	940,961	523.355	158.587	364.768	417.605
1953	983,167	549.916	169.627	380.289	433.251
1954	1,022,549	569.997	176.631	393.366	452.552
1955	1,065,442	589.818	184.247	405.570	475.624
1956	1,110,586	616.739	196.346	420.393	493.847
1957	1,157,798	655.921	215.316	440.605	501.877
1958	1,208,126	702.129	238.123	464.006	505.997
1959	1,247,053	734.316	251.774	482.542	512.737
1960	1,289,243	763.076	260.745	502.331	526.167
1961	1,342,642	802.501	276.405	526.095	540.142
1962	1,400,593	844.181	293.047	551.135	556.411
1963	1,472,314	891.183	303.799	587.384	581.131
1964	1,546,163	941.385	312.260	629.125	604.778
1965	1,607,914	983.126	318.537	664.589	624.788
1966	1,664,478	1.018.572	325.470	693.102	645.906
1967	1,722,005	1.056.214	336.903	719.310	665.792
1968	1,785,021	1.098.254	351.640	746.614	686.767
1969	1,855,445	1.142.517	367.769	774.748	712.928
1970	1,931,361	1.190.626	382.867	807.759	740.734
1971	2,006,749	1.235.769	394.637	841.131	770.980
1972	2,059,226	1.259.742	395.724	864.018	799.485
1973	2,087,779	1.269.446	392.462	876.984	818.334
1974	2,117,504	1.282.391	390.310	892.081	835.113
1975	2,136,667	1.288.356	386.710	901.645	848.311
1976	2,130,376	1.278.367	380.285	898.082	852.009
1977	2,124,671	1.272.409	378.756	893.653	852.262
1978	2,137,530	1.287.113	390.537	896.576	850.417
1979	2,168,314	1.317.730	411.808	905.923	850.584
1980	2,226,745	1.365.357	443.766	921.591	861.387
1981	2,319,492	1.442.312	488.158	954.154	877.180
1982	2,377,543	1.494.157	512.368	981.789	883.386
1983	2,373,276	1.494.504	501.620	992.885	878.771
1984	2,371,483	1.500.421	485.276	1.015.145	871.063
1985	2,392,784	1.526.083	476.346	1.049.737	866.701
1986	2,423,777	1.555.083	470.637	1.084.446	868.693
1987	2,473,149	1.597.622	473.621	1.124.000	875.527
1988	2,551,847	1.663.699	492.109	1.171.591	888.147
1989	2,667,628	1.758.516	528.499	1.230.017	909.111
1990	2,807,128	1.872.294	574.503	1.297.791	934.834
1991	2,938,631	1.974.881	612.654	1.362.226	963.750
1992	3,096,391	2.094.284	663.139	1.431.144	1.002.108
1993	3,314,028	2.260.875	743.908	1.516.967	1.053.153
1994	3,559,852	2.448.317	837.534	1.610.782	1.111.535

Net stocks — Non-residential column spans Total / M&E / Structures.

Table E.13 Chile 2. *Gross and Net Fixed Tangible Reproducible Capital Stocks by Type of Asset, 1950–94 (constant million 1980 international dollars)*

Mid-year	Total	Gross stocks			Res.
		Non-residential			
		Total	M&E	Structures	
1950	37,077	25,638	4.384	21.254	11.439
1951	38,379	26,513	4.683	21.829	11.866
1952	39,745	27,480	5.010	22.470	12.265
1953	41,143	28,441	5.294	23.146	12.703
1954	42,547	29,346	5.532	23.814	13.202
1955	44,212	30,421	5.806	24.615	13.791
1956	45,977	31,683	6.174	25.509	14.295
1957	47,746	33,173	6.731	26.442	14.573
1958	49,710	34,943	7.420	27.522	14.767
1959	51,541	36,500	7.987	28.513	15.041
1960	53,661	38,179	8.495	29.684	15.482
1961	56,197	40,287	9.101	31.186	15.910
1962	58,810	42,453	9.643	32.810	16.357
1963	61,822	44,843	10.052	34.791	16.979
1964	64,971	47,353	10.421	36.932	17.618
1965	67,748	49,490	10.751	38.739	18.258
1966	70,059	51,137	11.091	40.046	18.922
1967	72,292	52,786	11.484	41.302	19.506
1968	74,857	54,733	11.989	42.745	20.123
1969	77,538	56,660	12.615	44.045	20.878
1970	80,240	58,518	13.235	45.283	21.722
1971	83,192	60,502	13.724	46.778	22.690
1972	85,902	62,244	13.874	48.370	23.658
1973	88,021	63,599	13.836	49.762	24.422
1974	90,366	65,241	13.952	51.289	25.125
1975	92,401	66,687	14.102	52.585	25.713
1976	93,295	67,277	14.040	53.237	26.017
1977	94,040	67,777	14.011	53.765	26.263
1978	95,292	68,769	14.323	54.446	26.523
1979	97,110	70,302	14.860	55.442	26.808
1980	99,803	72,485	15.663	56.822	27.318
1981	103,575	75,553	16.729	58.825	28.021
1982	106,749	78,152	17.357	60.795	28.597
1983	108,521	79,574	17.246	62.329	28.947
1984	110,397	81,231	16.955	64.275	29.166
1985	112,696	83,311	16.771	66.540	29.385
1986	115,163	85,423	16.662	68.761	29.740
1987	118,177	87,987	16.895	71.092	30.191
1988	121,998	91,249	17.526	73.723	30.749
1989	126,768	95,314	18.532	76.782	31.453
1990	132,267	100,065	19.815	80.250	32.201
1991	137,762	104,759	21.076	83.684	33.003
1992	143,816	109,789	22.570	87.218	34.027
1993	151,244	115,942	24.502	91.440	35.302
1994	159,417	122,745	26.607	96.138	36.672

Table E.13 (continued)

Mid-year	Total	Net stocks Non-residential Total	M&E	Structures	Res.
1950	22.658	15.164	2.647	12.517	7.494
1951	23.572	15.813	2.869	12.944	7.759
1952	24.651	16.636	3.128	13.508	8.015
1953	25.744	17.428	3.346	14.083	8.316
1954	26.737	18.051	3.484	14.567	8.686
1955	27.782	18.653	3.634	15.019	9.129
1956	28.919	19.441	3.873	15.568	9.479
1957	30.196	20.563	4.247	16.316	9.633
1958	31.592	21.880	4.697	17.183	9.712
1959	32.677	22.835	4.966	17.869	9.841
1960	33.844	23.745	5.143	18.602	10.099
1961	35.301	24.934	5.452	19.482	10.367
1962	36.869	26.189	5.780	20.409	10.680
1963	38.898	27.744	5.992	21.752	11.154
1964	41.064	29.456	6.159	23.297	11.608
1965	42.886	30.894	6.283	24.611	11.992
1966	44.484	32.086	6.420	25.667	12.397
1967	46.061	33.282	6.645	26.637	12.779
1968	47.766	34.584	6.936	27.648	13.182
1969	49.628	35.944	7.254	28.690	13.684
1970	51.682	37.464	7.552	29.913	14.218
1971	53.730	38.932	7.784	31.148	14.798
1972	55.146	39.801	7.805	31.996	15.345
1973	55.924	40.217	7.741	32.476	15.707
1974	56.763	40.734	7.698	33.035	16.029
1975	57.299	41.017	7.627	33.389	16.282
1976	57.111	40.758	7.501	33.257	16.353
1977	56.922	40.564	7.471	33.093	16.358
1978	57.227	40.904	7.703	33.202	16.323
1979	57.996	41.670	8.122	33.548	16.326
1980	59.414	42.881	8.753	34.128	16.533
1981	61.799	44.962	9.628	35.334	16.836
1982	63.419	46.463	10.106	36.357	16.956
1983	63.529	46.662	9.894	36.768	16.867
1984	63.883	47.164	9.572	37.592	16.719
1985	64.904	48.269	9.395	38.873	16.635
1986	66.115	49.442	9.283	40.159	16.674
1987	67.770	50.965	9.342	41.623	16.805
1988	70.139	53.092	9.706	43.386	17.047
1989	73.423	55.973	10.424	45.549	17.449
1990	77.334	59.391	11.331	48.059	17.943
1991	81.027	62.529	12.084	50.445	18.498
1992	85.311	66.077	13.080	52.998	19.234
1993	91.062	70.848	14.673	56.176	20.214
1994	97.504	76.169	16.519	59.650	21.335

Table E.14 Chile 3. Capital Stock: Average Ages, Average Service Lives and Capital–Output Ratios, 1950–94 (on the basis of national currencies at constant 1980 prices)

| Mid-year | Average age capital stock | | | | Average service life capital stock | | Capital–output ratios | | | |
| | Total | | Non-residential | | Total | Non-residential | Total | | Non-residential | |
	Gross	Net	Gross	Net			Gross	Net	Gross	Net
1950	16.10	10.24	14.47	9.13	35.28	28.42	3.6	2.3	2.1	1.2
1951	15.90	10.11	14.09	8.87	35.07	28.28	3.6	2.3	2.1	1.2
1952	15.68	9.91	13.73	8.49	34.80	28.05	3.6	2.2	2.0	1.2
1953	15.51	9.87	13.50	8.44	34.51	27.63	3.5	2.2	2.0	1.2
1954	15.42	9.98	13.50	8.67	34.42	27.48	3.6	2.3	2.1	1.3
1955	15.38	9.87	13.56	8.58	34.71	27.68	3.8	2.4	2.2	1.3
1956	15.28	9.82	13.38	8.35	34.32	27.61	3.9	2.5	2.2	1.4
1957	15.05	9.69	12.95	7.97	34.18	27.80	3.7	2.3	2.1	1.3
1958	14.92	9.80	12.72	7.98	33.55	27.36	3.7	2.4	2.2	1.4
1959	15.00	9.99	12.77	8.20	32.80	26.49	3.9	2.5	2.3	1.5
1960	15.00	9.97	12.80	8.15	33.05	26.80	3.8	2.4	2.3	1.4
1961	15.00	9.96	12.85	8.08	32.69	26.68	3.8	2.4	2.3	1.4
1962	14.95	9.89	12.90	8.02	32.44	26.40	3.8	2.4	2.3	1.4
1963	14.78	9.75	12.80	7.90	32.57	26.54	3.7	2.3	2.3	1.4
1964	14.75	9.66	12.76	7.75	32.46	26.56	3.8	2.4	2.4	1.5
1965	14.77	9.67	12.70	7.75	32.31	26.35	3.9	2.5	2.5	1.5
1966	14.67	9.81	12.53	7.97	32.21	26.26	3.7	2.3	2.3	1.4
1967	14.63	9.87	12.47	8.03	32.22	26.36	3.7	2.3	2.3	1.4
1968	14.58	9.80	12.40	7.92	32.37	26.48	3.7	2.3	2.3	1.4
1969	14.44	9.79	12.20	7.94	32.20	26.25	3.7	2.3	2.3	1.4
1970	14.32	9.80	11.90	7.97	32.09	26.09	3.7	2.4	2.3	1.5
1971	14.40	9.81	11.94	8.04	32.06	25.94	3.5	2.3	2.2	1.4
1972	14.71	10.02	12.25	8.30	31.76	25.61	3.7	2.4	2.3	1.4
1973	15.02	10.28	12.54	8.60	31.91	25.81	3.9	2.4	2.4	1.5
1974	15.30	10.42	12.85	8.74	32.38	26.26	3.9	2.4	2.4	1.5
1975	15.61	10.76	13.19	9.10	32.00	25.95	4.6	2.8	2.8	1.7
1976	15.91	11.07	13.52	9.35	31.76	25.74	4.5	2.7	2.8	1.6
1977	16.17	11.36	13.73	9.61	32.14	26.12	4.2	2.5	2.6	1.5
1978	16.32	11.49	13.75	9.60	32.32	26.39	4.0	2.4	2.4	1.4
1979	16.43	11.51	13.82	9.53	32.35	26.45	3.8	2.2	2.3	1.4
1980	16.41	11.38	13.75	9.34	32.57	26.67	3.6	2.1	2.2	1.3
1981	16.34	11.15	13.52	9.05	32.50	26.70	3.5	2.1	2.2	1.3
1982	16.69	11.38	13.79	9.25	31.47	25.72	4.2	2.5	2.6	1.5
1983	17.12	11.66	14.17	9.48	31.31	25.58	4.4	2.6	2.7	1.6
1984	17.37	11.79	14.36	9.55	31.74	26.14	4.2	2.4	2.6	1.5
1985	17.52	11.83	14.45	9.54	32.01	26.44	4.1	2.3	2.6	1.5
1986	17.67	11.91	14.57	9.64	32.29	26.74	3.9	2.2	2.5	1.4
1987	17.64	11.72	14.50	9.41	32.75	27.31	3.8	2.2	2.4	1.4
1988	17.57	11.53	14.40	9.24	32.88	27.48	3.6	2.1	2.3	1.3
1989	17.28	11.13	14.10	8.87	33.08	27.79	3.4	2.0	2.2	1.3
1990	17.05	10.76	13.90	8.52	32.80	27.63	3.5	2.0	2.3	1.3
1991	16.86	10.55	13.78	8.39	32.47	27.32	3.4	2.0	2.2	1.3
1992	16.52	10.19	13.48	8.13	32.58	27.47	3.2	1.9	2.1	1.3
1993	16.07	9.78	13.09	7.83	32.49	27.45	3.1	1.9	2.1	1.3
1994	15.67	9.45	12.79	7.60	32.11	27.15	3.2	1.9	2.1	1.3

Table E.15 Chile 4. Capital Stock: Average Ages, Average Service Lives and Capital–Output Ratios, 1950–94 (on the basis of constant 1980 international dollars)

Mid-year	Average age capital stock Total Gross	Total Net	Non-residential Gross	Non-residential Net	Average service life capital stock Total	Non-residential	Capital–output ratios Total Gross	Total Net	Non-residential Gross	Non-residential Net
1950	16.44	10.49	15.62	9.95	36.55	32.26	2.8	1.7	1.9	1.1
1951	16.20	10.33	15.25	9.69	36.39	32.13	2.8	1.7	1.9	1.1
1952	15.95	10.05	14.90	9.27	36.19	31.94	2.7	1.7	1.9	1.1
1953	15.76	10.00	14.66	9.20	35.93	31.57	2.7	1.7	1.8	1.1
1954	15.69	10.15	14.65	9.44	35.84	31.43	2.8	1.7	1.9	1.2
1955	15.69	10.04	14.73	9.33	36.15	31.67	2.9	1.8	2.0	1.2
1956	15.58	9.92	14.56	9.08	35.79	31.54	3.0	1.9	2.0	1.3
1957	15.30	9.73	14.12	8.69	35.73	31.68	2.8	1.8	1.9	1.2
1958	15.16	9.84	13.89	8.74	35.24	31.30	2.8	1.8	2.0	1.2
1959	15.21	10.04	13.92	8.95	34.52	30.44	2.9	1.9	2.1	1.3
1960	15.22	10.00	13.94	8.90	34.89	30.87	2.9	1.8	2.0	1.3
1961	15.26	9.99	14.02	8.83	34.58	30.72	2.9	1.8	2.1	1.3
1962	15.24	9.91	14.08	8.75	34.43	30.53	2.9	1.8	2.1	1.3
1963	15.03	9.72	13.91	8.57	34.63	30.76	2.8	1.8	2.1	1.3
1964	14.98	9.57	13.83	8.36	34.51	30.74	2.9	1.8	2.1	1.3
1965	14.94	9.54	13.72	8.33	34.26	30.44	3.0	1.9	2.2	1.4
1966	14.80	9.73	13.52	8.58	34.08	30.25	2.8	1.8	2.1	1.3
1967	14.74	9.80	13.46	8.64	34.15	30.40	2.8	1.8	2.0	1.3
1968	14.69	9.72	13.38	8.54	34.26	30.47	2.8	1.8	2.1	1.3
1969	14.51	9.73	13.14	8.57	34.05	30.20	2.8	1.8	2.0	1.3
1970	14.30	9.75	12.79	8.61	33.96	30.07	2.8	1.8	2.1	1.3
1971	14.36	9.77	12.82	8.68	33.98	30.00	2.7	1.7	2.0	1.3
1972	14.68	10.00	13.15	8.95	33.71	29.72	2.8	1.8	2.0	1.3
1973	15.00	10.28	13.47	9.26	33.80	29.87	3.0	1.9	2.1	1.4
1974	15.29	10.41	13.78	9.40	34.27	30.35	3.0	1.9	2.2	1.4
1975	15.63	10.79	14.15	9.81	33.81	29.94	3.5	2.2	2.6	1.6
1976	15.96	11.09	14.52	10.07	33.58	29.74	3.5	2.1	2.5	1.5
1977	16.24	11.42	14.78	10.39	33.90	30.06	3.2	2.0	2.3	1.4
1978	16.38	11.55	14.83	10.44	34.08	30.31	3.0	1.8	2.2	1.3
1979	16.53	11.59	14.96	10.42	34.15	30.40	2.9	1.7	2.1	1.2
1980	16.54	11.50	14.95	10.29	34.37	30.59	2.8	1.6	2.0	1.2
1981	16.46	11.28	14.75	10.03	34.42	30.71	2.7	1.6	2.0	1.2
1982	16.80	11.49	15.04	10.22	33.46	29.76	3.2	1.9	2.3	1.4
1983	17.21	11.72	15.42	10.41	33.35	29.69	3.4	2.0	2.5	1.4
1984	17.41	11.78	15.58	10.41	33.82	30.30	3.2	1.9	2.4	1.4
1985	17.51	11.75	15.64	10.34	34.05	30.57	3.2	1.8	2.3	1.4
1986	17.63	11.81	15.74	10.41	34.31	30.85	3.1	1.8	2.3	1.3
1987	17.56	11.58	15.63	10.14	34.71	31.33	3.0	1.7	2.2	1.3
1988	17.48	11.39	15.54	9.98	34.86	31.52	2.8	1.6	2.1	1.2
1989	17.20	11.01	15.24	9.61	35.05	31.78	2.7	1.6	2.0	1.2
1990	16.98	10.64	15.05	9.25	34.86	31.66	2.7	1.6	2.1	1.2
1991	16.81	10.45	14.91	9.11	34.53	31.32	2.6	1.6	2.0	1.2
1992	16.50	10.15	14.62	8.87	34.66	31.46	2.5	1.5	1.9	1.1
1993	16.09	9.79	14.26	8.60	34.63	31.46	2.5	1.5	1.9	1.2
1994	15.75	9.50	13.99	8.38	34.31	31.18	2.5	1.5	1.9	1.2

Table E.16 Colombia 1. Gross and Net Fixed Tangible Reproducible Capital Stocks by Type of Asset, 1950–94 (constant 1980 pesos)

| | | Gross stocks | | | |
| | | Non-residential | | | |
Mid-year	Total	Total	M&E	Structures	Res.
1950	1,023,835	767.342	171.792	595.550	256.493
1951	1,066,845	797.915	189.032	608.883	268.930
1952	1,109,494	828.205	206.327	621.878	281.290
1953	1,163,273	867.632	230.005	637.627	295.641
1954	1,233,752	920.359	262.112	658.247	313.393
1955	1,314,488	980.835	298.435	682.400	333.653
1956	1,396,601	1.042.214	335.184	707.030	354.387
1957	1,466,379	1.092.500	362.948	729.552	373.879
1958	1,524,438	1.132.724	383.390	749.334	391.714
1959	1,582,015	1.171.985	402.409	769.575	410.031
1960	1,643,413	1.214.276	422.840	791.436	429.137
1961	1,707,663	1.261.579	443.875	817.704	446.084
1962	1,768,081	1.306.677	457.916	848.761	461.404
1963	1,822,812	1.346.620	468.203	878.417	476.192
1964	1,883,237	1.392.477	485.098	907.379	490.760
1965	1,944,143	1.438.402	502.164	936.238	505.741
1966	2,002,011	1.480.588	516.311	964.277	521.423
1967	2,066,503	1.526.530	529.499	997.031	539.973
1968	2,133,822	1.572.140	536.437	1.035.703	561.682
1969	2,206,466	1.620.873	540.796	1.080.078	585.593
1970	2,293,615	1.682.163	551.451	1.130.712	611.452
1971	2,396,446	1.758.674	573.539	1.185.135	637.772
1972	2,512,209	1.850.088	610.260	1.239.827	662.121
1973	2,643,160	1.954.138	656.111	1.298.027	689.021
1974	2,791,116	2.071.384	705.849	1.365.535	719.732
1975	2,936,893	2.188.398	753.211	1.435.187	748.495
1976	3,079,312	2.303.219	798.985	1.504.234	776.093
1977	3,229,466	2.423.837	848.569	1.575.268	805.629
1978	3,390,475	2.551.779	906.151	1.645.627	838.696
1979	3,561,144	2.689.656	974.153	1.715.504	871.488
1980	3,749,496	2.847.120	1.052.652	1.794.468	902.376
1981	3,961,202	3.026.109	1.139.536	1.886.572	935.094
1982	4,184,069	3.214.747	1.229.532	1.985.215	969.322
1983	4,409,268	3.402.315	1.317.760	2.084.555	1.006.953
1984	4,629,577	3.581.279	1.396.815	2.184.464	1.048.298
1985	4,832,434	3.741.846	1.454.077	2.287.769	1.090.588
1986	5,025,749	3.890.764	1.495.560	2.395.203	1.134.985
1987	5,225,926	4.043.541	1.549.255	2.494.285	1.182.385
1988	5,442,346	4.212.006	1.619.077	2.592.929	1.230.340
1989	5,665,823	4.389.532	1.690.395	2.699.137	1.276.291
1990	5,874,741	4.555.652	1.759.343	2.796.309	1.319.089
1991	6,063,918	4.699.082	1.816.184	2.882.897	1.364.836
1992	6,257,817	4.838.757	1.870.628	2.968.129	1.419.060
1993	6,518,999	5.030.308	1.976.179	3.054.129	1.488.691
1994	6,869,693	5.289.057	2.135.437	3.153.619	1.580.636

Table E.16 (continued)

Mid-year	Net stocks Total	Non-residential Total	M&E	Structures	Res.
1950	662,418	479.365	110.414	368.951	183.053
1951	687,788	496.627	122.709	373.918	191.161
1952	713,413	514.436	135.948	378.488	198.977
1953	750,277	541.706	155.934	385.772	208.572
1954	802,427	581.110	183.292	397.818	221.317
1955	861,074	624.821	211.654	413.167	236.252
1956	916,434	665.137	236.454	428.683	251.297
1957	953,661	688.934	247.151	441.783	264.726
1958	974,244	698.092	246.193	451.899	276.152
1959	993,395	705.648	243.338	462.310	287.747
1960	1,019,533	719.248	245.071	474.178	300.284
1961	1,053,639	742.815	252.552	490.263	310.824
1962	1,089,216	769.729	258.877	510.852	319.487
1963	1,119,163	791.755	262.107	529.648	327.408
1964	1,149,054	814.146	266.736	547.409	334.908
1965	1,179,530	836.905	271.274	565.631	342.624
1966	1,211,528	860.688	275.691	584.997	350.840
1967	1,252,608	890.894	280.299	610.595	361.714
1968	1,304,150	928.669	285.679	642.990	375.480
1969	1,367,905	976.780	296.966	679.813	391.125
1970	1,444,600	1.036.245	317.405	718.840	408.355
1971	1,531,335	1.105.688	347.425	758.263	425.646
1972	1,616,946	1.176.380	378.953	797.428	440.565
1973	1,703,757	1.246.081	407.358	838.723	457.676
1974	1,800,442	1.322.249	436.060	886.189	478.193
1975	1,895,550	1.400.009	464.924	935.085	495.541
1976	1,990,353	1.479.426	496.155	983.270	510.927
1977	2,089,439	1.560.821	528.391	1.032.430	528.619
1978	2,193,212	1.642.803	563.159	1.079.644	550.410
1979	2,304,656	1.732.423	606.593	1.125.830	572.232
1980	2,428,871	1.837.986	657.027	1.180.959	590.885
1981	2,568,982	1.959.307	711.629	1.247.678	609.676
1982	2,712,812	2.083.184	764.685	1.318.499	629.628
1983	2,853,368	2.199.930	811.623	1.388.306	653.438
1984	2,988,340	2.307.807	849.878	1.457.929	680.533
1985	3,108,790	2.400.956	870.511	1.530.445	707.834
1986	3,224,994	2.488.052	881.838	1.606.213	736.942
1987	3,346,846	2.577.714	905.593	1.672.121	769.132
1988	3,479,527	2.677.873	941.221	1.736.652	801.654
1989	3,611,862	2.779.542	977.043	1.802.500	832.320
1990	3,721,640	2.861.560	1.009.219	1.852.341	860.080
1991	3,808,601	2.919.093	1.030.216	1.888.878	889.507
1992	3,897,184	2.970.910	1.049.081	1.921.829	926.274
1993	4,055,565	3.077.720	1.121.264	1.956.456	977.845
1994	4,310,416	3.260.201	1.252.621	2.007.581	1.050.215

Table E.17 Colombia 2. Gross and Net Fixed Tangible Reproducible Capital Stocks by Type of Asset, 1950–94 (constant million 1980 international dollars)

		Gross stocks			
		Non-residential			
Mid-year	Total	Total	M&E	Structures	Res.
1950	42,962	29,876	3.135	26.741	13.086
1951	44,510	30,789	3.449	27.340	13.721
1952	46,040	31,688	3.765	27.923	14.352
1953	47,911	32,828	4.197	28.630	15.084
1954	50,329	34,339	4.783	29.556	15.989
1955	53,110	36,087	5.446	30.641	17.023
1956	55,944	37,863	6.117	31.747	18.081
1957	58,457	39,381	6.623	32.758	19.075
1958	60,628	40,642	6.996	33.646	19.985
1959	62,818	41,898	7.343	34.555	20.920
1960	65,147	43,253	7.716	35.537	21.895
1961	67,575	44,816	8.100	36.716	22.759
1962	70,008	46,467	8.356	38.111	23.541
1963	72,282	47,986	8.544	39.442	24.296
1964	74,634	49,595	8.852	40.743	25.039
1965	77,005	51,202	9.164	42.038	25.803
1966	79,322	52,719	9.422	43.297	26.603
1967	81,980	54,431	9.662	44.768	27.550
1968	84,951	56,294	9.789	46.505	28.657
1969	88,243	58,366	9.869	48.497	29.877
1970	92,030	60,834	10.063	50.771	31.197
1971	96,220	63,680	10.466	53.214	32.539
1972	100,588	66,806	11.136	55.670	33.782
1973	105,410	70,256	11.973	58.283	35.154
1974	110,916	74,195	12.880	61.314	36.721
1975	116,375	78,187	13.745	64.442	38.189
1976	121,719	82,122	14.580	67.542	39.597
1977	127,320	86,217	15.485	70.732	41.104
1978	133,217	90,427	16.536	73.891	42.791
1979	139,269	94,805	17.777	77.029	44.464
1980	145,823	99,783	19.209	80.574	46.040
1981	153,213	105,504	20.794	84.710	47.709
1982	161,031	111,576	22.437	89.139	49.455
1983	169,021	117,646	24.047	93.600	51.375
1984	177,060	123,575	25.489	98.086	53.485
1985	184,901	129,258	26.534	102.724	55.642
1986	192,747	134,839	27.291	107.548	57.907
1987	200,594	140,268	28.271	111.997	60.326
1988	208,744	145,971	29.545	116.426	62.772
1989	217,159	152,042	30.847	121.195	65.117
1990	224,964	157,663	32.105	125.558	67.300
1991	232,223	162,588	33.142	129.446	69.635
1992	239,810	167,409	34.136	133.273	72.401
1993	249,150	173,196	36.062	137.135	75.954
1994	261,215	180,570	38.968	141.602	80.645

Table E.17 (continued)

Mid-year	Total	Non-residential			Res.
		Total	M&E	Structures	
1950	27.921	18.581	2.015	16.566	9.339
1951	28.782	19.029	2.239	16.789	9.753
1952	29.627	19.475	2.481	16.995	10.152
1953	30.809	20.167	2.846	17.322	10.641
1954	32.499	21.207	3.345	17.863	11.292
1955	34.468	22.414	3.862	18.552	12.054
1956	36.385	23.563	4.315	19.248	12.821
1957	37.853	24.347	4.510	19.837	13.506
1958	38.873	24.783	4.493	20.291	14.089
1959	39.880	25.199	4.440	20.758	14.681
1960	41.084	25.763	4.472	21.291	15.321
1961	42.481	26.622	4.609	22.014	15.858
1962	43.962	27.662	4.724	22.938	16.300
1963	45.269	28.565	4.783	23.782	16.705
1964	46.534	29.447	4.867	24.579	17.087
1965	47.829	30.348	4.950	25.398	17.481
1966	49.198	31.298	5.031	26.267	17.900
1967	50.986	32.532	5.115	27.417	18.455
1968	53.241	34.084	5.213	28.871	19.157
1969	55.899	35.944	5.419	30.525	19.955
1970	58.903	38.069	5.792	32.277	20.834
1971	62.104	40.387	6.340	34.047	21.717
1972	65.199	42.721	6.915	35.806	22.478
1973	68.444	45.093	7.434	37.660	23.351
1974	72.146	47.748	7.957	39.791	24.398
1975	75.753	50.471	8.484	41.987	25.283
1976	79.272	53.204	9.054	44.150	26.068
1977	82.970	56.000	9.642	46.358	26.970
1978	86.836	58.754	10.277	48.478	28.082
1979	90.816	61.621	11.069	50.551	29.196
1980	95.164	65.016	11.990	53.027	30.147
1981	100.114	69.008	12.986	56.023	31.106
1982	105.281	73.157	13.954	59.203	32.124
1983	110.486	77.148	14.811	62.337	33.339
1984	115.693	80.972	15.509	65.463	34.721
1985	120.718	84.604	15.885	68.719	36.114
1986	125.812	88.213	16.092	72.121	37.599
1987	130.847	91.606	16.525	75.081	39.241
1988	136.054	95.154	17.176	77.978	40.901
1989	141.229	98.764	17.829	80.935	42.465
1990	145.471	101.589	18.416	83.173	43.882
1991	148.996	103.613	18.800	84.813	45.383
1992	152.696	105.437	19.144	86.293	47.259
1993	158.199	108.309	20.461	87.848	49.890
1994	166.584	113.001	22.858	90.143	53.582

Table E.18 Colombia 3. Capital Stock: Average Ages, Average Service Lives and Capital–Output Ratios, 1950–94 (on the basis of national currencies at constant 1980 prices)

Mid-year	Average age capital stock				Average service life capital stock		Capital–output ratios			
	Total		Non-residential		Total	Non-residential	Total		Non-residential	
	Gross	Net	Gross	Net			Gross	Net	Gross	Net
1950	14.35	9.58	14.02	9.07	34.18	30.58	2.9	1.9	2.2	1.3
1951	14.42	9.64	14.04	9.10	33.63	30.02	2.9	1.9	2.2	1.4
1952	14.45	9.66	14.02	9.07	33.21	29.53	2.8	1.8	2.1	1.3
1953	14.27	9.45	13.77	8.80	33.40	29.69	2.8	1.8	2.1	1.3
1954	14.01	9.20	13.45	8.52	32.97	29.19	2.8	1.8	2.1	1.3
1955	13.78	8.99	13.17	8.29	32.45	28.65	2.9	1.9	2.1	1.4
1956	13.67	8.96	13.04	8.26	31.61	27.79	2.9	1.9	2.2	1.4
1957	13.84	9.17	13.21	8.50	30.68	26.84	3.0	1.9	2.2	1.4
1958	14.05	9.38	13.43	8.73	30.41	26.55	3.0	1.9	2.3	1.4
1959	14.23	9.51	13.62	8.85	30.29	26.37	2.9	1.8	2.2	1.3
1960	14.30	9.57	13.68	8.90	30.28	26.35	2.9	1.8	2.2	1.3
1961	14.32	9.57	13.64	8.81	30.11	26.25	2.9	1.8	2.1	1.3
1962	14.37	9.59	13.62	8.75	29.87	25.99	2.8	1.8	2.1	1.2
1963	14.49	9.70	13.69	8.81	29.92	26.05	2.8	1.7	2.1	1.2
1964	14.55	9.72	13.70	8.75	30.15	26.32	2.8	1.7	2.0	1.2
1965	14.65	9.81	13.73	8.78	29.82	25.97	2.8	1.7	2.0	1.2
1966	14.63	9.77	13.64	8.66	29.94	26.08	2.7	1.6	2.0	1.2
1967	14.57	9.69	13.51	8.54	29.99	26.08	2.7	1.6	2.0	1.2
1968	14.41	9.58	13.26	8.40	30.09	26.13	2.6	1.6	1.9	1.1
1969	14.24	9.47	13.01	8.27	30.45	26.45	2.5	1.6	1.9	1.1
1970	14.05	9.28	12.75	8.06	30.90	26.90	2.5	1.6	1.8	1.1
1971	13.89	9.14	12.53	7.89	31.13	27.18	2.4	1.6	1.8	1.1
1972	13.78	9.08	12.36	7.82	31.19	27.34	2.4	1.5	1.8	1.1
1973	13.70	9.00	12.27	7.75	31.06	27.19	2.4	1.5	1.7	1.1
1974	13.60	8.90	12.16	7.66	30.98	27.18	2.4	1.5	1.7	1.1
1975	13.58	8.88	12.08	7.63	30.48	26.74	2.4	1.6	1.8	1.2
1976	13.52	8.89	11.96	7.66	30.46	26.77	2.4	1.6	1.8	1.2
1977	13.48	8.89	11.92	7.67	30.26	26.58	2.4	1.6	1.8	1.2
1978	13.41	8.86	11.86	7.67	30.25	26.60	2.4	1.5	1.8	1.1
1979	13.34	8.83	11.78	7.65	29.95	26.38	2.3	1.5	1.8	1.1
1980	13.23	8.74	11.63	7.55	29.92	26.43	2.4	1.5	1.8	1.2
1981	13.13	8.66	11.50	7.46	29.62	26.19	2.5	1.6	1.9	1.2
1982	13.07	8.61	11.43	7.43	29.39	26.03	2.6	1.7	2.0	1.3
1983	13.03	8.61	11.41	7.46	29.03	25.69	2.7	1.7	2.1	1.3
1984	13.02	8.64	11.40	7.52	28.81	25.49	2.7	1.7	2.1	1.3
1985	13.06	8.74	11.46	7.66	28.49	25.17	2.7	1.8	2.1	1.4
1986	13.08	8.76	11.49	7.70	28.64	25.31	2.7	1.7	2.1	1.3
1987	13.11	8.83	11.55	7.82	28.70	25.36	2.7	1.7	2.1	1.3
1988	13.09	8.82	11.54	7.82	28.80	25.49	2.7	1.7	2.1	1.3
1989	13.18	8.91	11.67	7.92	28.62	25.33	2.7	1.7	2.1	1.3
1990	13.32	9.05	11.84	8.08	28.50	25.24	2.7	1.7	2.1	1.3
1991	13.52	9.22	12.10	8.29	28.28	24.97	2.7	1.7	2.1	1.3
1992	13.66	9.32	12.29	8.41	28.49	25.13	2.7	1.7	2.1	1.3
1993	13.58	9.17	12.26	8.30	28.87	25.44	2.6	1.6	2.0	1.2
1994	13.35	8.89	12.08	8.06	28.89	25.39	2.6	1.6	2.0	1.2

Table E.19 Colombia 4. Capital Stock: Average Ages, Average Service Lives and Capital–Output Ratios, 1950–94 (on the basis of constant 1980 international dollars)

Mid-year	Average age capital stock				Average service life capital stock		Capital–output ratios			
	Total		Non-residential		Total	Non-residential	Total		Non-residential	
	Gross	Net	Gross	Net			Gross	Net	Gross	Net
1950	15.27	10.28	15.23	9.97	39.28	35,32	2,8	1,8	1,9	1,2
1951	15.42	10.41	15.36	10.08	38.87	34,86	2,8	1,8	1,9	1,2
1952	15.53	10.48	15.45	10.12	38.65	34,53	2,7	1,8	1,9	1,2
1953	15.47	10.36	15.35	9.95	38.86	34,65	2,7	1,7	1,8	1,1
1954	15.31	10.17	15.15	9.73	38.73	34,35	2,6	1,7	1,8	1,1
1955	15.16	9.99	14.97	9.52	38.39	33,90	2,7	1,7	1,8	1,1
1956	15.09	9.96	14.87	9.49	37.77	33,19	2,7	1,8	1,8	1,1
1957	15.21	10.10	14.99	9.67	37.05	32,39	2,8	1,8	1,9	1,1
1958	15.38	10.27	15.15	9.85	36.81	32,10	2,8	1,8	1,9	1,1
1959	15.51	10.34	15.27	9.90	36.78	31,98	2,7	1,7	1,8	1,1
1960	15.57	10.41	15.33	9.96	36.75	31,93	2,7	1,7	1,8	1,1
1961	15.60	10.43	15.26	9.85	36.67	31,96	2,6	1,7	1,8	1,0
1962	15.64	10.44	15.21	9.75	36.52	31,79	2,6	1,6	1,7	1,0
1963	15.76	10.56	15.25	9.79	36.47	31,78	2,6	1,6	1,7	1,0
1964	15.82	10.60	15.23	9.73	36.64	31,98	2,5	1,6	1,7	1,0
1965	15.91	10.69	15.23	9.75	36.37	31,68	2,5	1,6	1,7	1,0
1966	15.90	10.67	15.11	9.63	36.47	31,76	2,5	1,5	1,6	1,0
1967	15.80	10.57	14.90	9.46	36.64	31,87	2,4	1,5	1,6	1,0
1968	15.61	10.45	14.60	9.29	36.77	31,97	2,4	1,5	1,6	1,0
1969	15.44	10.34	14.33	9.16	37.12	32,33	2,3	1,5	1,6	1,0
1970	15.29	10.17	14.10	8.95	37.46	32,71	2,3	1,5	1,5	1,0
1971	15.18	10.05	13.92	8.80	37.59	32,93	2,3	1,5	1,5	1,0
1972	15.11	10.03	13.76	8.73	37.51	32,95	2,2	1,4	1,5	0,9
1973	15.03	9.94	13.66	8.66	37.52	32,89	2,2	1,4	1,4	0,9
1974	14.94	9.84	13.54	8.55	37.47	32,91	2,2	1,4	1,4	0,9
1975	14.94	9.82	13.46	8.51	37.00	32,49	2,2	1,4	1,5	1,0
1976	14.91	9.85	13.35	8.56	36.96	32,50	2,2	1,4	1,5	1,0
1977	14.88	9.84	13.30	8.56	36.80	32,32	2,2	1,4	1,5	1,0
1978	14.83	9.82	13.26	8.58	36.75	32,26	2,1	1,4	1,5	0,9
1979	14.79	9.83	13.20	8.59	36.45	32,03	2,1	1,4	1,4	0,9
1980	14.71	9.76	13.06	8.49	36.46	32,12	2,1	1,4	1,5	1,0
1981	14.64	9.68	12.92	8.40	36.23	31,93	2,2	1,4	1,5	1,0
1982	14.58	9.64	12.83	8.36	36.01	31,76	2,3	1,5	1,6	1,0
1983	14.53	9.63	12.79	8.39	35.72	31,43	2,4	1,5	1,6	1,1
1984	14.50	9.64	12.76	8.44	35.53	31,26	2,4	1,6	1,7	1,1
1985	14.50	9.70	12.76	8.54	35.30	31,02	2,4	1,6	1,7	1,1
1986	14.48	9.68	12.75	8.55	35.43	31,16	2,4	1,6	1,7	1,1
1987	14.51	9.76	12.82	8.69	35.37	31,07	2,4	1,5	1,6	1,1
1988	14.48	9.75	12.80	8.70	35.49	31,24	2,4	1,5	1,6	1,1
1989	14.58	9.85	12.95	8.83	35.30	31,07	2,4	1,5	1,7	1,1
1990	14.73	10.01	13.16	9.03	35.13	30,93	2,4	1,5	1,6	1,1
1991	14.94	10.20	13.45	9.28	34.97	30,67	2,4	1,5	1,7	1,1
1992	15.09	10.30	13.69	9.45	35.16	30,81	2,4	1,5	1,7	1,0
1993	15.07	10.24	13.78	9.47	35.46	30,96	2,3	1,5	1,6	1,0
1994	14.90	10.01	13.70	9.31	35.60	30,96	2,3	1,5	1,6	1,0

Table E.20 Mexico 1. Gross and Net Fixed Tangible Reproducible Capital Stocks by Type of Asset, 1950–94 (constant 1980 pesos)

		Gross stocks			
			Non-residential		
Mid-year	Total	Total	M&E	Structures	Res.
1950	1,161,610	937.095	145.880	791.215	224.514
1951	1,268,525	1.027.481	161.671	865.810	241.043
1952	1,390,508	1.131.796	179.234	952.562	258.712
1953	1,513,255	1.235.054	198.128	1.036.926	278.201
1954	1,636,803	1.337.211	218.484	1.118.728	299.592
1955	1,770,065	1.446.993	239.366	1.207.627	323.072
1956	1,922,487	1.573.605	262.773	1.310.832	348.882
1957	2,094,984	1.717.690	290.594	1.427.096	377.293
1958	2,270,575	1.862.028	320.044	1.541.984	408.547
1959	2,440,620	1.997.672	347.513	1.650.160	442.948
1960	2,611,295	2.130.511	372.630	1.757.881	480.784
1961	2,782,818	2.257.830	417.289	1.840.541	524.988
1962	2,958,803	2.382.598	484.317	1.898.281	576.205
1963	3,151,240	2.518.665	557.230	1.961.435	632.575
1964	3,382,527	2.687.910	646.452	2.041.458	694.617
1965	3,647,325	2.884.423	750.527	2.133.896	762.902
1966	3,932,193	3.094.136	860.843	2.233.293	838.057
1967	4,255,611	3.334.836	983.586	2.351.250	920.775
1968	4,622,027	3.610.212	1.122.677	2.487.535	1.011.815
1969	5,020,632	3.908.616	1.274.963	2.633.653	1.112.016
1970	5,452,064	4.231.240	1.439.565	2.791.675	1.220.824
1971	5,899,136	4.551.764	1.606.170	2.945.594	1.347.371
1972	6,374,235	4.883.600	1.779.878	3.103.722	1.490.635
1973	6,919,585	5.281.155	1.984.494	3.296.660	1.638.431
1974	7,526,375	5.739.992	2.222.361	3.517.631	1.786.383
1975	8,182,943	6.236.968	2.487.919	3.749.049	1.945.975
1976	8,846,168	6.718.111	2.739.228	3.978.883	2.128.057
1977	9,456,498	7.141.114	2.941.283	4.199.831	2.315.384
1978	10,090,874	7.598.454	3.142.044	4.456.410	2.492.419
1979	10,850,056	8.178.748	3.399.613	4.779.135	2.671.308
1980	11,741,821	8.879.384	3.727.202	5.152.182	2.862.437
1981	12,778,178	9.712.797	4.128.556	5.584.241	3.065.381
1982	13,779,896	10.502.372	4.476.686	6.025.686	3.277.524
1983	14,507,288	11.022.728	4.645.728	6.376.999	3.484.560
1984	15,091,096	11.401.141	4.738.662	6.662.479	3.689.955
1985	15,707,995	11.799.198	4.854.819	6.944.379	3.908.797
1986	16,283,479	12.149.478	4.963.156	7.186.322	4.134.001
1987	16,782,455	12.420.584	5.031.118	7.389.466	4.361.871
1988	17,271,368	12.678.575	5.088.368	7.590.207	4.592.793
1989	17,779,894	12.951.715	5.156.742	7.794.973	4.828.179
1990	18,337,334	13.250.678	5.248.563	8.002.115	5.086.656
1991	18,979,876	13.602.698	5.406.338	8.196.360	5.377.178
1992	19,746,221	14.046.770	5.669.903	8.376.868	5.699.450
1993	20,551,995	14.518.501	5.943.365	8.575.137	6.033.494
1994	21,321,983	14.945.535	6.146.195	8.799.340	6.376.448

Table E.20 (continued)

Mid-year	Total	Non-residential Total	M&E	Structures	Res,
1950	837,728	672,753	99,149	573,604	164,974
1951	917,855	738,870	110,451	628,419	178,986
1952	1,010,569	816,754	123,228	693,526	193,815
1953	1,099,558	889,413	135,338	754,075	210,145
1954	1,184,824	956,712	146,758	809,954	228,113
1955	1,277,148	1,029,276	158,390	870,885	247,872
1956	1,385,858	1,116,267	172,367	943,900	269,591
1957	1,509,139	1,215,688	188,295	1,027,393	293,451
1958	1,628,809	1,309,158	202,554	1,106,604	319,651
1959	1,738,697	1,390,288	214,059	1,176,229	348,409
1960	1,857,908	1,477,946	226,123	1,251,823	379,962
1961	1,986,207	1,570,363	261,152	1,309,211	415,844
1962	2,115,039	1,658,478	318,394	1,340,084	456,561
1963	2,255,129	1,753,722	378,428	1,375,294	501,407
1964	2,425,071	1,874,273	448,532	1,425,741	550,798
1965	2,621,441	2,016,251	526,902	1,489,349	605,190
1966	2,831,949	2,166,862	608,211	1,558,651	665,087
1967	3,068,589	2,337,546	697,119	1,640,427	731,044
1968	3,334,676	2,531,008	794,696	1,736,311	803,669
1969	3,620,755	2,737,122	896,766	1,840,357	883,633
1970	3,925,825	2,954,149	1,002,569	1,951,580	971,675
1971	4,228,568	3,152,163	1,103,137	2,049,026	1,076,405
1972	4,539,469	3,344,300	1,203,213	2,141,087	1,195,169
1973	4,902,308	3,586,452	1,322,803	2,263,649	1,315,857
1974	5,309,029	3,875,040	1,461,211	2,413,829	1,433,989
1975	5,747,732	4,186,815	1,613,843	2,572,971	1,560,917
1976	6,192,879	4,485,856	1,759,161	2,726,694	1,707,024
1977	6,588,529	4,733,601	1,863,662	2,869,939	1,854,927
1978	6,989,165	5,000,279	1,960,660	3,039,619	1,988,886
1979	7,500,284	5,379,317	2,116,013	3,263,305	2,120,966
1980	8,135,577	5,873,774	2,338,428	3,535,347	2,261,803
1981	8,897,611	6,486,681	2,622,645	3,864,037	2,410,930
1982	9,599,834	7,034,313	2,841,835	4,192,478	2,565,520
1983	10,004,214	7,293,099	2,875,582	4,417,517	2,711,115
1984	10,257,720	7,406,403	2,835,715	4,570,688	2,851,317
1985	10,550,531	7,549,248	2,826,762	4,722,486	3,001,283
1986	10,804,270	7,650,571	2,807,984	4,842,588	3,153,698
1987	10,987,777	7,682,992	2,752,222	4,930,770	3,304,784
1988	11,179,076	7,724,153	2,712,313	5,011,840	3,454,923
1989	11,402,865	7,797,090	2,712,170	5,084,920	3,605,775
1990	11,692,600	7,917,525	2,760,998	5,156,527	3,775,075
1991	12,076,453	8,105,362	2,880,048	5,225,314	3,971,091
1992	12,551,759	8,357,972	3,070,306	5,287,665	4,193,787
1993	13,042,359	8,619,734	3,258,858	5,360,876	4,422,626
1994	13,537,383	8,882,789	3,430,287	5,452,502	4,654,594

Table E.21 Mexico 2. *Gross and Net Fixed Tangible Reproducible Capital Stocks by Type of Asset, 1950–94 (constant million 1980 international dollars)*

Mid-year	Gross stocks				
	Total	Non-residential			Res.
		Total	M&E	Structures	
1950	61,878	48.020	6.881	41.138	13.859
1951	67,522	52.643	7.626	45.017	14.879
1952	73,952	57.982	8.454	49.527	15.970
1953	80,432	63.260	9.346	53.914	17.173
1954	86,966	68.473	10.306	58.167	18.493
1955	94,023	74.080	11.291	62.789	19.943
1956	102,086	80.550	12.395	68.155	21.536
1957	111,197	87.908	13.707	74.200	23.290
1958	120,489	95.270	15.096	80.174	25.219
1959	129,533	102.190	16.392	85.798	27.342
1960	138,654	108.976	17.577	91.399	29.678
1961	147,787	115.380	19.683	95.697	32.407
1962	157,113	121.544	22.845	98.699	35.568
1963	167,315	128.267	26.284	101.983	39.048
1964	179,514	136.637	30.493	106.144	42.878
1965	193,445	146.352	35.402	110.950	47.093
1966	208,456	156.724	40.606	116.118	51.732
1967	225,484	168.646	46.396	122.251	56.838
1968	244,751	182.293	52.956	129.337	62.458
1969	265,717	197.074	60.140	136.934	68.643
1970	288,414	213.054	67.904	145.150	75.359
1971	312,087	228.916	75.763	153.153	83.171
1972	337,346	245.331	83.956	161.375	92.015
1973	366,152	265.015	93.608	171.406	101.138
1974	397,994	287.724	104.828	182.896	110.271
1975	432,405	312.283	117.355	194.928	120.122
1976	467,448	336.087	129.209	206.878	131.362
1977	500,031	357.106	138.740	218.366	142.925
1978	533,769	379.916	148.210	231.706	153.853
1979	573,741	408.845	160.359	248.486	164.896
1980	620,387	443.694	175.811	267.882	176.694
1981	674,311	485.090	194.743	290.347	189.221
1982	726,780	524.464	211.164	313.299	202.316
1983	765,800	550.704	219.138	331.566	215.096
1984	797,706	569.931	223.522	346.409	227.775
1985	831,350	590.067	229.001	361.066	241.284
1986	862,942	607.757	234.111	373.645	255.185
1987	890,776	621.525	237.317	384.208	269.251
1988	918,168	634.662	240.017	394.645	283.506
1989	946,570	648.534	243.243	405.292	298.036
1990	977,627	663.635	247.574	416.062	313.991
1991	1,013,102	681.177	255.016	426.161	331.925
1992	1,054,813	702.995	267.448	435.547	351.818
1993	1,098,641	726.203	280.347	445.855	372.438
1994	1,141,035	747.427	289.915	457.513	393.608

Table E.21 (continued)

| | | Net stocks | | | |
| | | Non-residential | | | |
Mid-year	Total	Total	M&E	Structures	Res.
1950	44,684	34.501	4.677	29.824	10.184
1951	48,932	37.884	5.210	32.674	11.049
1952	53,836	41.872	5.813	36.059	11.964
1953	58,563	45.591	6.384	39.207	12.972
1954	63,116	49.035	6.923	42.113	14.081
1955	68,053	52.752	7.471	45.281	15.301
1956	73,849	57.208	8.131	49.077	16.641
1957	80,414	62.300	8.882	53.418	18.114
1958	86,823	67.091	9.554	57.537	19.732
1959	92,761	71.254	10.097	61.157	21.507
1960	99,208	75.753	10.666	65.087	23.454
1961	106,059	80.390	12.318	68.071	25.669
1962	112,878	84.695	15.019	69.676	28.183
1963	120,308	89.357	17.850	71.507	30.951
1964	129,287	95.287	21.157	74.130	34.000
1965	139,648	102.291	24.854	77.437	37.357
1966	150,784	109.730	28.689	81.040	41.055
1967	163,301	118.175	32.883	85.292	45.126
1968	177,373	127.763	37.486	90.278	49.609
1969	192,533	137.988	42.300	95.687	54.545
1970	208,741	148.761	47.291	101.470	59.980
1971	225,016	158.572	52.035	106.537	66.445
1972	241,855	168.079	56.755	111.324	73.776
1973	261,318	180.092	62.396	117.696	81.226
1974	282,947	194.430	68.925	125.505	88.518
1975	306,257	209.904	76.125	133.779	96.353
1976	330,123	224.751	82.979	141.772	105.372
1977	351,630	237.128	87.909	149.220	114.502
1978	373,297	250.526	92.484	158.042	122.771
1979	400,408	269.484	99.812	169.672	130.924
1980	433,737	294.120	110.303	183.817	139.617
1981	473,439	324.616	123.710	200.907	148.823
1982	510,398	352.032	134.049	217.984	158.365
1983	532,678	365.325	135.641	229.684	167.353
1984	547,416	371.408	133.760	237.648	176.007
1985	564,143	378.879	133.338	245.541	185.264
1986	578,910	384.237	132.452	251.785	194.673
1987	590,191	386.192	129.822	256.370	203.999
1988	601,792	388.525	127.939	260.585	213.267
1989	614,896	392.318	127.933	264.385	222.579
1990	631,373	398.344	130.236	268.108	233.029
1991	652,665	407.536	135.851	271.685	245.129
1992	678,628	419.752	144.826	274.927	258.876
1993	705,455	432.453	153.720	278.733	273.002
1994	732,624	445.303	161.806	283.497	287.321

Table E.22 Mexico 3. Capital Stock: Average Ages, Average Service Lives and Capital–Output Ratios, 1950–94 (on the basis of national currencies at constant 1980 prices)

Mid-year	Average age capital stock				Average service life capital stock		Capital–output ratios			
	Total		Non-residential		Total	Non-residential	Total		Non-residential	
	Gross	Net	Gross	Net			Gross	Net	Gross	Net
1950	11.64	7.81	11.06	7.50	37,08	34,52	1,7	1,2	1,4	1,0
1951	11.45	7.65	10.93	7.33	37,53	35,10	1,7	1,3	1,4	1,0
1952	11.34	7.51	10.87	7.17	37,16	34,73	1,9	1,3	1,5	1,1
1953	11.36	7.57	10.97	7.25	36,79	34,36	1,9	1,4	1,6	1,1
1954	11.41	7.64	11.11	7.34	36,47	34,00	2,0	1,4	1,6	1,1
1955	11.43	7.63	11.19	7.34	36,49	34,03	2,0	1,4	1,6	1,1
1956	11.38	7.56	11.19	7.26	36,59	34,16	2,0	1,5	1,7	1,2
1957	11.35	7.64	11.21	7.36	36,57	34,15	2,1	1,5	1,7	1,2
1958	11.45	7.73	11.38	7.48	36,00	33,52	2,1	1,5	1,7	1,2
1959	11.59	7.84	11.60	7.61	35,73	33,21	2,2	1,6	1,8	1,2
1960	11.46	7.85	11.47	7.62	35,54	32,95	2,2	1,6	1,8	1,2
1961	11.42	7.90	11.43	7.69	35,45	32,71	2,2	1,6	1,8	1,3
1962	11.40	7.99	11.40	7.82	34,75	31,87	2,3	1,6	1,8	1,3
1963	11.35	8.02	11.34	7.87	34,32	31,32	2,2	1,6	1,8	1,2
1964	11.23	7.94	11.20	7.78	34,13	31,06	2,1	1,5	1,7	1,2
1965	11.08	7.97	11.01	7.82	33,43	30,26	2,2	1,6	1,7	1,2
1966	10.98	7.94	10.88	7.79	32,89	29,63	2,2	1,6	1,7	1,2
1967	10.87	7.84	10.75	7.67	32,61	29,29	2,2	1,6	1,7	1,2
1968	10.77	7.75	10.63	7.57	32,16	28,79	2,2	1,6	1,7	1,2
1969	10.68	7.70	10.52	7.52	31,71	28,28	2,3	1,6	1,8	1,2
1970	10.62	7.68	10.47	7.49	31,31	27,85	2,3	1,7	1,8	1,3
1971	10.69	7.72	10.60	7.58	30,75	27,11	2,4	1,7	1,9	1,3
1972	10.74	7.70	10.71	7.56	30,64	26,95	2,4	1,7	1,8	1,3
1973	10.73	7.61	10.70	7.43	30,58	26,88	2,4	1,7	1,8	1,2
1974	10.72	7.56	10.66	7.32	30,26	26,60	2,5	1,7	1,9	1,3
1975	10.69	7.49	10.63	7.21	29,96	26,25	2,5	1,8	1,9	1,3
1976	10.71	7.52	10.66	7.23	29,34	25,54	2,6	1,8	2,0	1,3
1977	10.82	7.62	10.76	7.33	28,93	25,10	2,7	1,9	2,0	1,4
1978	10.91	7.64	10.81	7.27	29,15	25,36	2,7	1,8	2,0	1,3
1979	10.89	7.56	10.72	7.10	29,37	25,60	2,6	1,8	2,0	1,3
1980	10.80	7.46	10.54	6.91	29,40	25,70	2,6	1,8	2,0	1,3
1981	10.64	7.31	10.29	6.67	29,41	25,78	2,6	1,8	2,0	1,3
1982	10.73	7.40	10.34	6.73	28,51	24,89	2,9	2,0	2,2	1,5
1983	11.06	7.71	10.69	7.05	27,88	24,22	3,1	2,2	2,4	1,6
1984	11.36	7.97	10.99	7.31	28,13	24,39	3,1	2,1	2,4	1,5
1985	11.60	8.19	11.23	7.52	28,35	24,52	3,2	2,1	2,4	1,5
1986	11.90	8.47	11.52	7.80	28,25	24,34	3,4	2,3	2,6	1,6
1987	12.19	8.73	11.81	8.07	28,33	24,31	3,5	2,3	2,6	1,6
1988	12.46	9.02	12.07	8.37	28,54	24,44	3,5	2,3	2,6	1,6
1989	12.73	9.21	12.32	8.54	28,74	24,53	3,5	2,2	2,5	1,5
1990	12.91	9.31	12.49	8.61	29,00	24,67	3,4	2,2	2,5	1,5
1991	13.01	9.34	12.56	8.60	29,25	24,80	3,4	2,2	2,4	1,5
1992	13.07	9.33	12.59	8.57	29,44	24,89	3,4	2,2	2,4	1,4
1993	13.19	9.38	12.67	8.58	29,17	24,55	3,5	2,2	2,5	1,5
1994	13.26	9.38	12.70	8.55	29,15	24,41	3,5	2,2	2,4	1,4

Table E.23 Mexico 4. Capital Stock: Average Ages, Average Service Lives and Capital–Output Ratios, 1950–94 (on the basis of constant 1980 international dollars)

Mid-year	Average age capital stock				Average service life capital stock		Capital–output ratios			
	Total		Non-residential		Total	Non-residential	Total		Non-residential	
	Gross	Net	Gross	Net			Gross	Net	Gross	Net
1950	11.79	7.90	11.14	7.56	38.04	35.09	1.2	0.9	0.9	0.7
1951	11.59	7.75	11.00	7.38	38.48	35.68	1.2	0.9	1.0	0.7
1952	11.47	7.61	10.95	7.22	38.12	35.32	1.3	1.0	1.0	0.7
1953	11.48	7.66	11.05	7.30	37.74	34.92	1.4	1.0	1.1	0.8
1954	11.53	7.72	11.18	7.39	37.43	34.58	1.4	1.0	1.1	0.8
1955	11.53	7.72	11.27	7.39	37.46	34.61	1.4	1.0	1.1	0.8
1956	11.47	7.65	11.27	7.31	37.57	34.75	1.4	1.0	1.1	0.8
1957	11.44	7.72	11.29	7.41	37.54	34.74	1.5	1.1	1.2	0.8
1958	11.52	7.81	11.46	7.53	36.98	34.11	1.5	1.1	1.2	0.8
1959	11.65	7.91	11.67	7.66	36.73	33.79	1.6	1.1	1.2	0.9
1960	11.52	7.92	11.55	7.67	36.55	33.54	1.6	1.1	1.2	0.8
1961	11.49	7.98	11.52	7.76	36.43	33.23	1.6	1.1	1.2	0.9
1962	11.48	8.08	11.51	7.90	35.79	32.42	1.6	1.2	1.2	0.9
1963	11.44	8.12	11.47	7.97	35.40	31.89	1.6	1.1	1.2	0.8
1964	11.33	8.04	11.33	7.88	35.24	31.65	1.5	1.1	1.2	0.8
1965	11.20	8.07	11.16	7.94	34.57	30.85	1.5	1.1	1.2	0.8
1966	11.10	8.05	11.03	7.91	34.07	30.23	1.5	1.1	1.2	0.8
1967	11.01	7.95	10.91	7.80	33.81	29.90	1.6	1.1	1.2	0.8
1968	10.91	7.86	10.79	7.69	33.39	29.41	1.6	1.1	1.2	0.8
1969	10.83	7.82	10.68	7.64	32.95	28.89	1.6	1.2	1.2	0.8
1970	10.77	7.80	10.63	7.61	32.57	28.46	1.6	1.2	1.2	0.8
1971	10.82	7.83	10.77	7.70	32.05	27.71	1.7	1.2	1.2	0.9
1972	10.87	7.81	10.88	7.69	31.95	27.55	1.7	1.2	1.2	0.8
1973	10.86	7.72	10.87	7.56	31.89	27.48	1.7	1.2	1.2	0.8
1974	10.85	7.68	10.83	7.45	31.56	27.20	1.7	1.2	1.3	0.8
1975	10.82	7.62	10.80	7.34	31.27	26.84	1.8	1.3	1.3	0.9
1976	10.84	7.64	10.83	7.36	30.67	26.13	1.9	1.3	1.3	0.9
1977	10.95	7.75	10.93	7.45	30.27	25.69	1.9	1.3	1.4	0.9
1978	11.04	7.77	10.98	7.38	30.49	25.96	1.9	1.3	1.3	0.9
1979	11.03	7.71	10.89	7.22	30.70	26.20	1.9	1.3	1.3	0.9
1980	10.95	7.62	10.71	7.02	30.72	26.30	1.9	1.3	1.3	0.9
1981	10.81	7.49	10.45	6.78	30.72	26.38	1.9	1.3	1.3	0.9
1982	10.91	7.57	10.50	6.83	29.83	25.49	2.0	1.4	1.5	1.0
1983	11.24	7.88	10.84	7.15	29.20	24.80	2.2	1.5	1.6	1.1
1984	11.53	8.14	11.14	7.41	29.45	24.97	2.2	1.5	1.6	1.0
1985	11.77	8.36	11.38	7.62	29.68	25.11	2.3	1.5	1.6	1.0
1986	12.07	8.64	11.68	7.91	29.59	24.93	2.4	1.6	1.7	1.1
1987	12.36	8.90	11.96	8.18	29.69	24.90	2.5	1.6	1.7	1.1
1988	12.63	9.19	12.23	8.48	29.91	25.02	2.5	1.7	1.7	1.1
1989	12.90	9.38	12.48	8.66	30.12	25.12	2.5	1.6	1.7	1.0
1990	13.09	9.49	12.65	8.73	30.40	25.25	2.5	1.6	1.7	1.0
1991	13.20	9.53	12.74	8.75	30.66	25.38	2.4	1.6	1.6	1.0
1992	13.28	9.54	12.77	8.72	30.86	25.46	2.4	1.6	1.6	1.0
1993	13.40	9.59	12.87	8.75	30.60	25.12	2.5	1.6	1.7	1.0
1994	13.48	9.61	12.90	8.72	30.60	24.98	2.5	1.6	1.6	1.0

Table E.24 Venezuela 1. Gross and Net Fixed Tangible Reproducible Capital Stocks by Type of Asset, 1950–94 (constant 1980 bolívares)

		Gross stocks			
		Non-residential			
Mid-year	Total	Total	M&E	Structures	Res.
1950	128,678	112,340	50,564	61,776	16,338
1951	142,283	124,192	55,403	68,789	18,090
1952	157,815	137,135	60,709	76,426	20,680
1953	175,771	151,782	67,732	84,051	23,989
1954	195,894	168,408	75,919	92,489	27,486
1955	216,918	186,285	84,296	101,989	30,632
1956	238,672	204,481	92,175	112,306	34,191
1957	262,628	224,761	101,279	123,483	37,867
1958	287,513	245,494	111,752	133,742	42,019
1959	312,265	266,372	122,495	143,877	45,893
1960	333,325	284,677	130,439	154,238	48,648
1961	348,609	297,584	134,592	162,992	51,025
1962	361,003	307,457	137,301	170,156	53,546
1963	371,894	315,225	138,346	176,880	56,669
1964	384,093	323,595	139,129	184,466	60,499
1965	399,491	334,192	141,539	192,653	65,299
1966	416,621	345,912	145,331	200,581	70,709
1967	433,210	356,998	147,893	209,106	76,211
1968	450,128	368,323	148,561	219,763	81,804
1969	468,521	380,937	149,061	231,875	87,584
1970	487,600	393,940	149,953	243,987	93,660
1971	509,952	409,210	152,483	256,727	100,742
1972	536,703	427,396	156,070	271,326	109,307
1973	566,795	447,587	160,344	287,243	119,208
1974	597,296	468,033	165,104	302,929	129,264
1975	634,674	495,286	174,875	320,411	139,387
1976	687,762	536,684	193,783	342,901	151,078
1977	757,953	593,453	221,401	372,051	164,501
1978	839,186	660,021	254,056	405,964	179,166
1979	912,155	717,208	280,211	436,998	194,947
1980	969,938	759,418	298,010	461,407	210,520
1981	1,023,751	799,675	315,583	484,092	224,076
1982	1,077,832	843,244	334,989	508,255	234,588
1983	1,121,769	879,592	349,234	530,358	242,177
1984	1,150,897	903,202	356,761	546,441	247,695
1985	1,175,328	923,228	365,435	557,793	252,100
1986	1,200,945	944,620	376,805	567,815	256,325
1987	1,225,619	965,059	387,481	577,578	260,560
1988	1,249,739	985,123	397,592	587,531	264,617
1989	1,267,440	999,395	404,364	595,031	268,045
1990	1,274,380	1,004,002	401,679	602,323	270,379
1991	1,279,644	1,007,455	393,154	614,301	272,189
1992	1,287,588	1,013,062	381,576	631,485	274,526
1993	1,294,572	1,017,323	365,421	651,902	277,249
1994	1,298,099	1,018,624	350,643	667,980	279,475

Table E.24 (continued)

Mid-year		Net stocks			
			Non-residential		
	Total	Total	M&E	Structures	Res.
1950	94,446	82,822	35,519	47,302	11,625
1951	104,166	91,036	38,117	52,919	13,130
1952	115,783	100,343	41,352	58,991	15,440
1953	129,723	111,299	46,423	64,876	18,424
1954	145,399	123,866	52,482	71,384	21,533
1955	161,081	136,862	58,128	78,733	24,219
1956	176,189	148,937	62,277	86,660	27,252
1957	192,191	161,864	66,666	95,197	30,327
1958	207,903	174,096	71,546	102,550	33,807
1959	222,843	185,911	76,396	109,515	36,932
1960	234,134	195,247	78,809	116,438	38,887
1961	240,034	199,595	78,056	121,539	40,438
1962	244,215	202,120	77,272	124,848	42,095
1963	248,626	204,310	76,739	127,571	44,316
1964	254,919	207,735	76,521	131,213	47,184
1965	263,672	212,736	76,917	135,819	50,936
1966	273,072	217,872	77,242	140,631	55,199
1967	282,599	223,144	77,043	146,101	59,456
1968	293,921	230,216	76,969	153,247	63,705
1969	307,825	239,803	78,140	161,663	68,022
1970	322,133	249,630	79,802	169,828	72,503
1971	337,591	259,732	82,104	177,628	77,859
1972	356,986	272,424	86,059	186,365	84,562
1973	380,159	287,720	91,561	196,159	92,440
1974	403,810	303,519	97,931	205,589	100,291
1975	431,559	323,527	107,275	216,252	108,033
1976	471,331	354,164	122,467	231,697	117,168
1977	526,935	399,107	145,355	253,752	127,828
1978	591,630	452,126	171,871	280,255	139,504
1979	645,399	493,352	190,093	303,259	152,048
1980	681,484	517,387	198,882	318,504	164,097
1981	710,979	537,179	206,349	330,830	173,800
1982	738,193	558,039	214,206	343,833	180,155
1983	753,689	570,307	215,904	354,403	183,382
1984	754,736	570,331	211,224	359,107	184,405
1985	751,593	567,356	207,713	359,642	184,238
1986	750,588	566,715	207,020	359,696	183,823
1987	750,298	566,937	206,696	360,241	183,361
1988	751,097	568,420	206,881	361,539	182,677
1989	746,706	565,394	204,207	361,188	181,312
1990	734,378	555,578	194,915	360,663	178,800
1991	726,927	551,206	186,462	364,744	175,721
1992	731,945	558,844	184,481	374,363	173,100
1993	741,753	570,951	184,163	386,787	170,802
1994	743,377	575,361	180,183	395,178	168,015

Table E.25 Venezuela 2. Gross and Net Fixed Tangible Reproducible Capital Stocks by Type of Asset, 1950–94 (constant million 1980 international dollars)

| Mid-year | | Gross stocks | | | |
| | | | Non-residential | | |
	Total	Total	M&E	Structures	Res.
1950	26,144	23,195	11,162	12,033	2,949
1951	28,894	25,629	12,230	13,399	3,265
1952	32,021	28,288	13,402	14,886	3,733
1953	35,653	31,323	14,952	16,371	4,330
1954	39,736	34,774	16,759	18,015	4,961
1955	44,003	38,474	18,608	19,865	5,529
1956	48,394	42,223	20,348	21,875	6,172
1957	53,244	46,409	22,357	24,052	6,835
1958	58,304	50,720	24,669	26,050	7,585
1959	63,349	55,065	27,041	28,024	8,284
1960	67,618	58,837	28,795	30,042	8,781
1961	70,669	61,459	29,711	31,748	9,210
1962	73,118	63,452	30,309	33,143	9,665
1963	75,222	64,993	30,540	34,453	10,229
1964	77,563	66,643	30,713	35,930	10,920
1965	80,557	68,770	31,245	37,525	11,787
1966	83,914	71,151	32,082	39,069	12,763
1967	87,134	73,377	32,647	40,730	13,757
1968	90,366	75,600	32,795	42,805	14,766
1969	93,879	78,070	32,905	45,165	15,809
1970	97,532	80,626	33,102	47,524	16,906
1971	101,850	83,666	33,661	50,005	18,184
1972	107,032	87,301	34,452	52,849	19,731
1973	112,863	91,345	35,396	55,949	21,518
1974	118,784	95,451	36,447	59,004	23,333
1975	126,174	101,013	38,604	62,410	25,160
1976	136,838	109,568	42,778	66,790	27,270
1977	151,036	121,343	48,874	72,468	29,693
1978	167,497	135,157	56,083	79,074	32,340
1979	182,164	146,975	61,857	85,118	35,189
1980	193,659	155,659	65,786	89,873	38,000
1981	204,404	163,957	69,665	94,291	40,447
1982	215,291	172,947	73,949	98,998	42,344
1983	224,111	180,397	77,094	103,303	43,714
1984	229,901	185,191	78,755	106,436	44,710
1985	234,822	189,317	80,670	108,647	45,505
1986	240,047	193,779	83,180	110,599	46,268
1987	245,070	198,037	85,537	112,501	47,032
1988	249,973	202,208	87,769	114,439	47,765
1989	253,547	205,164	89,264	115,900	48,384
1990	254,796	205,991	88,671	117,320	48,805
1991	255,574	206,442	86,789	119,653	49,132
1992	256,787	207,234	84,233	123,001	49,553
1993	257,689	207,644	80,667	126,977	50,045
1994	257,961	207,514	77,405	130,109	50,447

Table E.25 (continued)

| Mid-year | Total | Non-residential | | | Res. |
		Total	M&E	Structures	
1950	19,153	17,054	7,841	9,214	2,098
1951	21,092	18,722	8,414	10,308	2,370
1952	23,406	20,619	9,129	11,490	2,787
1953	26,210	22,884	10,248	12,636	3,326
1954	29,376	25,490	11,585	13,904	3,887
1955	32,539	28,168	12,832	15,336	4,372
1956	35,546	30,627	13,748	16,880	4,919
1957	38,733	33,259	14,717	18,543	5,474
1958	41,871	35,768	15,794	19,975	6,102
1959	44,862	38,196	16,864	21,331	6,666
1960	47,096	40,077	17,397	22,680	7,019
1961	48,204	40,904	17,231	23,673	7,299
1962	48,974	41,376	17,058	24,318	7,598
1963	49,788	41,788	16,940	24,848	7,999
1964	50,967	42,450	16,892	25,558	8,517
1965	52,628	43,434	16,979	26,455	9,194
1966	54,407	44,443	17,051	27,392	9,964
1967	56,197	45,465	17,007	28,458	10,732
1968	58,339	46,840	16,991	29,849	11,499
1969	61,017	48,738	17,250	31,489	12,278
1970	63,783	50,695	17,616	33,079	13,087
1971	66,777	52,723	18,124	34,598	14,054
1972	70,562	55,298	18,998	36,300	15,264
1973	75,106	58,420	20,212	38,208	16,686
1974	79,766	61,663	21,618	40,045	18,103
1975	85,303	65,803	23,681	42,122	19,500
1976	93,314	72,165	27,035	45,130	21,149
1977	104,587	81,513	32,087	49,426	23,074
1978	117,710	92,529	37,941	54,588	25,181
1979	128,477	101,032	41,963	59,069	27,445
1980	135,562	105,942	43,903	62,038	29,620
1981	141,363	109,991	45,552	64,439	31,372
1982	146,777	114,258	47,286	66,972	32,519
1983	149,793	116,692	47,661	69,031	33,101
1984	149,861	116,575	46,628	69,947	33,286
1985	149,160	115,904	45,853	70,051	33,256
1986	148,942	115,761	45,700	70,061	33,181
1987	148,894	115,796	45,628	70,168	33,098
1988	149,064	116,090	45,669	70,421	32,974
1989	148,159	115,431	45,079	70,352	32,728
1990	145,552	113,278	43,028	70,250	32,274
1991	143,925	112,206	41,161	71,045	31,719
1992	144,888	113,643	40,724	72,918	31,246
1993	146,823	115,993	40,654	75,338	30,831
1994	147,076	116,748	39,776	76,973	30,328

Table E.26 Venezuela 3. Capital Stock: Average Ages, Average Service Lives and Capital–Output Ratios, 1950–94 (on the basis of national currencies at constant 1980 prices)

Mid-year	Average age capital stock				Average service life capital stock		Capital–output ratios			
	Total		Non-residential		Total	Non-residential	Total		Non-residential	
	Gross	Net	Gross	Net			Gross	Net	Gross	Net
1950	9.05	6.14	8.16	5.56	27.29	25.51	2.8	2.1	2.5	1.8
1951	9.01	6.13	8.24	5.65	27.01	25.05	2.8	2.0	2.4	1.8
1952	8.84	6.00	8.17	5.58	27.62	25.60	2.9	2.1	2.5	1.8
1953	8.70	5.92	8.15	5.59	27.56	25.37	3.0	2.2	2.6	1.9
1954	8.56	5.88	8.06	5.57	27.65	25.53	3.1	2.3	2.6	1.9
1955	8.59	5.99	8.14	5.71	27.14	25.03	3.1	2.3	2.7	2.0
1956	8.66	6.04	8.27	5.79	27.21	25.03	3.1	2.3	2.7	1.9
1957	8.77	6.14	8.41	5.89	27.29	25.17	3.1	2.2	2.6	1.9
1958	8.95	6.30	8.66	6.09	26.99	24.75	3.3	2.4	2.8	2.0
1959	9.14	6.43	8.84	6.19	26.70	24.61	3.3	2.4	2.8	2.0
1960	9.50	6.71	9.21	6.45	25.90	23.82	3.5	2.5	3.0	2.1
1961	9.91	7.09	9.63	6.80	25.66	23.60	3.5	2.4	3.0	2.0
1962	10.28	7.45	10.01	7.17	25.67	23.53	3.3	2.2	2.8	1.9
1963	10.61	7.75	10.36	7.47	25.71	23.49	3.2	2.1	2.7	1.8
1964	10.83	7.93	10.61	7.66	26.27	23.93	3.0	2.0	2.5	1.6
1965	10.99	8.04	10.80	7.79	26.65	24.19	3.0	2.0	2.5	1.6
1966	11.14	8.20	10.97	7.97	26.90	24.35	3.0	2.0	2.5	1.6
1967	11.27	8.33	11.10	8.11	26.85	24.22	3.0	2.0	2.5	1.6
1968	11.35	8.38	11.18	8.14	27.33	24.61	3.0	1.9	2.4	1.5
1969	11.36	8.40	11.15	8.13	27.67	24.87	3.0	2.0	2.4	1.5
1970	11.46	8.49	11.25	8.20	28.09	25.20	2.9	1.9	2.3	1.5
1971	11.57	8.48	11.37	8.19	28.65	25.64	2.9	1.9	2.3	1.5
1972	11.62	8.40	11.44	8.11	29.05	25.90	3.0	2.0	2.4	1.5
1973	11.60	8.32	11.45	8.03	29.45	26.18	3.0	2.0	2.3	1.5
1974	11.66	8.33	11.49	8.03	29.53	26.20	2.9	2.0	2.3	1.5
1975	11.61	8.19	11.43	7.84	30.43	27.09	2.9	2.0	2.3	1.5
1976	11.38	7.90	11.15	7.48	30.81	27.46	2.9	2.0	2.3	1.5
1977	10.98	7.51	10.67	7.01	31.02	27.75	3.0	2.1	2.4	1.6
1978	10.68	7.25	10.32	6.71	30.38	27.15	3.3	2.3	2.6	1.8
1979	10.71	7.31	10.36	6.79	29.17	25.88	3.5	2.5	2.8	1.9
1980	10.92	7.53	10.60	7.03	28.75	25.44	3.8	2.7	3.0	2.0
1981	11.16	7.71	10.82	7.18	28.75	25.49	4.0	2.8	3.2	2.1
1982	11.45	7.93	11.07	7.35	28.55	25.40	4.2	2.9	3.3	2.2
1983	11.90	8.31	11.48	7.66	27.93	24.82	4.7	3.1	3.7	2.4
1984	12.41	8.76	11.94	8.05	27.69	24.61	4.8	3.2	3.8	2.4
1985	12.87	9.17	12.35	8.41	27.75	24.70	4.9	3.2	3.9	2.4
1986	13.27	9.49	12.67	8.63	27.66	24.62	4.7	3.0	3.7	2.2
1987	13.64	9.79	12.97	8.85	27.50	24.47	4.7	2.9	3.7	2.2
1988	13.96	10.05	13.19	9.03	27.46	24.45	4.5	2.7	3.5	2.0
1989	14.38	10.44	13.53	9.34	27.08	24.07	5.0	2.9	3.9	2.2
1990	14.84	10.81	13.90	9.60	26.93	23.93	4.7	2.7	3.7	2.1
1991	15.14	11.00	14.07	9.67	27.24	24.23	4.3	2.4	3.4	1.9
1992	15.30	11.01	14.07	9.56	27.54	24.51	4.1	2.3	3.2	1.8
1993	15.51	11.10	14.12	9.57	27.89	24.85	4.1	2.4	3.2	1.8
1994	15.83	11.35	14.32	9.73	28.30	25.26	4.3	2.5	3.4	1.9

Table E.27 Venezuela 4. Capital Stock: Average Ages, Average Service Lives and Capital–Output Ratios, 1950–94 (on the basis of constant 1980 international dollars)

Mid-year	Average age capital stock				Average service life capital stock		Capital–output ratios			
	Total		Non-residential		Total	Non-residential	Total		Non-residential	
	Gross	Net	Gross	Net			Gross	Net	Gross	Net
1950	8.82	5.97	8.01	5.44	26.35	24.78	2.1	1.5	1.8	1.3
1951	8.80	5.99	8.10	5.54	26.02	24.30	2.0	1.5	1.8	1.3
1952	8.65	5.87	8.04	5.48	26.64	24.86	2.1	1.5	1.9	1.4
1953	8.52	5.80	8.01	5.49	26.57	24.65	2.2	1.6	1.9	1.4
1954	8.38	5.76	7.92	5.48	26.66	24.81	2.3	1.7	2.0	1.4
1955	8.42	5.88	8.00	5.62	26.16	24.31	2.3	1.7	2.0	1.5
1956	8.51	5.93	8.14	5.70	26.22	24.30	2.3	1.7	2.0	1.4
1957	8.62	6.03	8.28	5.80	26.32	24.46	2.2	1.6	2.0	1.4
1958	8.81	6.19	8.54	5.99	26.02	24.06	2.4	1.7	2.1	1.5
1959	9.00	6.32	8.72	6.09	25.75	23.92	2.4	1.7	2.1	1.5
1960	9.36	6.60	9.09	6.35	24.95	23.12	2.6	1.8	2.2	1.5
1961	9.77	6.97	9.50	6.69	24.71	22.91	2.6	1.7	2.2	1.5
1962	10.14	7.32	9.88	7.05	24.71	22.84	2.4	1.6	2.1	1.4
1963	10.46	7.62	10.21	7.35	24.73	22.79	2.3	1.5	2.0	1.3
1964	10.68	7.79	10.46	7.53	25.27	23.21	2.2	1.4	1.9	1.2
1965	10.84	7.91	10.64	7.65	25.64	23.47	2.2	1.4	1.8	1.2
1966	11.00	8.06	10.82	7.83	25.89	23.63	2.2	1.4	1.9	1.2
1967	11.12	8.20	10.95	7.97	25.81	23.48	2.2	1.4	1.8	1.1
1968	11.21	8.24	11.03	7.99	26.27	23.85	2.2	1.4	1.8	1.1
1969	11.21	8.26	11.00	7.98	26.59	24.10	2.2	1.4	1.8	1.1
1970	11.31	8.34	11.09	8.05	27.01	24.43	2.1	1.4	1.7	1.1
1971	11.42	8.33	11.21	8.03	27.55	24.86	2.1	1.4	1.7	1.1
1972	11.46	8.25	11.27	7.95	27.93	25.11	2.1	1.4	1.7	1.1
1973	11.44	8.17	11.26	7.87	28.32	25.38	2.1	1.4	1.7	1.1
1974	11.48	8.18	11.29	7.87	28.40	25.41	2.1	1.4	1.7	1.1
1975	11.42	8.03	11.21	7.67	29.31	26.31	2.1	1.4	1.7	1.1
1976	11.18	7.73	10.93	7.31	29.69	26.69	2.1	1.4	1.7	1.1
1977	10.77	7.33	10.44	6.85	29.91	26.97	2.2	1.5	1.7	1.2
1978	10.47	7.07	10.10	6.55	29.27	26.38	2.4	1.7	1.9	1.3
1979	10.50	7.14	10.14	6.64	28.06	25.12	2.5	1.8	2.0	1.4
1980	10.71	7.36	10.38	6.88	27.64	24.69	2.8	1.9	2.2	1.5
1981	10.95	7.54	10.60	7.03	27.66	24.75	2.9	2.0	2.3	1.6
1982	11.23	7.76	10.84	7.20	27.48	24.66	3.0	2.1	2.4	1.6
1983	11.68	8.14	11.25	7.52	26.86	24.08	3.4	2.2	2.7	1.7
1984	12.18	8.58	11.71	7.91	26.63	23.88	3.5	2.3	2.8	1.8
1985	12.63	8.98	12.11	8.25	26.70	23.97	3.6	2.3	2.9	1.8
1986	13.01	9.28	12.42	8.47	26.62	23.91	3.4	2.1	2.8	1.6
1987	13.38	9.57	12.72	8.68	26.45	23.76	3.4	2.0	2.7	1.6
1988	13.68	9.81	12.94	8.84	26.42	23.74	3.2	1.9	2.6	1.5
1989	14.09	10.19	13.28	9.14	26.04	23.36	3.6	2.1	2.9	1.6
1990	14.55	10.54	13.65	9.40	25.88	23.20	3.4	1.9	2.7	1.5
1991	14.84	10.72	13.82	9.47	26.17	23.49	3.1	1.8	2.5	1.4
1992	14.98	10.72	13.81	9.36	26.45	23.73	2.9	1.7	2.4	1.3
1993	15.17	10.81	13.86	9.37	26.79	24.05	3.0	1.7	2.4	1.3
1994	15.49	11.05	14.06	9.54	27.22	24.48	3.1	1.8	2.5	1.4

NOTES

1. Dollar with the same purchasing power parity over total GDP as the US dollar, but with a purchasing power over subaggregates and over detailed categories determined by average international prices rather than by US relative prices.
2. The exchange rates normally used are the (rf) series of the IMF, published in *International Financial Statistics*, various issues, which refer to period averages of market exchange rates for countries quoting in units of national currency per US dollar.

Appendix F. Foreign Trade[*]

Latin American involvement in the world economy and its role on economic development is a continuing theme in the debate on what development strategy should be chosen. In this appendix imports and exports series are presented, in current dollars and as indices representing volume movement only. For each country and each series I will give a detailed description of the sources used.

General sources

Imports and exports in current dollars for 1950–94 come from IMF (1995b). If not indicated otherwise current imports and exports for 1934–49 are from ECLAC (1976). ECLAC (1976) also provides the import volume for the 1934–59 period (with the exception of Colombia) and the export volume for Argentina, Chile and Mexico for 1934–72 and for 1934–55 in the cases of Brazil and Venezuela.

Argentina

Current exports: 1900–1913, Lewis (1981); 1914–33, Wilkie (1974).
Export volume: 1900–1933, Di Tella and Zymelman (1973); 1973–94, ECLAC, Statistics and Projections Division.
Current imports: 1900–1914, Di Tella and Zymelman (1973, pp. 100–121); 1915–33, Wilkie (1974, p. 259).
Import volume: 1900–1933, United Nations (1959); 1960–86, IMF (1988), p. 166; 1987–94, ECLAC, Statistics and Projections Division.

Brazil

Current exports: 1900–1913, Lewis (1981, p. 57). 1914–15, intrapolated; 1916–33, Wilkie (1974, p. 259).
Export volume: 1900–1933, ECLAC (1951).
Current imports: 1900–1915, APEC (1975); 1916–33, Wilkie (1974, p. 259).

---

[*] I am very grateful to John Hennelly who assisted me in the preparation of this appendix during his stay at ECLAC in Santiago de Chile

Import volume: 1900–1912, Villela and Suzigan (1977, p. 366); 1913–33, ECLAC (1951, p. 221); 1961–85, IMF (1988, p. 166); 1986–94, ECLAC, Statistics and Projections Division.

Chile

Current exports: 1900–1915, INE (various issues) linked for 1916–29 with Wilkie (1974, p. 262); 1930–34 from ECLAC (1976).
Export volume: 1900–1930, ECLAC (1951, p. 284); 1973–93, ECLAC, Statistics and Projections Division.
Current imports: 1900–1915, INE (various issues) linked for 1916–29 with Wilkie (1974, p. 262); 1930–34 from ECLAC (1976).
Import volume: 1900–1930, ECLAC (1951, p. 284); 1960–86, IMF (1988, p. 170); 1987–94, ECLAC, Statistics and Projections Division.

Colombia

Current exports: 1900–1904, Lewis (1981, p. 57). 1905–30, Colombia, Contraloria General de la República (1931), *Anuario de Comercio Exterior. Año 1930*, vol. XXIX, p. 234; 1931–33, Wilkie (1974, p. 259).
Export volume: 1900–1904: 1900, Maddison (1989, p. 138); 1901–04 are intrapolated; 1905–55, Colombia, Contraloria General de la República, *Anuario de Comercio Exterior*, (1926, p. 213; 1950, p. 3 and 1966, p. LIII); 1956–87, IMF (1988, p. 166); 1988–94, ECLAC, Statistics and Projections Division.
Current imports: 1905–30, Colombia, Contraloria General de la República (1931), *Anuario de Comercio Exterior. Año 1930*, vol. XXIX, p. 234; 1931–33, Wilkie (1974, p. 259).
Import volume: 1900–1904, not available; 1905–67, Colombia, Contraloria General de la República, *Anuario de Comercio Exterior*, (1937, p. 203; 1950, p. 2 and 1967, p. LIII); 1968–87, IMF (1988, p. 170); 1988–94, ECLAC, Statistics and Projections Division.

Mexico

Current exports: 1900–1913, Lewis (1981, p. 57); 1914–17, intrapolated; 1918–33, Wilkie (1974, p. 259).
Export volume: 1900–1933, ECLAC (1951, p. 424); 1973–94, ECLAC, Statistics and Projections Division.
Current imports: 1900–1917, INEGI (1990, vol. II, p. 679); 1918–33, Wilkie (1974, p. 259).
Import volume: 1900–1933, ECLAC (1951, p. 424); 1960–86, IMF (1988, p. 170); 1987–94, ECLAC, Statistics and Projections Division.

Venezuela

Current exports: 1900–1912, Lewis (1981, p. 57); 1913–49, Baptista (1991).
Export volume: 1900–1949, Baptista (1991, pp. 35, 63); 1950–56, ECLAC (1976); 1956–83, IMF (1988, p. 166); 1984–94, ECLAC, Statistics and Projections Division.
Current imports: 1900–1915, Baptista (1991); 1916–33, Wilkie (1974, p. 259).
Import volume: 1900–1933, Baptista (1991, pp. 61, 63); 1960–86, IMF (1988, p. 166); 1987–94, ECLAC, Statistics and Projections Division.

Table F.1 Latin American Exports, Six Countries, 1900–1994 (current dollars)

	Argentina	Brazil	Chile	Colombia	Mexico	Venezuela
1900	149	182	61	11	75	9
1901	162	194	63	11	77	9
1902	173	175	68	9	76	8
1903	213	177	71	12	83	7
1904	255	189	79	19	95	16
1905	312	215	97	12	97	14
1906	282	255	208	15	135	16
1907	286	263	202	15	124	16
1908	356	215	233	15	120	15
1909	386	310	228	16	115	16
1910	362	307	243	18	129	17
1911	316	325	250	22	146	19
1912	467	363	282	32	148	26
1913	515	317	292	34	150	32
1914	566	223	215	33	154	23
1915	622	262	241	32	157	26
1916	556	267	188	36	161	25
1917	534	298	260	37	165	26
1918	777	288	292	37	168	51
1919	1,000	571	116	79	180	57
1920	1,013	368	289	71	383	33
1921	651	220	162	63	339	23
1922	656	301	124	53	289	27
1923	748	336	198	60	254	31
1924	790	423	221	86	267	45
1925	793	491	229	85	203	76
1926	730	461	201	112	299	93
1927	972	431	206	109	268	110
1928	1,017	475	236	134	255	141
1929	907	465	279	127	255	203
1930	895	736	277	113	329	193
1931	814	432	173	142	258	106
1932	569	312	58	98	147	113
1933	475	282	49	71	121	88
1934	475	291	95	78	149	143
1935	501	272	96	70	207	143
1936	537	322	113	78	188	167
1937	758	350	193	86	221	208
1938	438	296	139	81	161	201
1939	466	305	136	78	150	185
1940	428	263	140	71	142	177
1941	455	358	159	76	138	258
1942	503	400	178	98	168	181
1943	610	466	179	125	231	221
1944	682	575	195	130	216	303
1945	739	655	205	141	258	393
1946	1,168	972	217	201	320	555
1947	1,612	1,131	279	255	414	718
1948	1,577	1,173	329	177	369	1,281

Table F.1 (continued)

	Argentina	Brazil	Chile	Colombia	Mexico	Venezuela
1949	1,011	1,089	296	321	381	1,164
1950	1,178	1,359	281	394	532	929
1951	1,169	1,771	370	463	644	1,187
1952	688	1,416	453	473	665	1,350
1953	1,125	1,539	408	596	591	1,463
1954	1,027	1,562	398	657	591	1,396
1955	929	1,423	472	584	785	1,819
1956	944	1,482	542	537	834	2,099
1957	975	1,392	455	511	735	2,542
1958	994	1,243	386	461	736	2,326
1959	1,009	1,282	495	473	753	2,214
1960	1,079	1,268	488	465	764	2,305
1961	964	1,403	506	435	826	2,225
1962	1,216	1,214	530	463	930	2,342
1963	1,365	1,406	522	446	985	2,343
1964	1,410	1,430	592	548	1,054	2,472
1965	1,493	1,596	637	539	1,145	2,455
1966	1,593	1,741	817	508	1,199	2,373
1967	1,465	1,654	847	510	1,145	3,077
1968	1,368	1,881	858	558	1,254	2,779
1969	1,612	2,311	1,075	708	1,430	3,083
1970	1,773	2,739	1,249	736	1,402	3,169
1971	1,740	2,904	997	690	1,504	3,124
1972	1,941	3,991	855	866	1,694	3,166
1973	3,266	6,199	1,231	1,177	2,250	3,298
1974	3,931	7,951	2,481	1,417	2,958	11,153
1975	2,961	8,670	1,552	1,465	2,904	8,800
1976	3,916	10,128	2,083	1,745	3,417	9,299
1977	5,652	12,120	2,190	2,663	4,167	9,551
1978	6,400	12,659	2,478	3,003	6,005	9,187
1979	7,810	15,244	3,894	3,300	8,982	14,317
1980	8,021	20,132	4,705	3,945	15,570	19,221
1981	9,143	23,293	3,837	2,956	19,646	20,980
1982	7,625	20,175	3,706	3,095	21,214	16,590
1983	7,836	21,899	3,831	3,081	21,819	13,937
1984	8,107	27,005	3,651	3,462	24,407	15,997
1985	8,396	25,639	3,804	3,552	22,112	14,438
1986	6,852	22,349	4,191	5,102	16,347	8,660
1987	6,360	26,224	5,224	4,642	20,887	10,577
1988	9,135	33,494	7,052	5,037	20,765	10,244
1989	9,579	34,383	8,080	5,717	23,048	13,286
1990	12,353	31,414	8,373	6,766	27,131	17,497
1991	11,978	31,620	8,942	7,232	27,318	15,155
1992	12,235	35,793	10,007	6,917	27,722	14,185
1993	13,118	38,597	9,199	7,116	30,241	14,066
1994	15,659	43,558	11,539	8,399	34,530	15,480

Table F.2 Latin American Imports, Six Countries, 1900–1994 (current dollars)

	Argentina	Brazil	Chile	Colombia	Mexico	Venezuela
1900	156	135	48	0	56	11
1901	140	110	52	0	59	12
1902	119	115	50	0	71	5
1903	159	119	53	0	72	11
1904	252	126	59	0	79	9
1905	246	112	71	12	97	9
1906	300	122	88	11	103	10
1907	303	158	110	12	98	10
1908	260	139	101	14	69	9
1909	289	145	99	11	88	10
1910	363	175	112	17	91	15
1911	388	195	131	18	80	20
1912	429	233	125	24	83	19
1913	477	247	123	29	46	17
1914	377	138	98	21	23	11
1915	298	143	57	18	42	17
1916	310	191	82	30	31	21
1917	410	201	128	25	89	24
1918	425	251	161	22	135	15
1919	556	350	137	48	138	37
1920	793	439	123	101	194	62
1921	635	217	110	33	242	18
1922	585	214	81	42	152	20
1923	736	231	117	61	155	31
1924	565	305	128	56	153	43
1925	700	412	137	89	189	60
1926	662	391	164	111	180	81
1927	721	388	132	126	160	71
1928	705	442	151	149	168	82
1929	717	417	203	126	180	89
1930	911	445	175	63	275	119
1931	513	245	145	67	153	62
1932	322	182	44	49	95	41
1933	329	238	38	55	89	37
1934	291	210	44	53	92	38
1935	301	226	61	60	113	44
1936	308	247	72	68	128	56
1937	427	335	88	85	170	92
1938	392	295	89	79	109	99
1939	312	241	103	96	121	105
1940	284	250	85	75	124	99
1941	241	278	104	86	188	90
1942	237	238	108	53	155	66
1943	181	317	128	76	177	67
1944	201	415	131	87	278	114
1945	266	446	144	142	330	184
1946	519	674	156	204	543	300
1947	1,188	1,217	197	323	661	568
1948	1,392	1,134	269	286	458	740

Table F.2 (continued)

	Argentina	Brazil	Chile	Colombia	Mexico	Venezuela
1949	1,036	1,115	304	234	440	724
1950	964	1,090	294	323	549	597
1951	1,480	1,987	391	371	822	765
1952	1,179	1,982	440	368	807	862
1953	795	1,319	398	484	808	961
1954	979	1,634	411	595	714	937
1955	1,173	1,307	448	592	874	1,098
1956	1,128	1,234	421	582	1,072	1,321
1957	1,310	1,489	525	483	1,155	1,869
1958	1,233	1,353	494	400	1,129	1,599
1959	993	1,374	491	415	1,007	1,578
1960	1,249	1,462	625	517	1,186	1,188
1961	1,460	1,460	711	557	1,139	1,197
1962	1,357	1,475	680	541	1,143	1,304
1963	981	1,487	663	508	1,240	1,238
1964	1,077	1,263	723	586	1,493	1,249
1965	1,199	1,096	718	454	1,560	1,421
1966	1,124	1,496	892	675	1,605	1,307
1967	1,096	1,667	819	497	1,748	1,445
1968	1,169	2,132	852	643	1,960	1,665
1969	1,576	2,265	1,028	685	2,080	1,720
1970	1,694	2,849	1,063	843	2,461	1,869
1971	1,868	3,701	1,109	929	2,407	2,103
1972	1,905	4,783	1,086	859	2,718	2,463
1973	2,230	6,999	1,290	1,062	3,814	2,812
1974	3,635	14,168	2,148	1,597	6,057	4,148
1975	3,947	13,592	1,525	1,495	6,580	6,000
1976	3,033	13,726	1,864	1,662	6,028	7,663
1977	4,162	13,257	2,539	1,880	5,489	10,938
1978	3,834	15,054	3,408	2,971	8,109	11,767
1979	6,700	19,804	4,808	3,364	12,086	10,670
1980	10,541	24,961	5,797	4,739	19,460	11,827
1981	9,430	24,079	7,181	5,201	24,068	13,106
1982	5,337	21,069	3,989	5,480	15,128	12,944
1983	4,504	16,801	3,085	4,963	8,023	6,419
1984	4,585	15,210	3,574	4,498	11,788	7,774
1985	3,814	14,332	3,072	4,141	13,993	8,106
1986	4,724	15,557	3,436	3,862	11,997	8,504
1987	5,818	16,581	4,396	4,322	12,731	9,659
1988	5,322	16,055	5,292	5,002	19,591	12,726
1989	4,203	19,875	7,144	5,004	24,438	7,803
1990	4,076	22,524	7,678	5,590	29,969	7,335
1991	8,275	22,950	8,094	4,906	38,124	11,147
1992	14,872	23,068	10,129	6,516	48,160	14,066
1993	16,784	27,740	11,125	9,832	50,147	12,200
1994	21,527	35,997	11,825	11,883	60,979	8,879

Table F.3 Latin American Export Volume Indices, Six Countries, 1900–1994 (1980 = 100)

	Argentina	Brazil	Chile	Colombia	Mexico	Venezuela
1900	16.3	0.0	23.6	0.8	8.3	4.3
1901	17.8	10.7	25.6	0.8	9.5	3.9
1902	19.0	10.2	24.3	0.7	9.8	3.1
1903	23.4	9.6	26.2	0.9	10.3	3.7
1904	27.6	7.7	28.9	1.4	10.3	4.6
1905	30.0	8.3	34.6	0.8	9.9	4.3
1906	26.3	10.6	87.2	1.0	10.3	4.0
1907	27.1	11.4	108.4	1.1	9.4	3.8
1908	33.0	9.3	99.6	1.0	9.8	3.9
1909	30.9	12.1	98.1	1.3	11.0	4.2
1910	29.6	7.9	110.6	1.5	12.6	4.2
1911	26.3	8.6	129.1	1.6	12.2	4.2
1912	38.9	9.2	123.4	1.6	12.5	4.4
1913	38.4	10.2	121.8	2.0	14.2	5.3
1914	41.7	9.1	97.0	1.9	15.8	5.5
1915	60.4	12.7	56.6	1.6	17.4	5.1
1916	52.6	10.8	81.0	1.6	19.0	5.1
1917	38.0	10.7	130.0	2.0	20.6	5.6
1918	54.6	9.1	159.0	2.0	22.2	6.5
1919	64.3	11.9	147.0	2.3	17.0	6.4
1920	62.3	10.9	166.0	2.4	36.8	6.3
1921	57.5	11.0	139.0	3.0	36.4	7.6
1922	73.0	11.6	87.0	2.6	39.9	7.6
1923	74.1	12.8	120.0	2.8	35.6	8.0
1924	91.5	11.5	133.0	3.2	32.4	9.1
1925	73.0	11.2	149.0	3.2	31.2	12.1
1926	81.8	10.9	157.0	9.0	32.4	13.7
1927	109.1	12.3	131.0	19.2	32.9	20.2
1928	101.3	11.6	146.0	25.6	31.3	29.1
1929	101.3	12.3	179.0	25.8	31.3	38.3
1930	70.1	13.5	288.0	26.6	25.2	38.2
1931	97.4	14.5	145.0	23.0	26.4	32.6
1932	89.6	9.9	44.0	21.9	18.6	32.2
1933	85.7	12.4	38.0	17.3	19.7	31.1
1934	72.5	13.6	44.0	23.2	26.2	35.7
1935	76.5	15.7	61.0	23.2	26.8	38.1
1936	69.2	17.4	72.0	23.8	29.4	42.1
1937	80.5	15.7	88.0	25.6	34.6	45.8
1938	51.9	19.0	89.0	27.0	15.4	46.1
1939	66.5	19.5	103.0	27.7	14.6	47.7
1940	56.5	16.2	85.0	30.7	12.5	40.1
1941	50.5	17.6	104.0	29.2	13.7	56.0
1942	49.2	13.4	108.0	11.7	14.0	37.6
1943	50.5	13.6	128.0	16.5	16.3	44.8
1944	55.2	16.0	131.0	25.7	13.4	60.3
1945	56.5	17.4	144.0	26.9	15.7	77.2
1946	58.5	21.4	156.0	25.1	16.0	91.7
1947	63.8	20.2	197.0	27.2	16.3	101.9
1948	57.9	21.2	269.1	26.6	12.8	113.9

Table F.3 (continued)

	Argentina	Brazil	Chile	Colombia	Mexico	Venezuela
1949	38.6	20.4	303.8	33.4	14.6	110.5
1950	47.9	16.5	31.7	38.8	16.6	124.7
1951	37.9	17.9	32.7	44.2	16.9	141.3
1952	25.9	15.0	34.0	42.8	17.5	152.4
1953	42.6	16.5	29.4	45.5	18.3	146.8
1954	45.9	14.6	33.6	42.8	18.6	157.9
1955	40.6	16.7	35.0	38.7	23.0	180.1
1956	45.2	21.3	38.2	37.0	23.6	208.2
1957	47.9	17.9	39.1	33.8	21.5	284.0
1958	51.9	19.0	37.3	39.5	23.3	251.4
1959	52.5	22.1	43.7	47.6	25.3	214.6
1960	53.2	22.3	40.0	45.8	25.0	213.0
1961	47.9	23.5	44.6	43.3	25.6	177.5
1962	58.5	23.3	45.1	50.3	28.8	187.1
1963	66.5	27.1	46.0	55.1	29.1	188.9
1964	64.5	23.1	50.6	56.7	29.4	192.7
1965	71.2	25.4	49.7	59.8	32.6	191.4
1966	73.8	29.0	52.9	69.4	34.0	185.0
1967	69.2	27.6	53.4	57.3	32.0	240.0
1968	66.5	31.7	53.8	61.6	33.5	217.4
1969	75.1	36.1	52.9	66.6	37.8	241.2
1970	81.0	45.4	49.2	69.9	38.0	182.1
1971	70.7	49.7	55.3	73.3	36.0	211.5
1972	65.2	58.8	49.3	81.6	40.5	209.4
1973	81.8	66.1	50.6	82.3	36.3	169.7
1974	78.5	62.3	61.0	75.9	38.2	145.8
1975	58.9	69.0	65.6	93.0	38.8	110.1
1976	84.7	69.4	84.7	86.0	46.9	111.4
1977	117.0	68.5	83.1	66.7	62.2	103.4
1978	123.7	75.5	79.2	88.9	66.0	100.6
1979	115.9	82.5	98.1	100.6	77.5	111.3
1980	100.0	100.0	100.0	100.0	100.0	100.0
1981	117.8	123.0	93.7	89.2	121.3	94.1
1982	105.4	114.5	100.7	84.9	152.9	74.2
1983	120.4	134.0	101.8	94.3	182.5	77.0
1984	119.7	160.1	107.6	103.1	198.7	88.0
1985	143.2	166.2	119.6	106.4	180.5	80.8
1986	125.1	143.2	122.7	125.2	185.4	92.0
1987	119.8	171.7	135.8	135.5	204.2	89.2
1988	150.0	193.3	150.5	130.4	219.7	99.9
1989	145.4	200.4	173.5	147.3	223.8	102.4
1990	198.1	186.9	191.1	180.1	233.2	117.1
1991	187.3	195.9	202.6	199.0	250.9	124.1
1992	188.1	230.1	238.7	214.9	258.4	119.6
1993	197.7	254.4	245.7	229.9	265.5	127.8
1994	232.6	268.4	266.8	226.7	291.5	140.9

Table F.4 Latin American Import Volume Indices, Six Countries, 1900–1994 (1980 = 100)

	Argentina	Brazil	Chile	Colombia	Mexico	Venezuela
1900	17.2	0.0	11.0	0.0	5.8	3.5
1901	17.9	8.7	13.5	0.0	6.1	3.5
1902	15.4	9.1	13.1	0.0	5.7	3.6
1903	20.0	9.3	13.8	0.0	7.1	3.8
1904	31.9	9.4	15.5	0.0	6.7	3.7
1905	30.1	11.0	19.9	1.9	9.5	3.9
1906	34.7	11.6	24.5	1.5	9.4	4.1
1907	33.6	13.3	29.7	1.5	11.2	4.3
1908	31.2	11.8	28.5	1.8	10.6	4.1
1909	36.1	12.6	24.2	1.5	8.2	4.2
1910	41.3	15.7	25.9	2.2	9.5	4.6
1911	44.8	19.3	29.3	2.5	9.7	4.8
1912	43.8	20.6	30.7	2.9	9.1	5.0
1913	48.0	20.4	30.5	3.4	9.7	5.2
1914	29.7	10.6	24.3	2.8	8.5	4.7
1915	22.4	6.7	14.7	2.3	7.4	4.7
1916	27.0	7.2	20.4	2.5	6.2	5.5
1917	23.5	6.1	25.0	2.2	5.1	5.0
1918	21.7	6.2	24.6	1.2	3.9	4.2
1919	26.6	8.6	19.4	2.1	5.2	5.5
1920	36.1	11.7	17.4	3.6	7.6	5.9
1921	34.0	7.8	17.5	2.7	11.2	4.4
1922	34.3	8.9	17.5	3.1	7.1	5.4
1923	44.8	10.0	24.9	4.5	8.6	5.9
1924	46.6	14.2	27.6	5.1	8.6	6.1
1925	53.9	18.0	29.9	7.3	12.3	6.4
1926	56.4	15.6	40.5	9.3	11.3	6.8
1927	60.2	15.6	28.2	11.6	9.4	6.9
1928	63.4	18.1	30.0	14.6	10.0	6.7
1929	64.4	18.3	38.1	14.1	10.7	7.3
1930	53.6	11.1	35.2	8.9	8.7	6.5
1931	35.0	7.3	19.0	5.4	5.5	5.8
1932	27.3	6.6	6.7	4.0	4.2	4.7
1933	31.9	9.1	7.5	4.7	5.0	4.8
1934	33.3	10.1	9.9	5.8	6.1	4.8
1935	34.4	11.5	15.0	5.9	6.3	3.6
1936	36.3	11.7	17.0	8.0	7.3	5.0
1937	47.6	14.4	19.0	8.6	9.4	7.3
1938	45.0	13.4	17.4	8.9	7.8	7.8
1939	37.8	12.3	22.1	11.4	7.1	9.0
1940	32.5	10.9	16.6	8.7	6.7	8.1
1941	25.7	10.9	19.4	8.5	10.0	6.2
1942	21.2	8.0	16.2	4.3	7.3	3.9
1943	14.0	10.4	16.6	5.2	8.8	3.6
1944	14.0	12.8	16.6	8.0	13.1	8.1
1945	15.5	12.5	17.8	11.7	15.5	10.4
1946	30.6	16.0	17.8	14.3	20.8	14.6
1947	55.6	23.0	18.6	20.7	21.0	24.6
1948	62.0	20.6	24.5	18.1	14.1	32.8
1949	42.3	20.0	29.6	15.5	12.2	32.2

Table F.4 (continued)

	Argentina	Brazil	Chile	Colombia	Mexico	Venezuela
1950	38.2	22.7	21.7	20.4	14.5	27.4
1951	43.5	35.2	24.5	23.0	18.8	28.3
1952	32.9	33.6	24.9	23.2	18.4	30.8
1953	25.7	23.0	24.1	32.8	17.7	33.3
1954	31.4	28.3	23.3	41.0	17.5	36.7
1955	36.7	21.4	25.3	37.2	19.0	38.6
1956	35.5	20.8	24.5	37.4	22.2	43.1
1957	40.8	26.4	32.0	31.8	23.1	60.2
1958	41.2	25.4	29.6	22.4	22.0	51.0
1959	35.2	27.2	28.0	21.5	20.4	50.1
1960	45.0	28.0	36.4	26.2	21.7	35.8
1961	51.0	25.0	41.8	31.2	20.8	36.1
1962	0.0	25.0	40.5	30.9	20.9	39.1
1963	33.0	24.5	38.7	24.9	22.4	36.4
1964	36.0	21.6	41.1	32.4	26.6	36.2
1965	40.0	18.6	40.7	23.3	27.3	40.3
1966	37.0	24.8	50.1	39.1	29.5	38.3
1967	36.0	26.8	49.0	26.6	29.7	40.5
1968	39.0	33.2	49.8	37.3	33.7	47.1
1969	50.0	24.6	58.7	39.1	34.5	46.9
1970	53.7	49.1	60.4	56.3	35.8	48.7
1971	57.9	58.7	59.1	60.3	34.6	51.6
1972	54.0	69.8	63.9	54.1	38.8	55.1
1973	55.0	86.3	71.1	51.2	46.5	52.5
1974	62.5	108.1	73.6	58.9	53.2	62.2
1975	59.0	101.5	47.3	49.6	51.8	81.1
1976	47.8	101.1	48.8	56.5	45.6	103.3
1977	60.9	92.6	59.7	67.6	41.6	135.5
1978	52.5	96.1	77.8	84.4	52.9	130.5
1979	77.0	103.8	89.7	84.8	68.3	102.5
1980	100.0	100.0	100.0	100.0	100.0	100.0
1981	89.6	87.0	120.1	105.8	122.2	115.7
1982	53.6	77.1	70.3	118.1	75.6	118.9
1983	47.9	64.5	61.2	108.5	54.9	82.8
1984	51.2	62.1	69.8	101.1	68.9	73.8
1985	41.7	61.3	65.3	89.5	84.8	81.4
1986	50.3	80.4	68.9	91.5	74.3	83.8
1987	54.8	78.3	82.3	97.0	77.4	92.3
1988	46.2	74.5	94.2	109.7	109.8	118.8
1989	34.4	81.6	119.2	104.8	133.7	71.6
1990	33.3	88.7	119.1	111.0	152.0	67.1
1991	61.6	99.3	126.3	105.6	176.8	99.6
1992	109.2	98.3	156.1	138.5	221.1	123.7
1993	125.9	127.7	176.0	211.1	214.9	109.9
1994	156.3	159.9	181.5	245.9	250.0	73.3

Appendix G. Prices

In this appendix the consumer prices evolution for the 1900–1994 period is presented. I have opted for a year-to-year inflation presentation because several countries present periods with very high or even hyperinflation, which makes an indices presentation quite difficult. If not mentioned otherwise I used IMF 1995c for the 1950–94 period. For the first half of the century sources were used as follows.

Argentina

1900–1913 not available, 1913–50, IEERAL (1986, Table 6, Consumer Price Index, pp. 122–3).

Brazil

1900–1957, Goldsmith (1986): Table III-3, p. 91 (1900–1913); Table IV-7, p. 158 (1913–45); Table V-9, p. 239 (1945–57).

Chile

1900–1950, Mamalakis (1983, vol.4, Table 4.6, p. 224).

Colombia

1900–1929, Ocampo (1981, Table 2, p. 134), representing nominal coffee prices which is a very rough approximation of the price level and 1929–50, Wilkie (1974, Table 1, p. 227).

Mexico

1900–1950, INEGI (1990, vol. II, Table 19.7, pp. 776–8) using the combined consumption and production price index, 1914–18 was interpolated.

Venezuela

1900–1950, Baptista (1991, Table VI-1, p. 287), which is an exports and imports price index.

Table G.1 Annual Change in Consumer Price Indices in Six Latin American Countries, 1900–1994 (annual % change)

	Argentina	Brazil	Chile	Colombia	Mexico	Venezuela
1900	n.a.	-6.0	18.5	-18.6	16.0	16.5
1901	n.a.	-21.3	-16.4	11.4	22.8	-2.1
1902	n.a.	-11.3	17.5	-29.5	2.8	-9.0
1903	n.a.	2.9	4.4	27.3	-0.5	-3.3
1904	n.a.	10.7	4.3	-1.4	-1.6	4.7
1905	n.a.	-8.7	9.6	7.2	10.6	3.0
1906	n.a.	2.2	-3.7	12.2	-1.0	16.9
1907	n.a.	-0.2	34.4	8.4	-1.0	-3.3
1908	n.a.	7.8	17.6	-8.9	3.6	-7.5
1909	n.a.	-1.4	-0.5	-2.4	6.5	3.2
1910	n.a.	2.8	6.3	0.0	17.3	12.7
1911	n.a.	6.7	4.1	10.0	-5.2	9.8
1912	n.a.	-0.2	-4.9	23.9	-0.8	4.7
1913	n.a.	-4.7	4.2	20.2	-0.8	-6.9
1914	-0.5	-13.1	8.4	-3.8	17.5	0.3
1915	7.6	13.1	16.3	-2.4	17.5	6.1
1916	7.5	20.9	-5.1	0.8	17.5	8.8
1917	17.2	8.9	1.9	-4.0	17.5	13.1
1918	25.9	8.2	-1.5	4.2	17.5	3.4
1919	-5.8	8.8	22.7	62.9	-20.0	16.5
1920	17.1	19.1	14.6	5.4	5.0	15.1
1921	-11.1	-15.4	-1.7	-29.6	-8.8	-24.5
1922	-15.9	9.2	4.1	2.7	-16.2	-9.0
1923	-2.0	30.0	2.3	9.1	7.4	-0.2
1924	2.1	11.1	4.6	19.0	-4.4	5.6
1925	-2.7	18.3	7.7	29.5	5.2	4.0
1926	-3.1	-18.1	-0.5	5.4	-1.9	3.7
1927	-1.1	-2.2	1.2	-4.8	-2.5	-4.2
1928	1.1	11.5	0.4	1.2	-3.7	-1.2
1929	-1.1	-3.6	1.3	7.2	-0.6	-4.0
1930	1.1	-12.4	0.7	-19.2	0.6	-6.3
1931	-13.9	-10.8	-5.4	-23.8	-10.4	-4.8
1932	-10.4	1.5	10.1	-18.8	-9.0	-6.9
1933	13.0	-2.0	24.1	38.5	6.2	-13.2
1934	-11.5	6.3	0.1	16.7	3.4	-9.9
1935	6.0	4.7	2.1	-4.8	0.7	0.2
1936	8.7	1.6	8.4	20.0	6.0	6.1
1937	2.4	6.5	12.6	0.0	18.7	3.3
1938	-0.4	6.1	4.4	12.5	4.5	-4.6
1939	1.6	2.0	1.4	3.7	2.8	1.3
1940	1.9	6.7	12.7	-3.6	0.5	0.4
1941	2.7	10.2	15.2	0.0	6.1	4.2
1942	5.9	16.3	25.6	7.4	10.6	5.2
1943	1.0	15.6	16.3	17.2	20.0	7.1
1944	-0.3	21.7	11.7	20.6	28.2	7.4
1945	19.8	15.7	8.8	9.8	8.1	8.6
1946	-69.3	13.9	15.9	8.9	18.8	10.9
1947	334.9	7.8	33.6	18.4	2.1	10.5
1948	13.0	8.8	18.0	17.2	6.2	24.4

Table G.1 (continued)

	Argentina	Brazil	Chile	Colombia	Mexico	Venezuela
1949	31.1	9.7	18.8	7.4	5.8	-5.0
1950	25.5	12.6	14.5	20.5	6.0	1.9
1951	36.7	20.8	22.5	9.0	12.6	7.1
1952	38.7	8.1	21.8	-2.4	14.3	1.2
1953	4.0	16.4	25.5	7.3	-1.5	-1.3
1954	3.8	22.2	72.2	8.7	4.9	0.1
1955	12.3	12.8	75.1	-0.8	16.0	-0.4
1956	13.4	33.6	56.1	6.5	4.8	0.9
1957	24.7	14.8	26.8	15.2	5.1	-2.1
1958	31.6	14.7	26.0	14.6	12.1	4.9
1959	113.7	39.3	38.7	7.2	2.6	5.0
1960	27.3	29.5	11.6	3.9	4.9	3.4
1961	13.4	33.4	7.7	8.7	1.6	-2.6
1962	28.3	51.8	14.0	2.5	1.2	-0.5
1963	23.9	70.1	44.1	32.0	0.6	1.1
1964	22.2	91.9	46.0	17.6	2.3	2.1
1965	28.6	65.7	28.8	3.5	3.6	1.7
1966	31.9	41.3	23.1	19.9	4.2	1.8
1967	29.2	30.5	18.8	8.2	3.0	-0.0
1968	16.2	22.0	26.3	5.8	2.3	1.3
1969	7.6	22.7	30.4	10.1	3.4	2.4
1970	13.6	22.4	32.5	6.8	5.2	2.5
1971	34.7	20.1	20.0	9.1	5.3	3.2
1972	58.4	16.6	74.8	13.4	5.0	2.8
1973	61.2	12.7	361.5	20.8	12.0	4.1
1974	23.5	27.6	504.7	24.3	23.8	8.3
1975	182.9	29.0	374.7	22.9	15.2	10.3
1976	444.0	42.0	211.8	20.2	15.8	7.6
1977	176.0	43.7	91.9	33.1	29.0	7.8
1978	175.5	38.7	40.1	17.8	17.5	7.1
1979	159.5	52.7	33.4	24.7	18.2	12.4
1980	100.8	82.8	35.1	26.5	26.4	21.5
1981	104.5	105.6	19.7	27.5	27.9	16.2
1982	164.8	97.8	9.9	24.5	58.9	9.6
1983	343.8	142.1	27.3	19.8	101.8	6.3
1984	626.7	197.0	19.9	16.1	65.5	12.2
1985	672.1	226.9	30.7	24.0	57.7	11.4
1986	90.1	145.2	19.5	18.9	86.2	11.5
1987	131.3	229.7	19.9	23.3	131.8	28.1
1988	343.0	682.3	14.7	28.1	114.2	29.5
1989	3079.8	1287.0	17.0	25.8	20.0	84.2
1990	2314.0	2937.8	26.0	29.1	26.7	40.8
1991	171.7	440.9	21.8	30.4	22.7	34.2
1992	24.9	1008.7	15.4	27.0	15.5	31.4
1993	10.6	2148.4	12.7	22.6	8.7	38.1
1994	4.2	2686.5	11.4	23.8	7.0	60.8

Appendix H. Previous Non-Standardised Capital Stock Estimates in Latin America

INTRODUCTION

The aim of this appendix is to examine in some detail the history of capital stock and national wealth estimation in Latin America in the twentieth century. The earliest estimates were made during the first half of the century. A second wave of estimates occurred early after World War II, influenced by the pioneering work of Goldsmith, Kuznets, Eisner, Fellner and Tinbergen. This appendix analyses all the major existing estimates. Chapter 5 presents new standardised estimates.

Reference will be made to earlier studies on capital and wealth estimates which are available in some countries such as Argentina and Chile. In Latin America no official time series of capital stock figures are prepared on a regular basis. The unofficial estimates were made by independent scholars and research institutes, and this explains why there are great differences in methodology and coverage.

Existing estimates can be useful for various types of analysis and comparisons within each country, but are difficult to use in international comparisons because of different underlying assumptions about the lives of assets, retirement patterns, and differences in the relative price of assets. Given the great difference in assumptions and methodology, this study concludes that the standardised estimates have the advantage of using the same methodology for all countries, and this facilitates comparisons between countries in terms of capital–output ratios, growth performance and the role of technical progress.

A first systematic approach to measuring capital stocks in Latin America was undertaken in the early 1950s in Argentina, Brazil, Chile, Colombia and Mexico with support from ECLAC.[1] Ganz (1959) provides an indication of the importance which ECLAC gave at the time to national wealth estimates:

> Investment and capital accumulation are the main basis for economic development . . . and the study of capital formation, capital accumulation, investment needs, the role of foreign capital and the use of investment resources has been undoubtedly the most important economic theme of concern to government economic policy, academic study as well as the work of international organisations such as ECLA. (p.217)

CAPITAL STOCK IN ARGENTINA

In the 1950s ECLAC made several efforts to estimate the Argentine capital stock. Before that time very few studies were available, with the exception of work carried out at the beginning of the century by Argentina's director general of statistics, Alejandro Bunge, who studied Argentina's wealth in comparative perspective, covering France, Germany, the United Kingdom and the United States (see Bunge, 1917). The first ECLAC study, ECLAC (1954), combined the gross investment estimates provided by an unofficial study of Belaúnde[2] with census benchmark estimates of the stock of capital.

Belaúnde defined gross investment as; machinery and equipment, including both domestical and imported; construction and improvements, including public works, railways, private buildings and agricultural improvements; and changes in the stock of cattle. He felt that his estimates probably underestimated (a) some types of durable equipment; (b) some investment in public services, such as trolley lines and telephones, and (c) some types of construction and improvements, such as mines.

ECLAC (1954) concluded that its estimates of gross investment probably understated the level of investment in Argentina. The gross investment series, expressed in current prices, were deflated through the use of the gross product deflator for the years after 1935. A cost-of-living index was used for the 1900–1935 period. The investment series were used to estimate the stock of capital defined as the depreciated replacement value (in 1950 prices) of reproducible tangible and durable capital goods. Land, consumer durable goods, inventories other than cattle, and monetary metal were excluded from the stock.

The main benchmark sources were the 1914 Census and the 1935 Census of Industry, direct estimates of producers' durable equipment in industry and buildings, and the value of railways. Sectors for which no comprehensive measures were available included imported vehicles and public works. The value of the capital stock for these groups was estimated for a base year by cumulating gross investment, in 1950 prices, beginning with the year 1900, for a number of years equivalent to one-half of the estimated useful life of the capital good. This methodology was based upon Goldsmith (1952). The estimates of the capital stock for benchmark years were extended by means of net annual investment series. The net investment series were derived by subtracting the estimated real depreciation of the capital stock from the gross investment series in accordance with the estimated useful life of each type of capital good. Table H.1 shows net capital stock, output and the capital–output ratio.[3]

Table H.1 Argentina: Net Capital Stock, GDP and Capital–Output Ratio, ECLAC Estimate, 1945–52 (thousand millions of pesos at 1950 prices)

Years	Net capital stock	GDP	Capital–output ratio
1945	116.0	40.9	2.84
1946	119.9	49.7	2.41
1947	125.9	56.8	2.22
1948	134.9	57.9	2.33
1949	142.7	53.1	2.69
1950	150.7	53.7	2.81
1951	157.3	53.3	2.95
1952	161.3	48.5	3.33

Source: ECLAC (1954).

A second major effort to study the historical trends in capital formation was initiated in 1956 with the establishment of a joint Argentine Government/United Nations study group to study the economic development of Argentina, United Nations (1959).[4] This group, which consisted of over 100 professionals, made sectoral evaluations in a historical perspective. The estimates generated by this project were relatively independent from those of the 1954 study and the differences are quite substantial (see Table H.2).

In the appendix to the study,[5] gross investment and capital stock estimates were given for the 1900–1955 period. The methodological explanation of how the data were obtained is very general. Reference to the studies of Ganz (1959) and Balboa and Fracchia (1959). The somewhat confused way of referring to other publications obscures the exact methodology used. Ganz stated that the differences between his estimates and those by Balboa/Fracchia were due to differences in classification and the inclusion of cattle stocks. Additionally, in the calculation of the long-term series from 1900 onwards, there was a slight difference in the treatment of depreciation (see Ganz, 1959, p. 242). However, it is not completely clear how the 1900–1935 series were calculated, as reference was also made to ECLAC (1954) and to the estimates made by Belaúnde, which were based, partially, on direct estimates.

United Nations (1959) concluded, after a critical analysis of all sources and available data, that it was not possible to obtain an estimate of fixed capital stock through direct estimation on the basis of census material. They used the perpetual inventory approach in which the estimates were based on accumulation of net annual investment. Reliable estimates were available for domestic production of investment goods.

Table H.2 Argentina: Net Capital, GDP and Capital–Output Ratio, ECLAC Estimate, 1900–1955 (millions of pesos at 1950 prices)

Years	Net capital stock	GDP[a]	Capital– output ratio	Years	Net capital stock	GDP[a]	Capital– output ratio
1900	39.989	8.865	4.51	1928	145.833	33.169	4.40
1901	42.862	9.615	4.46	1929	154.185	34.696	4.44
1902	44.709	9.425	4.74	1930	160.251	33.264	4.82
1903	46.758	10.773	4.34	1931	161.167	30.955	5.21
1904	49.711	11.919	4.17	1932	160.032	29.926	5.35
1905	54.908	13.499	4.07	1933	159.402	31.333	5.08
1906	61.064	14.108	4.31	1934	160.521	33.806	4.75
1907	68.769	14.481	4.75	1935	161.732	35.298	4.31
1908	74.941	15.898	4.71	1936	161.963	35.550	4.56
1909	81.689	16.686	4.89	1937	165.218	38.145	4.33
1910	89.969	17.898	5.03	1938	169.423	38.289	4.42
1911	97.683	18.220	5.36	1939	171.537	39.746	4.32
1912	103.261	19.707	5.24	1940	172.399	40.399	4.27
1913	108.592	19.914	5.45	1941	172.885	42.468	4.07
1914	111.150	17.849	6.23	1942	173.118	42.965	4.03
1915	111.414	17.945	6.21	1943	173.024	42.645	4.06
1916	111.227	17.429	6.38	1944	174.222	47.468	3.67
1917	110.355	16.014	6.89	1945	175.387	45.950	3.82
1918	109.232	18.952	5.76	1946	178.429	50.035	3.57
1919	108.528	19.651	5.52	1947	187.348	55.600	3.37
1920	110.022	21.079	5.22	1948	196.310	58.679	3.34
1922	114.330	23.346	4.90	1950	208.062	58.599	3.55
1923	120.087	25.919	4.63	1951	214.151	60.423	3.54
1924	124.925	27.942	4.47	1952	218.076	56.441	3.86
1925	129.266	27.824	4.65	1953	221.439	59.499	3.72
1926	133.325	29.164	4.57	1954	226.101	62.072	3.64
1927	138.790	31.233	4.44	1955	231.737	64.661	3.58

Note: [a] At factor costs.

Source: United Nations (1959, Annex I, p. 4 and Annex 3, p. 91).

Depreciation was estimated following Balboa and Fracchia (1959, pp. 280–83): (a) determination of the probable average life of groups of goods; (b) the assumption that goods would be completely worn out by the last year of their probable life (that is, they would have no scrap value); and (c) the assumption that annual depreciation would represent a constant proportion of the value when new (straight-line depreciation). In Table H.2, net capital stock, GNP and the capital–output ratio are shown for the period 1900–1955.

Recently several capital stock estimations have been published. One of these, prepared by IEERAL (1986), was based to a great extent on previous work, especially United Nations (1959). Again the methodological explanation is very general, and for details the reader is referred to other publications which are very hard to get, being, in some cases, mimeographed manuscripts at regional universities. It is somewhat surprising that the outcome, in terms of the capital–output ratio, is so different from the 1959 United Nations study. IEERAL (1986) presents total capital stock in australes at 1960 prices, equal to the sum of fixed capital in agriculture, non-agricultural activity (excluding government) and government. Table H.3 shows net capital stock, gross domestic product and the capital–output ratio for the 1950–84 period.

Table H.3 Argentina: Net Capital Stock, GDP and Capital–Output Ratio, IEERAL Estimate, 1950–84 (australes at 1960 prices)

Years	Net capital stock	GDP [a]	Net capital–output ratio	Years	Net capital stock	GDP [a]	Net capital–output ratio
1950	1,700	690	2.5	1970	3,168	1,412	2.2
1951	1,734	717	2.4	1971	3,349	1,480	2.3
1952	1,784	680	2.6	1972	3,538	1,526	2.3
1953	1,836	717	2.6	1973	3,739	1,620	2.3
1954	1,873	746	2.5	1974	3,926	1,724	2.3
1955	1,921	800	2.4	1975	4,134	1,709	2.4
1956	1,967	822	2.4	1976	4,348	1,705	2.5
1957	2,023	864	2.3	1977	4,570	1,808	2.5
1958	2,076	917	2.3	1978	4,849	1,729	2.8
1959	2,139	858	2.5	1979	5,055	1,852	2.7
1960	2,185	925	2.4	1980	5,292	1,878	2.8
1961	2,280	991	2.3	1981	5,428	1,761	3.1
1962	2,392	975	2.4	1982	5,504	1,662	3.3
1963	2,473	951	2.6	1983	5,549	1,713	3.2
1964	2,537	1,050	2.4	1984	5,543	1,748	3.2
1965	2,602	1,146	2.3				
1966	2,692	1,153	2.4				
1967	2,796	1,184	2.4				
1968	2,890	1,235	2.3				
1969	3,009	1,340	2.2				

Note: [a] At factor costs.

Source: IEERAL (1986).

Another study was the Goldberg and Ianchilovici (1986) estimation of the gross stock, derived on the basis of a perpetual inventory approach. This study has the advantage of a clear and transparent description of its methodology. They applied a rectangular retirement pattern in which all assets of the same vintage are scrapped simultaneously. Repairs and maintenance were deducted from total capital formation. The average service life of assets is rather high; fluctuating between 56–71 years for construction, 15–24 years for machinery and equipment, and 13–25 years for transport equipment; given the fact that the major part (75.2 per cent) of capital stock consists of construction, this gives an estimated average life for capital assets of about 52 years. Estimates of the total and non-residential capital stocks were presented. Table H.4 shows the relevant ratios.

Table H.4 Argentina: Capital–Output Ratios, Goldberg and Ianchilovici Estimates, 1970–86 (australes at 1970 prices)

Years	Total capital–output ratio	Non-residential capital–output ratio
1970	3.67	2.18
1971	3.69	2.22
1972	3.78	2.31
1973	3.80	2.35
1974	3.73	2.33
1975	3.88	2.45
1976	4.01	2.54
1977	3.90	2.49
1978	4.20	2.72
1979	4.06	2.65
1980	4.16	2.72
1981	4.64	3.05
1982	5.02	3.30
1983	4.96	3.25
1984	4.90	3.20
1985	5.17	3.37
1986	4.94	3.21

Source: Goldberg and Ianchilovici (1986).

Table H.5 compares the estimates presented in this chapter with the standardised estimates contained in Chapter 5.

The differences between the first three estimates are rather big in terms of levels and growth rates. The results of the Goldberg and Ianchilovici study are broadly similar to my own; the differences can largely be attributed due to different assumptions about average service life of assets, which produced a higher level of stocks and lower growth rates in the case of the Goldberg and Ianchilovici study.

Table H.5 Argentina: Capital–Output (C/O) Ratio, 1950–86, Comparison of Standardised and Existing Estimates (on the basis of national currencies)

Years	ECLAC United Nations (1954) Total net C/O ratio	ECLAC United Nations (1959) Total net C/O ratio	IEERAL (1986) Total net C/O ratio	Goldberg/ Ianchilovici (1986) Total gross C/O ratio	Goldberg/ Ianchilovici (1986) Gross non-res. C/O ratio	Standarised estimates of this study Total net C/O ratio	Standarised estimates of this study Total gross C/O ratio	Standarised estimates of this study Gross non-res. C/O ratio
1950	2.8	3.6	2.5			1.9	3.3	1.7
1951	3.0	3.5	2.4			1.9	3.2	1.7
1952	3.3	3.9	2.6			2.1	3.5	1.8
1953		3.7	2.6			2.0	3.4	1.8
1954		3.6	2.5			2.0	3.4	1.7
1955		3.6	2.4			1.9	3.2	1.7
1956			2.4			1.9	3.3	1.7
1957			2.3			1.9	3.2	1.7
1958			2.3			1.9	3.1	1.7
1959			2.5			2.1	3.4	1.9
1960			2.4			2.0	3.3	1.8
1961			2.3			2.0	3.2	1.8
1962			2.5			2.1	3.4	2.0
1963			2.6			2.3	3.6	2.1
1964			2.4			2.1	3.4	2.0
1965			2.3			2.0	3.2	1.9
1966			2.4			2.1	3.3	1.9
1967			2.4			2.1	3.4	2.0
1968			2.3			2.1	3.3	1.9
1969			2.3			2.0	3.2	1.9
1970			2.2	3.7	2.2	2.0	3.2	1.9
1971			2.3	3.7	2.2	2.1	3.3	1.9
1972			2.3	3.8	2.3	2.2	3.4	2.0
1973			2.3	3.8	2.4	2.2	3.4	2.0
1974			2.3	3.7	2.3	2.2	3.4	2.0
1975			2.4	3.9	2.5	2.3	3.5	2.1
1976			2.6	4.0	2.5	2.4	3.6	2.2
1977			2.5	3.9	2.5	2.3	3.6	2.1
1978			2.8	4.2	2.7	2.5	3.9	2.3
1979			2.7	4.1	2.7	2.5	3.7	2.3
1980			2.8	4.2	2.7	2.5	3.8	2.3
1981			3.1	4.6	3.1	2.8	4.3	2.6
1982			3.3	5.0	3.3	3.0	4.6	2.8
1983			3.2	5.0	3.3	2.9	4.6	2.8
1984			3.2	4.9	3.2	2.8	4.5	2.7
1985				5.2	3.4	2.9	4.8	2.9
1986				4.9	3.2	2.7	4.5	2.7

Source: Appendix E and sources indicated in headings.

CAPITAL STOCK IN BRAZIL

ECLAC (1954) provided the first capital stock estimates for Brazil. The general methodology was the same as for Argentina. 1940 wealth was estimated from the 1940 census. This benchmark, expressed in 1950 prices, was extended year by year, in combination with estimates of gross and net investment. For 1945 onwards, ECLAC (1954) gave figures for gross and net fixed investment that were deflated by the implicit gross product deflator. The results are shown in Table H.6.

Table H.6 Brazil: Net Capital Stock, GDP and Capital–Output Ratio, ECLAC Estimate, 1945–52 (thousands millions of cruzeiros at 1950 prices)

Years	Net capital stock	GDP	Capital–output ratio
1945	520.1	173.4	3.00
1946	535.5	190.9	2.81
1947	557.7	197.4	2.83
1948	576.3	209.8	2.75
1949	599.0	227.1	2.64
1950	624.6	240.6	2.60
1951	655.0	252.9	2.59
1952	693.1	271.9	2.55

Source: ECLAC (1954).

A second estimate was prepared shortly afterwards in a study of Brazil's economic development by ECLAC and the Brazilian National Bank for Economic Development (United Nations, 1956). An initial stock (for 1939) was updated on a yearly basis with net investment over the period 1939–53, giving a series of net fixed reproducible capital as shown in Table H.7. They were shown in 1952 rather than 1950 prices. There was a significant difference between the two estimates, as reflected in the capital–output ratio.

Carlos Geraldo Langoni undertook a third study to estimate the capital stock using different assumptions with respect to disaggregated growth and depreciation rates (Langoni, 1974). On the basis of an unpublished study by the Brazilian Economic Institute, Getúlio Vargas Foundation (1970), he disaggregated the capital stock into machinery and equipment (E), urban construction (U), rural construction (R) and imported capital goods (M). Table H.8 shows Langoni's capital–output ratios and a clearly downward trend can be observed.

Table H.7 Brazil: Net Capital Stock, GDP and Capital–Output Ratio, United Nations Estimate, 1939–53 (billions of cruzeiros at 1952 prices)

Years	Net capital stock	GDP	Capital–output ratio
1939	410	200.3	2.05
1940	421	200.3	2.10
1941	432	210.0	2.06
1942	443	203.5	2.18
1943	451	209.0	2.16
1944	458	219.4	2.09
1945	470	234.6	2.00
1946	477	257.7	1.85
1947	492	278.3	1.77
1948	519	294.1	1.76
1949	561	302.1	1.86
1950	593	324.1	1.83
1951	627	346.5	1.81
1952	667	360.9	1.85
1953	713	376.1	1.90

Source: United Nations (1956).

Table H.8 Brazil: GDP and Capital–Output Estimates, Langoni Estimate, 1948–69 (thousands of cruzeiros at 1953 prices)

Years	GDP	Capital–output ratio
1948	286,003	2.81
1949	306,308	2.74
1950	329,612	2.64
1951	342,081	2.65
1952	381,016	2.50
1953	384,560	2.62
1954	415,399	2.51
1955	355,679	2.38
1956	466,994	2.41
1957	507,845	2.30
1958	530,055	2.30
1959	550,462	2.31
1960	608,683	2.19
1961	689,691	2.03
1962	724,401	2.03
1963	737,971	2.10
1964	n.a.	n.a.
1965	759,041	2.23
1966	783,347	2.25
1967	853,089	2.17
1968	873,808	2.22
1969	951,790	2.17

Note: n.a. = not available. The 1964 estimate was not included as it was impossible to reproduce GDP for that year.
Source: Langoni (1974).

Raymond W. Goldsmith's (1986) book about Brazil's long-term development includes capital stock estimates for the 1913–80 period. These are based on Langoni's initial 1948 estimate which was adjusted by Goldsmith, incorporating updated estimates for GDP and capital formation made by the Getúlio Vargas Foundation. Goldsmith took Langoni's estimate as far back as 1913, using a rather ingenious aggregation procedure in which gross fixed capital formation is assumed to be 10 per cent of GDP[6] and net fixed capital formation 57 per cent of gross capital formation, the averages for the 1949–68 period. The 1972–80 estimates are by Goldsmith himself (see Table H.9).

Table H.9 Brazil: Capital Stock, Gross and Net Capital Formation and Capital–Output Ratio, Goldsmith Estimate, 1913–80 (millions of cruzeiros)

Years	Net capital stock	Capital formation		Capital–output ratio
		Gross	Net	
1913	366			3.21
1920	402	63	36	2.55
1924	429	48	27	2.13
1928	488	104	59	2.00
1932	525	65	37	2.45
1936	565	70	40	2.25
1940	647	143	82	2.10
1944	740	163	93	2.28
1948	841	178	101	2.11
1952	996	271	155	1.85
1956	1,165	312	169	1.72
1960	1,437	467	272	1.86
1964	1,831	648	394	2.04
1968	2,386	829	555	1.98
1972	3,281	1,316	895	1.77
1976	4,814	2,190	1,533	1.60
1980	6,758	2,700	1,944	1.96

Source: Goldsmith (1986).

Table H.10 shows a comparison of the different results and it becomes clear that the differences are rather substantial. The large difference between the Goldsmith and Langoni series is somewhat surprising. Goldsmith used the Langoni base year estimates, but his adjustment to this base year seems to have been significant.[7]

The standardised estimates and those of Goldsmith show similar levels around 1980, although his growth rate differs markedly. It is also difficult to compare the different performances as Goldsmith uses a four year moving average. My results are very different from those of Langoni and the earlier United Nations studies.

Table H.10 Brazil: Capital–Output (C/O) Ratio, 1950–80, Comparison of Standardised and Existing Estimates (on the basis of national currencies)

Years	ECLAC (1954) Total net C/O ratio	U. Nations (1959) Total net C/O ratio	Langoni (1974) Total net C/O ratio	Goldsmith (1986) Total net C/O ratio	This study Total net C/O ratio	Total gross C/O ratio	Gross non-res. C/O ratio
1950	2.6	1.8	2.6		0.9	1.4	0.9
1951	2.6	1.8	2.6		1.0	1.5	1.0
1952	2.5	1.8	2.5	1.8	1.1	1.6	1.0
1953		1.9	2.6		1.2	1.7	1.1
1954			2.5		1.2	1.6	1.1
1955			2.4		1.2	1.7	1.1
1956			2.4	1.7	1.3	1.8	1.2
1957			2.3		1.3	1.8	1.2
1958			2.3		1.3	1.8	1.2
1959			2.3		1.3	1.9	1.3
1960			2.2	1.9	1.3	1.8	1.3
1961			2.0		1.3	1.8	1.3
1962			2.0		1.3	1.8	1.3
1963			2.1		1.4	1.9	1.3
1964				2.0	1.4	2.0	1.4
1965			2.2		1.4	2.0	1.4
1966			2.2		1.4	2.0	1.4
1967			2.2		1.5	2.1	1.4
1968			2.2	2.0	1.4	2.0	1.4
1969			2.2		1.4	1.9	1.3
1970					1.5	2.1	1.4
1971					1.5	2.0	1.4
1972				1.8	1.4	2.0	1.4
1973					1.4	1.9	1.4
1974					1.5	2.0	1.4
1975					1.6	2.1	1.5
1976				1.6	1.6	2.1	1.6
1977					1.7	2.2	1.6
1978					1.7	2.3	1.7
1979					1.8	2.4	1.8
1980				2.0	1.8	2.4	1.8

Source: Appendix E and sources in headings.

CAPITAL STOCK IN CHILE

The first person to estimate capital stock in Chile was Raúl Simón (1935). He compared national income and wealth with the USA for 1929–34. His estimates of net capital stock cited in ECLAC (1954) were derived from a study by Hasche (1951). I only have at my disposal the aggregated values of the United Nations study, as the original Hasche study is no longer available (see Table H.11).

Apparently it estimated the depreciated replacement value of fixed capital, by activity for 1938–49, based on the 1938 census of industry and company balance sheets for that year. The benchmark estimate for 1938 took into account detailed information on the age composition of the capital stock by type of capital good. The estimate was extended year by year, by depreciating existing capital and adding new investment.

Table H.11 Chile: Net Capital Stock, GDP and Capital–Output Ratio, ECLAC Estimate, 1945–52 (billions of 1950 pesos)

Years	Net capital stock	GDP	Capital–output ratio
1945	241.2	125.6	1.92
1946	247.8	123.9	2.00
1947	253.9	117.2	2.17
1948	260.9	129.6	2.01
1949	270.7	123.4	2.19
1950	277.3	124.7	2.22
1951	284.7	131.3	2.17
1952	292.0	138.2	2.11

Source: ECLAC (1954).

The ECLAC (1954) study made various adjustments to the Hasche estimates. For the stock of capital of the agricultural sector, an estimate by the Corporación de Fomento de la Producción (CORFO) was used. Hasche's estimates were reworked to introduce different assumptions on the average length of life of assets. Unfortunately ECLAC did not give detailed information on the numerical implications of the different assumptions. ECLAC's stock of capital may be defined as the depreciated replacement value (in 1950 prices) of reproducible tangible and durable capital goods. Land, consumer durable goods, inventories and monetary metal were excluded from the stock of capital goods.

Recently, various estimates of net capital stock have been published (Gutiérrez, 1983) (see Table 5.12) and Haindl and Fuentes (1986) (see Table 5.13). These used the methodology developed by Harberger in his study on the rate of return to capital in Colombia (Harberger, 1972).

This methodology involved estimation of the initial capital stock, as follows:

$$GI = (\delta + y)K$$

Here GI refers to gross investment, y to the annual rate of growth of the capital stock, δ to the annual rate of depreciation and K to the capital stock at the beginning of the year. Harberger assumed the growth rate of capital stock to be equal to a normal growth rate of gross domestic product or national income, after allowing for depreciation. Based on this definition of the initial net capital stock, the stock in subsequent years consists of the initial stock minus depreciation plus gross investment during the year less one-half year's depreciation of new gross investment.

Table H.12 Chile: Net Capital Stock, GDP and Capital–Output Ratio, Gutiérrez Estimate, 1950–82 (billions of 1977 pesos)

Years	Net fixed capital stock		Total net capital stock	GDP	Capital–output ratio
	Construction/ other works	M&E			
1950	333.8	40.2	374.0	135.7	2.8
1951	342.1	43.5	385.7	141.6	2.7
1952	351.2	48.0	399.2	149.7	2.7
1953	361.1	52.3	413.5	157.3	2.6
1954	373.9	55.3	429.3	158.1	2.7
1955	387.7	57.0	444.8	157.9	2.8
1956	403.3	60.4	463.8	158.8	2.9
1957	411.2	65.0	476.3	175.5	2.7
1958	415.9	72.7	488.0	180.3	2.7
1959	419.5	79.0	499.1	178.4	2.8
1960	427.6	81.5	509.2	187.1	2.7
1961	442.2	85.8	528.1	196.0	2.7
1962	454.1	92.4	546.6	205.3	2.7
1963	471.4	97.5	568.9	218.3	2.6
1964	490.4	100.3	590.8	223.1	2.7
1965	516.7	104.1	620.8	224.9	2.8
1966	535.5	105.7	641.3	250.0	2.6
1967	552.3	110.0	662.3	258.1	2.6
1968	569.0	114.5	683.5	267.4	2.6
1969	587.8	120.8	708.7	277.3	2.6
1970	608.1	126.2	734.3	283.0	2.6
1971	630.8	132.0	762.8	308.4	2.5
1972	653.4	135.7	789.1	304.7	2.6
1973	668.3	134.9	803.2	287.7	2.8
1974	678.6	135.7	814.3	290.5	2.8
1975	697.7	135.3	833.1	253.0	3.3
1976	705.1	135.0	840.1	261.9	3.2
1977	707.9	133.4	841.3	287.7	2.9
1978	711.2	136.3	847.5	311.4	2.7
1979	717.2	142.5	859.8	337.2	2.6
1980	727.5	151.0	878.6	362.6	2.4
1981	744.2	163.5	907.8	381.8	2.4
1982	765.9	179.1	945.0	336.0	2.8

Source: Gutiérrez (1983).

Tables H.12 and H.13 give the estimates of capital stock, GNP and capital–output ratio for both studies. The initial stock in Table H.12 is based upon an assumed capital stock growth rate of 3 per cent, which is approximately the growth rate of GNP in 1940–60 (3.4 per cent). Estimates for depreciation were 2.5 per cent in construction and 10 per cent for machinery and equipment. Gross investment was calculated using national accounts. Normal investment was estimated by regression analysis of the national accounts investment series over the period 1940–80, excluding the period 1971–73. Once the initial stock estimation was made, the stock in subsequent years was estimated by the perpetual inventory method, although use was made of net fixed capital formation series.[8]

The initial stock in Table H.13 was based on a growth rate of 3.7 per cent (average growth during 1957–63, that is, three years before and three years after the base year), depreciation rates were 2.5 per cent for construction (40 years of service life) and 6.7 per cent for machinery and equipment (15 years). Normal investment was also estimated using regression analysis for the period 1960–70. In contrast with Harberger and Gutiérrez, Haindl and Fuentes did not depreciate gross investment for the previous year, when constructing their series.

Table H.13 Chile: Net Capital Stock, GDP and Capital–Output Ratio, Haindl and Fuentes Estimate, 1960–84 (billions of 1977 pesos)

| Years | Net fixed capital stock | | Total net capital stock | GDP | Capital–output ratio |
	Construction/ other works	M&E			
1960	430,525	125,330	555,855	187,229	2.97
1961	445,374	130,050	575,424	196,039	2.94
1962	457,542	137,260	594,802	205,169	2.90
1963	475,044	143,163	618,207	218,351	2.83
1964	500,440	146,841	647,281	223,443	2.90
1965	521,086	151,506	672,592	225,030	2.99
1966	540,184	154,012	694,196	250,329	2.77
1967	557,237	159,357	716,594	258,598	2.77
1968	574,164	165,032	739,196	267,286	2.77
1969	592,787	172,672	765,459	277,157	2.76
1970	613,871	179,482	793,353	282,695	2.81
1971	636,906	186,860	823,766	308,799	2.67
1972	659,858	191,913	851,771	304,586	2.80
1973	674,969	192,551	867,520	287,793	3.01
1974	685,423	194,709	880,132	290,257	3.03
1975	704,892	195,549	900,441	252,793	3.56
1976	712,387	196,321	908,708	262,027	3.47
1977	715,261	195,700	910,961	287,651	3.17
1978	718,630	199,684	918,314	311,226	2.95
1979	724,775	207,203	931,978	337,168	2.76
1980	735,288	217,281	952,569	363,028	2.62
1981	751,910	231,824	983,734	383,804	2.56
1982	773,902	250,350	1,024,252	329,621	3.11
1983	785,365	252,213	1,037,578	327,169	3.17
1984	795,062	248,074	1,043,136	347,923	3.00

Source: Haindl and Fuentes (1986).

Table H.14 Chile: Capital–Output (C/O) Ratio, 1950–84, Comparison of
Standardised and Existing Estimates (on the basis of national currencies)

Years	ECLAC (1954) Total net C/O ratio	Gutiérrez (1983) Total net C/O ratio	Haindl/Fuentes (1986) Total net C/O ratio	Standarised estimate of this study Total net C/O ratio	Total gross C/O ratio	Total non-res. C/O ratio
1950	2.2	2.8		2.3	3.6	2.1
1951	2.2	2.7		2.3	3.6	2.1
1952	2.1	2.7		2.2	3.6	2.0
1953		2.6		2.2	3.5	2.0
1954		2.7		2.3	3.6	2.1
1955		2.8		2.4	3.8	2.2
1956		2.9		2.5	3.9	2.2
1957		2.7		2.3	3.7	2.1
1958		2.7		2.4	3.7	2.2
1959		2.8		2.5	3.9	2.3
1960		2.7	3.0	2.4	3.8	2.3
1961		2.7	2.9	2.4	3.8	2.3
1962		2.7	2.9	2.4	3.8	2.3
1963		2.6	2.8	2.3	3.7	2.3
1964		2.7	2.9	2.4	3.8	2.4
1965		2.8	3.0	2.5	3.9	2.5
1966		2.6	2.8	2.3	3.7	2.3
1967		2.6	2.8	2.3	3.7	2.3
1968		2.6	2.8	2.3	3.7	2.3
1969		2.6	2.8	2.3	3.7	2.3
1970		2.6	2.8	2.4	3.7	2.3
1971		2.5	2.7	2.3	3.5	2.2
1972		2.6	2.8	2.4	3.7	2.3
1973		2.8	3.0	2.4	3.9	2.4
1974		2.8	3.0	2.4	3.9	2.4
1975		3.3	3.6	2.8	4.6	2.8
1976		3.2	3.5	2.7	4.5	2.8
1977		2.9	3.2	2.5	4.2	2.6
1978		2.7	2.9	2.4	4.0	2.4
1979		2.6	2.8	2.2	3.8	2.3
1980		2.4	2.6	2.1	3.6	2.2
1981		2.4	2.6	2.1	3.5	2.2
1982		2.8	3.1	2.5	4.2	2.6
1983			3.2	2.6	4.4	2.7
1984			3.0	2.4	4.2	2.6

Source: Appendix E and sources in headings.

Table H.14 compares the different results. The estimates are quite close, especially when compared with the outcomes for most of the other countries. The estimate for 1950 included in the 1954 ECLAC estimate is very similar to mine. The Gutiérrez and Haindl and Fuentes estimates show somewhat higher levels. However, the performance with respect to growth rates and changes between years is very similar. The differences in level are to a large extent attributable to the procedure followed to calculate the initial capital stock. These cannot be explained by the differences in average asset life, which are rather small.

CAPITAL STOCK IN COLOMBIA

ECLAC's study of Colombia's economic development included a long-term estimate of fixed capital stock (ECLAC, 1957). This was defined as the depreciated replacement value (at 1950 prices) of reproducible, tangible and durable capital goods, including construction, agricultural improvements and livestock. The total estimate was based partly on direct calculations for the different sectors performed by ECLAC, and partly on accumulated gross investment over a period that corresponds to the average life of the respective capital category. Table H.15 shows capital, output and capital–output ratio for 1950–53 in millions of 1950 pesos.

Table H.15 Colombia: Capital, GDP and Capital–Output Ratio, ECLAC Estimate, 1950–53 (millions of 1950 pesos)

Years	Capital stock	GDP	Capital–output ratio
1950	20,197	6,322	3.23
1951	20,725	6,702	3.13
1952	21,264	7,164	2.94
1953	22,262	7,751	2.80

Source: United Nations (1957a).

In an influential paper first published in 1969, Harberger developed a methodology to estimate the stock of fixed capital in Colombia, in view of the fact, as he stated, that there were no estimates of the total fixed capital stock of Colombia – or even of major segments of it such as fixed reproducible capital – for any year (Harberger, 1972). He was obviously unaware of the studies made by ECLAC in the 1950s. His basic methodology was to estimate stock of capital through gross investment and, especially, assumptions about the growth of the capital stock and its depreciation rate (see also Harberger, 1972, p. 119). The growth rate of the capital stock was assumed to be the same as some other proxy growth rate.

For Colombia, Harberger used the growth rate of GDP of almost exactly 5 per cent per annum from 1950 to 1953. He assumed that the normal rate of growth of capital in the form of buildings and other construction works was also 5 per cent for that time. However, because of the likelihood that war-induced shortages of machinery and equipment had not been completely overcome, he assumed that stocks of those assets had a slightly higher normal growth rate of some 6 per cent per year during this period. Harberger used two sets of assumptions with regard to depreciation. He distinguished between asset lives of 40 to 50 years in construction and 12.5 to 20 years in machinery and equipment. The depreciation rates he chose, together with the abovementioned growth rates and gross investment data, generated the capital stocks shown in Table H.16.

Table H.16 Colombia: Alternative Capital Stock Estimates, GDP and Capital–Output Ratio, Harberger Estimate, 1952–67 (billions of 1958 pesos)

Years	(1)	(2)	(3)	(4)	(5)
	Total fixed capital stock		GDP	Capital–output ratios	
	a	b		(1)/(3)	(2)/(3)
1952	31.64	36.59	16.1	1.97	2.27
1953	33.00	38.28	17.1	1.93	2.24
1954	35.30	40.91	18.3	1.93	2.24
1955	38.13	44.09	19.0	2.01	2.32
1956	41.05	47.42	19.7	2.08	2.41
1957	43.58	50.39	20.2	2.16	2.49
1958	45.83	53.08	20.7	2.21	2.56
1959	46.85	54.56	22.2	2.11	2.46
1960	48.09	56.24	23.1	2.09	2.43
1961	49.95	58.51	24.3	2.06	2.41
1962	52.08	61.04	25.6	2.03	2.38
1963	54.14	63.55	26.5	2.04	2.40
1964	55.77	65.61	28.1	1.98	2.33
1965	57.85	69.13	29.1	1.99	2.38
1966	59.58	71.30	30.7	1.94	2.32
1967	61.61	73.72	31.9	1.93	2.31

Notes:
a asset lives: construction, 40 years and machinery and equipment, 12.5 years
b asset lives: construction, 50 years and machinery and equipment, 20 years

Source: Harberger (1972).

In a recent study, Henao presented an alternative approach to Harberger's initial capital stock estimation methodology (Henao, 1983). Equations (1) and (2) disaggregate the capital stock in machinery and equipment and equations (3)–(5) generate the total capital stock. Table H.17 shows Henao's estimates and the resulting capital–output ratio.

(1) $KPTt = KMEt + KCt$ 　　　　　　　$KPTt$ = total fixed private capital stock in year t

(2) $Dt = \delta a KMEt + \delta b KCt$ 　　　　　$KMEt$ = fixed private capital stock in machinery and equipment in year t

(3) Dt $= \delta cKPTt$ KCt = total fixed private capital in construction in year t

(4) $KPTt$ $= KPTt\text{-}1 + Ibt - Dt$ $\delta a, \delta b, \delta c$ = depreciation rates

(5) $KPTt\text{-}1 = DT(1/\delta c + 1) - Ibt$ Ibt = gross investment in year t

Table H.17 Colombia: Total Fixed Capital Stock, GNP and Capital–Output Ratio, Henao Estimate, 1950–81 (thousands of 1970 pesos)

Years	Fixed capital stock	GNP	Capital–output ratio
1950	168,039		
1951	172,831	51,325	3.38
1952	177,312	54,556	3.27
1953	182,378	57,853	3.25
1954	191,222	61,816	3.15
1955	202,122	64,288	3.09
1956	213,504	66,859	3.19
1957	223,375	63,395	3.27
1958	228,310	70,063	3.26
1959	232,421	75,147	3.09
1960	237,372	78,298	3.03
1961	244,572	82,352	2.97
1962	252,860	86,750	2.91
1963	260,871	89,614	2.91
1964	267,159	95,134	2.80
1965	275,227	98,569	2.79
1966	281,943	103,040	2.71
1967	289,777	108,180	2.68
1968	298,543	114,829	2.60
1969	309,680	122,128	2.53
1970	321,283	130,861	2.46
1971	335,592	137,889	2.43
1972	350,972	148,630	2.36
1973	365,461	159,195	2.20
1974	380,770	168,787	2.26
1975	398,098	175,226	2.27
1976	414,936	183,296	2.27
1977	432,058	192,187	2.25
1978	450,094	209,369	2.15
1979	468,573	220,006	2.13
1980	493,511	228,805	2.15
1981	520,081	235,054	2.21

Source: Henao (1983).

Table H.18 Colombia: Capital–Output (C/O) Ratio, 1950–81, Comparison of Standardised and Existing Estimates (on the basis of national currencies)

Years	ECLAC (1957) Total net C/O ratio	Harberger (1972) Total net C/O ratio	Henao (1983) Total net C/O ratio	Standarised estimates of this study Total net C/O ratio	Total gross C/O ratio	Gross non-res. C/O ratio
1950	3.2			1.9	2.9	2.2
1951	3.1		3.4	1.9	2.9	2.2
1952	2.9	2.0	3.3	1.8	2.8	2.1
1953		1.9	3.2	1.8	2.8	2.1
1954		1.9	3.1	1.8	2.8	2.1
1955		2.0	3.1	1.9	2.9	2.1
1956		2.1	3.2	1.9	2.9	2.2
1957		2.2	3.3	1.9	3.0	2.2
1958		2.2	3.3	1.9	3.0	2.3
1959		2.1	3.1	1.8	2.9	2.2
1960		2.1	3.0	1.8	2.9	2.2
1961		2.1	3.0	1.8	2.9	2.1
1962		2.0	2.9	1.8	2.8	2.1
1963		2.0	2.9	1.7	2.8	2.1
1964		2.0	2.8	1.7	2.8	2.0
1965		2.0	2.8	1.7	2.8	2.0
1966		1.9	2.7	1.6	2.7	2.0
1967		1.9	2.7	1.6	2.7	2.0
1968			2.6	1.6	2.6	1.9
1969			2.5	1.6	2.5	1.9
1970			2.5	1.6	2.5	1.8
1971			2.4	1.6	2.4	1.8
1972			2.4	1.5	2.4	1.8
1973			2.2	1.5	2.4	1.7
1974			2.3	1.5	2.4	1.7
1975			2.3	1.6	2.4	1.8
1976			2.3	1.6	2.4	1.8
1977			2.2	1.6	2.4	1.8
1978			2.1	1.5	2.4	1.8
1979			2.1	1.5	2.3	1.8
1980			2.1	1.5	2.4	1.8
1981			2.2	1.6	2.5	1.9

Source: Appendix E and sources in headings.

Formula (5) gives capital stock and the only dependent variables are depreciation, the depreciation rate and gross investment. Thus, the main difference with the Harberger methodology is that no assumption is necessary regarding growth of the capital stock. An initial estimate was made with the depreciation rates of ECLAC (1957) ($\delta c = 0.0346$, $\delta a = 0.05733$ and $\delta b = 0.02862$), resulting in a total stock of \$141,305,9 million for 1950. Given this stock, Henao estimated the depreciation rates which 'minimized' the differences between depreciation in this estimated capital stock and the depreciation estimates in the national accounts. The result was $\delta c = 0.036$, $\delta a = 0.0659$ and $\delta b = 0.0269$.

For public capital, a long series from 1925–81 of public investment was available. Henao first estimated the initial capital stock in 1925 and this initial capital stock was then updated. From the 1950s onwards the original error in the 1925 estimate does not affect the total series to any great extent.

Table H.18 compares the different results. The capital stock levels are rather different. The results of the Harberger study and my results coincide, but they differ by a constant factor as both capital–output ratios remain almost the same, while the Henao estimate shows a clear downward trend.

CAPITAL STOCK IN MEXICO

In the early 1950s ECLAC published some estimates of the capital stock in Mexico which were based upon the accumulation of gross investment data for a number of years equivalent to one-half of the estimated useful life of the stock of capital (ECLAC, 1954). The methodology was based upon the perpetual inventory method described in Goldsmith (1952). Investment data for the period 1925–38 was obtained from ECLAC (1951) and for 1939–50 from the Combined Mexican Working Party (1953) (see Table H.19).

In 1957, ECLAC published another study which contained rather different figures, especially with regard to capital stock (see Table H.20). It consisted of a preliminary estimate of Mexico's geographical assets in 1950, defined narrowly as 'tangible reproducible wealth' (United Nations, 1957b). In 1969, the Banco de México published a comprehensive system of national accounts which included capital stock (Banco de México, 1969). The information was based upon national censuses and data obtained from the Statistics Division of the Ministry of Industry and Trade. Additional information was obtained through surveys or directly from public and private enterprises. However, the methodological explanation given for this study is very vague. It remains quite unclear how the initial stock was measured. Table H.21 shows the basic information at constant 1960 prices.

Table H.19 Mexico: Net Capital Stock, GDP and Capital–Output Ratio, ECLAC Estimate, 1950–52 (billions of 1950 pesos)

	Net capital stock	GDP	Capital–output ratio
1950	77.3	43.2	1.79
1951	83.8	45.1	1.86
1952	89.6	45.8	1.96

Source: ECLAC (1954).

Table H.20 Mexico: Net Capital Stock, GDP and Capital–Output Ratio, ECLAC Estimate, 1950–55 (billions of 1950 pesos)

Years	Net capital stock	GDP	Capital–output ratio
1950	93.5	43.3	2.16
1951	96.4	47.8	2.02
1952	100.9	47.4	2.13
1953	105.5	49.3	2.14
1954	109.1	53.4	2.04
1955	112.9	57.7	1.96

Source: United Nations (1957b).

Table H.21 Mexico: Total Fixed Net Capital Stock, Banco de Mexico Estimate, 1950–67 (millions of 1960 pesos)

Years	Total fixed net capital stock	Construction	M&E	Permanent crops livestock	GDP	Capital– output ratio
1950	235,857	140,246	79,936	15,675	85,319	2.76
1951	248,873	147,395	85,456	16,022	91,732	2.71
1952	262,323	155,444	90,312	16,567	94,480	2.78
1953	273,413	161,365	94,922	17,126	99,587	2.75
1954	285,427	168,332	99,408	17,687	105,012	2.72
1955	298,637	175,756	104,502	18,379	113,315	2.64
1956	314,871	185,128	110,858	18,885	119,372	2.64
1957	331,885	194,767	117,407	19,711	128,335	2.59
1958	347,297	203,919	123,098	20,280	134,225	2.59
1959	362,825	212,902	129,000	20,923	140,058	2.59
1960	380,692	223,696	135,359	21,637	150,511	2.53
1961	399,480	234,354	142,455	22,671	156,664	2.55
1962	417,907	245,570	149,110	23,227	165,518	2.52
1963	439,482	258,672	156,977	23,833	179,920	2.44
1964	467,245	274,479	168,173	24,593	199,609	2.34
1965	495,964	289,765	181,051	25,148	212,139	2.34
1966	528,508	307,654	195,060	25,794	229,151	2.31
1967	565,805	328,082	211,245	26,478	245,499	2.30

Source: Banco de México (1969).

For the period 1960–85, I obtained six diskettes from the Banco de México containing very detailed information, in current and constant prices, on capital formation. Table H.22 gives a summary of the information on capital stock and depreciation. These diskettes do not give any methodological explanation, and analysis of the period covered by both, 1960 and 1970 base-year Banco de México series, brings one to the conclusion that there are great discrepancies between the two series. It is probable that the Banco de México diskettes contain some kind of error, as the capital stock is very low compared, for example, with the stock in

1960 prices presented in Table H.21 and, therefore, the results are not presented in the summary Table H.23.

Table H.22 Mexico: Gross and Net Capital Stock, Banco de Mexico Estimate, 1960–85 (millions of 1970 pesos)

	Total Stock		Construction		M&E	
	Gross	Net	Gross	Net	Gross	Net
1960	97,304	60,304	57,586	36,469	39,718	23,835
1961	105,061	65,634	62,167	39,671	42,894	25,963
1962	112,154	69,010	64,817	40,572	47,337	28,438
1963	123,036	75,834	69,649	43,445	53,381	32,389
1964	135,387	83,286	74,377	46,058	61,010	37,228
1965	145,893	88,860	78,108	47,738	67,785	41,122
1966	156,874	95,715	81,039	48,467	75,835	47,248
1967	171,387	104,526	85,972	51,242	85,415	53,284
1968	181,674	109,109	89,474	53,326	92,200	55,783
1969	195,532	116,433	93,426	54,959	102,106	61,474
1970	222,241	134,742	104,720	63,658	117,521	71,084
1971	242,038	145,916	111,489	67,740	130,549	78,176
1972	260,358	156,690	118,128	71,572	142,230	85,118
1973	283,092	170,166	124,995	75,750	158,097	94,416
1974	300,485	177,349	130,177	77,801	170,308	99,548
1975	323,956	190,802	133,617	79,356	190,339	111,446
1976	355,915	209,363	143,441	85,270	212,474	124,092
1977	378,471	218,481	150,324	88,709	228,147	129,772
1978	399,354	227,553	152,704	87,732	246,649	139,821
1979	419,416	237,844	155,845	87,686	263,571	150,158
1980	444,374	250,815	162,857	90,982	281,517	159,832
1981	478,776	276,886	170,082	95,343	308,694	181,543
1982	527,167	306,424	177,438	98,022	349,730	208,402
1983	536,173	297,402	180,617	96,588	355,557	200,814
1984	538,302	284,509	182,176	93,632	356,126	190,877
1985	543,941	276,046	182,175	89,994	361,767	186,053

Source: Banco de México (1986a).

Table H.23 compares the results of the different studies. It is clear that growth rates as well as levels of capital stock differ substantially according to the study used.

Table H.23 Mexico: Capital–Output (C/O) Ratio, 1950–67, Comparison of Standardised and Existing Estimates (on the basis of national currencies)

Years	ECLAC (1954) Total Net C/O Ratio	ECLAC (1957) Total net C/O ratio	Banco de Mexico (1969) Total net C/O ratio	Standarised estimates of this study		
				Total net C/O ratio	Total gross non-res. C/O ratio	Total net C/O ratio
1950	1.8	2.2	2.8	1.2	1.7	1.4
1951	1.9	2.0	2.7	1.3	1.7	1.4
1952	2.0	2.1	2.8	1.3	1.9	1.5
1953		2.1	2.7	1.4	1.9	1.6
1954		2.0	2.7	1.4	2.0	1.6
1955		2.0	2.6	1.4	2.0	1.6
1956			2.6	1.5	2.0	1.7
1957			2.6	1.5	2.1	1.7
1958			2.6	1.5	2.1	1.7
1959			2.6	1.6	2.2	1.8
1960			2.5	1.6	2.2	1.8
1961			2.5	1.6	2.2	1.8
1962			2.5	1.6	2.3	1.8
1963			2.4	1.6	2.2	1.8
1964			2.3	1.5	2.1	1.7
1965			2.3	1.6	2.2	1.7
1966			2.3	1.6	2.2	1.7
1967			2.3	1.6	2.2	1.7

Source: Appendix E and sources in headings.

CAPITAL STOCK IN VENEZUELA

Information regarding Venezuela's capital stock is scarce. The only available sources are the reports by the Central Bank of Venezuela (Banco Central de Venezuela, 1958, 1968 and 1991) and the interesting work by Asdrubal Baptista (1991). The Central Bank of Venezuela gives net fixed capital stock estimates for the period 1950–65. The methodology used for the estimation of depreciated renewable fixed capital was based on a measure of gross investment, depreciation and inventories of machinery and equipment, infrastructure, construction works, buildings and livestock in each of twelve different sectors. The base year of the series was 1957 for which the best data on prices were available. To obtain a capital stock estimate for 1950, the Central Bank extended several series retroactively (see Table H.24). Unfortunately, I have not been able to obtain these series, which might facilitate estimation of a gross fixed capital stock for the period 1950–85.

Table H.24 Venezuela: Capital Stock, GDP and Capital–Output Ratio, Banco Central Estimate, 1950–65 (millions of 1957 bolívares)

Years	Net capital Stock	GDP	Capital–output ratio
1950	26,523	12,728	2.08
1951	28,484	14,212	2.00
1952	31,326	15,248	2.05
1953	34,342	16,190	2.12
1954	37,840	17,749	2.13
1955	40,821	19,325	2.11
1956	44,033	21,366	2.06
1957	47,485	23,848	1.99
1958	50,032	24,164	2.07
1959	53,442	26,065	2.05
1960	55,250	26,433	2.09
1961	56,370	26,881	2.10
1962	57,499	28,585	2.01
1963	58,800	29,765	1.98
1964	60,769	32,326	1.88
1965	63,512	33,966	1.87

Source: Banco Central de Venezuela (1958, 1968 and 1991).

A very complete source of information is the study by Asdrubal Baptista (1991) who gives net and gross capital stock estimates based upon the perpetual inventory method (see Table H.25). He also presents his basic investment series, making it possible to reproduce his results using different assumptions on service life, depreciation and mortality. His assumptions about service life are somewhat lower than those of the standardised method: 15 years for machinery and equipment in general; 12 years for machinery and equipment in the oil sector; 10 years for transport equipment; and 35 years for railroad equipment.

Non-residential structures have a service life of 35 years (with the exception of non-residential structures in the oil sector whose service life is 25 years). Finally, residential structures have a service life of 50 years. Baptista presents a brief but careful description of methodology and limitations of capital stock estimation. He obtained estimates of net fixed capital stock by using straight-line depreciation. In Table H.26 the summary information on Venezuela is presented.

Table H.25 Venezuela: Total Capital Stock, GDP and Capital–Output Ratio,
Baptista Estimate, 1950–89 (millions of 1984 bolívares)

Years	Total fixed capital stock		GDP	Capital–output ratio	
	Gross	Net		Gross	Net
1950	204,484	151,885	118,302	1.73	1.28
1951	223,583	166,212	131,064	1.71	1.27
1952	245,283	182,771	141,209	1.74	1.29
1953	268,080	197,327	145,476	1.84	1.36
1954	291,738	214,292	159,396	1.83	1.34
1955	315,967	230,748	176,458	1.79	1.31
1956	341,693	249,444	195,804	1.75	1.27
1957	374,083	277,869	223,881	1.67	1.24
1958	409,104	302,504	221,948	1.84	1.36
1959	440,611	323,005	236,235	1.87	1.37
1960	466,434	332,950	236,538	1.97	1.41
1961	486,443	336,272	234,296	2.08	1.44
1962	502,735	339,685	250,428	2.01	1.36
1963	516,716	343,271	259,343	1.99	1.32
1964	531,818	350,269	278,625	1.91	1.26
1965	550,662	358,814	293,438	1.88	1.22
1966	568,546	366,443	295,567	1.92	1.24
1967	585,913	375,994	309,508	1.89	1.21
1968	607,822	391,681	326,847	1.86	1.20
1969	634,611	409,621	333,407	1.90	1.23
1970	663,990	428,450	356,089	1.86	1.20
1971	697,217	451,744	359,015	1.94	1.26
1972	734,131	481,329	357,839	2.05	1.35
1973	775,080	512,125	378,642	2.05	1.35
1974	819,734	541,515	377,397	2.17	1.43
1975	871,163	585,101	374,377	2.33	1.56
1976	934,716	642,443	403,266	2.32	1.59
1977	1,019,109	722,758	427,309	2.38	1.69
1978	1,121,236	805,062	439,127	2.55	1.83
1979	1,222,748	865,201	440,823	2.77	1.96
1980	1,313,760	909,513	418,811	3.14	2.17
1981	1,393,171	949,957	419,643	3.32	2.26
1982	1,459,407	979,308	423,378	3.45	2.31
1983	1,502,188	983,066	408,989	3.67	2.40
1984	1,528,847	969,200	391,765	3.90	2.47
1985	1,546,119	958,178	396,319	3.90	2.42
1986	1,562,588	955,273	419,977	3.72	2.27
1987	1,577,165	950,411	431,714	3.65	2.20
1988	1,601,080	961,136	463,540	3.45	2.07
1989	1,615,436	940,778	427,011	3.78	2.20

Source: Baptista (1991).

Table H.26 Venezuela: Capital–Output (C/O) Ratio, 1950–89, Comparison of Standardised and Existing Estimates (on the basis of national currencies)

Years	Banco Central de Venezuela	Baptista	(1991)	Standarised estimates of this study		
	Total net C/O ratio	Total gross C/O ratio	Total net C/O ratio	Total net C/O ratio	Total gross C/O ratio	Gross non-res. C/O ratio
1950	2.1	1.7	1.3	2.1	2.9	2.5
1951	2.0	1.7	1.3	2.1	2.9	2.5
1952	2.0	1.7	1.3	2.2	3.0	2.6
1953	2.1	1.8	1.4	2.3	3.1	2.7
1954	2.1	1.8	1.3	2.3	3.2	2.7
1955	2.1	1.8	1.3	2.4	3.2	2.8
1956	2.1	1.7	1.3	2.4	3.2	2.7
1957	2.0	1.7	1.2	2.3	3.1	2.7
1958	2.1	1.8	1.4	2.5	3.4	2.9
1959	2.1	1.9	1.4	2.4	3.4	2.9
1960	2.1	2.0	1.4	2.5	3.6	3.1
1961	2.1	2.1	1.4	2.4	3.5	3.0
1962	2.0	2.0	1.4	2.2	3.3	2.8
1963	2.0	2.0	1.3	2.1	3.2	2.7
1964	1.9	1.9	1.3	2.0	3.0	2.5
1965	1.9	1.9	1.2	2.0	3.0	2.5
1966		1.9	1.2	2.0	3.0	2.5
1967		1.9	1.2	2.0	3.0	2.5
1968		1.9	1.2	1.9	3.0	2.4
1969		1.9	1.2	2.0	3.0	2.4
1970		1.9	1.2	1.9	2.9	2.3
1971		1.9	1.3	1.9	2.9	2.3
1972		2.0	1.3	2.0	3.0	2.4
1973		2.0	1.3	2.0	3.0	2.3
1974		2.2	1.4	2.0	2.9	2.3
1975		2.3	1.6	2.0	2.9	2.3
1976		2.3	1.6	2.0	2.9	2.3
1977		2.4	1.7	2.1	3.0	2.4
1978		2.5	1.8	2.3	3.3	2.6
1979		2.8	2.0	2.5	3.5	2.8
1980		3.1	2.2	2.7	3.8	3.0
1981		3.3	2.3	2.8	4.0	3.2
1982		3.4	2.3	2.9	4.2	3.3
1983		3.7	2.4	3.1	4.7	3.7
1984		3.9	2.5	3.2	4.8	3.8
1985		3.9	2.4	3.2	4.9	3.9
1986		3.7	2.3	3.0	4.7	3.7
1987		3.6	2.2	2.9	4.7	3.7
1988		3.4	2.1	2.7	4.5	3.5
1989		3.8	2.2	2.9	5.0	3.9

Source: Appendix E and sources in headings.

NOTES

1. The United Nations Economic Commission for Latin America and the Caribbean undertook a series of studies on economic development and capital stock estimation which included four of our countries (Argentina, Brazil, Colombia and Mexico), in ECLAC (1954) some estimates were also given for Chile.
2. Apparently this study by Belaúnde, who formed part of the Alejandro Bunge group which studied Argentina's wealth at the beginning of the twentieth century (see Bunge, 1917), was never published.
3. The length-of-service-life assumptions used for estimating depreciation were as follows: agricultural improvements, 50 years; agricultural machinery, 20 years; producers durable equipment (non-agricultural), 20 years; vehicles, 20 years; buildings, 50 years; railroad equipment and construction and improvements, 33 years; public works, 50 years.
4. The study was carried out in Argentina and at the United Nations Economic Commission for Latin America and the Caribbean, under the direction of Raúl Prebisch.
5. Anexo III, 'Inversión Bruta y Capital Existente en la Argentina, por Sectores Económicos y por Tipo de Inversión y Capital, 1900–1955', pp. 77–105.
6. Goldsmith used the GDP estimates of Haddad (1980).
7. See Goldsmith (1986, p. 154).
8. See Gutiérrez (1983, pp. 205–10).

References

Abramovitz, Moses (1986), 'Catching Up, Forging Ahead and Falling Behind', *The Journal of Economic History*, Vol. 46, No. 2, June, Cambridge.

Abramovitz, Moses (1989), *Thinking about Growth*, Cambridge, Massachusetts, Cambridge University Press.

Abramovitz, Moses (1990), 'The Catch-Up Factor in Postwar Economic Growth', *Economic Inquiry*, Vol. 28, January.

Abramovitz, Moses (1991), 'The Postwar Productivity Spurt and Slowdown: Factors of Potential and Realization', in OECD (Organization for Economic Co-operation and Development), *Technology and Productivity: The Challenge for Economic Policy*, Paris.

Abramovitz, Moses (1993), 'The Search for the Sources of Growth: Areas of Ignorance, Old and New', *The Journal of Economic History*, Vol. 53, No. 2, June, Cambridge.

Altimir, Oscar (1987), 'Income Distribution Statistics in Latin America and their Reliability', *Review of Income and Wealth*, Series 33, No. 2, New Haven, Connecticut, June.

Altimir, Oscar (1997), 'Desigualdades, empleo y pobreza en América Latina', *Desarrollo económico,* vol. 37, No. 145, April–June, Buenos Aires.

Altimir, Oscar (1998), 'The Long-term Evolution of Inequality and Poverty in Argentina, Colombia and Mexico', background paper to Rosemary Thorp.

Altimir, Oscar and André A. Hofman (1990), 'Latin American Development Problems in Historical Perspective', paper presented at the ECLAC/University of Lund Symposium, Santiago, Chile, ECLAC (Economic Commission for Latin America and the Caribbean).

Annino, Antonio (1995), 'Reflections on Spanish American History', *Itinerario. European Journal of Overseas History*, Vol. XIX, No. 2, Leiden.

APEC (Análise e Perspectiva Econômica) (1975), *A Economia Brazileira e Suas Perspectivas*, Year XIV, Rio de Janeiro.

Arriagada, Irma (1994), 'Changes in the Urban Female Labour Market', *CEPAL Review*, No. 53, Santiago, Chile, ECLAC.

Arthur, W. Brian (1988), 'Self-Reinforcing Mechanisms in Economics' in P.W. Anderson, K. Arrow, and D. Pines (eds), *The Economy as an Evolving Complex System*, Reading, Addison-Wesley.

Bacha, Edmar L. (1989), 'Economic Trends in Latin America' in Seiji Naya, Miguel Urrutia, Shelley Mark and Alfredo Fuentes (eds), *Lessons in Development: A Comparative Study of Asia and Latin America*, San Francisco, California, ICEG (International Center for Economic Growth).

Balassa, Bela, Gerardo M. Bueno, Pedro Pablo Kuczynski and Mario Henrique Simonsen (1986), *Towards Renewed Economic Growth in Latin America*, Washington, DC, IIE (Institute for International Economics).

Balboa, Manuel and Alberto Fracchia (1959), 'Fixed Reproducible Capital in Argentina, 1935–55', *Income and Wealth*, series VIII, London, Bowes and Bowes.

Ballesteros, M.A. and T.E. Davis (1965), 'El crecimiento de la producción y el empleo en sectores básicos de la economía chilena, 1908–1957', *Cuadernos de Economía*, Year 2, No. 7, Santiago, Chile, Catholic University of Chile, September–December.

Banco Central de Chile, *Boletín Mensual*, various issues, Santiago, Chile.

Banco Central de Chile (1993), *Cuentas Nacionales de Chile, 1985–1992, Síntesis anticipada*, Santiago, Chile, Gerencia de División Estudios.

Banco Central de Chile (1994), *Cuentas Nacionales de Chile, 1985–1992*, Santiago de Chile.

Banco Central de la República Argentina (1976), *Cuentas Nacionales, Series Históricas*, Vol. III, Buenos Aires.

Banco Central de la República Argentina (1991), 'Informe Final de la CEPAL', Proyecto Revisión de las Cuentas Nacionales y de la Distribución del Ingreso, Buenos Aires, December, mimeo.

Banco Central de la República Argentina (1993), *Estimaciones Anuales de la Oferta y Demanda Globales. Periodo 1980–1992*, Buenos Aires, April.

Banco Central de Venezuela (1958), *Memoria Correspondiente al Ejercicio Anual 1958*, Caracas.

Banco Central de Venezuela (1968), *Informe Económico 1968*, Caracas.

Banco Central de Venezuela (1978), *La Economía Venezolana en los Últimos Treinta y Cinco Años*, Caracas.

Banco Central de Venezuela (1991), *Informe Económico 1990*, Caracas.

Banco de México (1969), *Cuentas Nacionales y Acervos de Capital, Consolidadas y por Tipo de Actividad Económica, 1950–1967*, Mexico City, Departamento de Estudios Económicos, June.

Banco de México (1986a), *Acervos y Formación de Capital*, Mexico City, Subgerencia de Precios.

Banco de México (1986b), *Indicadores Económicos, Acervo Histórico V*, Mexico City, May.

Baptista, Asdrubal (1991), *Bases Cuantitativas de la Economía Venezolana: 1830–1989*, Caracas, Comunicaciones Corporativas D.

Barbera, Mattia (1990), 'Latin America's Place in World Trade', *CEPAL Review*, No. 41, Santiago, Chile, ECLAC, August.

Baumol, W.J., R.R. Nelson and E.N. Wolf (eds) (1994), *International Convergence of Productivity*, New York, Oxford University Press.

Becker, Gary S. (1964), *Human Capital*, NBER General Series, No. 80, New York, NBER (National Bureau of Economic Research, Inc.).

Belaúnde, César H., 'Estudio de la Capitalización Bruta de la Argentina, 1900 −1950', Buenos Aires, University of Buenos Aires, *mimeo*.

Bernstein, Jeffrey and Anwar Shah (1993), 'Corporate Tax Structure and Production', *Policy Research Working Papers*, No. 1196, Washington, DC, World Bank, September.

Bianchi, Andrés and Takashi Nohara (1988), *A Comparative Study on Economic Development between Asia and Latin America*, JRP Series, No. 67, Tokyo, Institute of Developing Economies.

Blades, Derek (1989), *Capital Measurement in the OECD Countries: An Overview*, Paris, OECD.

Blakemore, Harold (1992), 'Chile, Desde la Guerra del Pacífico hasta la Depresión Mundial, 1880−1930', in Leslie Bethell (ed.), *Historia de América Latina*, Barcelona, Editorial Crítica.

Bonelli, Regis (1976), *Tecnología e Crescimento Industrial: A Experiencia Brasileira nos Anos 60*, Rio de Janeiro, IPEA (Institute of Economic and Social Planning)/INPES (Instituto de Pesquisas).

Borges, J.G. and F.P. Vasconcellos (1974), *Habitação para o Desenvolvimento*, Rio de Janeiro, Block Editores.

Borah, Woodrow (1951), *New Spain's Century of Depression*, Berkeley, California, University of California Press.

Bresser Pereira, Luis (1984), *Development and Crisis in Brazil, 1930–1983*, Boulder, Colorado, Westview Press.

Brito Figueroa, Federico (1966), *Historia Económica y Social de Venezuela: Una Estructura para su Estudio*, Caracas, Central University of Venezuela.

Bruton, Henry (1967), 'Productivity Growth in Latin America', *American Economic Review*, Vol. VII, No. 5, Washington, DC, December.

Buffon, G.L.L. (1761), *Histoire Naturelle*, as quoted in A. Annino (1995).

Bulmer-Thomas, Victor (1994), *The Economic History of Latin America since Independence*, Cambridge Latin American Studies, No. 77, New York, Cambridge University Press.

Bunge, Alejandro E. (1917), *Riqueza y Renta de la Argentina: Su Distribución y su Capacidad Contributiva*, Buenos Aires.

Bushnell, D. and N. Macauly (1988), *The Emergence of Latin America in the Nineteenth Century*, New York, Oxford University Press.

Campbell, Colin (1977), 'Capacity Capital Formation in the New Zealand Manufacturing Industries, 1952–1973', *Occasional Paper,* No. 31, Wellington, Victoria University of Wellington.

Campos, Roberto (1967), *Reflections on Latin America Development,* Latin American Monographs, No. 8, Austin, Texas, University of Texas, Institute of Latin American Studies.

Cardoso, Eliana and Ann Helwege (1992), *Latin America's Economy: Diversity, Trends, and Conflicts,* Cambridge, Massachusetts, MIT Press.

Cardoso, F.H. and Enzo Faletto (1969), *Dependencia y Desarrollo en América Latina,* Mexico City, Siglo XXI Editores.

Cardoso de Mello, Joao M. and Maria da Conceicao Tavares (1985), 'The Capitalist Export Economy in Brazil, 1884–1930', in Roberto Cortés Conde and Shane J. Hunt (eds), *The Latin American Economies,* New York, Holmes and Meier.

Cariola, Carmen and Osvaldo Sunkel (1985), 'The Growth of the Nitrate Industry and Socioeconomic Change in Chile: 1880–1930', in Roberto Cortés Conde and Shane J. Hunt (eds), *The Latin American Economies,* New York, Holmes and Meier.

Cavallo, Domingo and Yair Mundlak (1982), *Agriculture and Economic Growth in an Open Economy: The Case of Argentina,* Washington, DC, IFPRI (International Food Policy Research Institute).

CELADE (Latin American Demographic Center) (1985a), *Demographic Bulletin,* Year XVIII, No. 35, Santiago, Chile.

CELADE (1985b), *Demographic Bulletin,* Year XVIII, No. 36, Santiago, Chile.

CELADE (1990), *La Mortalidad en las Américas: Progresos, Problemas y Perspectivas,* Santiago, Chile, CELADE/PAHO (Pan American Health Organization), unpublished.

CELADE (1992), 'Economically Active Population', *Demographic Bulletin,* Year XXV, No. 49, Santiago, Chile, January.

CELADE (1993), *Demographic Bulletin,* Year XXVI, No. 51, Santiago, Chile, January.

CELADE (1995), *Demographic Bulletin,* Year XXVIII, No. 55, Santiago, Chile.

CELADE, *Demographic Bulletin,* various issues, Santiago, Chile.

CELADE/ECLAC (1993), *Population, Social Equity and Changing Production Patterns,* Santiago, Chile.

Chenery, Hollis B. (1965), 'The Structuralist Approach to Economic Development', *American Economic Review,* Vol. IV, No. 2, Washington, DC, May.

Clark, Colin (1940), *Conditions of Economic Progress,* London, Macmillan.

Coeymans, Juan Eduardo (1992), 'Productividad, Salarios y Empleo en la Economía Chilena: Un Enfoque de Oferta Agregada', *Cuadernos de Economía,* Year 29, No. 87, Mexico City, August.

Coeymans, Juan Eduardo and Yair Mundlak (1993), *Sectorial Growth in Chile: 1962–82*, Research report, No. 95, Washington DC, IFPRI.

Collver, Andrew O. (1965), *Birth Rates in Latin America: New Estimates of Historical Trends and Fluctuations*, res. ser. No. 7, Berkeley, California, Institute of International Studies, University of California.

Colombia, Contraloría General de la República, *Anuario de Comercio Exterior*, various issues, Santa Fe de Bogotá.

Combined Mexican Working Party (1953), *The Economic Development of Mexico*, Washington, DC, World Bank.

Corbo, Vittorio (1988), 'Problems, Development Theory, and Strategies of Latin America', in Gustav Ranis and T. Paul Schultz (eds), *The State of Development Economics. Progress and Perspectives*, Cambridge, Massachusetts, Basil Blackwell.

CORFO (Corporación de Fomento de la Producción) (1957), *Cuentas Nacionales de Chile, 1940–1954*, Santiago, Chile.

CORFO (1963), *Cuentas Nacionales de Chile, 1940–1962*, Santiago, Chile.

Correa, Héctor (1970), 'Sources of Economic Growth in Latin America', *The Southern Economic Journal*, Vol. XXXVII, No. 2, July.

Cortés Conde, Roberto (1985), 'The Export Economy of Argentina, 1880–1920', in Roberto Cortés Conde and Shane J. Hunt (eds), *The Latin American Economies*, New York, Holmes and Meier.

Cortés Conde, Roberto and Shane J. Hunt (eds) (1985), *The Latin American Economies*, New York, Holmes and Meier.

Council for Economic Planning and Development (1994), *Taiwan Statistical Data Book – 1994*, Seoul, Korea.

DANE (Departamento Administrativo Nacional de Estadística) (1956), *Anuario General de Estadística. Colombia – 1956,* Santa Fe de Bogotá.

DANE (1986), *XV Censo Nacional de Población y IV de Vivienda*, Características Económicas, Vol. IV, Santa Fe de Bogotá.

DANE, *Anuario de Comercio Exterior*, various issues, Santa Fe de Bogotá.

David, Paul A. (1975), *Technical Change, Innovation and Economic Growth*, Cambridge, Massachusetts, Cambridge University Press.

David, Paul A. (1985), 'Clio and the Economics of QWERTY', *American Economic Review*, Vol. 75, No. 1, Washington, DC.

De Gregorio, José (1991), 'Economic Growth in Latin America', paper presented at the Fourth Annual Interamerican Seminar on Economics, Santiago, Chile.

Denison, Edward F. (1962), *The Sources of Economic Growth in the United States and the Alternatives before us*, New York, Committee on Economic Development.

Denison, Edward F. (1967), *Why Growth Rates Differ*, Washington, DC, The Brookings Institution.

Denison, Edward F. (1974), *Accounting for United States Economic Growth 1929–1969*, Washington, DC, The Brookings Institution.

Denison, Edward F. (1985), *Trends in American Eonomic Growth, 1929–1982*, Washington, DC, The Brookings Institution.

Denison, Edward F. (1993), 'The Growth Accounting Tradition and Proximate Sources of Growth', in Adam Szirmai, Bart van Ark and Dirk Pilat (eds), *Explaining Economic Growth – Essays in Honour of Angus Maddison*, Amsterdam, Elsevier/North-Holland.

Denison, Edward F. and William K. Chung (1976), *How Japan's Economy Grew so Fast: The Sources of Postwar Expansion*, Washington, DC, The Brookings Institution.

Devlin, Robert (1989), *Debt and Crisis in Latin America: The Supply Side of the Story*, Princeton, New Jersey, Princeton University Press.

Díaz-Alejandro, Carlos F. (1970), *Ensayos sobre la Historia Económica Argentina*, Buenos Aires, Amorrortu Editores.

Díaz-Alejandro, Carlos (1983), 'Argentina, Australia and Brazil before 1929', New Haven, Connecticut, Yale University, January, mimeo.

Díaz-Alejandro, Carlos (1984), 'No Less Than Hundred Years of Argentine Economic History Plus Some Comparisons' in Gustav Ranis, Robert L. West, Mark W. Leiserson and Cynthia Taft Morris (eds), *Comparative Development Perspectives*, Boulder, Colorado, Westview Press.

Di Tella, Guido and Manuel Zymelman (1973), *Ciclos Económicos Argentinos*, con la colaboración de Alberto Petrecolla, Buenos Aires, Paidos.

Domínguez, Loreto M. (1947), 'National Income Estimates of Latin American Countries', *Studies in Income and Wealth*, Vol. 10, New York, NBER.

Dornbusch, Rudiger and S. Edwards (1990), 'El Populismo Macroeconómico', in Edmar Bacha and Sebastián Edwards (eds), *Sector Externo, Políticas Financieras y Proceso de Ajuste Macroeconómico. El Trimestre Económico*, Vol. LVII, Número especial, Mexico City, FCE (Fondo de Cultura Económica), December.

Dornbusch, Rudiger and Mario Henrique Simonsen (1987), 'Estabilización de la Inflación con el Apoyo de una Política de Ingresos', *El Trimestre Económico*, Vol. 54, No. 2, Mexico City, FCE, April–June.

ECLAC (1951), *Economic Survey of Latin America, 1949*, New York, United Nations.

ECLAC (1954), *Economic Survey of Latin America, 1951–52*, New York, United Nations.

ECLAC (1957), *Statistical Annex*, to 'The Economic Development of Colombia', Geneva, United Nations.

ECLAC (1958), *El Desarrollo Económico de la Argentina*, Annex, Santiago, Chile.

ECLAC (1963), *A Measurement of Price Levels and the Purchasing Power of Currencies in Latin America, 1960–1962*, Santiago, Chile.

ECLAC (1965a), *External Financing in Latin America*, New York, United Nations.

ECLAC (1965b), 'El Proceso de Industrialización en América Latina. Anexo Estadístico', ST/ECLA/Conf.23/L.2/Add.2, Santiago, Chile, mimeo.

ECLAC (1972), *Statistical Bulletin for Latin America*, Vol. IX, No. 1–2, New York, United Nations.

ECLAC (1976), *América Latina: Relación de Precios del Intercambio*, Cuadernos Estadísticos de la CEPAL, Santiago, Chile.

ECLAC (1985), *Evolución de las Tasas Específicas de Participación de la Población en la Actividad Económica por Sexo y Grupo de Edades. América Latina: 1950, 1960, 1970 y 1980*, LC/IN.37, Santiago, Chile.

ECLAC (1989), *Antecedentes sobre la Transformación Productiva y la Competitividad de la Economía Chilena en el Período 1939–1989*, Santiago, Chile.

ECLAC (1990a), *Changing Production Patterns with Social Equity*, LC/G.1601-P, Santiago, Chile. United Nations publication, sales N°E.90.II.G.6.

ECLAC (1990b), *Magnitud de la Pobreza en América Latina en los Años Ochenta*, Santiago, Chile, April.

ECLAC (1990c), *Latin America and the Caribbean: Options to Reduce the Debt Burden*, Santiago, Chile.

ECLAC (1992), *Economic Survey of Latin America and the Caribbean 1991*, Santiago, Chile.

ECLAC (1994a), *Latin America and the Caribbean: Policies to Improve Linkages with the Global Economy*, LC/G.1800, Santiago, Chile.

ECLAC (1994b), *Open Regionalism in Latin America and the Caribbean. Economic Integration as a Contribution to Changing Production Patterns with Social Equity*, Santiago, Chile.

ECLAC\UNESCO (United Nations Educational, Scientific and Cultural Organization) (1992), *Education and Knowledge: Basic Pillars of Changing Production Patterns with Social Equity*, Santiago, Chile.

Edwards, Sebastian (1995), *Crisis and Reform in Latin America: From Despair to Hope*, Washington, DC, World Bank.

Eisner, Robert (1952), 'Depreciation Allowances, Replacement Requirements and Growth', *American Economic Review*, Vol. XLII, No. 5, Washington, DC, December.

Elías, Victor J. (1978), 'Sources of Economic Growth in Latin American Countries', *The Review of Economics and Statistics*, Vol. LX, Amsterdam, North-Holland, August.

Elías, Victor J. (1992), *Sources of Growth. A Study of Seven Latin American Economies*, San Francisco, A Joint Research Project of the Fundación del Tucumán and the International Center for Economic Growth (CEG).

Fajnzylber, Fernando (1990), *Unavoidable Industrial Restructuring in Latin America*, Durham, NC, Duke University Press.

FAO (Food and Agriculture Organization of the United Nations) (1995), *Production Yearbook*, FAO Statistical Series, No. 125, Rome.

FAO, *Production Yearbook*, various issues, Rome.

Ferrer, Aldo (1977), *Crisis y Alternativas de la Política Económica Argentina*, Mexico City, FCE.

Ffrench-Davis, Ricardo (1973), *Políticas Económicas en Chile 1952–1970*, Santiago, Chile, CIEPLAN (Economic Research Corporation for Latin America).

Ffrench-Davis, Ricardo (1991), 'Formación de Capital' in Osvaldo Sunkel (ed.), *El Desarrollo desde Dentro. Un enfoque neoestructuralista para la América Latina*, Lecturas, No. 71, Mexico City, FCE.

Ffrench-Davis, Ricardo (1994), 'The Macroeconomic Framework for Investments and Development: The Links between Financial and Trade Reforms' in Colin I. Bradford (ed.), *The New Paradigm of Systemic Competitiveness: Toward More Integrated Policies in Latin America*, Paris, OECD Development Centre.

Ffrench-Davis, Ricardo and Stephany Griffith-Jones (eds) (1995), *Las Nuevas Corrientes Financieras hacia la América Latina – Fuentes, Efectos y Políticas*, Lecturas, No. 81, Mexico City, FCE.

Ffrench-Davis, Ricardo and Oscar Muñoz (1992), 'Economic and Political Instability in Chile' in Simón Teitel (ed.), *Towards a New Development Strategy for Latin America*, Washington, DC, IDB (Inter-American Development Bank)/The Johns Hopkins University Press.

Ffrench-Davis, Ricardo, Oscar Muñoz and Gabriel Palma (1994), 'The Latin American Economies, 1950–1990', in Lesley Bethell (ed.), *The Cambridge History of Latin America*, Vol. VI, Cambridge, Massachusetts, Cambridge University Press.

Fishlow, Albert (1972), 'Origins and Consequences of Import Substitution in Brazil', in L.E. Di Marco (ed.), *International Economics and Development: Essays in Honor of Raúl Prebisch*, New York, Academic Press.

Fitzgerald, E.V.K. (1984), 'Restructuring Through the Depression: The State and Capital Accumulation in Mexico 1925–40', in Rosemary Thorp (ed.), *Latin America in the 1930s: The Role of the Periphery in World Crisis*, New York, St. Martin's Press.

Foxley, Alejandro (1983), *Latin American Experiments in Neoconservative Economics*, Berkeley, California, University of California Press.

Furtado, Celso (1963), *The Economic Growth of Brazil*, Berkeley, California, University of California Press.

Ganz, Alexander (1959), 'Problems and Uses of National Wealth Estimates in Latin America', *Income and Wealth*, Series VIII, London, Bowes and Bowes.

García, Norberto (1992), *Cambio Estructural y Mercado de Trabajo. Chile: 1973–1992*, Santiago, Chile, PREALC (Regional Employment Programme for Latin America and the Caribbean), ILO (International Labour Organization), September.

Getúlio Vargas Foundation (1970), 'Formaçâo Bruta de Capital', Rio de Janeiro, mimeo.

Goldberg, Samuel and Beatriz Ianchilovici (1986), *El Stock de Capital en la Argentina: Medición y Problemas Conceptuales*, Buenos Aires, Secretaría de Planificación.

Goldsmith, Raymond W. (1951), 'A Perpetual Inventory of National Wealth', *Studies in Income and Wealth*, Vol. 14, New York, NBER.

Goldsmith, Raymond W (1952), 'The Growth of Reproducible Wealth in the United States of America from 1805 to 1950', *Income and Wealth*, Series II, London, International Association for Research in Income and Wealth/Bowes and Bowes.

Goldsmith, Raymond W. (1986), *Brasil 1850–1984, Desenvolvimento Financiero sob um Sécolo de Inflação*, São Paulo, Brazil, Harper and Row do Brasil.

Goldsmith, Raymond W. and Robert Lipsey (1963), *Studies in the National Balance Sheet of the United States*, Vol. 1, Princeton, New Jersey, NBER/Princeton University Press.

Gordon, Robert J. (1990), *The Measurement of Durable Goods Prices*, Chicago, Illinois, University of Chicago Press.

Griffin, Keith (1989), *Alternative Strategies for Economic Development*, London, OECD Development Centre/Macmillan Press.

Griffith-Jones, Stephany and Osvaldo Sunkel (1989), *Debt and Development Crises in Latin America – The End of an Illusion*, Oxford, UK, Clarendon Paperbacks/Oxford University Press.

Griliches, Zvi (1996), 'The Discovery of the Residual: A Historical Note', *Journal of Economic Literature*, Vol. XXXIV, No. 3, Nashville, Tennessee, September.

Gunder Frank, André (1969), *Capitalism and Underdevelopment in Latin America*, New York, Monthly Review Press.

Gutiérrez, Mario (1983), 'Ahorro y Crecimiento en Chile en el Período 1960–81', *Monetaria*, Vol. VI, No. 2, Santiago, Chile, April–June.

Haddad, C.L.S. (1975), 'Crescimento do produto real brasileiro – 1900/1947', *Revista Brasileira de Economia*, Vol.29, No.1, January–March.

Haddad, C.L.S. (1980), 'Crescimento Econômico do Brasil, 1900–1976', in Paulo Neuhaus (ed.), *Economia Brasileira: Uma Visâo Historica*, Rio de Janeiro, Campus.

Haindl, Erik and Rodrigo Fuentes (1986), 'Estimación del Stock de Capital en Chile: 1960–1984', *Estudios de Economía*, Vol. 13, No. 1, Santiago, Chile, University of Chile, April.

Harberger, Arnold C. (1972), 'On Estimating the Rate of Return to Capital in Colombia', in Arnold C. Harberger (ed.), *Project Evaluation–Collected Papers*, Chicago, Illinois, University of Chicago Press.

Harbison, F. and C. Myers (1964), *Human Resources, Education and Economic Growth*, New York, McGraw Hill.

Hasche S. Ewald (1951), *El Proceso de Capitalización en Chile, 1938–1950*, Santiago, Chile, Institute of Economics, University of Chile.

Hegel, Georg W.F. (1820), *Philosophie der Geschichte*, Leipzig.

Henao Morales, Rafael (1983), *La Acumulación de Capital Fijo y los Precios: Una Aproximación Estructural. El Caso de Colombia*, Santa Fe de Bogotá, Facultad de Ciencias Económicas y Administrativas, Pontificia Universidad Javeriana.

Hibbert, J., T.J. Griffin and R.L. Walker (1977), 'Development of Estimates of the Stock of Fixed Capital in the United Kingdom', *Review of Income and Wealth*, Series 23, No. 2, New Haven, Connecticut, June.

Hofman, André A. (1982), 'Mexico's Current Economic Problems in Historical Perspective', Groningen, The Netherlands, mimeo.

Hofman, André A. (1991a), 'Fasi Diversa di Crescita Economica', *Politica Internazionale*, Anno XIX (nuova serie), Rome, November–December.

Hofman, André A. (1991b), 'The Role of Capital in Latin America: A Comparative Perspective of Six Countries for 1950–89', Working paper, No. 4, Santiago Chile, ECLAC.

Hofman, André A. (1992a), 'International Estimates of Capital: A 1950–1989 Comparison of Latin America and the USA', Research memorandum, No. 509, Groningen, The Netherlands, Institute of Economic Research, University of Groningen.

Hofman, André A. (1992b), 'Capital Accumulation in Latin America: A Six Country Comparison for 1950–89', *Review of Income and Wealth*, series 38, No. 4, New Haven, Connecticut, December.

Hofman, André A. (1993a), 'Economic Development in Latin America in the 20th Century – A Comparative Perspective', in Adam Szirmai, Bart van Ark and Dirk Pilat (eds), *Explaining Economic Growth, Essays in Honour of Angus Maddison*, Amsterdam, Elsevier/North-Holland.

Hofman, André A. (1993b), 'Chile, Latin America and the World: Economic Growth in the 20th Century in a Comparative Perspective', Encuentros Anuales de Economistas de Chile, Santiago, Chile, Department of Economics, University of Chile.

Hofman, André A. (1993c), 'Chile, Latin America and the World: Economic Growth in the 20th Century in a Comparative Perspective', *Estudios de Economía*, Vol. 20, Special Issue on Economic Growth, Santiago, Chile, Department of Economics, University of Chile, June.

Hofman, André A. (1996), 'The Historical Experience: Growth Accounting' in Ruud Buitelaar and Pitou van Dijck (eds), *Latin America's New Insertion in the World Economy – Towards Systemic Competitiveness in Small Economies*, London, Macmillan.

Hofman, André A. (forthcoming), 'Capital Stocks Estimates in Latin America – A 1950–1994 Update', *Cambridge Journal of Economics*, Oxford, UK, Oxford University Press.

Hudson, H.R. and Russell Mathews (1963), 'An Aspect of Depreciation', *The Economic Record*, June.

Hulten, Charles R. (ed.) (1981), *Depreciation, Inflation, and the Taxation of Income from Capital*, Washington, DC, The Urban Institute Press.

Hulten, Charles R. (1990), 'The Measurement of Capital' in Ernst R. Berndt and Jack E. Triplett (eds), 'Fifty Years of Economic Measurement', *Studies in Income and Wealth*, Vol. 54, Chicago, Illinois, NBER.

Hulten, Charles R. (1992), 'Growth Accounting When Technical Change Is Embodied in Capital', *American Economic Review*, Vol. 82, No. 4, Washington, DC.

Hulten, Charles R. and Frank C. Wykoff (1980), 'Economic Depreciation and the Taxation of Structures in United States Manufacturing Industries: An empirical Analysis', in Dan Usher (ed.), *The Measurement of Capital*, Studies in Income and Wealth, Vol. 45, Chicago and London, The University of Chicago Press.

IBGE (Instituto Brasileiro de Geografia e Estatística), *Censo Demográfico*, various issues, Brazil.

IBGE (1990), *Anuário Estatístico do Brasil, 1990*, Rio de Janeiro.

IBGE (1992), *Anuário Estatístico do Brasil, 1992*, Rio de Janeiro.

IDB (1993), *Economic and Social Progress in Latin America, 1993 Report. Special Section: Human Resources*, Washington DC.

IEERAL (1986), 'Estadísticas de la Evolución Económica de Argentina, 1913–1984', *Estudios*, Year IX, No. 39, Córdoba, Argentina, Fundación Mediterránea, July–September.

ILO (1982), *Conditions of Work, A Cumulative Digest 2*, Geneva.

ILO (1986), *Economically Active Population: Estimates, Projections 1950–2025* Geneva.

ILO (1995), *Yearbook of Labour Statistics – 1995*, Geneva.

IMF (1988), *International Financial Statistics*, Supplements on Trade Statistics, No. 15, Washington DC.

IMF, (1995a), *International Financial Statistics*, Washington, DC, September.

IMF, (1995b), *International Financial Statistics*, No. 10, Washington, DC, October.

IMF, (1995c), *International Financial Statistics*, Washington, DC, February.

IMF, *International Financial Statistics*, various issues and CD-ROM, Washington, DC.

INE (Instituto Nacional de Estadística), *Estadísticas Comerciales de la República de Chile*, various issues, Santiago, Chile.

INEGI (Instituto Nacional de Estadística Geografia e Informática) (1992), *XI Censo General de Población y Vivienda, 1990. Resumen General*, Mexico City.

INEGI (1985), *Estadísticas Históricas de México*, Tomo I, Mexico City, August.

INEGI (1990), *Estadísticas Históricas de México*, Aguascalientes, Mexico, June.

Jain, Shail (1975), *Size Distribution of Income, A Comparison of Data*, Washington, DC, World Bank.

Jorgenson, Dale W. (1974), 'The Economic Theory of Replacement and Depreciation', in Willy Sellekaerts (ed.), *Econometrics and Economic Theory – Essays in Honour of Jan Tinbergen*, London, Macmillan.

Jorgenson, Dale W. (1990), 'Productivity and Economic Growth' in Ernst R. Berndt and Jack E. Triplett (eds), 'Fifty Years of Economic Measurement', *Studies in Income and Wealth,* Vol. 54, Chicago, Illinois, NBER.

Jorgenson, Dale W. and Martin A. Sullivan (1981), 'Inflation and Corporate Capital Recovery', in Charles R. Hulten (ed.), *Depreciation, Inflation, and the Taxation of Income from Capital*, Washington, DC, The Urban Institute Press.

Junguito, Roberto (1990), 'El Programa de Ajuste de Colombia: Su Impacto Económico y Social', in PREALC, ILO, *Colombia – La Deuda Social en los 80*, Informe de la misión PREALC/OIT, Colombia, Programa Mundial del Empleo.

Kaldor, H. (1961), 'Capital Accumulation and Economic Growth, in F.A. Luti and D. Hague (eds), *The Theory of Capital*, London, MacMillan.

Kendrick, John W. (1961), *Productivity Trends in the United States*, New York, NBER.

Kravis, Irving B., Zoltan Kenessey, Alan Heston and Robert Summers (1975), *A System of International Comparisons of Gross Product and Purchasing Power*, Baltimore, Pennsylvania, Johns Hopkins.

Kravis, Irving B., Alan Heston and Robert Summers (1978), *International Comparisons of Real Product and Purchasing Power*, Baltimore, Pennsylvania, Johns Hopkins.

Kravis, Irving B., Alan Heston and Robert Summers (1982), *World Product and Income*, Baltimore, Pennsylvania, Johns Hopkins.

Krugman, Paul (1994), 'The Myth of Asia's Miracle', *Foreign Affairs*, Vol. 73, No. 6, New York, Council on Foreign Relations, November–December.

Kuznets, Simon (ed.) (1952), 'Income and Wealth of the United States – Trends and Structure', *Income and Wealth*, Series II, Cambridge, Massachusetts, Bowes and Bowes.

Kuznets, Simon (1955), 'Economic Growth and Income Inequality', *American Economic Review*, Vol. XLV, No. 1, Washington, DC, March.

Kuznets, Simon (1961), *Capital in the American Economy, Its Formation and Financing*, Princeton, New Jersey, Princeton University Press.

Kuznets, Simon (1974), *Population, Capital and Growth*, London.

Langoni, Carlos Geraldo (1974), *As Causas do Crescimiento Económico do Brasil*, Rio de Janeiro, APEC.

Lewis, Arthur (1981), 'The Rate of Growth of World Trade, 1830–1973' in Sven Grassman and Erik Lindberg (eds), *World Economic Order: Past and Prospects*, London, Macmillan Press.

Lewis, Stephen R. (1984), 'Development Problems of Mineral-Rich Countries' in Moshe Syrquin, Lance Taylor and Larry E. Westphal (eds), *Economic Structure and Performance – Essays in Honor of Hollis B. Chenery*, Academic Press.

Lin, Ching-Yuan (1988), 'East Asia and Latin America as Contrasting Models', *Economic Development and Cultural Change*, Vol. 36, No. 3, Supplement, Chicago, Illinois, April.

Lucas, Robert E. (1988), 'On the Mechanics of Economic Development', *Journal of Monetary Economics*, Vol. 22, Amsterdam.

Lustig, Nora (1992), *Mexico: The Remaking of an Economy*, Washington DC, The Brookings Institution.

Lynch, John (1991), 'Los Orígenes de la Independencia Hispanoamericana', in Leslie Bethell (ed.), *Historia de América Latina*, Vol. 5, Barcelona, Editorial Crítica.

Maddison, Angus (1972), 'Explaining Economic Growth', *Banca Nazionale del Lavoro Quarterly Review*, Rome, September.

Maddison, Angus (1980), 'Monitoring the Labour Market. A Proposal for a Comprehensive Approach in Official Statistics', *Review of Income and Wealth*, Series 26, No. 2, New Haven, Connecticut, June.

Maddison, Angus (1982), *Phases of Capitalist Development*, Oxford, UK, Oxford University Press.

Maddison, Angus (1985), *Two Crises: Latin America and Asia 1929–38 and 1973–83*, Paris, OECD Development Centre.

Maddison, Angus (1987), 'Growth and Slowdown in Advanced Capitalist Economies: Techniques of Quantitative Assessment', *Journal of Economic Literature*, Vol. XXV, No. 2, Nashville, Tennessee, June.

Maddison, Angus (1989), *The World Economy in the 20th Century*, Paris, OECD Development Centre.

Maddison, Angus (1991a), *Dynamic Forces in Capitalist Development: A Long-Run Comparative View*, Oxford, UK, Oxford University Press.

Maddison, Angus (1991b), 'Economic and Social Conditions in Latin America, 1913–1950' in Miguel Urrutia (ed.), *Long-Term Trends in Latin American Development*, Washington, DC, IDB/The Johns Hopkins University Press.

Maddison, Angus (1993), *Standardised Estimates of Fixed Capital: A Six Country Comparison*, Essays on Innovation, Natural Resources and the International Economy, Montedison, Milan, Ferrazi Montedison Group.

Maddison, Angus (1994), 'Explaining the Economic Performance of Nations 1820–1989', in W.J. Baumol, R.R. Nelson and E.N. Wolf (eds), *International Convergence of Productivity*, New York, Oxford University Press.

Maddison, Angus (1995), *Monitoring the World Economy, 1820–1992*, Paris, OECD Development Centre.

Maddison, Angus (ed.) (1986), *Latin America, the Caribbean and the OECD*, Paris, OECD Development Centre.

Maddison, Angus and associates (1992), *The Political Economy of Poverty, Equity, and Growth – Brazil and Mexico*, A World Bank Comparative Study, Oxford, UK, Oxford University Press.

Mamalakis, Markos J. (1976), *The Growth and the Structure of the Chilean Economy: From Independence to Allende*, New Haven, Yale University Press.

Mamalakis, Markos J. (1983), *Historical Statistics of Chile, Money, Prices and Credit Services*, Westport, Greenwood Press.

Marcel, M. and P. Meller (1986), 'Empalme de las Cuentas Nacionales de Chile, 1960–1985, Métodos Alternativos y Resultados', *Colección Estudios CIEPLAN*, No. 20, Santiago, Chile, CIEPLAN.

Marichal, Carlos (1989), *A Century of Debt Crises in Latin America: From Independence to the Great Depression, 1820–1930*, Princeton, New Jersey, Princeton University Press.

McGreevey, William P. (1985), 'The Transition to Economic Growth in Colombia', in Roberto Cortés Conde and Shane J. Hunt (eds), *The Latin American Economies*, New York, Holmes and Meier.

Merrick, Thomas W. and Douglas H. Graham (1979), *Population and Economic Development in Brazil 1800 to the Present*, Baltimore, Pennsylvania, Johns Hopkins University Press.

Mingat, A. and J.P. Tan (1988), 'The Economic Returns to Investments in Project-Related Training: Some Empirical Evidence', *International Review of Education*, Vol. 34, No. 2.

Moguillansky, Graciela (1995), *Reformas Económicas en América Latina: Una Síntesis de la Experiencia en 11 Países*, Santiago, Chile, ECLAC.

Nelson, Richard R. (1981), 'Research on Productivity Growth and Differences', *Journal of Economic Literature*, Vol. XIX, No. 3, Nashville, Tennessee, September.

North, Douglas C. (1990), *Institutions. Institutional Change and Economic Performance*, Cambridge, Massachusetts, Cambridge University Press.

North, Douglas C. (1993), 'The Ultimate Sources of Economic Growth', in Adam Szirmai, Bart van Ark and Dirk Pilat (eds), *Explaining Economic Growth – Essays in Honour of Angus Maddison*, Amsterdam, Elsevier/North-Holland.

Ocampo, José Antonio (1981), 'El Mercado Mundial del Café y el Surgimiento de Colombia como País Cafetero', *Desarrollo y Sociedad*, No. 5, Sante Fe de Bogotá, CEDE (Centro de Estudios sobre Desarrollo Económico), January.

Ocampo, José Antonio (1984), *Colombia y la Economía Mundial – 1830–1910*, Santa Fe de Bogotá, FEDESARROLLO (Fundación para la Educación Superior y el Desarrollo)/Siglo Veintiuno Editores.

Ocampo, José Antonio (ed.) (1987), *Historia Económica de Colombia*, Santa Fe de Bogotá, FEDESARROLLO/Siglo Veintiuno Editores.

OCEI (Oficina Central de Estadística e Informática) (1990), *Indicadores de la Fuerza de Trabajo – Total Nacional y por Entidades Federales, 1985–1990*, Caracas, May.

ODEPLAN (Oficina de Planificación Nacional) (1976), *Cuentas Nacionales de Chile, 1960–1975*, Santiago, Chile.

OECD (1991a), *Technology and Productivity: The Challenge for Economic Policy*, Paris, TEP (Technology Economy Programme).

OECD (1991b), *Main Economic Indicators*, Paris.

OECD (1993), 'Methods Used by OECD Countries to Measure Stocks of Fixed Capital', *National Accounts: Sources and Methods*, No. 2, Paris, Statistics Directorate, Economic Statistics and National Accounts Division.

OECD, *Main Economic Indicators*, various issues, Paris.

Okhawa, Kazushi and Henry Rosovski (1973), *Japanese Economic Growth*, Stanford, California and London, Stanford University Press and Oxford University Press.

Orlando Melo, Jorge (1987), 'Las Vicisitudes del Modelo Liberal, 1850–1899', in José Antonio Ocampo (ed.), *Historia Económica de Colombia*, Santa Fe de Bogotá, FEDESARROLLO/Siglo Veintiuno Editores.

Palma, Gabriel (1979), 'Growth and Structure of the Chilean Manufacturing Industry from 1830 to 1935', Ph.D. dissertation, Cambridge, UK, Cambridge University.

Palma, Gabriel (1984), 'From an Export-Led to an Import-Substituting Economy: Chile 1914–39', in Rosemary Thorp (ed.), *Latin America in the 1930s: The Role of the Periphery in World Crisis*, New York, St. Martin's Press.

Patterson, K.D. and Kerry Schott (eds) (1979), *The Measurement of Capital: Theory and Practice*, Macmillan Press Ltd.

Pauw, Abbé de (1768), *Recherches Philosophiques sur les Américains*, as quoted in A. Annino (1995).

Pilat, Dirk (1993), *The Economics of Catch Up: The Experience of Japan and Korea*, Monograph Series, No. 2, Groningen, The Netherlands, Groningen Growth and Development Centre

Pilat, Dirk (1994), *The Economics of Rapid Growth. The Experience of Japan and Korea*, Aldershot, UK, Edward Elgar.

Pilat, Dirk and André A. Hofman (1990), 'Comparing Real Output, Purchasing Power and Labour Productivity: A Case Study for Argentina and the United States, 1973–1985', in J. Salazar-Carrillo and D.S. Prasada Rao (eds), *Comparisons of Prices and Real Products in Latin America, Contributions to Economic Analysis 194*, Amsterdam, North-Holland.

PREALC (1993), *Deuda Social: Desafío de la Equidad*, Santiago, Chile, ILO.

PREALC/ILO (1990), *Colombia: La Deuda Social en los 80*, Informe de la misión PREALC/OIT, Santa Fe de Bogotá, Programa Mundial del Empleo.

Prebisch, Raúl (1988), 'Dependence, Development and Interdependence', in Gustav Ranis and T. Paul Schultz (eds), *The State of Development Economics – Progress and Perspectives*, Oxford, UK, Basil Blackwell.

Prebisch, Raúl (1991), *Obras, 1919–1948*, Buenos Aires, Fundación Raúl Prebisch.

Psacharopoulos, George (1984), 'The Contribution of Education to Economic Growth: International Comparisons', in John W. Kendrick (ed), *International Comparisons of Productivity and Causes of Slowdown,* Cambridge, Massachusetts, Ballinger.

Psacharopoulos, George (1993), 'Returns to Investment in Education – A Global Update', *Policy Research Working Papers*, No. 1067, Washington, DC, World Bank, January.

Psacharopoulos, George and Zafiris Tzannatos (1992), *Women's Employment and Pay in Latin America: Overview and Methodology*, Washington, DC, World Bank Regional and Sectoral Studies.

Psacharopoulos, George and E. Vélez (1992), 'Schooling, Ability and Earnings in Colombia, 1988', *Economic Development and Cultural Change*, Vol. 40, No. 3, Chicago, Illinois, April.

Quero Morales, Constantino (1978), *Imagen–Objetivo de Venezuela: Reformas Fundamentales para su Desarrollo*, Caracas, Banco Central de Venezuela.

Ramos, Joseph (1986), *Neoconservative Economics in the Southern Cone of Latin America, 1973–83*, Baltimore, Pennsylvania, The Johns Hopkins University Press.

Reisen, Helmut (1985), *Key Prices for Adjustment to Less External Indebtedness*, Paris, OECD Development Centre.

Reisen, Helmut (1986), 'The Latin American Transfer Problem in Historical Perspective' in Angus Maddison (ed.), *Latin America, the Caribbean and the OECD*, Paris, OECD Development Centre.

Reynolds, Lloyd G. (1983), 'The Spread of Economic Growth to the Third World', *Journal of Economic Literature*, Vol. XXI, No. 3, Nashville, Tennessee, September.

Romer, Paul M. (1989), 'Capital Accumulation in the Theory of Long-Run Growth', in Robert J. Barro (ed.), *Modern Business Cycle Theory*, Cambridge, Massachusetts, Harvard University Press.

Romer, Paul M. (1990), 'Human Capital and Growth: Theory and Evidence', in Allan H. Meltzer (ed.), *Carnegie–Rochester Conference Series on Public Policy*, Vol. 32, Amsterdam, North-Holland.

Safford, Frank (1976), *The Ideal of the Practical: Colombia's Struggle to Form a Technical Elite*, Austin, Texas.

Salter, W.E.G. (1960), *Productivity and Technical Change*, Cambridge, Massachusetts, Cambridge University Press.

Sánchez-Albornoz, Nicolás (1991), 'The Population of Latin America, 1850–1930', in Leslie Bethell (ed), *Historia de América Latina*, Barcelona, Editorial Crítica.

Schultz, Theodore W. (1961), 'Investment in Human Capital', *American Economic Review*, Vol. 51, No. 1, Washington, DC, March.

Secretaría de Planificación (1991), *Stock de Capital y Productividad*, Buenos Aires, Presidencia de la Nación.

Simón, Raúl (1935), *Determinación de la Entrada Nacional de Chile*, Santiago, Chile, Editorial Nascimiento.

Simonsen, Mario Henrique (1964), 'Comment', in Werner Baer and Isaac Kerstenetzky (eds), *Inflation and Growth in Latin America*, New Haven, Connecticut, The Economic Growth Center, Yale University.

Singer, Hans W. (1950), 'The Distribution of Gains between Investing and Borrowing Countries', *American Economic Review*, Vol. 40, No. 40, Washington, DC, May.

Smith, Adam (1776), *The Wealth of Nations*, 1937 edition, New York, The Modern Library, Random House.

Solow, Robert M. (1956), 'A Contribution to the Theory of Economic Growth', *The Quarterly Journal of Economics*, Vol. LXX, No. 1, Cambridge, Massachusetts, February.

Solow, Robert M. (1957), 'Technical Change and the Aggregate Production Function', *The Review of Economics and Statistics*, Vol. XXXIX, No. 3, Amsterdam, North-Holland, August.

Solow, Robert M. (1962), 'Technical Progress, Capital Formation and Economic Growth', *American Economic Review*, Vol. LII, No. 2, Washington, DC, May.

Solow, Robert M. (1988), 'Growth Theory and After', *American Economic Review*, Vol. 78, No. 3, Washington, DC, June.

Stallings, Barbara (1987), *Banker to the Third World*, Berkeley, California, University of California Press.

Studenski, Paul (1958), *The Income of Nations, Theory, Measurement, and Analysis: Past and Present*, New York, New York University Press.

Summers, Robert and Alan Heston (1991), 'The Penn World Table (Mark 5): An Expanded Set of International Comparisons, 1950–1988', *Quarterly Journal of Economics*, Vol. CVI, Issue 2, Cambridge, Massachusetts, May.

Sunkel, Osvaldo (1960), 'Inflation in Chile: An Unorthodox Approach', *International Economic Papers*, No. 10, August.

Sunkel, Osvaldo (ed.) (1991), *El Desarrollo desde Dentro*, Lecturas, No. 71, Mexico City, FCE.

Suzigan, Wilson (1976), 'Industrialization and Economic Policy in Historical Perspective', *Brazilian Economic Studies*, No. 2, Rio de Janeiro, Brazil, IPEA/INPES.

Swan, Trevor W. (1956), 'Economic Growth and Capital Accumulation', *The Economic Record*, Vol. 32.

Syrquin, Moshe, Lance Taylor and Larry E. Westphal (eds) (1984), *Economic Structure and Performance – Essays in Honor of Hollis B. Chenery*, Orlando, Florida, Academic Press, Inc.

Szirmai, Adam, Bart van Ark and Dirk Pilat (eds) (1993), *Explaining Economic Growth – Essays in Honour of Angus Maddison*, Amsterdam, Elsevier/North-Holland.

Terborgh, George (1954), *Realistic Depreciation Policy*, Chicago, Illinois, Machinery and Allied Products Institute.

Thomas, Vinod (1985), *Linking Macroeconomic and Agricultural Policies for Adjustment with Growth: The Colombian Experience*, Washington, DC and Baltimore, Pennsylvania, World Bank/The Johns Hopkins University Press.

Thorp, Rosemary (ed.) (1984), *Latin America in the 1930s: The Role of the Periphery in World Crisis*, New York, St. Martin's Press.

Tinbergen, Jan (1942), 'Zur Theorie der Langfristigen Wirtschaftsentwicklung', *Weltwirtschaftliches Archiv*, Vol. 55, No. 1, Tubingen.

Tinbergen, Jan and Hendricus C. Bos (1965), 'A Planning Model for the Educational Requirements of Economic Development', in OECD, *Econometric Models of Education: Some Applications*, Paris.

UNCTAD (1992), *Trade Liberalization in Chile: Experiences and Prospects*, Trade Policy Series, No. 1, New York.

United Nations (1956), *Analysis and Projections of Economic Development – The Economic Development of Brazil*, study prepared by the Joint Working Group of the Banco Nacional do Desenvolvimento Econômico (Brazil) and ECLAC, Department of Economic and Social Affairs, New York.

United Nations (1957a), *Análisis y Proyecciones del Desarrollo Económico III, El Desarrollo Económico de Colombia*, Mexico City, Departamento de Asuntos Económicos y Sociales.

United Nations (1957b), *El Desequilibrio Externo en el Desarrollo Económico Latinoamericano. El Caso de México*, study prepared by ECLAC and Economic and Social Council, New York.

United Nations (1959), *Análisis y Proyecciones del Desarrollo Económico V. El Desarrollo Económico de la Argentina*, Mexico City, Departamento de Asuntos Económicos y Sociales.

United Nations (1968), 'A System of National Accounts', *Studies in Methods*, series F, No. 2, Rev. 3, New York.

United Nations (1993), *Demographic Yearbook, 1991*, New York, March.

United Nations/EUROSTAT (1987), *World Comparison of Purchasing Power and Real Product for 1980, Phase IV of the International Comparison Project, Part Two: Detailed Results for 60 Countries*, New York.

Urquidi, Victor (1985), 'The World Crisis and the Outlook for Latin America' in Wionczek Miquel S. (ed.), *Politics and Economics of External Debt Crisis, The Latin American Experience*, Boulder, Colorado, Westview Press.

Urrutia, Mario G. (1983), 'Ahorro y Crecimiento en Chile en el Período 1960–81', *Monetaria*, Vol. VI, No. 2, Santiago, Chile, April–June.

Urrutia, Miguel (ed.) (1991), *Long-Term Trends in Latin American Development*, Washington, DC, IDB/The Johns Hopkins University Press.

US Bureau of Labor Statistics (1983), *Trends in Multifactor Productivity, 1984–81*, Bulletin 2178, Washington, DC.

US Department of Commerce, Bureau of Economic Analysis (1987), *Fixed Reproducible Tangible Wealth in the United States, 1925–85*, Washington, DC, U.S. Government Printing Office, June.

US Department of Commerce (1993), *Fixed Reproducible Tangible Wealth in the United States, 1925–89*, U.S. Washington, DC, Government Printing Office, January.

Usher, Dan (ed.) (1980), 'The Measurement of Capital', *Studies in Income and Wealth*, Vol. 45, Chicago, Illinois, The University of Chicago Press.

Van Ark, Bart (1993), *International Comparisons of Output and Productivity – Manufacturing Productivity Performance of Ten Countries from 1950 to 1990*, Monograph Series, No. 1, Groningen, The Netherlands, Groningen Growth and Development Centre.

Veblen, Thorstein (1915), *Imperial Germany and the Industrial Revolution*, New York, Macmillan.

Villela, Annibal V. and Wilson Suzigan (1977), 'Government Policy and the Economic Growth of Brazil, 1889–1945', *Brazilian Economic Studies*, No. 3, Rio de Janeiro, IPEA/INPES.

Viner, Jacob (1950), *The Customs Union Issue*, New York, Carnegie Endowment for International Peace.

Von Furstenberg, George M. (ed.) (1980), *Capital, Efficiency and Growth*, Cambridge, Massachusetts, Ballinger Publishing Company.

Ward, Michael (1976a), *The Measurement of Capital*, Paris, OECD.

Ward, Michael (1976b), 'Problems of Measuring Capital in Less Developed Countries', *The Review of Income and Wealth*, series 22, No. 3, New Haven, Connecticut, September.

Wilkie, James W. (1974), *Statistics and National Policy*, Supplement 3, UCLA Statistical Abstract of Latin America, Los Angeles, Latin American Center, UCLA.

Wilkie, James W. and Enrique Ochoa (eds) (1989), *Statistical Abstract of Latin America*, Vol. 27, Los Angeles, Latin American Center, UCLA.

Williamson, John (ed.) (1990), *Latin American Adjustment: How Much Has Happened?*, Washington DC, IIE.

Winfrey, Robley (1935), 'Statistical Analyses of Industrial Property Retirements', *Bulletin*, No. 125, Ames, Iowa, Iowa Engineering Experiment Station, December.

World Bank (1953), *The Economic Development of Mexico, Report of the Combined Mexican Working Party*, Baltimore, Pennsylvania, The Johns Hopkins Press.

World Bank (1991), *Proceedings of the World Bank Annual Conference on Development Economics 1990*, Washington, DC.

World Bank (1993a), *The East Asian Miracle – Economic Growth and Public Policy*, Washington, DC.

World Bank (1993b), *Latin America and the Caribbean – A Decade after the Debt Crisis*, Washington DC, Latin American and the Caribbean Regional Office, September.

World Bank (1995), *World Development Report*, Washington DC.

Young, Allan H. and John C. Musgrave (1980), 'Estimation of Capital Stock in the United States' in Dan Usher (ed.), 'The Measurement of Capital', *Studies in Income and Wealth*, Vol. 45, Chicago, Illinois, The University of Chicago Press.

Young, Alwyn (1994), 'The Tyranny of Numbers: Confronting the Statistical Realities of the East Asian Growth Experience', *NBER Working Paper,* No. 4680, Cambridge, Massachusetts, NBER, March.

Young, Alwyn (1995), 'The Tyranny of Numbers: Confronting the Statistical Realities of the East Asian Growth Experience', *The Quarterly Journal of Economics*, Cambridge, Massachusetts, August.

Zerkowsky, R. and M.A. de Gusmao Veloso (1982), 'Seis Décadas de Economia a través do PIB', *Revista Brasileira de Economía*, Vol. 26, No. 3, Rio de Janeiro, July–September.

Index